JOHN AND QUMRAN

John and Qumran

Edited by
JAMES H. CHARLESWORTH

Raymond E. Brown, s.s.

James L. Price

A. R. C. Leaney

A. Jaubert

James H. Charlesworth

Gilles Quispel

Marie-Émile Boismard, o.p.

William H. Brownlee

 GEOFFREY CHAPMAN
LONDON 1972

Geoffrey Chapman Publishers
35 Red Lion Square
London, WC1 4SJ

Geoffrey Chapman (Ireland) Publishers
5–7 Main Street
Black Rock, County Dublin

ISBN 0 225.66101.2

First published 1972

This book is set in 10 pt Times
Made and printed in Great Britain by Willmer Brothers Limited, Birkenhead

Contents

Contents

Abbreviations

AER	*American Ecclesiastical Review*
AGSU	Arbeiten zur Geschichte des Spätjudentums und Urchristentums
ALUOS	*The Annual of Leeds University Oriental Society*
APOT	R. H. Charles, *The Apocrypha and Pseudepigrapha of the Old Testament*, 2 vols, Oxford, 1913; reprinted 1963–68
AsSt	*Asiatische Studien*
ATD	Acta Theologica Danica
AThANT	Abhandlungen zur Theologie des Alten und Neuen Testaments
AusBR	*Australian Biblical Review*
AVTR	Aufsätze und Vorträge zur Theologie und Religionswissenschaft
BA	*Biblical Archaeologist*
BASOR	*Bulletin of the American Schools of Oriental Research*
BBB	Bonner Biblische Beiträge
BHT	Beiträge zur historischen Theologie
Bib	*Biblica*
BiViChr	*Bible et Vie Chrétienne*
BJRL	*Bulletin of the John Rylands Library*
BNTE	*The Background of the New Testament and its Eschatology*, ed. W. D. Davies and D. Daube, Cambridge, 1956 [C. H. Dodd Festschrift]
BO	Biblica et Orientalia
BWANT	Beiträge zur Wissenschaft vom Alten und Neuen Testament
BZ	*Biblische Zeitschrift*

BZNW	Beihefte zur Zeitschrift für die Neutestamentliche Wissenschaft
CB	*Cultura Bíblica*
CBQ	*Catholic Biblical Quarterly*
ChCen	*The Christian Century*
ChQR	*Church Quarterly Review*
ColHef	Colwer Hefte
CTM	*Concordia Theological Monthly*
DAWB	Deutsche Akademie der Wissenschaften zu Berlin
DJD	Discoveries in the Judaean Desert, 1955–
DSS	Dead Sea Scrolls
En	*Encounter*
Ét	*Études*
ÉtBib	Études Bibliques
ET	English Translation
ETL	*Ephemerides Theologicae Lovanienses*
EvT	*Evangelische Theologie*
Ev. Ver.	*Gospel of Truth*
ExpT	*Expository Times*
FT	*Faith and Thought.* Journal of the Victorian Institute
FV	*Foi et Vie*
GCS	Die griechischen christlichen Schriftsteller der ersten drei Jahrhunderte
HE	Eusebius, *Historia Ecclesiastica*
HR	*History of Religions*
HTR	*Harvard Theological Review*
ICC	International Critical Commentary
IDB	*The Interpreter's Dictionary of the Bible*, ed. G. A. Buttrick *et al.*, 4 vols, New York, Nashville, 1962
IEJ	*Israel Exploration Journal*
Int	*Interpretation*
Int. Bible	*The Interpreter's Bible*
ITQ	*Irish Theological Quarterly*
JAAR	*Journal of the American Academy of Religion*
JBL	*Journal of Biblical Literature*
JJS	*Journal of Jewish Studies*
JQR	*Jewish Quarterly Review*
JSS	*Journal of Semitic Studies*
JTS	*Journal of Theological Studies*
Leiturgia	*Leiturgia: Handbuch des Evangelischen Gottesdienstes*
MTZ	*Münchner Theologische Zeitschrift*

Mus	*Muséon*
NovTSup	Novum Testamentum Supplement (Leiden)
NRT	*Nouvelle Revue Théologique*
NT	*Novum Testamentum*
NTRG	New Testament Reading Guide
NTS	*New Testament Studies*
NTT	*Nederlands Theologisch Tijdschrift*
PEF	*Palestine Exploration Fund*
PelGosCom	Pelican Gospel Commentaries
PEQ	*Palestine Exploration Quarterly*
PG	Patrologiae Cursus Completus. Series Graeca, ed. J.-P. Migne
PO	Patrologia Orientalis
PP	*La Parola di Passato*
PTR	*Princeton Theological Review*
RB	*Revue Biblique*
RechBib	Recherches Bibliques
RevQ	*Revue de Qumran*
RevTh	*Revista de Theología*
RHR	*Revue de l'Histoire des Religions*
RiB	*Rivista Biblica*
RL	*Religion in Life*
RocTK	*Roczniki Theologiczno-Kanoniczne*
RScRel	*Revue des Sciences Religieuses*
RSR	*Recherches de Science Religieuse*
RTh	*Revue Thomiste*
SANT	Studien zum Alten und Neuen Testament
SBL	Society of Biblical Literature
SBT	Studies in Biblical Theology
ScE	*Sciences Ecclésiastiques* (now called *Science et Esprit*)
SE	*Studia Evangelica*, ed. F. L. Cross. *SE* 1=TU 73, Berlin, 1959; *SE* 2=TU 87, Berlin, 1964; *SE* 3=TU 88, Berlin, 1964; *SE* 4=TU 102, Leipzig, Berlin, 1968
SEA	*Svensk Exegetisk Årsbok*
SH	*Scripta Hierosolymitana*
SHR	Studies in the History of Religions
SIMSVD	Studia Instituti Missiologici Societatis Verbi Divini
SJT	*Scottish Journal of Theology*
SNTS	Studiorum Novi Testamenti Societas
ST	Studia Theologica
StCa	*Studia Catholica*
STDJ	Studies in the Texts of the Desert of Judah

Str-B	H. L. Strack and P. Billerbeck, *Kommentar zum Neuen Testament aus Talmud und Midrasch*, 6 vols, Munich, 1922–61
SUNT	Studien zur Umwelt des Neuen Testaments
Sym	*Symbolon: Jahrbuch für Symbolforschung*
Tarb	*Tarbiz*
TBT	*The Bible Today*
TLZ	*Theologische Literaturzeitung*
Tôk	*Tôkyô-shingaku-daigaku-hô*
TR	*Theologische Rundschau*
TrInstCaP	Travaux de l'Institut Catholique de Paris
TS	*Theological Studies*
TU	Texte und Untersuchungen zur Geschichte der altchristlichen Literatur
TZ	*Theologische Zeitschrift*
UUA	Uppsala Universitets Årsskrift
VD	*Verbum Domini*
VDBS	F. Vigouroux, *Dictionnaire de la Bible, Supplément*, Paris, 1928–
VigChr	*Vigiliae Christianae*
VoxTh	*Vox Theologica*
WUZNT	Wissenschaftliche Untersuchungen zum Neuen Testament
ZNKUL	*Zeszyty Naukowe Katolickiego Uniwersytetu Lubelskiego*
ZNW	*Zeitschrift für die Neutestamentliche Wissenschaft*
ZTK	*Zeitschrift für Theologie und Kirche*

MISCELLANEOUS ABBREVIATIONS

Apart from usual abbreviations for the biblical books, the following have been used

Ant.	Josephus, *Jewish Antiquities*
Apoc. Abr.	Apocalypse of Abraham
JB	Jerusalem Bible
Jub	Book of Jubilees
LXX	Septuagint
MT	Massoretic Text
NAB	New American Bible
NEB	New English Bible
RSV	Revised Standard Version
Test. Asher, Judah etc.	Testament of Asher, Judah etc.

Dedicated to

Rev. Dr and Mrs Thomas Charlesworth

and

Rev. Dr and Mrs Arthur R. Charlesworth

Editor's Foreword

The stone thrown by Muhammed ed-Dîb through the opening of what is now designated Qumran Cave 1 shattered the silence of almost two thousand years as it cannoned off earthen jars containing unimagined treasures. The clatter created by that stone was soon lost, but the echoes generated by the tossing of that stone have carried around the world. The noise of Ta'âmireh Bedouin clambering up to the cave in search of gold soon ebbed, and was followed by the crackle of flames from camp fires that cast flickering streams of light on ancient parchment. Stranger sounds followed: the screech of the sawing machine invented to cut the copper scrolls into decipherable sections, and the pitch of angry voices from businessmen caught in the web on an international intrigue. Above the pandemonium one sound persists: that of the scholars' typewriters.

From the four corners of the earth and from the major faiths, concurring conclusions regarding the Scrolls have evolved independently. From Scotland (Black), Australia (Morris), Russia (Livshits) and the United States (Brown), Protestants, Catholics and Jews have slowly come to agree that ideas contained in the Dead Sea Scrolls influenced portions of the Gospel according to John.

This important conclusion climaxes voluminous research. From 1950 to 1970 more than 170 works were published in the attempt to discover the possible relationships between John and Qumran.

Père Jean Carmignac has kindly permitted me to draw attention to a discovery he has just made. He has completed an article entitled "Les apparitions de Jésus ressucité et le calendrier biblico-qumrânien", which is to be published in the *Revue de Qumran*, number 28. Père Carmignac sent a French abstract of his research; an idiomatic translation is found below.

According to the biblical-Qumranic calendar the Passover feast always commenced on Wednesday and terminated the following Wednesday, a day which was strictly observed. In order to return to Galilee after the crucifixion of their Master on Friday, the apostles should have departed very early Sunday morning, because it took three days to travel from Jerusalem to Galilee. This explains why Jesus strongly insisted that they depart immediately. The apostles, however, who did not at first believe in the resurrection of their Master, did not depart; it was Jesus who came to them Sunday evening in an apparition that is now recorded in Jn 20: 19–25. By Sunday evening, however, it was too late for them to reach Galilee before Wednesday, which as stated above was a holy day. The following Thursday and Friday would not have provided sufficient time to complete the journey before the commencement of the Sabbath rest. The following Sunday, according to the Qumran calendar, was the feast of Unleavened Bread, hence the apostles would again have to postpone their departure until the morning of the following Monday. These necessary postponements explain why the second apparition, in the presence of Thomas, occurred the second Sunday, just prior to the departure for Galilee. Consequently, the apparitions in Jerusalem neither contradict the apparitions in Galilee nor the return to Galilee. Everything had been conditioned by the biblical-Qumranic calendar; the narratives in John are surprisingly faithful.

One of the purposes of the present book is to report some of the consensus that has been reached among scholars. Another is to examine possibilities that have been felt, though not necessarily published, to see if they are verifiable probabilities. The research found below helps to dispel the darkness from the greatest enigma in Christian origins, the origin of the Gospel according to John.

I wish to express my gratitude to the trustees and editorial boards of *The Expository Times* and *New Testament Studies* for the permission to republish the material found in chapters one and five. Also, I wish to thank Charles D. Myers, Jr and Joe W. Russell, Jr for their indefatigable work on the bibliography, and to recognize John W. Wilson for his help in translating some of the chapters. Finally, I wish to acknowledge the excellent and amiable relationship enjoyed with Geoffrey Chapman Publishers.

JHC
Easter 1971
Duke University

1

The Dead Sea Scrolls and the
New Testament[1]

RAYMOND E. BROWN, S.S.

Almost twenty-five years have now passed since that Arab boy
stumbled into a cave near Qumran and found the first of the Dead
Sea Scrolls.[2] The dust raised in the caves by the archaeologists and
the Bedouin has long since settled, and so to some extent has the
furore of first reactions. Particularly on the question of the relation
of the Scrolls to the New Testament these reactions covered a spec-
trum which ran from a judgment of no relationship to hysterical
claims that now one could see that there was nothing original in
either Jesus or the New Testament. Here we shall attempt to isolate
and evaluate the suggestions that have survived the scholarly
criticism of the intervening years.[3]

Let us first state the presuppositions of this survey. Most of the
Qumran literature was composed and copied before the composition
of the first Christian literature (c. A.D. 50). A dating of the Scrolls to
the Middle Ages or to the period after the destruction of the Second
Temple is untenable. The identification of the sectarians who composed the Scrolls with the Essenes approaches certainty in our judgment, but this identification is not absolutely necessary for discussing
relationships with the New Testament. What is certain is that the
sectarians were not Christians, nor is there any evidence of Christian
influence on their writings. They were Jews of strict legal observance,
strongly apocalyptic in outlook, with a strain of ethical and eschatological dualism that ultimately may have been of Iranian origin.
The most important figure in the history of the community, the
Teacher of Righteousness, who in all probability lived in the second
half of the second century B.C., was an anti-Hasmonean priest of
Zadokite lineage. In protest against cultic and calendric innovations
at Jerusalem and in pietistic zeal for the pure observance of the Law,

---

[1]Originally published in *ExpT* 78 (1966–67) 19–23.
[2]In this article the term "Dead Sea Scrolls" is confined to the discoveries at
Qumran.
[3]The literature is enormous. Two anthologies are worthy of note: *The Scrolls
and the New Testament*, ed. K. Stendahl (New York, 1957); and *The Scrolls and
Christianity*, ed. M. Black (SPCK Theological Collections; London, 1969). The
most comprehensive study is a passage by passage comparison of the New Testament
with the Scrolls done by Herbert Braun, *Qumran und das Neue Testament* (2 vols;
Tübingen, 1966).

he went into exile at the Qumran desert site where his religion and theology influenced greatly all the subsequent adherents to the sect. There is no evidence that he claimed to be a Messiah, nor *a fortiori* that he claimed to be divine. He was persecuted, but for all we know he died a natural death. There is no evidence that he was crucified or that he rose from the dead, although it is possible that the sectarians expected his return at the time of God's final intervention (CD 6:10–11). Thus, all the theories that the Qumran Teacher was a "Christ before Christ"[4] or that Qumran thought anticipated the truly distinctive contributions of Christianity belong to the domain of over-enthusiastic popularization rather than to that of serious scholarship.

If the relationships between the Scrolls and the New Testament are not by way of anticipated Christianity among the Qumran sectarians, neither are these relationships by way of direct Christian dependency on the Scrolls. In no passage of the New Testament is there a direct citation of a known Qumran work, and there is no evidence that Jesus or his followers had direct contact with the sectarians or their writings. On geographical, chronological and ideological grounds one may propose seriously that John the Baptist must have encountered the Qumran sectarians, as we shall see below; but we have no way of knowing if John was a sectarian at any period of his life.[5] The fact that in the New Testament and Josephus John is presented as an isolated phenomenon suggests that he was not popularly remembered as having belonged to an Essene or sectarian group.

Thus, as far as we can see, the plausible relationships between Qumran and the New Testament are indirect and must be cautiously stated.[6] We may distinguish two kinds of relationships. (a) The broadest relationship is where the Scrolls are a witness of the *general Jewish background*. The paucity of late pre-Christian Jewish literature means that any body of such literature, even sectarian, enlightens us on the vocabulary, thought, and customs common among Jews in Jesus' time. Undoubtedly much of what comes before us for the first time in the Scrolls was not at all peculiar to Qumran and is simply illustrative of a broader background familiar to Jesus and his followers.[7] Much of the light that the Scrolls have thrown on the

---

[4]A thorough discussion of this may be found in J. Carmignac, *Christ and the Teacher of Righteousness* (Baltimore, 1962); and G. Jeremias, *Der Lehrer der Gerechtigkeit* (Göttingen, 1963).

[5]Lk 1:80 is cited to show that John grew up in the desert; and Josephus, *War*, II, viii, 2, par. 120, is cited to the effect that Essenes had the custom of adopting children. It is also noted that John was of priestly lineage and that the Qumran sectarians gave strong emphasis to the priesthood; yet, of course, John's father was a priest loyal to the Jerusalem Temple and hence an object of Qumran scorn.

[6]As will be seen in the following chapters, other scholars accept the possibility of direct Qumran influence on the Fourth Gospel.

[7]Not only did the Qumran sectarians have a heritage of common Jewish ideas and vocabulary, but even some of their peculiar doctrines were probably well known outside their community. Josephus, *War*, II, viii, 4, par. 124, says that there were large numbers of Essenes in every town, and he himself shows a familiarity with Essene ideas. The Scrolls censure those who report community secrets to others, and the existence of the censure warns us that such betrayal must have occurred.

Synoptic Gospels and on the Pauline Epistles would, in our judgment, be by way of this general background. (*b*) A more precise relationship between the Scrolls and the New Testament arises where elements representing *peculiar sectarian Jewish thought* are involved. Long before the discovery of the Scrolls, scholars like Renan suggested that Christianity had been heavily influenced by Essenism, precisely because there were elements in New Testament thought not conformable with Pharisee and Sadducee Judaism. Since the discovery of the Scrolls, we are in a better position to evaluate such influence; but even now we must be careful in assuming that all sectarian ideas in the Scrolls were the peculiar property of the Qumran (Essene) community, for Qumran probably shared some of its peculiarities with other groups of baptizing sectarians reputed to have flourished in Judaism at this time.[8] Therefore we cannot be certain that even the most characteristic Qumran features found in the New Testament came to Christianity from Qumran, and it is best to attribute the influence to a type of Judaism of which Qumran is exemplary.

Having clarified our general presuppositions and attitudes toward Qumran-Christian relationships, we shall organize the most important parallels between the Scrolls and the New Testament under six headings below. We shall confine ourselves to those parallels which seem to have plausibility, leaving aside more ingenious suggestions which are unfortunately incapable of proof. We must insist too that in speaking of "parallels" we do not restrict ourselves to ideas or features that are exactly the same in the Scrolls and the New Testament.[9] In almost all the "parallels" there was an adaptation to Christian theological patterns.

(1) *Parallels in Jesus' words and deeds* (*as found in the Synoptic Gospels*). The most characteristic features of Jesus' teachings have little or no parallel at Qumran: freedom with regard to details of the Law and the Sabbath; parabolic teaching; mission to the social outcastes. The relationships between the Scrolls and Jesus' sayings belong principally to our classification (*a*) wherein the Scrolls enlarge the general background for understanding Jesus. Just as many of Jesus' words (e.g. the petitions of the Lord's Prayer) have parallels in fragments of Pharisaic material preserved in the later rabbinical writings, so, for instance, do parts of the Sermon on the Mount, especially those concerned with legal observance, have parallels in the Scrolls.[10] In particular, the "poor in spirit" can be better under-

---

[8]J. Thomas, *Le mouvement baptiste en Palestine et Syrie* (150 *av. J.C.*–300 *ap. J.C.*) (Gembloux, 1935). M. Black, *The Scrolls and Christian Origins* (London, 1961) Part I. By way of example, opposition to the Jerusalem Temple was shared by the Qumran group, the Samaritans, the Hellenists (Acts 6:1–7:60), etc. See O. Cullmann, *ExpT* 71 (1959–60) 8–12.

[9]Reacting to wild claims about Christian dependence on Qumran, some writers have contented themselves with pointing out differences between the Scrolls and the New Testament and seem to think that thus they have refuted any claim of Christian dependency on the thought represented at Qumran. Dependency, however, is not eliminated by the fact that one changes an idea gained from another.

[10]K. Schubert, "The Sermon on the Mount and the Qumrân Texts", *The Scrolls and the New Testament*, ed. K. Stendahl, 118–28; W. D. Davies, *The Setting of the Sermon on the Mount* (Cambridge, 1964) 208–56.

stood now that we encounter the Hebrew phrase in context at Qumran.[11] The strong eschatological outlook of Jesus and his early followers is not unlike that of the Dead Sea sectarians, giving substance to an eschatological interpretation of a petition like, "Lead us not into temptation" [i.e., the final trial].[12] Some scholars would go further in evaluating the relations between the Scrolls and Jesus and see the influence on Jesus of clearly sectarian ideas and practices (classification b). Here the evidence is less certain. The process of correcting straying brethren proposed by Jesus in Mt 18:15-17 is quite like the Qumran rule for correction within the community (1QS 5:25-6:1). Of course, here we may be dealing with a parallel between Matthew and the Scrolls rather than between Jesus and the Scrolls, for it is worth noting that Matthew has more parallels to the Scrolls than Mark (very few) or even than Luke (numerous in infancy narrative). Whether the Qumran eschatological meals of bread and wine throw much light on the Last Supper[13] is an open question. Several authors[14] have sought to solve the chronological discrepancy between John and the Synoptics about the date of Jesus' Last Supper and death on the basis of the Qumran solar calendar wherein Passover fell on Tuesday evening-Wednesday. Yet there are formidable difficulties,[15] for it is doubtful whether Jesus could have conformed to a peculiarly sectarian calendar without being a sectarian himself.

(2) *Parallels in the career of John the Baptist.* The ministry of the Baptist in the Desert of Judea in the 20s brought him into close geographical proximity to the Qumran settlement at a time when it flourished. He is described in the New Testament with a phrase from Is 40:3 ("In the wilderness prepare the way of the Lord") also used by the Qumran sectarians to describe their role in the desert (1QS 8:12-14). His characteristic action of baptizing shares common features with the initiatory lustrations at Qumran: (a) the external ablution is useless without repentance; (b) it is given to Jews, not to pagan converts; (c) it is designed to set up a penitent nucleus in Israel for the coming of God; (d) it is preliminary to a dispensation of God's spirit.[16] Of course, there are differences too, for John's baptism is on a more universal scale and without the trappings of

[11]J. Dupont in *Neutestamentliche Aufsätze*—J. Schmid Festschrift, ed. J. Blinzler (Regensburg, 1963) 53–64.

[12]K. G. Kuhn, "New Light on Temptation, Sin, and Flesh in the New Testament", *The Scrolls and the New Testament*, ed. K. Stendahl, 94–113. Also R. E. Brown, *New Testament Essays* (London, Milwaukee, 1966) 248–53, or (Garden City, N.Y., 1968) 314–20.

[13]K. G. Kuhn, "The Lord's Supper and the Communal Meal at Qumran", *The Scrolls and the New Testament*, ed. K. Stendahl, 65–93; M. Delcor, "Repas cultuels esséniens et thérapeutes", *RevQ* 6 (1968) 401–25.

[14]A. Jaubert, *The Date of the Last Supper* (New York, 1965)—see also her chapter below; E. Ruckstuhl, *Chronology of the Last Days of Jesus* (New York, 1965).

[15]The objections of scholars like P. Benoit, P. Gaechter, J. Jeremias and J. Blinzler are summed up in Raymond E. Brown, *New Testament Essays*, 164–7, 214–17.

[16]J. A. T. Robinson, "The Baptism of John and the Qumran Community", *HTR* 50 (1957) 175–91.

monasticism. It is not implausible that the Baptist received his general orientation from baptizing sectarians such as those at Qumran,[17] and then in the light of his own prophetic call adapted these ideas to a more universal eschatological mission. We may also note that the *Benedictus* (Lk 1:68–79)—a hymn in praise of John the Baptist which many scholars suggest was composed by his followers but subsequently adapted by Christians—is similar in its structure and mosaic style to Qumran hymns pieced together from the Old Testament.

(3) *Parallels in the Pauline Epistles.*[18] Here there are good relationships of class (*a*). The recurrence in the Scrolls of various types of "mysteries", including God's mysterious plan of salvation, suggests strongly that the Pauline concept of *mystērion* has its roots in Semitic thought rather than in the Hellenistic mystery religions.[19] A better knowledge of Jewish angelology gained through the Scrolls throws light on the veiling of women's heads because of angels in 1 Cor 11:10: the presence of heavenly angels at earthly liturgical gatherings is expected, and a bodily defect is unworthy of their sight.[20] The Scrolls make use of ideas and terms found frequently in Paul, like flesh,[21] power,[22] spirit,[23] and truth;[24] and studies of such terms at Qumran have been very fruitful. Are there also relationships of class (*b*) between the Scrolls and the Pauline writings? One passage that has a very definite Qumran ring is 2 Cor 6:14–7:1; and J. A. Fitzmyer[25] has argued persuasively that the passage resembles "a paragraph in which Qumran ideas and expressions have been reworked in a Christian cast of thought". However, this Qumran colouring, along with the fact that the passage seems out of context, leads Fitzmyer to regard it as a *non-Pauline* interpolation. The interpretation of the faith of Hab 2:4 as faith in the Teacher ('s interpretation of the Law) in 1QpHab 8:1–3 may be a halfway step toward the Pauline usage wherein it becomes faith in Jesus Christ, but one can scarcely claim that Paul is dependent here on the Scrolls. The dualism between flesh and spirit and the lists of the works of the flesh and the fruits of the spirit in Gal 5:16–23 resembles closely the literary form of 1QS 3:13–4:26 with its description of the ways

---

[17]C. Scobie, *John the Baptist* (London, 1964) gives a well-balanced evaluation of John's relationship to the Jewish Baptist sectarian movement illustrated by Qumran. We prefer his caution to the over-Qumranization of the Baptist in works by W. H. Brownlee and J. Daniélou.

[18]See especially *Paul and Qumran: Studies in New Testament Exegesis*, ed. J. Murphy-O'Connor (London, Chicago, 1968).

[19]R. E. Brown, *The Semitic Background of the Term "Mystery" in the New Testament* (Facet Biblical Series 21; Philadelphia, 1968).

[20]J. A. Fitzmyer in *Paul and Qumran*, 31–47.

[21]R. E. Murphy in *Sacra Pagina*, ed. J. Coppens (Paris, 1959) 60–76. Also W. D. Davies in *The Scrolls and the New Testament*, ed. K. Stendahl, 157–82.

[22]R. E. Murphy in *Lex Tua Veritas*—Junker Festschrift, ed. H. Gross (Trier, 1961) 137–43.

[23]F. Nötscher in *Vom Alten zum Neuen Testament* (Bonn, 1962) 178–87. This volume collects many of Nötscher's important studies on the Scrolls and the New Testament.

[24]J. Murphy-O'Connor in *Paul and Qumran*, 179–230.

[25]*CBQ* 23 (1961) 271–80.

of the two spirits that govern man. Perhaps the Epistles that have the closest parallels to the Scrolls are Colossians and (especially) Ephesians.[26] If we do not resort to an explanation based on deutero-Pauline authorship, part of the explanation may be that the opponents in these Epistles seem to be Jewish sectarians whose thought has some of the same features as Qumran thought—they are strict legalists who pay excessive honour to angels (Col 2:16ff.; Eph 6:12ff.). The strong "mystery" language of these Epistles and the moral admonitions which bear strong resemblance to Qumran paraenesis may represent the author's attempt to speak in a language that the opponents would understand.

(4) *Parallels in the Epistle to the Hebrews.* These are numerous and have suggested to some that the author was familiar with Qumran thought.[27] It has even been proposed that the unnamed addressees of the Epistle were Christian converts from Qumran (Essene) ranks whom the author was trying to persuade against returning to their former practices. The early chapters where Jesus is shown to be superior to the angels and to Moses could be seen as an effective argument for sectarians whose chief guide in the apocalyptic struggle was the Archangel Michael and who put heavy stress on an ultra-pure observance of the Law of Moses. The theme that Christ was a priest (5:5) takes on importance in the light of the Scrolls, which attest the highest reverence for the priesthood and the expectation of a priestly messiah.[28] The theme of the Christian replacement of the Tabernacle (not the Temple) could well have been addressed to a group like that of Qumran where the Jerusalem Temple was rejected and the sectarians modelled themselves on the Exodus community grouped around the Tabernacle.[29] Attractive as this hypothesis is, it is still no more than a hypothesis. We have no knowledge that any sizeable number of the Qumran (Essene) sectarians became Christians; and there is no proof that the generalization in Acts 6:7 concerning the many priests who became obedient to the faith is a reference to Essene priests. The caution made above that Qumran ideas were shared by other Jewish sectarians is very important here.

(5) *Parallels to the Church organization in Acts (and Pastorals).* The Lucan description of the Jerusalem Church in Acts with its close community life, daily sacred meals, and shared goods has close parallels with Qumran life.[30] Even more striking similarities may

---

[26]K. G. Kuhn and F. Mussner in *Paul and Qumran,* 115–31, 159–78.

[27]Cf. Y. Yadin in *SH* 4 (1958) 36–55; C. Spicq, *RevQ* 1 (1959) 365–90.

[28]This has been disputed but remains well substantiated in our view. See *The Scrolls and Christianity,* ed. M. Black, 41–4.

[29]A general comparison of Qumran and Christian attitudes toward the Temple is found in B. Gärtner, *The Temple and the Community in Qumran and the New Testament* (SNTS Monograph Series 1; Cambridge, 1965).

[30]S. E. Johnson, "The Dead Sea Manual of Discipline and the Jerusalem Church of Acts", *The Scrolls and the New Testament,* ed. K. Stendahl, 129–42. See qualifications in M. Black, *The Scrolls and Christian Origins,* and in J. A. Fitzmyer, "Jewish Christianity in Acts in Light of the Qumran Scrolls", *Studies in Luke-Acts,* ed. L. E. Keck and J. L. Martyn (Nashville, London, 1966) 233–57, reprinted with

be found in the details of organization.[31] The most important ruling elements at Qumran seem to have been: (a) a cabinet of twelve or fifteen men within the community council, endowed with some legislative authority; (b) the Assembly of all the mature members of the community, called "the Session of the Many", endowed with judicial and executive authority; (c) the priest who presided over the Assembly and is called "the Supervisor" or "Inspector of the Many" (*mᵉbaqqēr* or *pāqîd*). The Christian parallel for (a) is found in the Twelve; indeed the same imagery of foundation walls is used for both groups (1QS 8:7–8; Rev 21:14). The Christian parallel for (b) is the assembly of "the multitude" (*plēthos*) mentioned in passages like Acts 6:2; 15:12, 30, where matters of policy were decided. The parallel for (c) is the Christian overseer or *episkopos* (the LXX uses *episkopein* to translate the Hebrew verbs related to *mᵉbaqqēr* and *pāqîd*). The precise functions of steward and teacher of sound doctrine which the Pastoral Epistles attribute to the *episkopos* are also the functions of the Qumran *mᵉbaqqēr*. Such parallels are not really surprising, for it is quite logical that in organizing itself the Christian community would pattern itself on extant Jewish models. The Qumran community offers the most plausible model yet proposed. If the parallelism is valid, then Luke's description of Church organization in the 30s and 40s has to be taken more seriously in terms of history than some critics have admitted.

(6) *Parallels in the Johannine Gospel and Epistles.* Many writers[32] have recognized that here we have the most impressive relationships of class (b) between the Scrolls and the New Testament. John's pervading ethical and eschatological dualism with its contrasts between light and darkness, truth and falsehood, finds a very plausible background in Qumran dualism;[33] and in our judgment the Scrolls consistently offer better parallels to John than do any of the non-Christian elements in the Mandaean documents emphasized by Bultmann or the examples in Philo and the *Hermetica* offered by Dodd. The angelic figure in the Scrolls who as prince of lights and spirit of truth leads the sons of light has been adapted in John to the figure of Jesus (the light of the world, the truth) and to the Paraclete (the Spirit of truth).[34] The Christian community is constituted, not by faith in an interpretation of the Law which is truth for Qumran, but by faith in Jesus who embodies truth. Why the

revisions in J. A. Fitzmyer, *Essays on the Semitic Background of the New Testament* (London, 1971) 271ff.

[31]For details and qualifications see our *New Testament Essays*, 27–30 (or 49–53).

[32]See the bibliography below, pp. 195ff. We have listed important parallels in an article in *The Scrolls and the New Testament*, ed. K. Stendahl, 183–207, reprinted in our *New Testament Essays*, 102–31 (or 138–73). The impact of Qumran on Johannine interpretation is visible in our commentary on John, *The Gospel According to John* (2 vols; Anchor Bible 29 and 29a; Garden City, New York, 1966, 1970; London, 1971).

[33]O. Böcher, *Der johanneische Dualismus im Zusammenhang des nachbiblischen Judentums* (Gütersloh, 1965); see also the chapters by J. Charlesworth below, pp. 76ff. and 107ff.

[34]R. E. Brown, "The Paraclete in the Fourth Gospel", *NTS* 13 (1966–67) 122–3. See also the chapter by A. R. C. Leaney below, pp. 38ff.

relationship between sectarian thought like that of Qumran and the Johannine writings should be so much closer than that between the Scrolls and the other Gospels is not clear. If one attributes to John the son of Zebedee a role in supplying the ancient tradition behind the Gospel, then possibly he was influenced by his master John the Baptist who would have been the bridge between Qumran or sectarian thought and Christian thought. If one holds that the Johannine writings were composed at Ephesus, then the relationship between the Scrolls and the Epistles to the Ephesians and the Colossians is significant. But these are little more than guesses. The critical import of the parallels between the Scrolls and John is that one can no longer insist that the abstract language spoken by Jesus in the Fourth Gospel *must* have been composed in the Greek world of the early second century A.D. What Jesus says in John would have been quite intelligible in the sectarian background of first-century Palestine. Yet this observation does not in itself establish that Jesus actually did speak in the way in which he is quoted by John, for it remains perfectly possible that much of the Qumran colouring came from the Evangelist.

Obviously, both the extent and the meaning of the important relationships between John and Qumran thought need further study, and the pages that follow undertake that task. This collection of essays, along with its companion volume *Paul and Qumran*, constitutes a model of how each of the six areas mentioned above can and should be investigated. These essays reflect the past twenty-five years of research on the relations of the Scrolls to the New Testament and, at the same time, open up promising vistas for future work. Not until much more of such investigation has been completed will the Dead Sea Scrolls have told their story.

2

Light from Qumran upon Some Aspects of Johannine Theology

JAMES L. PRICE

The earliest comparisons of the Dead Sea Scrolls and New Testament books drew attention to the remarkable similarities in terminology and thought between the writings from Qumran and the Gospel and Epistles of John. That these affinities should immediately have attracted an unusual amount of interest is not surprising. Prior to Qumran the debate concerning the cultural milieu of the Johannine books and their historical position in early Christianity had resulted in a disconcerting stalemate. Many of the attempts to reconstruct the conceptual backgrounds of these books had relied upon sources later than the writings themselves, some much later. It was evident to all that the writer of the Fourth Gospel had interested himself in traditions reporting the controversies of Jesus and his disciples with "the Jews", and had some reasons for advancing them. Yet his most typical and most important modes of discourse seemed remote from those exhibited in extant Jewish documents. At long last, there were discovered in Palestine pre-Christian Jewish writings disclosing a native soil which could have produced the flowering of Johannine theology.[1] It was asserted, or at least strongly implied, that there must have been a direct influence from Qumran upon Johannine teaching—that its apologetic was directed against Essene doctrines. Credibility was now given to the second-century tradition (which had become for many critics indefensible) that the Fourth Gospel, and the First Epistle of John as well, had been written by Jesus' disciple, John the son of Zebedee.[2]

Extravagant claims of direct contact, or at least literary dependence, led some scholars to make a prompt and unqualified denial of the alleged similarities, or to discount their value in affording clues to the origin of the Johannine tradition or of the theological doctrines which these books contain.[3] Fortunately, with the passage of time, the debate has moved to more defensible, possibly more productive,

---

[1]M. Burrows, *The Dead Sea Scrolls* (New York, London, 1956) 338ff.; J. A. T. Robinson, "The New Look on the Fourth Gospel", *Twelve New Testament Studies* (SBT 34; London, 1962) 98ff.

[2]W. F. Albright, "Recent Discoveries in Palestine and the Gospel of John", *The Background of the New Testament and Its Eschatology*, ed. W. D. Davies and D. Daube (Cambridge, 1956) 153ff.

[3]H. M. Teeple, "Qumran and the Origin of the Fourth Gospel", *NT* 4 (1960) 6ff.

ground. Most critics would now acknowledge that one can neither establish nor refute the direct contact of Jesus, or of any of his disciples or of those formerly belonging to John the Baptist, with the Qumran settlement. Nor can one prove or disprove a literary dependence of the author or authors of the Johannine gospel and letters upon documents found at Qumran. Moreover, it is commonly conceded that even though the Qumran discoveries enable one to postulate an early Palestinian provenance for much of the Jewish-Christian tradition peculiar to John's Gospel, the evidence which the canonical book itself provides supports the hypothesis of a complicated development of this tradition.[4]

Sound methods of comparison must therefore be directed toward more modest objectives. The most important methodological procedure is to identify teaching peculiar to the Qumran and Johannine writings which exhibits a similar development of concepts, or common emphases. But having so narrowed the scope of inquiry the critic faces the moot question of the nature of the relationship. The most striking similarities may only establish that the Qumran and Johannine communities independently derived inspiration from elements in the Old Testament, or from later Jewish writings antedating the documents from Qumran and the Johannine circle, under the influence of their group situations and experiences.[5]

It is important to stress the probability of this wider, interim development within Judaism between the Old Testament and Qumran. Some of the documents partially recovered at Qumran, e.g. 1 Enoch and the Testaments of the Twelve Patriarchs, were known before the Dead Sea Scroll discoveries, through later, somewhat expanded versions preserved by Christians in antiquity (the so-called Pseudepigrapha). Since it is unlikely that these books were composed by the men of Qumran, or expressed the views of the sectarians only, it is quite possible that some of the scrolls recovered from the Qumran caves were written by other Jews and express beliefs by no means held exclusively by the Qumran settlers. The books of the Qumran community were not subject to any strict theological censorship. Moreover, the classical descriptions of the beliefs and practices of important Jewish parties provided by Josephus cannot have been all-inclusive. The same cultural influences—deriving from the East and the West—which impinged on Palestine as well as diaspora Judaism, and which produced the Qumran phenomena, probably gave rise to similar ephemeral Jewish sectarian groups, one or more of which may have interacted with the Johannine community.

The practical inference to be drawn from these considerations is that one should not leap to the conclusion that certain important ideas which John and Qumran seem to have in common were ideas derived from Qumran. These ideas may have characterized a much

---

[4]R. E. Brown, "The Qumran Scrolls and the Johannine Epistles", *New Testament Essays* (Milwaukee, 1965; London, 1966) 104ff.; *idem, The Gospel According to John: I–XII* (Anchor Bible 29; Garden City, New York, 1966; London, 1971) lxiiff.

[5]This point is developed by P. Benoit in his essay, "Qumran and the New Testament", *Paul and Qumran*, ed. J. Murphy-O'Connor (London, Chicago, 1968) 1ff.

wider cultural movement flourishing in an environment shared by Jewish groups and John's community.

These cautions should not, however, suggest a foreclosure of comparisons between the books of John and Qumran, or lead to a denial that important conclusions can result from a careful scrutiny of similarities and differences. The purpose of this essay is to suggest ways in which Johannine theology can be elucidated by juxtaposing Qumran parallels or near parallels. The writer does not seek to make a case for or against literary dependence, but he has found intensely interesting and rewarding the examination of some of these affinities. The scrolls do provide a literary corpus antedating John's books and *exhibiting a type of Jewish sectarian thought resembling specific aspects of teaching found in the Gospel and Letters of John.* From this particular historical perspective new light is shed upon familiar but none the less obscure features of Johannine theology.

A word of justification is needed for using both the Gospel and the Letters of John in these comparisons, as well as for the repeated references to a "Johannine community". Many modern critics accept the view of a common authorship of these Johannine books, but there are others who dispute this on the ground that significant differences may be detected in vocabulary and theology. While doubts remain as to the identity of authorship, the present writer is confident that the Gospel and Letters of John derive from the same "school" or "circle" of Christian writers.[6] He therefore considers these writings a corpus in much the same way most scholars view the Qumran materials. Differences are surely to be found in the theological formulations of Qumran's Rule (1QS), the Thanksgiving Hymns (1QH), and War Scroll (1QM), as examples, but it is commonly assumed that these three documents reflect basic beliefs of the sect. Unique features of the Fourth Gospel persuade some readers that the thought of the evangelist can be known only through this writing, that he may well have been a maverick in his theology. Yet, if it is a sound assumption that the writer or writers of the Johannine Gospel and Letters belonged to the same community, it is more probable that their basic ideas, attitudes and perception of mission were similar. One may speak therefore of a Johannine as well as a Qumran theology recognizing that, within each corpus, documents of different types and purposes may be expected to exhibit different concerns and emphases, and employ common language and modes of expression in slightly different ways. With the proper reservations, one may use ideas which come to clear expression in one document to explain unclear passages in another. An important guideline is that one make the basic comparisons between documents which are most nearly alike with respect to their writer's intentions.

In the study of passages which follows, principal attention is

---

[6]No treatment of The Revelation to John will be attempted. The source problems of the Apocalypse are especially complicated and, as R. E. Brown notes, the peculiar literary genre of the book possesses "so many stereotyped qualities that it offers great difficulties for establishing interrelationship" (*New Testament Essays*, 103, n. 3). It is of course probable that the Apocalypse originated in the Johannine community. See C. K. Barrett, *The Gospel According to St John* (London, 1955) 51f., 113f.

focused upon a single document from each collection, the Gospel of
John and the Thanksgiving Hymns of Qumran (the Hodayoth or
1QH). Within the Gospel, primary consideration will be given to
the Prologue (1:1–18) and to the discourses, especially the so-called
"farewell discourses" (14–17). While the Hodayoth of Qumran and
the Johannine discourses are in many ways dissimilar with respect
to their literary forms, content and purpose, there are features of
both which invite comparison, and raise similar problems for
their interpreters. The theological teaching of both documents comes
to expression as the testimony of speakers who, having experienced
a direct and passionate personal relationship with God, talk mostly
about themselves, and yet throughout intend to instruct disciples,
even when their speech is directed toward God in prayer and praise.
Speakers in both celebrate the revelation of divine mysteries—a
disclosure of God's saving "knowledge" or "truth". Doxological
language serves a variety of purposes: to clarify, to correct misunderstanding, to console, to declare the things that are to come, etc.
As mediators of divine revelation, the words of the speakers draw
together before God a community of his worshippers who believe
that they are his "chosen ones".

In describing the nature of the Hodayoth, J. Licht observes
that the themes of the hymns are few "and repetitive to the point of
monotony"; the same things are said over and over again, "either in
the same words or with some variations". Whereas the theological
doctrines of the Hodayoth are not always explicit, "the basic and
most important notions recur almost constantly" and "the insertion
of speculative sentences or of single, sharply phrased statements of
belief into the lyrical flow of praise" enables the reader to reconstruct
the theology which underlies the text.[7]

The above sentences are reminiscent of comments frequently voiced
by students of John's Gospel, and to some extent of 1 John. The
Gospel's themes are few and developed in a repetitive style which
sometimes reaches the point of monotony. Yet the evangelist's
theology unfolds as complementary themes are developed through
their restatement with important nuances.

There is, however, in the Gospel a concreteness which one does
not find in the Hodayoth. According to Licht, the poetry of the
Hodayoth "proves to be to some extent a lyrical elaboration of
speculative themes". The human story of the writer or writers
remains unknown, only the life of the inner man is exhibited, a
spiritual odyssey unfolded. But John's teaching arises out of a con-
tinuum of events, and dramatic narration in which everything focuses
upon Jesus' historic ministry, his words and work. Man's ultimate
blessedness is to know him and to believe in his words and work.[8]
All threads of John's theology are drawn through the pattern of his
Christology. The speaker in the Hodayoth affirms confidently that
God has manifested his "marvellous mysteries" to him, taught him
"the counsel of his truth", and given him "understanding of his

---

[7]J. Licht, "The Doctrine of the Thanksgiving Scroll", *IEJ* 6 (1956) 2f.
[8]Jn 17:3, 24; also 3:36; 5:24f.; 6:28f.; 20:30f.; cf. 1QH 2:30f.; 4:5f.; 7:26ff.
See also 1 Jn 3:1ff.; 5:20; 1QS 11:8ff., 43ff.

wonderful works", in nature and history, so that he may testify to God's glory. But there are no parallels in the Qumran hymns to words of the Johannine Christ such as these: "I am the way and the truth and the life: no one comes to the Father except through me. If you really knew me, then you would recognize my Father too. From now on you do know him and have seen him." Or again, there is no praise like the following: "I glorified you on earth by completing the work you have given me to do; so now glorify me, Father, in your presence with that glory which I had with you before the world existed."[9] The sectarians of Qumran evidently scorned all spiritual guides except their own maśkîl and revered especially their Teacher of Righteousness. Yet one searches in vain in the Qumran documents for anything comparable to the belief to which Jesus' disciples are called, a belief in the absolute finality—the eschatological significance—of Jesus' person, his words and his work.[10]

God the Creator: of the world, of man, and of the two spirits

The Qumran sectarians affirmed the Old Testament faith in God as Creator.[11] Yet associated with this traditional faith was their intense belief in divine foreknowledge and predestination which they expressed with a fervour and certainty unparalleled in the Jewish literature of late antiquity. All things exist and everything happens because God in his wisdom wills them, and always for his own glory.

By Thy wisdom [all things exist from] eternity,
   and before creating them Thou knewest their works
   forever and ever.
[Nothing] is done [without Thee]
   and nothing is known except Thou desire it. . . .
Thou hast spread the heavens for Thy glory. . . .
   Thou hast created the earth by Thy power
   and the seas and deeps [by Thy might].
Thou hast fashioned [all] their [inhabi]tants
   according to Thy wisdom. . . .
Thou hast allotted to them (i.e. to men) tasks
   during all their generations. . . .
In the wisdom of Thy knowledge
   Thou didst establish their destiny
   before ever they were.
All things [exist] according to [Thy will]
   and without Thee nothing is done.[12]

The Hodayoth begin with this meditation upon God's unlimited power and glory evidenced in his creation. Likewise a passage in the

9Jn 14:5f.; 17:4f. (R. E. Brown's translations); also Jn 1:1–4, 14; 1 Jn 5:20.
10 1QH 2:11ff.; 4:22f.; 7:11f., 20f.; 1QpHab 2:8f.; 7:4f.; 1QpMicah; 4QpPs 37 2:15f. Cf. Jn 6:61ff.; 10:1ff.; 13:13; 17:6ff.; 1 Jn 1:4f.; 5:20.
11Gen 1:1ff.; Ps 33:5; Is 40:28; 42:5; Pr 8:30.
12 1QH 1:7f., 13f., 19f. See also 1QH 10:12; 16:8; 18:21f.; and 1QM 10:12ff. All translations, unless otherwise noted, are from G. Vermes, The Dead Sea Scrolls in English (Harmondsworth, Baltimore, 1968).

Rule, which seems to introduce a credal statement, begins as follows:

> From the God of Knowledge comes all that is and shall be.
> Before ever they existed He established their whole design, and
> when, as ordained for them, they came into being, it is in accord
> with His glorious design that they accomplish their task without
> change.[13] The laws of all things are in His hand and He provides
> them with all their needs.[14]

In both documents from Qumran these statements concerning God
the Creator make reference to his having created "the spirits". As one
would expect, in view of their different intentions, the statement in
the Rule proclaims this teaching in greater detail and clarity than the
passage in the first hymn, or indeed in any of the Hodayoth that
follow. The celebrated passage from the Rule is excerpted below:

> He (i.e. God) has created man to govern the world, and has
> appointed for him two spirits in which to walk until the time of
> His visitation: the spirits of truth and falsehood. Those born of
> truth spring from a fountain of light, but those born of false-
> hood spring from a source of darkness. All the children of righteous-
> ness are ruled by the Prince of Light and walk in the ways of
> light, but all the children of falsehood are ruled by the Angel of
> Darkness and walk in the ways of darkness.
>
> The Angel of Darkness leads all the children of righteousness
> astray, and until his end, all their sin... and all their unlawful
> deeds are caused by his dominion in accordance with the mysteries
> of God... for all his allotted spirits seek to overthrow the sons of
> light. But the God of Israel and His Angel of Truth will succour
> all the sons of light....

This is followed by descriptions of the opposing "ways" of the two
spirits, as manifested in the virtues and vices of the sons of light
and of darkness, respectively; and brief statements of an eschatology
of bliss or of calamity awaiting those who walk in one or the other
way. And then we read:

> The nature of all the children of men is ruled by these (two
> spirits), and during their life all the hosts of men have a portion
> in their divisions and walk in (both) their ways. And the whole
> reward for their deeds shall be, for everlasting ages, according to
> whether each man's portion in their two divisions is great or small.
> For God has established the spirits in equal measure until the final

[13]Or perhaps, with P. Wernberg-Møller, one should read: "...they carry
through their activity according to His glorious design. Nothing can be changed";
see *Manual of Discipline* (STDJ 1; Leiden, Grand Rapids, 1957) 25.

[14]1QS 3:15ff. See also 1QS 11:11. H. Ringgren shows that the Qumran sectarians'
belief in God's predestination in ordering the universe was accompanied by "a
similar deterministic view of history", citing CD 1:3f. and 1QM 11:1ff. While
Jewish apocalyptic literature also expresses a more or less deterministic view of
history (e.g. 2 Esdras 6:5f.), "this doctrine has never been presented elsewhere
within Judaism as consistently" as in the Qumran corpus; see *The Faith of Qumran*
(Philadelphia, 1963) 58ff., 55.

age, and has set everlasting hatred between their divisions....[15]

Is it possible to define with precision this dualistic position? Efforts by scholars have resulted in divergent views. Terms such as metaphysical, cosmological, psychological, ethical—to note but a few —have been employed, which seem to mean different things to different scholars, and one or more of these adjectives have been used to the exclusion of others. Much attention also has been given to the cultural derivation of this particular type of dualistic thought, and to the question whether or not the development resulted in a faith essentially compatible with or alien to Judaism.[16] There is, however, agreement on one point. The dualism of Qumran was certainly not an absolute dualism, either in the sense of affirming a limitless coexistence and coequality of good and evil beings or forces, or of spirit and matter. Belief in "the God of Israel" as Creator led the sectarians to espouse a "modified dualism", or perhaps one should say, a qualified or relative system.

Much interest has centred on the question: to what do the "two spirits" have reference? Does the Qumran dualism merely express, in mythological language, a belief similar to that set forth in rabbinic literature, that God created in man two impulses or propensities, a good and an evil $y\bar{e}t\!ser$?[17] Attempts have been made to limit the meaning of the text to a "psychological dualism".[18] But references to the "dominions" of "the Angel of Darkness" (elsewhere given the personal name "Belial"[19]) and to God's "Angel of Truth" or "Prince of Light" (probably "Michael" of 1QM),[20] and to the baneful or helpful influences which these powers exert upon men, seem to demand a dualism that is cosmic in its dimensions. This is strongly supported by evidence that the sectarians believed in the existence of "angels" and "demons" as cosmic beings. Although they gave the term "spirit" manifold meanings, it is sometimes used to refer to angels, as it was by writers of other apocalyptic documents.[21] One

---

[15]1QS 4:15ff. Cf. 1QH 1:15ff. and 23ff. (passages difficult to reconstruct because of damage to the scroll). For clearer expression of this dualism in the Hodayoth, see 14:8ff., and 15:12ff.; also, 1QM 13:9ff. J. Painter's statement is surprising: "The conflict between the two spirits is absent from the Hymn Scroll." But he is correct in calling attention to the writer's "unsystematic use of the term spirit"; see "Gnosticism and the Qumran Texts", *AusBR* 17 (1969) 3f. From 1QH alone it could not be demonstrated that there was a real *hypostasis* of the spirit in Qumran doctrine.

[16]The most comprehensive survey of these divergent views may be found in J. Charlesworth, "A Critical Comparison of the Dualism in 1QS III, 13–IV, 26 and the 'Dualism' Contained in the Fourth Gospel", *NTS* 15 (1969) 389ff. This article is reprinted below, pp. 76ff.

[17]Note especially the statement in 1QS 4:23. See also G. F. Moore, *Judaism* (Cambridge, 1927) vol. 1, 479ff. For references in intertestamental literature to the two inclinations, see Sir 15:14; Test. Asher 1:3ff.

[18]See especially P. Wernberg-Møller, "A Reconsideration of the Two Spirits in the Rule of the Community (1Q Serek III, 13–IV, 26)", *RevQ* 3 (1961) 413ff.

[19]1QS 1:18, 24 *et al.*; 4QTest 2:3. Note also the reference to subordinates in 1QS 3:24; 1QM 13:11f.; and CD 14:5: "the spirits of Belial"; cf. 1QM 1:5.

[20]1QM 17:6ff.; cf. 13:10.

[21]See A. A. Anderson, "The Use of 'Ruah' in 1QS, 1QH and 1QM", *JSS* 7 (1962) 293; J. Pryke, " 'Spirit' and 'Flesh' in the Qumran Documents and Some New Testament Texts", *RevQ* 5 (1965) 345ff.; Ringgren, *The Faith of Qumran*, 81ff.

may agree that while in the passage from the Rule Qumran's dualistic teaching is applied primarily to man's moral life and destiny, so that the ethical aspect predominates, human existence is viewed here and elsewhere as only part of a cosmic warfare ordained by the Creator, and finally resolved, not by men, but by God in his mighty power and for his own glory.[22]

Predestinarian themes are corollaries of this "qualified dualism" with ethical and cosmic dimensions. Some scholars have concluded that the men of Qumran espoused an absolute determinism and drew the logical conclusions therefrom: at birth a man was assigned "the lot" either of the righteous or the wicked. His nature and fate were predetermined by the divine will. "The children of righteousness" could only exult in God's unmerited favour and assurances to them and, being upheld by his grace, walk according to "the counsels of the spirit to the sons of truth". Accordingly, they accepted without questioning the "mysteries" of the divine will which, for a limited time, delivered a part of the world of men to the rule of Belial. They offered no reason for this rigid division of mankind other than that it manifested the glory of God.[23]

It is unlikely that the Qumran sect wholly rejected belief in man's freedom, or in the necessity for his making genuine ethical decisions. The righteous were ever being subjected to the onslaughts of "the spirit of falsehood", which called for a resistance of man's will. Is it possible that the sectarians remained "unaware of the problem of moral responsibility", as some have claimed?[24] The rules of the community clearly imply otherwise. Punishments were meted out to individuals who disobeyed God's laws, for "deliberate sins" as well as unwitting sins; and the possibilities for repentance and reform were emphasized.[25] Given the unsystematic way in which doctrine is expressed in the Hodayoth, it is not surprising to find in these hymns a logically inconsistent juxtaposition of determinism and freedom:

> Thou alone didst [create] the just
>   and established him from the womb
>   for the time of goodwill,
> that he might hearken to Thy covenant
>   and walk in all [Thy ways]. . . .
> But the wicked Thou didst create
>   for [the time] of Thy [wrath],

[22]Charlesworth, see below, pp. 82 ff. J. T. Milik makes the important observation: "although each day's life was a struggle between the forces of good and evil", the sectarians' "main interests were in the moral and human aspects of this conflict; in contrast to the author of the Book of Enoch, they did not become fascinated by its cosmic character"; see *Ten Years of Discovery in the Wilderness of Judaea*, trans. J. Strugnell (SBT 26; London, Naperville, 1959) 121.

[23]Licht, *IEJ* 6 (1956) 9, and 5ff.; M. Mansoor, *The Thanksgiving Hymns* (STDJ 3; Leiden, Grand Rapids, 1961) 55f.

[24]*Ibid.*, 7. M. Burrows, *More Light on the Dead Sea Scrolls* (New York, 1958) 292f.

[25]R. E. Brown points to 1QS 5:11, and cites also CD 3:7; 4:9f., in *New Testament Essays*, 115. Note other paradoxical statements in 1QS 5:1; 10:12f.

Thou didst vow them from the womb
  to the Day of Massacre,
  for they walk in the way that is not good.
They have despised [Thy Covenant]
  and their souls have loathed Thy [truth];
they have taken no delight in all Thy commandments
  and have chosen that which Thou hatest. . . .[26]

Divine grace is primarily emphasized in the Hodayoth in the light
of which the writer can only deplore his sinfulness and inert frailty.
Yet one reads:

But those who please Thee
  shall stand before Thee forever,
Those who walk in the way of Thy heart
  shall be established forevermore. [27]

Neither in theory nor in practice were the men at Qumran "wholly
deterministic or wholly voluntaristic".[28] This conclusion seems to be
borne out by the way in which eschatological sanctions are developed
in the doctrine of the "two spirits".[29] Each person is conceived to
be a mixture of those qualities which distinguish absolutely the
sons of darkness and of light. God's eschatological judgment alone
will separate the righteous from the wicked according to their "lot",
as aggregates of men. Of course the men of Qumran believed themselves already "the sons of light" because of divine favour. Yet the
process of their purification by the spirit of truth was not yet completed. They must ever be alert to the possibility that the evil spirit
which threatened them would gain ascendancy in their hearts. They
must seek by their own wills to remove the evil portion within them.
"The precise factor in the [Qumran] community which sanctifies
its members is their acceptance of, and obedience to, the teaching of
the sect." "Refusal to do God's will makes one a son of darkness."[30]
In any statement of their doctrines it cannot be overlooked that
Qumran was a community of "the Covenant".[31] It could be affirmed,
in summary fashion, by one writer that the righteous are those "who
observe the Law in the House of Judah, whom God will deliver from
the House of Judgment, because of their suffering [or 'their labour'],
and because of their faith in the Teacher of Righteousness" (i.e. their
fidelity to their revered teacher's exposition of the Torah).[32]

26 1QH 15:15ff.
27 1QH 4:21f.
28P. Hyatt, "The View of Man in the Qumran '*Hodayoth*' ", *NTS* 2 (1955–56)
203. J. Van der Ploeg, *The Excavations at Qumran*, trans. K. Smyth (London,
New York, Toronto, 1958) 112ff.
29Charlesworth calls attention to the intensification of the eschatological sanction
in the delineation of this doctrine, with emphasis falling upon the final judgment.
See below, pp. 81ff.
30R. E. Brown, *New Testament Essays*, 117. An active not a passive acceptance.
The community demanded of its sectarians that they do good works in conformity
to the Rule.
31*Ibid.*, 116.
32 1QpHab 8:1.

Johannine dualism

Attention is now drawn to the Gospel and Letters of John. When we compare poetry with poetry, the themes of the first hymn of the Hodayoth with those of the Prologue to the Gospel of John (and note their development, chiefly in the Johannine discourses) we find some interesting parallels. Central to both documents is the thought of God revealing himself—his divine "glory" and "name"—making himself known to the world of men.[33] In both, the speakers acknowledge that it is only because God, in his grace and truth, has willed it that some men come to know him and receive this knowledge in faith, and are thus enabled to live perpetually before him and proclaim his glory.[34]

Of course, in the Gospel, God's self-revelation is through the Logos, "the Son" of the Father. The enlightenment of those bearing witness to the divine glory does not consist in their having received unprecedented insights into God's "marvellous mysteries" through their meditation upon the Law and the Prophets, or through a new revelation of the divine will in the form of law such as Moses had received,[35] but in the fact that the Logos had become "flesh" and lived among men, speaking "the truth" but also in his manhood personifying Truth itself.[36]

Clearly John's theological conviction that God had revealed himself definitively in his "unique Son" makes his Gospel and the Qumran community theology incommensurable, but do we not find that a similar conceptual framework underlies both proclamations of divine revelation?

Qumran's "qualified dualism", with its ethical and cosmic dimensions, its deterministic teaching and eschatological sanctions, is developed in the Scrolls by an extensive use of a light-versus-darkness motif. Indeed, "the most conspicuous characteristic" of the sect's dualism is the predominance of this motif.[37] The Prologue to the Fourth Gospel also introduces the theme of conflict between light and darkness in association with the thought of the Creator's self-revelation to the world. One might expect to find here Johannine dualism in its cosmic aspect. But the struggle between light and darkness is presented as a conflict within creation, within "the world" of men. On the one side is the uncreated Logos "of God" become man, and "children" who are also "of God", having been given the right to be called his children because they are begotten by his will and believe in his name. On the other side, according to the Prologue, is "the darkness" of the world which not only fails to receive "the true light" of God being manifested, but actively opposes

---

[33] Jn 1:18 (note that the best manuscript evidence supports "God the only Son", i.e. only God can reveal God; the variants do not change the sense, according to John's oft repeated claim that the one seeing Jesus sees God, Jn 17:3). "I glorified thee . . . I manifested thy Name" (17:4, 6, 25f.). Cf 1QH 10:20f. Note also the poetic apostrophe, 1QS 11:17ff.

[34] Jn 1:12f., 14b, 16. Cf. 1QH 1:21, 29ff.; 4:27ff.; 9:35f.

[35] E.g., 1QH 7:26f.

[36] Jn 1:14, 17f.; 8:31f., 40; 14:6; 18:37f.

[37] Charlesworth, see below, pp. 78ff.

it. In this context it is implied that it is God's "own people"—some of his own creation—who typify or represent this darkness. In the Gospel it is made clear that Jesus is the uncreated Light, who has "come", or been "sent", into this world to be "the light of men".[38] And the believing disciples of Jesus are these "children", born of God and summoned to "walk in the light", lest they be overtaken by the darkness, so that they may become "sons of light".[39] Those among "the Jews" who do not believe in Jesus are identified as representatives of "this world" (of darkness).[40]

The above observations might lead one to describe the dualism of the Gospel as soteriological and ethical. Both of these aspects are also present in 1 John, although in an epistolary document of its type, as one might expect, emphasis is given to the ethical aspect, an emphasis which receives only slight development in the Gospel. But an important question remains unanswered. Does Johannine theology presuppose a dualism in its cosmic aspect?

Many scholars have found that an essential feature of John's dualism is expressed in his frequent allusions to two realms or worlds: "the above" and "the below".[41] The earliest Christians, it is said, employed the commonplace contrast within Jewish eschatology between "this (present) age, or world" and "the world to come", as the conceptual framework for interpreting their gospel of fulfilment; John either substituted a vertical and spatial dualism for this linear, horizontal and temporal one of the traditional Gospel, or combined the two. The Gospel's cosmic dualism consists of coexistent worlds, "the above" (characterized by light, life, truth, spirit) and "the below" (characterized by darkness, death, error, flesh). This cosmological framework is parallel to the metaphysical dualism of the Greeks and, others would add, is proto-gnostic in its statement.

Clearly John assumes a two-world *Weltanschauung*. It provided an important assumption for positions taken concerning Christ's origin and essential nature. Thus Jesus is presented as one having "come from God" or "descended from heaven".[42] John evidently found the two-world schema also helpful in his expositions of the "already fulfilled" aspects of Christian eschatology.[43] None will deny that John's "two worlds" provide a distinguishing feature of his Gospel, especially when one compares its Christology and eschatology with the Synoptic Gospels. Yet it is probable that John's two-world dualism was already a commonplace conceptual framework in Jewish apocalyptic and wisdom theology which was sometimes substituted for, or combined with, the linear division between the present and future ages or worlds. In any case, it seems that a soteriological and ethical dualism is more fundamental to the theology of the Fourth Gospel than its two-world dualism, and that in the development of the former a cosmic aspect is disclosed which is more typically Johannine.

38Jn 8:12; 9:5; 12:46, also 3:18ff.
39Jn 12:35f., also 8:12b.
40Jn 9:39ff., also 3:18ff.
41E.g. Charlesworth, see below, pp. 89ff.
42Jn 3:11ff., 31; 6:33ff.; 8:23; 13:3; 16:28ff.
43Jn 3:3ff.; 6:37ff.; 15:19; 17:13ff.

B

When the two-world cosmology of John is compared with
Hellenistic or specifically gnostic models, significant differences
appear. The Gospel excludes the idea that "this world" ("the below")
is essentially a realm of darkness; that only "the above" is a realm
of light. God's creation through the Logos includes the world below;
his light shines in the darkness, so that light and darkness are
opposed to one another *in this world*. Moreover, John does not seem
to teach that men, by virtue of their human existence, are children
of darkness. Some men "love" the darkness rather than the light,
"walk" or "work" in it, or are "overtaken" by it, but all men are
not fated to live in darkness.[44] It may seem that the "man born
blind" signifies this state of man's darkness, of man's congenital
sinfulness. But the Johannine Christ declares: "if I had not come
and spoken to them (i.e. those who are identified as 'of the world'),
they would not have sinned; but now they have no excuse for their
sins".[45] Those men are blind who claim that they see while they are
in the process of rejecting the light.[46] Again it may seem that John's
references to those who "remain" in darkness imply that darkness is
a condition of man's existence *qua* man. But, as we have noted, this
being-in-darkness derives from man's preference for it rather than
light, or a wilful refusal to come to the light.

The Johannine equation of the darkness of the world with man's
unbelief in God self-revealed in Jesus is given special development in
the controversial discourse of chapter eight. Here the contrast between
men who "have the light of life" and those who "walk in darkness"
is further explained as the fateful opposition of those who know and
tell "the truth", and those who will have nothing to do with it and
who "lie" about their origin, present situation and destiny. Employing
these complementary pairs of opposite terms (light/darkness; truth/
error), John explicates an essential cosmic dimension of the Gospel's
dualism.

An early hint is given of this aspect of Johannine theology. The
dictum that "he who does what is true comes to the light" is accompanied by the explanation that such a man's deeds are manifestly
"wrought in God".[47] We are now told that "he who is *of God*
hears the words of God", words spoken by the Son, himself taught
by the Father and sent into the world to bear witness to the truth,
and thereby to free men from their bondage to sin and death.[48] But
opposed to him and to his disciples is another group of men, those
who walk in darkness wilfully refusing to come to the light. These
are not "of God" but "of [their] father the devil, and [their] will is
to do [their] father's desires". It is affirmed that this evil one was
"a murderer from the beginning"; that he has "nothing to do with
the truth because the truth is not in him"; that he is "a liar and the
father of lies".[49]

44Jn 3:19ff.; 8:12b; 9:4.
45Jn 15:22.
46Jn 9:39f.
47Jn 3:21.
48Jn 8:47; see also vv. 31ff.
49Jn 8:44; also vv. 38, 41.

It is noteworthy that while John's presupposition of the coexistence of two worlds (the above/the below) appears in the development of this discourse, the dualism which interests him most remains a this-worldly struggle, and is restated as a soteriological and ethical ✓ conflict. The life-or-death encounter between light and darkness is depicted as a collision between two cosmic powers and two groups of men: the one, representing the truth; the other, perverse error. On the one hand, God makes his appeal to men through him who is "the light of the world", offering them freedom from sin and death; on the other hand, the devil is the source of man's falsehood and opposition to the truth. He holds dominion over some men destined "to die in their sins", unless they are made free by the Son.[50] This threatening power is elsewhere identified in the Gospel as "the ruler of the (or this) world", and Satan.[51]

The tantalizingly brief references to this cosmic dimension of Johannine dualism probably bring the theology of the Fourth Gospel closer to Qumran dualism than many scholars have allowed. It has been claimed that while John clearly found the concept of the devil as world-ruler in primitive Christian apocalyptic thought, he demythologized the concept; that since the Fourth Gospel does not portray the devil as a cosmic "spirit" or "angel", references to the evil one are only symbolical.[52] But should one expect to find in the Gospel an explicit interest in the origin, nature and influence of "the ruler of this world", comparable to that shown in the Qumran Rule? The Hodayoth offer no cosmological explanation of man's wickedness, yet few would deny the presence therein of a cosmological dualism. The hymn writer's preoccupation with the blessedness of the righteous, both as present experience and future hope, adequately explains the scant or imprecise references in the Hodayoth to the cosmic "spirits".

A somewhat similar reason may explain why the fourth evangelist does not develop this cosmic dimension of the Johannine dualism. If, as we believe, the Gospel was written to confirm the faith of Christians in Jesus Christ, the Son of God, who has "overcome the world", then the writer's overriding interest in heralding Christ's victory, and in dwelling upon the benefits of his death and resurrection, is understandable. Thus Jesus is presented as celebrating the imminent

---

[50] Jn 8:43ff., also 21, 24. Cf. 1QS 3:19, 21; 4:12. Note that the angel or spirit is identified by the three terms "falsehood, darkness, destruction (death)".

[51] Jn 12:31; 13:2, 27ff.; 14:40; 16:11. The term Satan was not unknown at Qumran, 1QM 13:2.

[52] E.g. Charlesworth, see below, pp. 92ff. R. Bultmann, *Theology of the New Testament*, trans. K. Grobel (New York, London, 1955) vol. 2, 17, observes correctly that the devilish power "is not gnostically conceived as a cosmic power . . . . Rather, *the world is the creation of God.*" But Qumran and Johannine theology allow the limited world rule of a cosmic evil power *within* God's creation and destined for destruction. It seems clear to the present writer that John's references to the "ruler of this world" (Satan) are to a cosmic spirit. Note Jn 13:7: "Satan entered into him" (i.e. Judas). In the light of this, can one be sure that 6:70 can have a symbolical meaning only? Cf. 1QS 3:22f.; 4:23f. It is not inconsistent to shift from the thought of a man's action as revealing his dominant spirit to the thought of an impersonal cosmic spirit exercising rule over him. Note the terminology in 8:13ff.: Jesus' opponents claim that he has "a demon". Cf. 10:19ff.

defeat of "the ruler of this world".[53] As the "glorified Son" of the
Father, he calls upon men to "believe in the light" that they may
become "sons of light".[54] The struggles between the risen Lord
and the devil could no longer be depicted as an unresolved, cosmic
conflict between light and darkness, truth and error, *on equal terms*.
At the same time, the ascending Christ prays that those whom the
Father has given him may be kept in this world from "the evil
one". Only as God wills to "sanctify them in the truth" will their
victory as a community of faith be fully realized.[55] Moreover,
Jesus promises his disciples—and this is often overlooked—that when
"the Spirit of truth comes", his own forensic work in the contest
with darkness and error will be carried forward. In their own forthcoming struggles the disciples will become convinced that, because
of Jesus' accomplished mission, "the ruler of this world is judged".[56]

One finds in 1 John, as one might expect, a clearer statement of
this cosmic aspect of Johannine dualism. It is with 1 Jn 3:7-10 and
4:1-6 that one should compare 1QS 3:17ff. Some while ago Frank
Cross observed that "in both the Rule and 1 John we recognize a
similar 'spirit-spirit' dualism ... which allots some to God or the Spirit
of Truth, others to the devil or the Spirit of Deceit. In both, the
diabolical spirit struggles against the children of God (or of light).
In both, the children of light have knowledge which permits them to
distinguish between the spirits of truth and deceit. Because of the aid
of God or the Spirit of Truth, the children of light do righteousness,
but those under the dominion of the devil walk in ways of darkness."[57]

Two explanations may be given for the relative lack of interest of
the writer of the Fourth Gospel in the cosmic dimension of this
Johannine dualism: the distinctive emphasis within his community
upon the realized aspects of Christian eschatology decisively affected
his theological perspective and brought into prominence the thought
of Christ's cosmic victory (not conflict); and the evangelist's interest
in the this-worldly struggle between Christ and his foes led him to
develop especially the soteriological aspect of his community's
dualistic theology and, to lesser extent, its ethical dimension. Yet the
similarity of Johannine and Qumran dualism in their cosmic aspects
is striking, and differences are not satisfactorily explained as grounded
in disparate conceptual backgrounds. The impact of the early
Christian kerygma accounts for the substantive differences: the proclamation that God had acted in history through his Son, a person of
unequalled authority in heaven and on earth, whose victory over sin
and death revealed the eschatological glory of God and made certain
the accomplishment of his will. In the idiom of the Fourth Gospel,
the personal leader of "the sons of light" is the uncreated Logos
whom God sent into the world to be its light and life, to dispel its
darkness (sin and death) and, finally, to overcome the threatening
power of "the ruler of this world".

[53] Jn 12:27ff. 1 Jn 2:13f.; 3:8.
[54] Jn 12:36.
[55] Jn 17:15ff.
[56] Jn 16:7ff. Cf. 1QH 6:8ff.; 11:6ff.
[57] F. M. Cross, Jr, *The Ancient Library of Qumran and Modern Biblical Studies*,
rev. ed. (Garden City, New York, London, 1961) 212f.

Whether or not some of the terms used by the Qumran sectarians in the exposition of their cosmic dualism, and not found in the Gospel, were known to the Johannine community is a purely speculative question. One may judge that if the designation "Prince of Light" had currency, John might have considered it wholly inadequate as applied to Christ in view of his convictions concerning the origin and historical manifestation of Christ's "kingdom".[58] Likewise the term "Angel of Truth" would have seemed inappropriate since John's narrative stresses that Jesus' regal authority was manifested in his *manhood,* especially in his death and resurrection. It is noteworthy, however, that one term found in Qumran's dualistic teaching—"the Spirit of Truth"—is an important concept in the Gospel's theology. As Raymond Brown observes, John seems to have chosen the term "light" as a fitting symbol for Jesus, the Logos incarnate, and "the Spirit of Truth" as "an apt description of the Holy Spirit, the true witness to Christ".[59]

According to the Qumran dualistic teaching, as we have seen, God appointed "the Spirit of Truth" to "help" or to "succour" all the sons of light.[60] It has been suggested by some scholars that the most adequate translation for the Johannine loan-word *paraklētos* is the term "helper". But neither this word nor the archaic phrase, "the one who gives succour", connotes the variety of functions assigned to the Spirit in the Johannine community.[61] The Gospel proclaims that "the Spirit of Truth" will console the disciples in the absence of their teacher and Lord;[62] that he will dwell with them, guide and teach them, bringing to their remembrance all that Jesus said to them, as well as declaring to them "the things that are to come".[63] The remaining functions of the *paraklētos* may be described as forensic: in the face of the world's hatred, "the Spirit of Truth" will witness in defence of Jesus, becoming a spokesman for him when his claims are in dispute.[64]

The only certain, pre-Christian parallel to this assignment of forensic activity to "the Spirit of Truth" is found in the Qumran documents.[65] In general it may be concluded that Jewish apocalyptic and wisdom books provide an intelligible background for John's conception of the divine Spirit as a quasi-personal teacher, guide

---

[58]Note the emphasis in John's passion story upon Jesus as "king", 18:33ff., 39; 19:1ff.

[59]*New Testament Essays*, 121.

[60] 1QS 3:24. (The priestly prayer in the War Scroll provides a particularly interesting parallel to the priestly farewell discourses of Jesus. Cf. 1QM 13, which describes the elect company—the high priest and the people of God's inheritance who "know" him by faith—rejoicing in the "help" and "peace" which God has given them: "Thou hast decreed for us a destiny of Light according to Thy truth. And the Prince of Light Thou hast appointed from ancient times to come to our support; [all the sons of righteousness are in his hand], and all the spirits of truth are under his dominion." Cf. Jn 14:16; 17:7ff.

[61]See R. E. Brown, *The Gospel According to John: XIII–XXI* (Anchor Bible 29a; Garden City, New York, 1970; London, 1971) 1136f.

[62]Jn 14:16.

[63]Jn 14:17b, 26; 16:12f.

[64]Jn 15:26; 16:7ff.

[65]The text history of the several parallels in Test. Judah 20:1ff. is uncertain.

and revealer of God's mysteries to his chosen ones.[66] But the
Qumran complex of ideas which defines the Spirit both as a God-
appointed, cosmic-defender and advocate, and as a witness within
certain men to "the truth" (a spirit which opposes the spirit of deceit
in the sons of darkness) affords a particularly close analogy to the
forensic activities of John's *paraklētos*. The doctrine of the Holy
Spirit in the Fourth Gospel is not as unique as some have supposed,
when one compares with other New Testament teaching the functions
which John assigns the Spirit within the life and mission of the
Christian community. Yet when one juxtaposes Qumran and
Johannine passages relating to the forensic activity of "the Spirit of
Truth", distinctive emphases and original elements in the Johannine
theology of the Spirit are brought into sharp focus.

The impression must not be given that John's understanding of
the work of "the Spirit of Truth" developed under the direct impact
of ideas such as those expressed in Qumran's dualistic teaching,
although it is quite probable that these ideas provided him with
congenial modes of expression. The description of the work of the
paraklētos in the Fourth Gospel parallels closely its portrayal of
Jesus' person and work. It is therefore likely that the direct inspiration
for John's "Spirit of Truth" arose from his conviction that in becoming "flesh", God's unique Son had revealed "the Truth" and mediated
to men "the light of life", and that through Jesus' indwelling spirit,
God continues to console and to teach his own, and also to convince
the world that men are saved and judged through testimony to the
Son.

Brief comment must be made on the predestinarian element in
Johannine theology since, as we have seen, a marked determinism was
a corollary of the cosmic dualism of Qumran. Bultmann calls attention to the numerous passages in the Gospel which pose the problem:[67]
"Is it not true that only he whom the Father 'draws' comes to Jesus,[68]
only he to whom it is 'given' by the Father?[69] Is it not said that only
he can 'hear his voice' who is 'of the truth', who is 'of God'[70]—
that only he can believe who belongs to his 'sheep'?[71] And is it not
solely 'his own' whom he calls to himself,[72] whom he knows and
who know him?[73] And does not the prophet's word confirm the
opinion that unbelief rests upon the hardening imposed by God?"[74]
One might also call attention to the explanation given in John for
the defection of Judas.[75]

Numerous efforts have been made to show that John's Gospel
does not teach predestination. By contrasting the Gospel's teaching
with the determinism of later Gnosticism, grounded in a belief that

66R. E. Brown, *John* (Anchor Bible 29b) 1138f.
67*Theology*, vol. 2, 21.
68Jn 6:44.
69Jn 6:65; also 6:37, 39; 17:2, 6, 9, 12, 24; 18:9.
70Jn 18:37; 8:47.
71Jn 10:26.
72Jn 10:3f., 15.
73Jn 10:14, 27.
74Jn 12:39f. (Is 6:10).
75Jn 6:70; 13:11, 21ff.; 17:12.

men possess different natures, Bultmann declares that John's "pre-destinatory formulations" only define his understanding of Christian faith as "a surrender of one's own self-assertion".[76] Other scholars are content to say that for John belief or disbelief conditions whether one is of the light or the darkness.[77] The present writer is not persuaded that the apparent paradox of predestination and freedom of man's will in the Fourth Gospel is so readily resolved, either by an existentialist or voluntarist solution. The logical inconsistency which characterizes Qumran's qualified dualism is found also in John's. The form and substance of the Gospel's discourses make improbable a systematizing of theological statements bearing on the subject, for much the same reasons one finds them ambiguous in the Hodayoth. One finds in John, as in the Hodayoth, the teaching that the righteous must be purified by a divine power external to men, but that they must also consecrate themselves. In the Jewish and Christian documents men are "confirmed in the truth" both by acknowledging that God in his "truth" or Spirit of Truth directs the steps of his chosen ones, and by doing or practising the truth.[78]

One finds in 1 John more explicitly predestinarian statements, without the qualifications one finds in the Gospel, a determinism more closely akin to that set forth in the Rule, in the proportion that 1 John approximates the Rule's doctrine of the "two spirits". Again one must add, however, that logical consistency is eschewed: the elect of God are warned that they must "walk in the light" as God is in the light;[79] that they must "keep his commandments",[80] "confess [their] sins" (i.e. their "lawlessness"),[81] "purify" themselves,[82] and "love the brethren".[83] One suspects that within the Johannine community the perception of and emphasis upon the *love* of God manifested in his Son, struggled with a strong tendency toward predestinarian thought inherent in its dualistic theology. More successfully than the writer of 1 John, perhaps, the fourth evangelist found that the disciple's experience of "abiding in [Christ's] love" afforded a perspective for understanding, if not explaining, this paradox.[84]

Qumran's spokesman for God: The Teacher as revealer and example

Attention is now directed to the characteristics of the righteous man and of his vocation as they are portrayed in Qumran's Hodayoth. Even though the speaker's identity is never disclosed, his personal convictions and emotions are vividly displayed. These poems record the outpouring of a man's gratitude to God for the special revelations

---

[76] Bultmann, *Theology*, vol. 2, 23.
[77] Cf. Charlesworth, below, pp. 91f., 94f.
[78] 1QH 4:14; 6:7ff.; 7:14; 11:9ff.; 14:15 (cf. 1QS 1:11ff.; 5:10; CD 13:10); Jn 14:6; 16:13ff.; 17:16ff.; also 3:21; 8:31f. (cf. 1 Jn 3:1ff.; also 2:26f.; 1:6; 2:4).
[79] 1 Jn 1:7.
[80] 1 Jn 2:3f.; 5:3.
[81] 1 Jn 1:8f.; 2:1f.; 3:4.
[82] 1 Jn 3:2f.
[83] 1 Jn 2:9ff.; 3:14ff.; 4:7ff.
[84] Jn 15:1ff.

which have been granted him; for having put into his heart "teaching
and understanding" so that he might bear witness to the divine power
and glory in the midst of "the congregation of the Sons of Heaven".[85]

> What am I, that Thou shouldst [teach] me
>   the counsel of Thy truth
> and give me understanding
>   of Thy marvellous works;
> that Thou shouldst lay hymns of thanksgiving
>   within my mouth
> and [praise] upon my tongue ... ?
> I will bless Thy Name evermore.
> I will declare Thy glory in the midst of
>   the sons of men
> And my soul shall delight in Thy great goodness.

> I know that Thy word is truth,
>   and that righteousness is in Thy hand;
> that all knowledge is in Thy purpose,
> and that all power is in Thy might,
>   and that every glory is Thine.[86]

These lines clearly express the psalmist's consciousness of man's
utter dependence upon God. Even his ability to praise the Lord is a
divine gift.[87] But it is the granting of "knowledge", of "insight"
into God's "marvellous mysteries", which he celebrates most
frequently in the hymns. It may be that the gift of knowledge is
mentioned so often only to emphasize that everything that the teacher
proclaims has been revealed to him by God. But it is more likely
that the psalmist's constant references to knowledge refer to his personal rapport with God and to the particular understanding which has
been granted him. Several times he declares: "I know through the
understanding which comes from Thee ..." or, "I know through the
Spirit which Thou hast given to me...."[88] Our writer seems to
believe that a special, direct revelation from God has been vouchsafed
him. These exceptional tokens of divine grace fill him with deep
thankfulness.

Knowledge of God, of his truth or true nature, is the *summum
bonum* of this man's life.[89] Yet in the Hodayoth knowledge of God

---

[85] Some believe that the Hodayoth were written by, or at least about, Qumran's
môrēh haṣṣedeq—"the teacher of righteousness" (or the righteous or true teacher):
1QpHab 1:3; 2:1f.; 5:9; 7:1ff.; CD 1:3ff.; 19:35ff.; 20:14f.; 4QpPs 37:32f.
Ostensibly the autobiographical passages in 1QH reflect the beliefs and experiences
of an individual (and are not merely a collective expression) whether or not composed by this person or by his disciples. Since there is only one person revered in
the Qumran text, whose mission corresponds to the speaker in 1QH, it is a reasonable assumption that many if not all of the hymns were authored by "the teacher
of righteousness". However, these vexing questions of identity need not be answered
for the purposes of this section.
[86] 1QH 11:1ff. See also 4:27ff.
[87] Note 1QH 12:33ff.
[88] 1QH 14:12; 15:12; 13:18f.
[89] 1QH 12; 9:9f.; 11:7.

brings true knowledge of man, of his frailty and insignificance, his loathsome sin and wretchedness, his despair and death apart from God's saving mercy and grace:

> I know through the understanding which comes from Thee that righteousness is not in a hand of flesh, [that] man [is not master of] his way and that it is not in mortals to direct their step.[90]

The perception that God is righteous in all his actions, always truthful to his word,[91] carries with it the unqualified confession that "man is not righteous except through [God]", only God can "purify" by his Spirit all those whom he "draws near" to himself according to his gracious will.[92]

No reader of the Hodayoth can fail to be impressed with the mercurial contrasts one finds in these poems between despondency and terror on the one hand, and joy, peace and assurance on the other. Hope in God stirs the poet to the shuddering depths of emotion as he ponders the dark fate from which he is being rescued:

> As for me, shaking and trembling seize me
>   and all my bones are broken;
> my heart dissolves like wax before fire
>   and my knees are like water
>   pouring down a steep place.
> For I remember my sins
>   and the unfaithfulness of my fathers . . .
> But calling to mind the might of Thy hand
>   and the greatness of Thy compassion,
> I rose and stood,
>   and my spirit was established
>   in face of the scourge.
> I lean on Thy grace
>   and on the multitude of Thy mercies,
> for Thou wilt pardon iniquity,
>   and through Thy righteousness
>   [Thou wilt purify man] of his sin.
> Not for his sake wilt Thou do it
>   [but for the sake of Thy glory].[93]

In several passages from the Hodayoth, like the one above, forgiveness and cleansing are parallel: God will pardon and purify those "who repent of their sin".[94] J. Licht observes that ritual purity is never mentioned in the Hodayoth and explains that the speaker is not concerned about particular offences. Rather he is oppressed with a consciousness of the universal burden of man's sin. Thus God's forgiveness or atonement is perceived to be "a purification from the

90 1QH 15:12.
91 1QH 13:18f.
92 1QH 16:11f.
93 1QH 4:33ff.; also 3:19ff.; 6:5f.; 9:10ff.; 11:15ff.
94 1QH 7:30; 11:30f.; 14:24.

contaminating filth of humanity".[95] Although the hymn writer
knows that the elect of God, including himself, have not yet been
purified or made perfect, he praises God for his salvation, speaking
of a future hope as though it were present experience.

> What shall a man say
>   concerning his sin? ...
> And how shall he reply
>   to righteous judgment?
> For thine, O God of Knowledge,
>   are all righteous deeds
>   and the counsel of truth;
> but to the sons of men is the work of iniquity
>   and deeds of deceit....
> By Thy mercies and by Thy great goodness
> Thou ... hast purified [the erring spirit]
>   of a multitude of sins,
> that it may declare Thy marvels
>   in the presence of all Thy creatures.[96]

The writer's strong sense of mission or vocation has been revealed
in the passages already cited. One reads in the poems repeatedly
that God had "unstopped" the speaker's "ears" to his "marvellous
mysteries" in order that he might bear witness. Yet it would seem
that the teacher's knowledge was not to be imparted directly to
everyone. His special responsibility was for "the sons of God's
favour".[97] Several passages suggest a limitation of the speaker's
mission to the congregation or council in order to inform, instruct
and discipline the latter for its mission to other men:

> Through me Thou hast illumined
>   the face of the congregation (lit. "the many")
> and hast shown Thine infinite power.
> ... that they may make known Thy mighty deeds
>   to all the living.[98]

It is also clear that the speaker is aware of the need for the
separation of "the sons of God's favour", "the sons of truth", from
the works of "the men of deceit", "the sons of Belial". The obligation
falls upon him to love the former and nurture their piety, and to
"despise all the ways of error".[99]

The idea of separation of those who come into the covenant from
"the assembly of error" is also present in the teacher's belief that
the sectarians are constituted a "congregation of the Sons of Heaven"
as together they praise God and strive to do his will.[100] In some way

---

[95] J. Licht, *IEJ* 6 (1956) 96.
[96] 1QH 1:25ff., 32ff.; also 3:19ff.; 5:5f.
[97] 1QH 11:9. Note the explicit statement in 1QS 10:24f.
[98] 1QH 4:27f. "Thou hast made me a father to the sons of grace", 1QH 7:20.
See also 1:28ff.; 2:13f.; 11:1ff.
[99] 1QH 11:9, 11; 4:20; 2:22; 14:17ff.; 1QS 1:10.
[100] 1QH 3:22; 4:24f.; 11:10ff.; 1QS 8:21.

those who enter the Qumran community were believed to "share a common lot with the angels of the Face" (or "angels of the Presence").[101]

Of special interest to interpreters of the Hodayoth is the question of the teacher's understanding of his sufferings, chiefly caused by the abuse he has received from enemies of the sect and the traitorous actions of some of its members. It would seem that he considered his troubles to be evidence of God's "righteous judgment" which he does not wish to contest, a divine chastisement and means of purification which he accepts with thanksgiving for, in the midst of his suffering, divine grace is experienced:

Thy just rebuke accompanies my [faults]
    and Thy safeguarding peace delivers my soul.
The abundance of (Thy) forgiveness is with my steps
    and infinite mercy accompanies Thy judgment of me.[102]

In the same hymn, however, the writer speaks of his afflictions as somehow related to the fulfilment of the "mystery", of God's (final?) visitation of salvation and judgment:

For it is according to the mystery of Thy wisdom
    that Thou hast rebuked me.
Thou wilt conceal the truth until [its] time,
    [and righteousness] until its appointed moment.
Thy rebuke shall become my joy and gladness,
    and my scourges shall turn to [eternal] healing and everlasting [peace].
The scorn of my enemies shall become a crown of glory,
    and my stumbling (shall change) to everlasting might.
For in Thy...
    and my light shall shine forth in Thy glory.
For as a light from out of the darkness,
    so wilt Thou enlighten me....[103]

The author of this poem calls himself "the servant" of God, and in these lines describes his afflictions in language reminiscent of Is 53. It has been observed that the text of Is 53:12 in 1QIs[a], as well as in the LXX, reads: "from the travail of his soul *he shall shed forth light* and be satisfied".[104] Perhaps another passage from Is 53 is echoed in the phrase, "my scourges shall turn to... healing and peace". One is reminded of the hymn writer's words elsewhere: "I have been a snare to those who rebel, but healing to those of them who repent. To traitors Thou hast made of me a mockery and scorn, but a counsel of truth to the upright of way."[105]

101 1QH 6:13; 1QS 11:7f.
102 1QH 9:33f.
103 1QH 9:23ff.
104 M. Black, *The Scrolls and Christian Origins* (London, Edinburgh, Paris, New York, 1961) 143. Black calls attention to 1QH 4:27. Note also 4:22ff.
105 1QH 2:8ff., 23ff.; 7:12. Cf. Is 53:4f.

In summary we may say that the writer regarded all his troubles
as sent by God to chastise, test and purify him for his special
vocation.[106] "He therefore declares, with inverted pride: 'the con-
tempt of my foes has become for me a crown of glory'."[107] Despised
and derided by men, this man claims to know God "in [His] power as
perfect light". Through his servant's suffering, God has "illumined
the face of the congregation" of his elect.[108] The teaching of the
servant is likened to "a fountain of living water", bringing salvation
to the sons of God's favour.[109] But his teaching also provokes bitter
opposition: murmuring and betrayal from within the community;
harassment, and treacherous attempts upon his life from enemies
without.[110]

The Johannine "Son" as spokesman for God:
Jesus as revealer and example

C. H. Dodd has written that when one examines closely what is
said in the Fourth Gospel about the Son of God it would appear
"that John has deliberately moulded the idea of the Son of God in
the first instance upon the prophetic model. . . . The human
mould, so to speak, into which the divine sonship [of Jesus] is poured
is a personality of the prophetic type."[111]

Possibly a more extensive analogy or correspondence may be
drawn between Christ in the Fourth Gospel and the type of the
righteous teacher portrayed in the Hodayoth of Qumran. The fact
that in John's Gospel Jesus is presented as the Son who is "sent" by
the Father, who lives in strict subordination to his will, proclaiming
the words and work of God, is indeed reminiscent of the Old Testament prophets. The author of the Hodayoth likewise perceived his
vocation as being, in part, a prophetic one. But it is the Qumran
teacher's priesthood that is especially prominent. Similarly, the
Johannine Christ is distinguished by the priestly functions which he
exercises, in relation to God and to men. In mediating the knowledge
and life of God, Jesus speaks in terms reminiscent of those used by
the spokesman in the Qumran Hodayoth. This is seen in passages
from the Hodayoth and from the Gospel in which both teachers
speak of their missions, and of their relationships to disciples and of
their gratitude for them.

In the Fourth Gospel, Jesus is constantly referring to what he
"knows", and bearing witness to what he has experienced. The Father
has "shown" the Son what he is doing, and the Son bears witness to
what he has "seen", that men may "marvel".[112] This claim to have
special knowledge of God, coupled with a passionate concern to
share it, so that men may gain eternal salvation, is most

106 1QH 17:21ff.; 5:15f.
107 J. Licht, *IEJ* 6 (1956) 95.
108 1QH 4:22ff.
109 1QH 4:27f.; 8:16f.: one of many scriptural metaphors used by the author.
110 1QH 5:22ff.; 1QpHab 5:9ff.; 1QH 2:31ff.; 7:18f.; 1QpHab 2ff.; 11:8ff.
111 C. H. Dodd, *The Interpretation of the Fourth Gospel* (Cambridge, 1953) 253f.
112 Jn 5:20; also 3:11, 32; 7:29; 8:26f., 40, 55; 10:15a; 12:49f.; 15:15; 17:8,
14, 25f.; 18:37.

characteristic of the speaker in the Gospel, as in the Hodayoth. To this end, Jesus is the teacher of "his own", of the disciples whom God has "given" him, "chosen out of the world".[113] Jesus is not called the Righteous Teacher, although he is frequently addressed as teacher.[114] His sole function as the Son is to reveal the Father who has sent him. Thus his teaching as well as his action is described as the "work" of God.[115] In his whole life, in his rejection, suffering and death, Jesus manifests the divine power and glory.[116] Jesus repeatedly reminds his disciples that the Father has "commanded" everything that he says and does. At the time of his departure Jesus praises the Father, acknowledging that the disciples "have come to know" that he has given the Son "everything".[117] Thus, in summary, the Johannine Christ proclaims as he prays: "This is life eternal that they know thee, the only true God, and Jesus Christ whom thou hast sent."[118]

As is the case with the writer of the priestly hymns, a corollary of Jesus' personal knowledge of God is his acknowledgment that man cannot hope for freedom from bondage to sin and death, or for eternal life, unless God "purify" him by his Spirit, and "draw near" to himself those whom he wills.[119]

When the Qumran writer considered the human condition he became deeply distraught. His emotions oscillated between terror and despondency, joy and peace. Jesus is portrayed in the Fourth Gospel as a man visibly moved by his emotions.[120] A comparison of the situations which gave rise in both men to expressions of anguish discloses some striking differences. Jesus was deeply troubled when confronted with the loss of a friend, when he experienced the human sadness which accompanies death or a betrayal of trust. The hymn writer was tormented by the thought of his own, helpless involvement in man's depravity. His anguished self-deprecation accords with the confessions of true saints in other times and places. Although Jesus testified that the "works" of men of the world are "evil", and in so doing incurred their hatred, Jesus' piety reveals no trace of self-condemnation.[121] Yet both spokesmen interpret the particular situations which grieve them as occasions for manifesting to men God's glory and power.[122] Moreover, both spokesmen reflect a similar cause for thanksgiving and elevation of spirit. God is always a present help in their moments of anguish. He does not abandon

---

113 Jn 13:13f.; also 11:28.
114 Although in 1 Jn 2:1 Jesus is designated "the righteous (one)". Jn 3:3; 11:28; 13:13f. Also 7:14ff., 28; 8:20; 14:26; 18:19.
115 Jn 17:25; also 1:18; 5:19, 30; 6:38.
116 Jn 12:23f., 27f.; 17:1; also 13:1, 31ff.
117 Jn 17:8; also 8:28f.; 13:49.
118 Jn 17:3; cf. 20:30f.
119 The common use of the rare expression that God "draws", or "draws near", men to himself is noteworthy.
120 Jn 11:33, 35, 38; 12:27; 13:21. Some writers seem to ignore these passages, speaking only of the superhuman passivity of the Johannine Son of God.
121 Jn 7:7. Jesus challenges his opponents who judge that his words and work are the speech and action of one who is demon possessed: "Which of you convicts me of sin?" (8:44ff.).
122 Jn 11:3f., 41f.; 12:27f., 30; 1QH 1:31ff.; 4:28f.

them to their tormentors, or leave them alone when their friends
fail them. The conviction of both men is that they exist in such
personal rapport with God that in agony or loneliness of spirit they
experience an incomparable joy, peace and serenity.[123]

Both spokesmen affirm that men must experience a divine renewal,
described as a washing or cleansing, if joy and peace are to attend
their ways. In the Fourth Gospel, as in the Hodayoth, these
references to purification are not to ritual or ceremonial lustrations
for the purpose of removing individual transgressions: both writings
envision a radical change in human nature. Jesus speaks of the
absolute necessity of rebirth, or birth from above.[124] All men—including "a ruler of the Jews" as well as Jesus' chosen disciples, his
"friends"—have need of a cleansing by the divine Spirit.[125] God is
glorified, and his name manifested, through the purity of the lives of
those men whom he "draws" to himself. The writer of the Hodayoth
can speak both of the purity of "the sons of truth" and of their need
for further purification. So also the Johannine Son of God speaks of
his "own" as being "already clean", as already having their "part"
or lot in him, yet also of their need to be "consecrated in truth",
of their need to "abide" in him if they are not to perish, if indeed
they are "to bear fruit" and so "prove" themselves to be his
disciples.[126]

The conviction of Jesus and of his disciples that they must be
separated from "the world" is a puzzling aspect of Johannine
theology, when viewed in conjunction with the Gospel's patent
universalistic teaching. It is true that the all-inclusive scope of the
Father's love, and of the Son's saving work, are frequently asserted
in the Johannine discourses.[127] John's dualistic and predestinarian
statements need not be taken as contradictions of this universalism,
if, as has been noted, their soteriological context is recognized,
although they are logically inconsistent with it. Nevertheless one
must not overlook the following: Jesus explicitly claims that he is
not, and that his disciples cannot be, "of this world";[128] in his
priestly prayer Jesus limits his intercession for men to his disciples
("I am *not* praying for the world");[129] and he commands them to
"love one another" (saying nothing about love for "enemies", or
even for one's "neighbour").[130] Are we to conclude that in the
Fourth Gospel "the world is the object of mission only in so far as
it is necessary to gather the elect"?[131]

A similarly paradoxical teaching in the Hodayoth provides a
partial parallel to, but also a revealing contrast with, this aspect of
John's theology. When the Qumran hymn writer celebrated the

---

123 Jn 16:31f.; 17:21ff.; 1QH 2:34ff.; 5:1ff.; 9:6ff.; 11:29ff.
124 Jn 3:3, 6.
125 Jn 13:8; 15:3.
126 Jn 12:10; 15:3, 5f.; 17:18; 1 Jn 1:7f.; 3:5ff.
127 Jn 3:16f.; 4:42; 6:33, 40; 8:12; 9:5; 12:46.
128 Jn 8:23; 15:18f.
129 Jn 17:6ff.
130 Jn 13:33ff. Cf. Lk 6:32ff.; 10:25ff.
131 E. Käsemann, *The Testament of Jesus*, trans. G. Krodel (London, Philadelphia,
1968) 65. Note Jn 11:52; 10:15f.; 12:32.

"great lovingkindness" of God, "the multitude of [His] mercies", and "the abundance of [His] pardon", and reflected upon the witness of his own community to the "marvels" of God, he was led to affirm: "all the nations shall acknowledge Thy truth, and all the people Thy glory".[132] Yet along with this hope, resting upon his keen perception of the gracious, forgiving love of God for men, the hymn writer was bound to confess the reality of every man's capacity to do evil, and of some men's resistance to, and intense hatred of, God and his truth. The responses of "the sons of men" to the saving knowledge of God, revealed through the teacher's doctrine, convinced him that the eschatological judgment of the world had begun, or at least was being anticipated. The sons of God's favour were being separated from those who were hostile to him, including some within Israel who, by moving over to the side of the enemy, had forfeited their position as his covenant people.[133] Consequently, the spokesman in the Hodayoth acknowledges that he is bound to love the "men of his Council" whom God has "drawn near", and to hate those whom God has "removed" far from himself, including those of his people who have "turned from [His] covenant". Apocalyptic images of annihilation of the wicked in battle, or of their destruction in a fiery judgment or by other violent means, are used to express the teacher's fury against the damned who are destined to "perish without understanding".

Jesus' "knowledge" also led him to proclaim God's salvation to everyone. Testimony to the universality of salvation is more evident in the Gospel than in the Hodayoth. Yet like the hymn writer, Jesus proclaimed a salvation that could be appropriated only by those who are separated from the ways of the world and who inherit its hatred. His disciples were instructed accordingly.[134] The universality of Christ's saving action was to be their gospel; they were to witness to his victory, the victory of light over darkness, a light which would continue to shine in the darkness. Yet in sending his disciples into the world, and speaking of the forensic activity of the *parakletos* in and through their witness, Jesus forecasts a separation of the community of faith from the world.[135] Our conclusion is that the fourth evangelist teaches coordinate mandates: the Christian Church must continue Christ's mission to the world, and maintain its independence of the world. The two conceptions are held in tension in the Gospel.

The First Letter of John may reflect a situation in which this truth-in-tension became intolerable, for in the letter the line seems to be drawn more rigidly between Church and world. The universalism of the Gospel is formally proclaimed,[136] but the characteristic Johannine motif contrasting light and darkness is developed in a different way. The belief that the darkness is passing away is not used to proclaim Christ's victory as overcoming the world, but in

132 1QH 6:9ff.
133 1QH 14:13ff.
134 Jn 15:18f.; 17:14ff., 25.
135 Jn 16:7ff.
136 1 Jn 2:2; 4:9, 14.

order to admonish Christians not to walk in it.[137] This shift in emphasis to separation from the world is supported by the absence of any statement in 1 John concerning a mission to the world. In 1 John believers are warned not to love the world.[138] The subsequent statement concerning the hatred of the world suggests that this writer in the Johannine community judged that some persons fell outside the scope of Christ's mandate to love. Love of the brethren is distinguished specifically from love of the world.[139] This exclusivistic ethic may be said to approximate the teaching of Qumran. According to the Rule, members of the sect were commanded to "love all the sons of light" and "to hate all the sons of darkness".[140]

The fourth evangelist, however, seems far removed from the letter or the spirit of this Qumran rule. According to John, Christ commands his disciples to love one another as he has loved them, which was to be a sign to all men.[141] The logical extension of this commandment is a disinterested love for the undeserving. The evangelist does not explicitly draw this conclusion, yet there is a complete absence of any expressions of vindictiveness or hatred toward his enemies on the part of the Johannine Jesus, in sharp contrast to the bitter denunciations voiced by the writer of the Hodayoth.

An important comparison between the Johannine Jesus and the Qumran teacher may be drawn from the interpretations which both men gave of suffering as essentially a part of their vocations. It is interesting that the sorrows which the two righteous men had to bear were caused by the murmurings and disloyal actions of disciples, as well as by the abuse and murderous threats of representatives of Judean officialdom. Like the spokesman in the Hodayoth, Jesus viewed his afflictions as portending the eschatological salvation and judgment, and, again like the Qumran teacher, Jesus drew upon the language and imagery of Isaiah's servant of the Lord in interpreting the meaning of his mission.

A striking parallel to Jn 12:23f. appears in Is 52:13ff.: "Behold, my servant shall prosper, and be lifted up and glorified."[142] With the Johannine conception of Jesus as "the light of the world" one may compare the references in the Isaianic songs to the servant who is "given" by God to his people as "a light to the nations".[143] It may also be noted that a major function of the servant, according to the prophet, was the gathering of the scattered sheep or children of God.[144]

Comparisons of this common use of the servant imagery bring into sharp relief, however, a central aspect of the Johannine theology which one does not find in the Qumran literature. In fulfilling their

137 1 Jn 2:8ff.
138 1 Jn 2:15ff.; 3:13.
139 F. Hahn, *Mission in the New Testament*, trans. F. Clarke (London, 1965) 160ff.
140 1QS 1:9f.
141 Jn 15:12f. See also 13:12ff.; 17:26.
142 Jn 12:32 (Is 53:11); Jn 13:31 (Is 49:13 LXX).
143 Jn 8:12; 12:26 (Is 49:6; 42:6f.).
144 Is 49:5f. (Jn 11:52; 12:32f.).

vocations, both the Qumran teacher and the Johannine Jesus were despised and rejected of men. Both believed themselves to be chosen by God, endowed by his Spirit. Both believed that it was God's will that they be humiliated and reviled, and both taught that, in and through their sufferings, God would be glorified, and men would receive enlightenment and expiation from sin. Nevertheless, there is one specific characteristic of the suffering servant which is predominant in the Fourth Gospel but is conspicious by its absence in the Hodayoth: Jesus explicitly declares that he is to lay down his own life for his friends, knowing at the time that they are to abandon him.[145] As we have seen, the Qumran author was tormented by his sinfulness, his lack of fitness for his servant-vocation, his constant need of divine pardon and purification. His own dedicated life, lived in company with the sons of light, in conformity to the Torah as interpreted through the truth revealed in the teacher's doctrine, constitutes an acceptable sin-offering, a more efficacious means than animal sacrifices in atoning for the defilements of God's people. There is, however, no claim on the part of the Qumran teacher that his suffering is in place of sinners. Israel's apostates are to be condemned along with all sinners. They are to receive from the Lord their just retribution. Clearly the Johannine Jesus disclaimed any need for such self-purgation from sin. In the priestly prayer Jesus prepares himself for his final human act, his devotion to the Father's will in death, by means of which he becomes the vicarious sin-offering: "And for their sake I consecrate myself, that they also may be consecrated in truth."[146]

The unique significance for mankind which the writer of the Fourth Gospel assigns to the death of Jesus as saving event is one decisive way in which the Johannine Jesus is to be distinguished from the Qumran model of the true revealer. But it is the Gospel's teaching concerning Jesus' relation to God, the uniqueness of his person as "the Son", which radically sets apart Johannine from Qumran theology. Since we have noted this from time to time, one comparison may suffice as the conclusion to this study.

Important parallels have been drawn between the Johannine ideal of Jesus' "oneness" with his disciples and the Qumran ideal of *yaḥad*, "community" or "unity". The author of the Hodayoth often expresses his sense of the profound spiritual unity, created by the revelation of God's "marvellous mysteries", among fellow members of the company of the elect. We may notice first some passages in which the teacher asserts that his own salvation is not to be perceived apart from the *yaḥad*, and in which his vocation is identified with the aims and life of the gathered community to which, by God's grace, he belongs:

For the sake of Thy glory
    Thou hast purified man of sin
that he may be made holy for Thee . . .

145 Jn 14:11f.; 16:31f.
146 Jn 17:19; 1:29, 35; 6:51. Cf. 1QH 5:15f.; also 1QS 4:20ff.

that he may be one [with] the children of Thy truth
and partake of the lot of Thy Holy Ones....[147]

Other passages in 1QH stress the special calling of the author to
instruct this community, his own obligation to nurture disciples, and
his conviction that it is God's will that the community acknowledge
his crucial leadership:

... to the elect of righteousness
Thou hast made me a banner,
and a discerning interpreter of wonderful mysteries....[148]
All those who are gathered in Thy covenant
inquire of me...
Through me Thou hast illumined
the face of the Congregation (lit. "the many").[149]

... Thou wilt condemn in Judgment
all those who assail me,
distinguishing through me
between the just and the wicked....[150]

The following words of Jesus in the Fourth Gospel can be said to
summarize also the expressed purpose of the author of the Hodayoth
with respect to the sons of God's favour:

I have manifested thy name to the men whom thou
gavest me out of the world;
thine they were, and thou gavest them to me,
and they have kept thy word....
I have given them the words which thou gavest me,
and they have received them...
and they have believed that thou didst send me....[151]
Holy Father, keep them in thy name...
that they may be one... that they may become perfectly
one....[152]

Yet is it clear from explicit statements, associated with the above
passages, that a quite remarkable distinction must be made between
the Qumran teacher's understanding of the saved, and saving, community and Johannine ecclesiology. It is not altogether clear in the
Qumran hymns how the role of the teacher is to be distinguished
from that of the community.[153] At times it appears that he is only a
man *primus inter pares* within the elect community, that his knowledge and doctrines are only the knowledge and doctrines of the
sect; that his personal piety only exemplifies the life-style of "the

---

147 1QH 11:10ff.; 2:20; 3:19ff.
148 1QH 2:13, 17f.; 8:16.
149 1QH 4:24, 27.
150 1QH 7:12. See also 14:18ff.
151 Jn 17:6ff.
152 Jn 17:22f.
153 J. Licht, *IEJ* 6 (1956) 101.

sons of truth". At other times his leadership is described in imagery which almost ascribes to him a messianic office.[154]

In John's Gospel there is to be found no such ambiguity. Only as the crucified and risen Messiah continues to abide with his own or, to express it differently, only as he continues to lead and nourish his own by means of "the Spirit of Truth", can Jesus' disciples attain and experience a viable life in community.[155] Yet this spiritual togetherness of Jesus and his friends has a more ultimate or ontological foundation. It is only because Jesus and God are one, that Jesus' words and work are constitutive of the eschatological community. The unity that God wills for the disciples of Jesus is therefore grounded upon the unity of God the Father and his only Son, a unity sustained in love. Thus in directing his priestly intercession for men to his Father, Jesus' assumption—"even as we are one"[156]—is the essential basis for the prayer of assurance respecting his disciples, as well as all those who "are to believe through their word"—that they "may be one", that they "may become perfectly one".

---

[154] For a judicious discussion of the self-understanding and role(s) of the Teacher of Righteousness, see M. Burrows, *More Light on the Dead Sea Scrolls*, 324ff.; W. H. Brownlee, *The Meaning of the Qumrân Scrolls for the Bible* (New York, 1964) 138ff.
[155] Jn 15:1ff.
[156] Jn 17:11, 22; also 17:5 (1:1f.), 24; 8:19c; 10:30; 14:7, 11.

3

The Johannine Paraclete and the Qumran Scrolls

A. R. C. LEANEY

The Paraclete in the Fourth Gospel must be studied, as the relevant passages make obvious, in relation to the Spirit, the Holy Spirit and the Spirit of Truth. This essay will look first at the Paraclete as a distinct and individual concept, and then in relation to these other and related notions.

In his magisterial work *Der Paraklet*[1] Otto Betz opened up the path for subsequent writers on this subject, and much that follows is in debt to him. This acknowledgment may perhaps make constant reference to this book unnecessary, but certain points, especially disagreements with it, will be pointed out. A paraclete is an advocate. As such he not only intercedes for his client but also indicts the adversary. Such indictment is extended to the spiritual and moral spheres, and indeed indictment is in general the function of a paraclete; when the term is used metaphorically of a being properly belonging to another world who exercises protection over an inhabitant of this world, he specifically condemns wrong wherever it appears. Hence, a member of the Qumran sect, or the sect acting corporately, can act as a paraclete—and must so act—to rebuke a fellow-member, and thus help to remove his guilt, if the latter has been discovered in some breach of the *hᵃlākāh* of the sect. Betz would regard the Teacher of Righteousness as *par excellence* one who rebukes and convicts, and the whole sect expected to be a corporate rebuker and convicter, that is a paraclete, at the final judgment.

Such an interpretation throws light upon the manner in which the ministry of Jesus is presented in the Fourth Gospel; there a trial is taking place behind the scenes. The actual trial of Jesus by the Jews is a symbol and, as it were, but one instance of this constant "trial" of strength between the two opposing parties. The victory apparently goes to the Jews, but in reality to Jesus who in this way fulfils what the author of the Hodayoth trusted would be his destiny: each reveals his sense of being on trial and expresses his trust that he will be vindicated.

As in the history of the Jews a great emissary from God was often

[1] *Der Paraklet, Fürsprecher im häretischen Spätjudentum, im Johannesevangelium und in neu gefundenen gnostischen Schriften* (AGSU 2; Leiden, 1963).

followed by another who continued the previous great man's work, so in the Fourth Gospel the Paraclete follows Jesus to complete his work, basing his own as teacher on that of Jesus (14:26; 15:26; 16:13). The Paraclete will act in this way as indwelling power and is therefore appropriately identified with the Spirit of Truth (14:17). This brings the author's conception of the Spirit of Truth close to his conception of Jesus himself, and according to the usually adopted reading at 14:23, close to Jesus and the Father together. The relation of Jesus to the Paraclete is a most fascinating subject, in view of the implication in 14:16 that Jesus himself is a, or the, Paraclete; the other Paraclete whom he promises will by his work also identify himself with Jesus by recalling to the disciples the body of doctrine which Jesus taught them (14:26). This body of doctrine is "my words" or even "the word", which is really that of the Father (14:24). Hence the Paraclete will teach what comes from the Father who is the original source of all true doctrine. This is implied more clearly still in 16:14f. Jesus stands therefore in the same relation to the Father as the Paraclete stands to both the Father and to himself; but there is no warrant for saying with Betz that the Paraclete, so long as he is in heaven, is identifiable with the Logos. Indeed we shall argue that God himself (in Johannine language the Father) is the true Paraclete, and that Jesus is so called because he is the incarnation of God, the Paraclete of Israel, and that both Jesus and the Paraclete are equally those "whom the Father has sent".

I

There is no exact Hebrew equivalent of the Greek *paraklētos* which later Jewish writings borrowed and transliterated (e.g. Aboth 4:11); but our task must include investigation of some words more or less closely associated with the concept as well as some quite general considerations of our subject.

We may begin with the Teacher of Righteousness. Did his contemporaries or those who looked back on his life and work with admiration regard him as in any way the equivalent of a paraclete? Did he see himself as a leader who may be described in this way? Not all references to the, or a, Teacher of Righteousness are necessarily to one historical character. Some at least may well be to the holder of an office who was accordingly a different person at different times; but there are some, notably in the Habakkuk Commentary, to a manifestly particular historical person. Unfortunately in none of these is there any description of him which brings out his character other than the general implication that he was at this time the leader of the sect, persecuted by the Wicked Priest. The case is similar with the references in the Damascus Document, and there remain for investigation the Hodayoth, where indeed no actual reference is made to the Teacher; but some commentators confidently identify the author and the Teacher, very largely because passages in the hymns appear to reflect the experiences of a leader who worked and suffered in the creation of a body of followers whose task was to remain faithful through persecution to their God by adherence to the right way or *ʰᵃlākāh*. For our purpose it is unnecessary to enter this controversy since we are seeking evidence only for the foreshadowing of the idea of the Paraclete. Such evidence may lie in any historical person, or imaginative concept or personification in the literature of the Scrolls; it is of no consequence whether such a person actually existed when we seek to determine whether this literature inspired the figure of the Paraclete in the Fourth Gospel.

Whether or not, therefore, the author of the Hodayoth may be identified with the Teacher of Righteousness, the great man of the sect who apparently arose about twenty years after its foundation, whether or not the hymns reflect his own experience (or their own experience if the collection had more than one author) or that of the people whom he seeks to represent or personify, we may properly use these poems in our enquiry. In doing so, we shall write as if the author were one person since the details of the question of authorship clearly do not concern us.

The writer shows utter personal trust and confidence in God and on the basis of his own religious experience believes that God will carry out his divine purpose through him (1QH 2:8–19), this purpose being the creation of a company of holy people at the end of the age (5:20–7:5; cf. CD 1:9).[2] He is as devoted to his followers as he is to God (14:14ff.). The author trusts in God through persecution, and believes that during and after it God will deliver him (2:20–30; 31–32; 3:19–36; 5:5–19). Indeed it is his task to bring to birth a community out of the present suffering (3:3–18; and especially 8:4–9:36). One of the reasons for thinking that the hymns are written by a leader out of his own experience is that he seems to see himself as a well of knowledge (2:18; 11:19; 12:29; 18:10ff.; 1QS 10:12; 11:3). One of the main reasons for his trust in God is that God has revealed to him his marvellous secrets, almost certainly those contained in the scriptures which awaited a specially gifted interpreter (4:22–29; 7:4f.). If he is to be identified with the Teacher of Righteousness, according to a probable restoration of 1QpHab 2:2f., he speaks what he hears from the mouth of God. There were certainly prominent and effective enemies either of the sect or of the Teacher himself (4:7–12a; cf. CD 8:21), or of both, some being previously supporters and therefore called "traitors" in CD 8:21. Again, if references to the historical Teacher are allowable in this connection we must add 1QpHab 5:9; 11:4ff.; cf. 4QpPs 37. In his edition of the Hodayoth Holm-Nielsen expresses grave doubt as to whether the "I" of these hymns is a person with a special relation to the community, although he gives on page 285 a summary of the relevant passages if after all this is the case.[3] He points out rightly that such a person remains a fallible and sinful man conscious of the fact that righteousness belongs to God alone (16:9; 17:20, cf. 11:18 and 1QS 10:24; cf. also Dan 9:7); and the author longs for cleansing for himself no less than for others, from the God who alone can offer this blotting out of his sins (4:37; 16:12).

---

[2] Betz and others would go further and say that the author believed God had a special destiny for him as an individual.

[3] *Hodayot: Psalms From Qumran* (ATD 2; Aarhus, 1960).

It is hardly necessary to point out the correspondences between Jesus and his ministry and that of the leader revealed in the hymns, if indeed it is right to interpret them as the utterances of a historical person in this way. Otherwise, Jesus could be regarded as "fulfilling" the aspirations of a poet or poets who wrote partly as representatives of their own experience, partly as those of others in the same group or community. In the latter case the way in which the ministry of Jesus is represented, not only in the Fourth Gospel but also in the Synoptics and elsewhere, reflects the scriptures not only of the Old Testament but, naturally enough, those of the sect. Naturally enough, for both the Scrolls and the New Testament have the same spiritual ancestors. Both the "I" of the hymns and Jesus have apparently the same trust in God and in God's intention to carry out the divine purpose through themselves; both are concerned with the creation of a community at the end of the age, both teach a high interpretation of suffering and its creative function. Jesus too endures much opposition, stylized and dramatically presented in Jn 7–9, although of course to be found elsewhere in this gospel, opposition which includes defectors (Jn 6:64–66) and a traitor. Enthusiasts may even compare the "well of knowledge" in the hymns with Jn 4:13ff.

On the other hand, the differences are all the more eloquent for the manifest possibility of comparison. Jesus' confidence in God goes beyond that of the author (or authors) of the hymns, for he claims to be one with God, whom he calls Father. It is insufficient to say of him that he was the object of persecution, for his suffering is dramatized in the actual historical fact of the crucifixion and in the rich theology which surrounds it; his power to reveal, including as it does the unique power to reveal heavenly things (3:12f.), is identical with being the object of that revelation at its highest, and showing that in the climax of his suffering he reveals the true nature both of himself and of God (8:28). Consistently, the traitor in the case of Jesus himself possesses a cosmic significance, being "a devil" (6:70; cf. 13:27); and the creation of a new community shows a further theological dimension which places it at a distance from any thought found in the Scrolls by being a consequence of the resurrection of Jesus and taught enigmatically in the form of a "sign" (Jn 2:19–21).

While it is clearly fair to say that for the hymns (and similar passages in other Qumran sources) the Paraclete, understood as the person standing behind the scenes and watching over his people, is God himself, in the Fourth Gospel Jesus could not only be called the Paraclete, but is by implication actually so called (14:16). It might well be claimed that the sense in which Jesus is himself the Paraclete at least includes that of being a, or the, Teacher of a particular group, imparting a $h^a l\bar{a}k\bar{a}h$ no less than that imparted to the Qumran community by some leader or leaders and now found in large measure in the Rule and the Damascus Document; but, as already implied, it would be inadequate to describe the teaching of Jesus as $h^a l\bar{a}k\bar{a}h$; some of the teaching of the Scrolls goes beyond such a category, but that of the Jesus of the Fourth Gospel goes beyond even such more profound—or more ambitious—teaching of the Scrolls.

In the Fourth Gospel he is more than a teacher, he is a, or rather the, Revealer. With this warning it is certainly right to see in Jesus as the Paraclete Jesus the Teacher. It is indeed a primary function of the Paraclete to teach (14:26; 16:13), so if Jesus is the first Paraclete of the disciples we may expect to find that in the Fourth Gospel Teacher is one of the important titles given to Jesus. There are a number of such instances; in some the word merely translates "Rabbi" (1:39 and 20:16; cf. 11:28 and [8:4]) but its association with "Lord" in 13:13f. suggests that like the latter title it is used, at least in this Gospel, of a divinely appointed teacher, and this is the idea put into the mouth of Nicodemus who calls Jesus, no doubt in flattery but if so with true dramatic irony, a teacher come from God, or more accurately, acclaims him with the assurance that "we know" (itself often a form of introduction to an important assertion in this Gospel, 4:42; 9:31; 16:30; 21:24; cf. 3:11; 4:42) "that thou art come from God (as) Teacher". In contrast Nicodemus himself is a "Teacher of Israel" but does not understand what Jesus has tried to teach him (3:10). From the outset it is assumed that Nicodemus desires to see the kingdom of God (3:3) although he has so far stated only his belief that Jesus is a teacher from God and that God is clearly with Jesus because he is able to perform the signs. Responding to this, Jesus expresses surprise that a "teacher of Israel" cannot understand even "earthly things" and then claims his own personal knowledge of heavenly things and implies that he is the Son of Man who has descended to earth with this revelation (3:11-13). Jesus as Teacher therefore is far removed from the Teacher of Righteousness or the author of the hymns for whom no such divine authority or content of teaching is claimed.

It is worthwhile to consider a little further the content of the teaching which Nicodemus sought and which Jesus came to give. The assumption that Nicodemus was seeking the kingdom of God may provide us with a clue to the person of Jesus which is presented here and answer at least tentatively the question, "If Jesus is here approached as the divinely sent and divinely authorized Teacher, in view of the fact that imparting truth is the function of Jesus and the other Paraclete, is there any hint that Jesus is for Nicodemus the Paraclete or a figure who might be so described?" The question cannot be answered for certain, but a possible link may be found if we consider not the noun *paraklētos* but the verb *parakalein*. The classical instance of God calling on his emissary to *parakalein* his people in the Greek scriptures is Is 40:1, where the original Hebrew verb is from the root *nhm*, "comfort", a word used little in the Scrolls. There are, however, two significant passages where the word occurs, 1QH 11:32 and fragment 21:3, and in these God is the Comforter. It is possible that these two passages reflect a tradition otherwise not found in the Scrolls and which may be described in the terms of Strack-Billerbeck who say that for the "teachers of Israel", "the word *nehāmāh* became a general term for the messianic redemption"[4] which it was hoped would fulfil the expectation raised by Is 40:1.

---

[4] Str-B 2, 125.

In later literature this is reflected in 2 Baruch 44:7, and in Lk 2:25 where *paraklēsis* seems to be a synonym for *lytrōsis* in Lk 2:38. Simeon and Anna represent faithful Judaism waiting for this "comfort" or redemption of their country and people, contrasting with those who later failed to see this redemption or *paraklēsis* in Jesus. Joseph of Arimathea is another faithful Jew of the same kind and Luke says of him that he was awaiting the kingdom of God (cf. Mk 15:43), illustrating neatly that the phrases used to describe the object of the hopes of Simeon and Anna in Luke's second chapter are synonymous with the kingdom of God. The specifically Jewish national character of such hopes as those of Simeon, Anna and Joseph of Arimathea were shared by the disciples, according to Luke, for they hoped that Jesus would have "redeemed Israel" (24:21) and persisted in this hope after the resurrection (Acts 1:6). The men of Qumran entertained parallel patriotic expectations to which they gave a strongly eschatological form, but they do not appear to have used any vocabulary which would connect them with expectation of the fulfilment of Is 40:1, and the word *neḥāmāh* does not occur in the extant Scrolls. Two conclusions emerge, of which the first must remain very tentative. It is that Nicodemus, who is brought into association with Joseph of Arimathea in Jn 19:39, in awaiting the kingdom of God may be regarded as awaiting the *paraklēsis* of Israel and that he is faced with the claim that here in effect is the Paraclete who is its incarnation. The second conclusion is firmer: if the former is correct, the line of thought here pursued does not come to the author of the Gospel through Qumran but along channels much closer to what is usually for convenience termed orthodox Judaism, in the time of the historical Jesus represented by the Pharisees to whom Nicodemus belonged. The relation of this passage to the Johannine teaching about the spirit will be considered later.

In terms of tracing origins among the Scrolls for the concept of and vocabulary associated with the Paraclete, results are so far meagre and tentative. Betz would connect the Paraclete in the Fourth Gospel with the Prince of Lights (1QS 3:20 and CD 5:18) and the similar title Prince of Light in 1QM 13:10, where in all three instances the Hebrew word translated "prince" is *śar*, as in Dan 10:21; 12:1. This heavenly being is one of those elsewhere called angels, beings who according to intertestamental literature were created by God early in the creative process and whose existence and tasks seem in such accounts to be integral and vital to the function of the universe. Jubilees 2:2 makes the importance of their creation abundantly clear, as does 1 Enoch (*passim*) that of their position as intermediaries for the functioning of the universe. Whether to be identified with a particular angel such as Michael or Uriel, the Prince of Light or Lights in the Scrolls appears to wear a double aspect: in the War Scroll (1QM 13:10) it is natural to envisage him as in part a contender in the heavenly sphere on behalf of Israel, like Michael in the book of Daniel. But even in the War Scroll the other aspect is unmistakable: his dominion consists of "spirits of truth" and the conflict in which Israel is engaged and in which he assists her sons is a moral and spiritual conflict, even if it comes to a cosmic climax in

the physical and earthly sphere. In 1QS 3:20 there is no missing
this spiritual side, for the title is clearly an alternative to that of
Spirit of Truth (3:18f.). Here, therefore, we have a bridge between
the concept of an angel who assists Israel in battle and a similar
spiritual being who assists Israel in the life of obedience to God
which alone will deserve victory in the final judgment. For the men of
Qumran the final *dénouement* of the story of creation was to be the
War of the Sons of Light against the Sons of Darkness, enacting on
earth a decision in the good versus evil battle which has throughout
the ages proceeded in both earth and heaven, sometimes thought of
as armed conflict, sometimes as a scene in a court of law. In the
Fourth Gospel this final clash is similarly enacted on earth but not
in the form of a battle; it is enacted in the form of the crucifixion.
Part of the final action of God according to 1QS 4:21 will be the
cleansing of the righteous by the aspersion of "a spirit of truth like
waters for purification". As the passage which follows shows clearly,
it is after this apparently eschatological act that those who receive
this benison from God begin to "understand knowledge of the highest".
We are already in the realm of symbols which outrun the ability of
the mind to translate them fully into rational terms. We are in the
realm of poetry rather than prose, illustrated by the fact that the
author of this passage of the Rule can use the old levitical idea of
the "waters of *niddāh*" to express so great a spiritual event. If we
agree that we must refrain from attempting to re-express poetry in
prose, it is fair to compare this aspersion of water promised by the
Rule to the water which issued from the side of the crucified Jesus in
Jn 19:34, and to reflect that for the author of this Gospel water is
the symbol of the spirit (7:38f.) which Jesus was to bestow and
without which (or whom) the work of Jesus even after the crucifixion
was incomplete (Jn 16:7). In examining therefore the meaning of
the phrase Prince of Light (or Lights) we discover a foreshadowing of
that process of thought by which an angel, a presumably tangible,
certainly visible being, may be identified with a spirit. This process
is clearly exemplified by the author of the Fourth Gospel when
according to him Jesus identifies the Paraclete with the Spirit of
Truth (14:16f.; 15:26; 16:13); it is in this sphere that the familiarity
of the author with the thought of Qumran becomes most obvious.
It is obvious also that the Fourth Gospel, however much it is
"influenced" by a manner of thought and vocabulary close to that of
the Qumran sect, introduces as of paramount importance ideas which
owe nothing to Qumran and everything to the conviction that Jesus
the Paraclete has come in the flesh. Not the least of the consequences
which flow from this conviction unique to Christianity is the further
conviction that the spirit given by Jesus is the fulfilment of the promise
of the *paraklēsis* which Judaism believed God was to bestow. How
the author of the Gospel thinks of the spirit in connection with the
Paraclete will be the subject of a further section of this essay.

One or two other expressions deserve some examination. Part of
the function of the Paraclete whom Jesus will send in place of himself
is to convince or convict (*elenchein*). One meaning shades off into
the other in the notoriously difficult passage Jn 16:7-11, whose

difficulty arises largely from this fact. The basic necessity for understanding it seems to be the realization that in a situation actually or metaphorically forensic the chief protagonist of a case aims to convict the opposite side so thoroughly that the latter is also convinced of his own guilt and of the rightness or "righteousness" of the accuser. That the sinner should be convinced of his own guilt is often the most important aim, and the nearest parallel to this aim of the Paraclete in Jn 16:7ff. which we can find in the Scrolls is associated with the verb *hôkîaḥ* (Hiph. form of the root *ykḥ*), which more or less corresponds to the Greek *elenchein*. The meaning of the passages where the verb is used in the Scrolls is often best indicated by the word "rebuke", especially in the context of the duty of a member of the sect to rebuke his neighbour in order that the latter may purge his guilt in good time. This duty is enjoined in 1QS 5:24, 26; CD 9:3, 7f., 20:4. CD 9:18 concerns a formal rebuke in the presence of the *meḇaqqēr* (superintendent or guardian) and 8:27f. seems to envisage the community acting as a corporate prosecutor. The meaning varies a little when we come to the hymns: in 1QH 6:4 the text is uncertain but appears to reflect the situation in which the community are again to act as corporate prosecutor; 1QH 1:25 uses the verb metaphorically, and Holm-Nielsen comments that it "derives from legal language, and probably has the sense of 'defend a case'". Although not all commentators agree, this suits the context and suggests that the verb may be used of the activity of the defence as well as of that of the prosecution. In 1QH 9:23 God in his wisdom is the subject of the sentence; Vermes[5] translates the verb and its object as "rebuked me", but the general sense requires something like the slightly inelegant "set me to rights" of Holm-Nielsen who gets nearer to the heart of the meaning in 1QH 12:28 which asks the question, "How will dust stand its ground in the face of him who *môkîaḥ bô*?" Here the latter translates the last two words "pronounceth judgment over it" and Vermes, "reproves it". It is in a similarly metaphorical way that Jn 3:20f. speaks of an evildoer fearing the light lest his deeds be "shown up" (*elenchthē*).

The use of the Hebrew verb in the Scrolls and the practice with which it is associated may well help us to understand the assertion that it is a duty to "rebuke" one's neighbour, for his sake (Eph 4:26 and Heb 3:13 illustrate the point in the New Testament), but there is no evidence that any person at Qumran is specially to be regarded as rebuker or convictor unless it be God himself, who is regarded naturally in this way because of his universally acknowledged position as Judge of the world. In the two passages cited from the hymns he is in 9:23 regarded as a Judge in earthly matters after the style of many passages, such as 1 Kings 8:31f., and in 12:28 as the eternal or eschatological Judge. 1QH 18:12 is not altogether easy to interpret but does nothing to alter the impression gained from other passages and may be left on one side. The Rule offers two further interesting passages: 1QS 10:11 suggests that in effect the author "convicts himself" (like Job) and the use of the verb in

5 G. Vermes, *The Dead Sea Scrolls in English* (Harmondsworth, Baltimore, 1962).

1QS 9:16, 17 illustrates the claim that true argument means to contend not only *against* the other side but also *for* knowledge of the truth. In the great cosmic trial where good is pitched against evil this is a vital element; it is unsatisfactory to have so thoroughly won the case that the adversary is convicted unless the course of the controversy has brought out at the same time the final truth, the truth of God.

In his recent monograph on the Paraclete[6] G. Johnston commends the Hebrew word *mēlîṣ* as providing a substantial clue to understanding the Fourth Gospel's use of the Greek *paraklētos* without apparent introduction. His main argument is that the Targum on Job used the Greek loan-word in an Aramaic form to translate *mēlîṣ*, a discovery of N. Johannson. Thus the Greek word must have had a wide currency in Greek and Palestinian Judaism during the first century A.D. and later. This is indeed an important argument and suggests that the author of the Fourth Gospel may have adopted the term from either Greek or Palestinian Judaism; but it is not so certain that *mēlîṣ* should be regarded as the main Hebrew counterpart of the word. Johnston appears to imply that it occurs in the sense of "mediator" and in other related meanings in three passages of Job. In fact the word occurs only at Job 33:23 in a meaning of this kind, and in the plural in Is 43:27 in a perhaps similar way. Again, of the occurrences in the hymns (1QH 2:13, 14, 31; 4:7, 9; 6:13, 19; 18:11; fragment 2:6) and in 1QpHab 8:6 (where the MT has *melîṣāh*) only 1QH 2:13 and 18:11 support the argument, for the others are either too fragmentary or (as in 1QH 2:14, 31; 4:7, 9) are cases where the word is used of false interpreters.

One other term from the Scrolls deserves consideration, less because it is directly reflected in the Fourth Gospel or can be regarded as parallel to *paraklētos* than because it illustrates a function of a religious leader in a Jewish setting at that time. This is the term *maśkîl* occurring at 1QS 3:13; 9:12; 9:21; 1QSb 1:1; 3:22; 5:20; CD 12:21; 13:22 (1QH fragment 8:10 may be mentioned for completeness but is too fragmentary to help). In all these passages it evidently means some kind of leader, in 1QS at least in his capacity as instructor of others, thus one who is himself instructed and able to instruct others, very probably in the sense of instructing them in some not generally known information or religious knowledge, which is the nuance that seems to attach itself to the use of the term in Dan 11:33; 12:3, 10. Whether or not *maśkîl* is to be taken always in this way, its use sometimes in such a connection reminds us of the fact that a religious leader, for example the Teacher of Righteousness and perhaps the author of the Hodayoth (who may be identical) instruct their followers in a *hᵃlākāh* or Way embodied in a set of regulations held to have the same divine authority enjoyed by the laws delivered to Moses. It follows, where eternal salvation is taken to depend on obedience to such regulations, that the teacher of them is in some sense a saviour by his word. We shall see presently

---

[6] G. Johnston, *The Spirit-Paraclete in the Gospel of John* (SNTS Monograph Series 12; Cambridge, 1970).

both the likeness and the difference between religious leader or leaders at Qumran and Jesus in this respect.

We may now consider Jesus as Paraclete. The question has already been asked whether possibly Nicodemus was in effect looking for the *paraklēsis* of Israel and therefore Jesus was for him God's *paraklēsis* incarnate, or *the* Paraclete. This is indeed uncertain, but Jn 14:16 establishes clearly that in this Gospel Jesus is a Paraclete. It will be well to clarify the importance, which is probably not great, of the fact that whereas Jesus is *a* paraclete by the implication of his promise of another paraclete in Jn 14:16, and by the anarthrous use of the word in 1 Jn 2:1, he who is to be sent on the departure of Jesus is unequivocally *the* Paraclete. The correct balance in understanding this matter may be won by remembering that for Judaism God himself is the Paraclete, he who brings final *paraklēsis* to his people. No documentation is needed for the claim that according to the Fourth Gospel God has come to his people in Jesus: the Paraclete has taken flesh and offered his final consolation and redemption by his sacrifice of himself, which is emphasized as a deed as well as a revelation of the Father in Jn 8:28. It is well-known that in the thought of Paul "Christ" often appears in the sense of "all that God did through Christ" (e.g. 2 Cor 5:19). Jesus in the Fourth Gospel is paraclete in this sense, the embodiment of the activity of God (the Father) as bringer of comfort and redemption. It was the purpose of God that Jesus should die, rise again and ascend to share the glory of God which he enjoyed before the incarnation. Inevitably therefore he is *for this world* a temporary manifestation of the Paraclete and it is in this sense that the Father is greater than he (14:28). *The* Paraclete will be with the disciples of Jesus "for ever"; but there is no question of the Paraclete being superior to Jesus for the Paraclete will be given by his prayer (14:16), and will be sent by the Father in his name (14:26) or even by Jesus himself from the Father (15:26); even if 16:7 almost seems to suggest that one main task of Jesus is to cause him to be sent, when he comes he will give honour to Jesus (16:14).

The phrase "for ever" attached to the Paraclete in Jesus' promise in 14:16 must be understood in the context of the two spheres, this world and the world above. Jesus does not cease to act as, that is to be, Paraclete, but ceases to be so in this world. 1 Jn 2:1 makes plain that his work and being as Paraclete is *pros ton patera,* an expression which may be compared with *pros ton theon* in Jn 1:1. He no less than the other Paraclete whom he promises to send is a paraclete "for ever", and is so in his capacity as propitiation, as the context shows (1 Jn 2:2).

Emphasis has been given to the fact that for Judaism God himself is Paraclete. The Fourth Gospel contrasts with this less by contradicting the identification than by a discrimination which in later theology might be described as correctly distinguishing the "persons" of the Godhead; even the later technical language seems to be adumbrated when in 15:26 the Paraclete is identified with the Spirit of Truth who is then said to "come forth from" or "proceed from the Father". Nevertheless the contrast exists and throws up the concept

of "the Father" as a distinct person of the Godhead no less than
that of the Son or the Holy Spirit.

It is in a relatively minor fashion that Jesus may be compared as
saviour with the religious teachers of the past who could be regarded
as in some sense also saviours through the word which they delivered.
The main sense in which he is saviour involved far more than can
be discussed here, and the subject has been touched upon already at
several points. In a less important sense he is like the teachers of
Judaism in that he too cleanses by his word, as is cryptically
suggested by Jn 15:3. If the instructor at Qumran had said to his
pupils that they were clean by the word which he had uttered to
them, he would have meant his interpretation of the Law and the
regulations which he had derived from it, adherence to which would
have rendered them "clean" in a levitical and moral sense, neither
sense being more important than the other. The content of Jesus'
"word" is quite different in the gospel: it declares his own paramount place and that of the Paraclete or Spirit in God's plan of
salvation; only by a great extension of meaning can it be called
$h^a l\bar{a}k\bar{a}h$, though it is in effect so called when Jesus says in 14:6
that he is the Way ($h^a l\bar{a}k\bar{a}h$). Yet there is a manner in which the word
of Jesus is for the author of the Gospel like that of the Qumran
legislator or legislators for the sectarians: it is decisive and critical.
It is God's own word (14:24) and it will be the means of judging at
the last day (12:48–50). Not only is it God's word but it renders
those who accept it distinct from "the world" (17:14). It is God's
word and as such is truth (17:17). A picture is suggested of two
groups of people, one steadfast followers of the Law, excluding
those who understood it differently, and the other a group in one
sense just as exclusive but believing that the Law in the ancient sense
was superseded and that the word of God had appeared incarnate.

Even if the word of Jesus concentrates for the most part on the
subject of who he himself is and on his revelation of the Father, far
more important than such revelation is his action as eternal
Paraclete, which goes quite beyond the value of teaching, essential as
that is. In the foot-washing scene in Jn 13:1–11 Peter along with the
other disciples present is the subject of an enacted parable, probably
reflecting a baptismal eucharist, for the scene is the Last Supper and
the action can hardly escape being compared to baptism, baptism at
the hands of one who by his self-disrobing enacts his giving up
his life by crucifixion. Johnston draws attention to the fact that the
words of Jesus to Peter which explain that he will understand later
the purport of the acted parable, suggest the work of the Paraclete,
for it is his function "to teach disciples the meaning of what Jesus
did and what Jesus said". The meaning of this passage is nowhere
drawn out specifically but seems to be that the disciples are "baptized
into his death" (cf. Rom 6:3), so that the First Epistle can be
confident about the work of Jesus: his blood cleanses us from all sin
(1:7). The Paraclete (the spirit) has taught the author that the Paraclete (Jesus) is the eternal cleansing sacrifice, as is clear in the passage
which follows (1 Jn 1:8–2:2). The efficacy of this sacrifice depends
on one thing alone—the confession of sins; at Qumran such con-

fession was necessary along with the acceptance of such penalty as the council decided; in many cases cleansing would be necessary also. Because of the action of Jesus the eternal Paraclete, no penalty and no further "washing" is needed than that which he has wrought. "A man who has bathed needs no further washing" (Jn 13:10). It is therefore by his action that Jesus the Paraclete transcends any *paraklēsis* offered hitherto, whether at Qumran or elsewhere. The final "word" of Jesus is the cross.

II

In one passage, Jn 14:26, the Paraclete is apparently identified with the Holy Spirit. In this sole passage where the full phrase *to pneuma to hagion,* familiar from Paul and elsewhere in the New Testament, is used in this Gospel, we may suspect that the original, like the Sinaitic Syriac, omitted *to hagion.*[7] The passage will then read, "The Paraclete, the spirit whom the Father will send in my name ...", an expression consistent with belief in the existence of a number of spirits. This concept of plurality in the spirit world is prominent in the Qumran writings (e.g. 1QS 3:24; 1QH 3:18; 1QM 10:12) and was natural to Paul (1 Cor 12:10; 14:12) and to the author of 1 John (4:1; cf. 1 Pet 3:19). In fact, the idea of the Holy Spirit as it developed in later theology is unknown to the author of the Fourth Gospel, although everything that he says pertinent to such theology agrees verbally with the orthodox development of it. Indeed it was inevitable that the idea of "holy spirit" with which John is familiar should grow into that of "the Holy Spirit". This less specific phrase, "holy spirit" occurs at 1:33 and 20:22, and the Qumran literature can help us to understand it. Johnston's simple definition of the primary meaning of the word "spirit" in the Old Testament as the energy or power of God makes a good starting-point.[8] Since God is the source of all energy and power and indeed of all beings and creatures, it is natural enough to summarize his being as Spirit, so that the spirit of God, active in creation, in enabling men to do more than they naturally could, in communicating his word, in saving his people, can be said to declare what God in his essence is. God is Spirit (Jn 4:24 where, however, the meaning is probably correctly paraphrased by "God is of the realm of spirit, not of this world"). Such a direct statement is nowhere made in the extant Scrolls but God is said often to do things by his spirit. The only occasion where *rûah* is not used in such a connection seems to be 1QH 1:13, where God is praised because "Thou hast created the earth by thy might" and this word (*kôah*) illustrates an important point: to say that God is spirit is to imply that God is power, or the source of all power.

The other great attribute of God according to the Bible and the whole tradition of Judaism and Christianity is his holiness, meaning not only his otherness from creation but also what follows from that, his unquestionable moral sovereignty and purity, a purity conceived of in the Old Testament and in Judaism to this day partly on the

---

7 See Johnston, *The Spirit-Paraclete,* 31.
8 Johnston, *The Spirit-Paraclete,* 4.

model of ritual purity, since the being of God is the ultimate *raison d'être* for all laws of cleanness, ritual no less than moral. Lev 19:1, "You shall be holy, because I, the LORD your God, am holy", sums up better than any other text the deepest demand of the biblical tradition. Thus for Qumran God is the holy one who demands holiness and also graciously bestows it. In CD 5:11 some are blamed for having defiled their holy spirit (cf. Ps 51:10) and 7:4 lays it down that "no man shall defile his holy spirit", implying that he possesses a holy spirit because he is a member of the sect whose special pursuit was holiness, to be derived and deserved from God by obedience to his regulations and commands. 1QS 3:7 implies similarly that man can have a holy spirit or spirit of holiness, 8:16 the belief that the prophets revealed God's will by his holy spirit; and 9:3 states that a spirit of holiness is to be founded in Israel. God helps man with his holy spirit in 1QH 7:6 and 9:32, and according to 1QH 12:12 and 14:13 a God-given spirit of man enables him to listen to God (cf. 1 Cor 2:10f.). Finally 1QS 4:21 promises that God will purify some men with a spirit of holiness (or holy spirit), as also in 1QH 12:12.

1 Jn 4:1, it was claimed above, shares with Qumran the belief in a number of spirits. In the same passage it is implied that the spirit of God is one of them (4:2); indeed the whole section 4:1–6 has links with Qumran vocabulary. "Holy spirit" does not occur in the Epistle, and the absence (if we are right about 14:26) of the phase *to pneuma to hagion* in the Gospel suggests that we should interpret the two occurrences of *pneuma hagion*[9] in 1:33 and 20:22 according to the guidance given by the Qumran passages. Thus the assertion that the One on whom John sees the spirit descend is he who baptizes "with holy spirit" means that the one designated thus baptizes with power, power given by God.[10] When therefore, in the other passage in the Fourth Gospel where this expression occurs, Jesus imparts holy spirit to the disciples (20:22), this is clearly to give them the necessary power to continue his work. He does not say to them, "Receive the Holy Spirit", for in the author's mind this would be a manifest impossibility like saying, "Receive God in his fulness", whereas to say as he does, "Receive holy spirit", meaning, "Receive the power of God", is intelligible. We may compare Acts 8:15, 17 where Peter and John pray for the converts of Samaria that they may receive holy spirit. Such a conclusion has useful and clarifying results for understanding baptism and its relation to the holy spirit, for Jn 20:22 is obviously a fulfilment, and the only fulfilment narrated, of 1:33.[11]

God may be called Spirit and also the Holy One. Jesus, God incarnate, because he has come in the flesh, cannot of course be

---

[9] It is assumed that *hagion* is omitted in the correct reading of 7:39.

[10] The Fourth Gospel here "follows" Mk 3:8, a slightly refined version of the Q account of John's baptismal teaching (Mt 3:11; Lk 3:16) whose phrase "with holy spirit and fire" unmistakably denotes a divisive and destructive judgment and has little to do with the holy spirit in any of the usual NT senses. John 1:33 adds "and fire" only in the first hand of the fifth-century Alexandrian text MS. C.

[11] See J. D. G. Dunn, *Baptism in the Holy Spirit* (SBT Ser. 2, 15; London, 1970) 176.

called Spirit; but he can be called the Holy One. The title is rare, but occurs in Mk 1:24; Lk 4:34; Jn 6:69; Acts 3:14; 1 Jn 2:20; Rev 3:7 (cf. Lk 1:35; 2:23; Acts 4:27, 30; 1 Pet 1:15; Rev 4:8). In Jn 6:69 it is a formal messianic title, and in this Gospel messiah means much more than in the Synoptics (cf. 20:28 and 31). As the Holy One of God Jesus is sanctified by the Father (10:36) and sanctifies himself (17:19). Such a conception goes far beyond anything which the author of the hymns of Qumran or any other writer of their extant literature would say of himself or of any other. The central action of Jesus is once more seen to transcend his word. In this prayer in which he says that he sanctifies himself he also says that he has completed the work which the Father gave him to do (17:4), but this work is not finally completed until the crucifixion for which he is sanctifying himself. When it is and he gives up his life he says that it is completed (19:30). In one respect this sanctification is like the dedication of the author of the Hodayoth to his task: it is for the sake of his followers (1QH 6:6–9; Jn 17:19). In the case of Jesus it is said that "I sanctify myself, that they may be sanctified in the truth", a phrase not found in the Qumran literature, but which echoes its vocabulary and ideas.

The absence of the phrase the Holy Spirit in its full form in this Gospel (apart from the admittedly usually adopted text in 14:26) does not then mean that the spirit is an unimportant conception, but that where it is used it is to be understood with the aid of the passages of early contemporary Judaism which employ the notion of the spirit of the Holy One, that is, God, as we have attempted to explain it above. This way of explanation helps when an approach is made to the famous demand made of Nicodemus that to see the kingdom of God a man must be born again, that is of water and spirit.[12] Here too it is the spirit of God which gives power that is meant, and from making this distinction we can gain an understanding into the insistence of Jesus that a man must be born of water and spirit. To be born of spirit is to receive the spirit of God as the disciples do in 20:22, and this is their baptism in the spirit. It is indeed to be born again; to quote Dunn,[13] drawing attention to the use of *enephusēsen* in 20:22, "It is the word used in Gen 2:7, Ezek 37:9 and Wisd 15:11 to describe the creation of man —the divine breath (*pneuma*—in Gen 2:7 *pnoē*) which brings life to what was otherwise a corpse. In other words, John presents the act of Jesus as a new creation: Jesus is the author of the new creation as he was of the old (1:3)."

We may incidentally insert here our solution of the question why Jesus says that it is necessary to be born of *water and* spirit; briefly the problem is that the Gospel would lead us to expect that baptism in the spirit is essential but water-baptism unnecessary. The reason why water-baptism is still necessary is that it retains the

---

[12] Spirit is anarthrous but no doubt means "spirit of God". It has the article in Jn 3:6.
[13] *Baptism in the Holy Spirit*, 180. On this page (note 12) Dunn lists numerous scholars who support the view of the connection of 1:33 with 20:22 and of the significance of these passages.

C

lesser function of cleansing ceremonially from sin and acting as a psychological aid to repentance without which forgiveness is impossible; for it was one of the most interesting advances in thought shown by the men of Qumran that for them moral sin defiled no less than ritual transgression. This is shown in 1QS 3:4; 5:13f.; and 8:16–19. Dunn aptly quotes Josephus, *Ant.* 18:117:[14] John's baptism was "not to beg for pardon for sins committed, but for the purification of the body, when the soul had previously been cleansed by right behaviour". The author of the Gospel had not quite left behind this notion but usually for him water as cleanser is a powerful symbol of the spirit, and he thinks along the lines suggested by Ezek 36:25f. (a most important passage since it brings together water and spirit); Zech 13:1; 1QS 4:21. Hence water is "living water" and wells up to give life (Jn 4:14) and rivers of it (expressly identified with the spirit) flow from the believer (7:38f.) as from the side of the crucified Jesus.[15]

To sum up so far, it seems that the Fourth Gospel regarded the Paraclete as primarily God himself, Jesus as Paraclete because he was God incarnate, and as such the bestower of spirit in the sense of the power of God for cleansing and giving rebirth which enables a man to achieve in the service of God that of which he would otherwise be incapable, and without which he would be unable to see the kingdom of God, the sovereignty of God, God at work in the world, unable, that is, to see that Jesus is precisely this, i.e. God active in the world. Unless we are wrong about the original reading in 14:26, the evangelist does not think in terms of the Holy Spirit but in those of holy spirit in a way very like that of the men of Qumran. Nevertheless, in Jn 14:26, with the reading which we have adopted, the author says, "the Paraclete, the spirit which the Father will send in my name...", and this cannot be made to sound quasi-impersonal, as though the Paraclete—certainly personal—were being equated with the spirit power of God of which the author speaks elsewhere. Here then he must intend a spirit in the sense of a personal being and be using the term as it is so often used in the inter-testamental literature of beings whom we should loosely call "angels". The term is applied to both good and bad angelic powers in such literature, including the Scrolls. In the following passages the "spirits" are those on the side of God (beginning with two references from the Old Testament to bring out the continuity of the concept): Num 27:16; Ps 104:4; 1QH 3:22f.; 8:12 ("spirits of the holy one"); 10:8; 13:8 ("thy host of spirits" as in 1QM 12:8); 1QM 13:2, and 10 ("spirits of truth"). There is therefore no difficulty whatever in understanding John 14:26: the Paraclete is pre-eminently the spirit which, or rather in this case whom, the Father will send in the name of Jesus. There are others whom he may send to the Christian congregation as we have already seen implied in 1 Jn 4:1. There is just as clearly no difficulty in identifying in Scroll and Johannine

---

[14] *Baptism in the Holy Spirit*, 16.
[15] The best explanation of Jn 7:38 seems to be provided by G. Widengren, *The King and the Tree of Life in Ancient Near Eastern Religion* (*King and Saviour IV*) (UUA 4; Uppsala, Wiesbaden, 1951).

terms this spirit whom the Father will send in the name of Jesus; he is the Paraclete and the Spirit of Truth in Johannine terms, in Scroll terms the Spirit of Truth.

Since no term exactly corresponding to Paraclete is found in the Scrolls the identification of Paraclete and Spirit of Truth could not be made there, but in discussing some of the terms which might foreshadow the idea of Paraclete, we found that this literature afforded evidence that some minds were ready for personifying a figure who fulfilled the functions of *paraklēsis* and for identifying this figure with the Spirit of Truth. The Fourth Gospel has done this explicitly in 14:16f.; 15:26; 16:13. We have therefore to examine the use made by this Gospel of the Spirit of Truth and his relation to the Paraclete in the light of the ancestry of the terms, chiefly as they are illustrated in the Scrolls.

III

The Testament of Judah alone of intertestamental literature outside the Scrolls appears to use the terms in which we are interested, speaking of the Spirit of Truth and the Spirit of Deceit in 20:1, and saying in 20:5, "... the Spirit of Truth testifieth all things, and accuseth all; and the sinner is burnt up by his own heart, and cannot raise his face to the judge". Nothing could be closer to the function of the *paraklētos* as convincer and convictor. We have already seen that the phrases exist also in the plural. It is only in 1QS 3:13–4:26 among the Qumran writings that the Spirit of Truth and the Spirit of Deceit are opposed clearly to one another and the doctrine deriving from belief in their existence worked out and presented. This is not the place for an extended discussion of the doctrine, but the main points which afford parallels with, or otherwise throw light upon the Fourth Gospel, may well be listed and briefly discussed. First, the Rule and the Gospel have in common belief in the existence of these two spirits. The most obvious evidence for this is the passage always quoted in this connection, 1 Jn 4:6, where the phrases of the Testament of Judah and of the Rule appear in exact Greek equivalents; but we shall see that the correspondence goes further than this. Secondly, both clearly fail to reconcile the existence of these two spirits and their influence over mankind with any possibility of individual repentance, or indeed of individual choice; for both combine this dualistic and apparently deterministic doctrine inconsistently with the simpler doctrine that there is a choice for all men like that assumed by Dt 30:15–20. Thirdly, the role of God in the situation described by this dualistic doctrine is in the Gospel taken over largely by Jesus. Fourthly, there are a number of further elements in the Gospel way of thinking about the Spirit of Truth which were not possible for the Rule; and these must be discussed.

The existence of the common belief may be accepted in the light of 1QS 3:19–25 and 1 Jn 4:6, and the essay elsewhere in this volume devoted to the Rule passage will treat of the doctrine in detail.[16] Here must be mentioned the cognate idea of the existence

---

16 See J. H. Charlesworth's chapter below, pp. 76ff.

in the world of two sorts of men as this idea is used in the Fourth Gospel and the First Epistle. The most obvious place from which to start is 1:12. It illustrates at once the particular feature of the Gospel which takes it out of the milieu of thought represented by the Rule. The two sorts (the Gospel does not use any word to denote categories such as "lots", used by the Scrolls) are distinguished by one kind being "born of God" and the other being able to claim only a natural birth. The passage is close to the beginning of the Gospel and thereby shows the importance of the idea for the author. Developing this theme, the author uses in 3:6 a different vocabulary from that which contrasts truth and deceit, opposing spirit and flesh and characterizing men according to these categories. It is already obvious that the men of Qumran, along with other contemporaries, did not sharply oppose these two as though spirit were necessarily good and flesh necessarily evil, since they think of evil in the spiritual sphere also, but, like Paul, they reject a life controlled by flesh, so that 1QH can speak of a "spirit of flesh" (13:13) as the wrong kind of spirit to control one's life. In John 3:6 it is clear that the two are not opposed as good to evil, but that spiritual things can be discerned only by someone who is born of the spirit, that is, of God. This passage should then probably be left on one side in our discussion, and not be too readily regarded as dualistic.

More to our purpose is 3:18–21, showing a main theme of the Gospel, that the appearance of the incarnate *logos* actuates a division already latent in mankind: there are those who accept and those who reject him, and these reactions reveal their already existing dispositions. At first sight it might seem that this passage illustrates rather that men must, faced with Jesus, decide for or against him, and that this decision determines their destiny; but the accusation that men loved darkness rather than light (the vocabulary is unmistakably akin to that of the Scrolls) is followed by the explanation that "their deeds were evil" (cf. 1 Jn 3:12). The judgment which Jesus' arrival brings is to operate very soon according to 5:28f., and we meet in this passage the reason for the author's preoccupation with the existence already of the two kinds of men, righteous and wicked: like the author of Daniel (12:2) he is concerned for past generations, assuming that it is known which of them were good and which bad; indeed the fate of each category is already determined. Nevertheless the Gospel and Epistle think also of those who have given their allegiance to Jesus as *par excellence* those who are righteous and belong to him. They are the true worshippers who worship in spirit and in truth, an impossibility if they have not been endowed with these gifts in baptism, receiving spirit and instruction in the truth. From at least chapter 5 onwards the enemies of Jesus become implacable and the battle seems to be less between two "lots" of men than between him and "the Jews". Jn 8:23 sums up the situation from the point of view of the Johannine Jesus: "You are from below, I am from above; you are of this world, I am not of this world". In 8:33, 39 "they" (one cannot resist the modern idiom) claim to be sons of Abraham but Jesus argues that their father is the devil (v. 44):

"He was a murderer from the beginning, and is not rooted in the truth, because the truth is not in him." It appears then that the spirit according to which one must be born (or reborn) has strong affinities with the truth, a conception which will be discussed further presently. Moreover, it is clear from this passage that the author believed in the existence of one kind of men belonging to the truth and the other to the "father of falsehood" (v. 44, end). That Judas is thought of as a "devil" (6:70; cf. 13:2, 27) is in accordance with the author's belief in a plurality of devils or evil spirits under the command of Satan. He probably did not think out to the end whether men could be regarded as "devils" (6:70) or whether they should be seen as possessed by devils (13:2, 27), but in any case his thought is more concrete and exact than the passage in the Rule which seeks to explain the way in which the two main different and opposed spirits influence the conduct of men; for in 1 Jn 2:18 he can refer to "many antichrists", evidently meaning recognizable contemporaries, but here too there is an affinity with the vocabulary of the Rule: in verses 21 and 26 the author writes of truth, falsity and deception. The theme of deception is taken up again in 3:7 which introduces a passage contrasting the children of God with the children of the devil. Like that from Jn 8:33–44 it uses a number of different contrasted pairs, the doer of righteousness and the doer of sin, God and the devil, children of God and children of the devil, those who love their brethren and those who do not love their brethren, and Cain and Abel (though Abel is not mentioned by name). Both Jn 8:33–44 and 1 Jn 3:7–12 seem to reflect themes according to which Cain became the first in a line of wicked men who derived their disposition from him, which reflected an origin in which the devil had played a decisive role. To be born of God, though understood in a profoundly spiritual sense in the Johannine literature, thus contrasts with being descended from the devil in a quasi-literal sense. Nothing like this appears in any of the extant literature of Qumran, and we thus find another instance of the multiple character of the sources and thought-forms upon which the author of the Fourth Gospel drew.

We have established that the Scrolls, however, either were one of the sources used by the Gospel or themselves shared with it some material not extant elsewhere. We pass on now to consider the second point made above, the failure of both to reconcile the contradiction inherent in the belief that mankind is divided into two opposed "lots" whose nature is fixed by the influence of immutable supernatural powers with the censure and exhortation consistent only with the view that all men have some freedom to choose. The famous passage of the Rule (3:13–4:26) appears to teach that every individual is a mixture of the two spirits, both of whom have been created by God, who would therefore be responsible for the unchangeable destiny of each; but there are hints elsewhere that God takes the place of the Spirit of Truth while the Spirit of Perversity or Falsehood will be his adversary rather than the adversary of a supernatural being of the same status as himself. Thus in the initiatory rite of

1QS 1:16–3:12 it is God and Belial who are opposed (cf. 1QH 4:5f., 23 for God himself enlightening his faithful servant). In this case God assures ultimate victory to those who are loyal to him. The parallel mixture of the two outlooks in the Fourth Gospel and the First Epistle has already been described.

We come to the third point. Whether it is by his own agency or that of the Spirit of Light or Truth which he has created for this purpose, it is God who in the Scrolls literature is expected finally to put an end to evil and give the triumph to his people. This could not be gainsaid by any reader of the final passage of the War Scroll as it has come down to us. From 18:2 it is clearly God who is the champion of Israel in the final battle of good and evil. The point needs no further documentation. When we seek a parallel for this final contest in the Gospel tradition, while it would be natural to consider the coming of the Son of Man in glory to inaugurate the final judgment, it will be agreed that in the whole of the New Testament including all four gospels the final action of God is understood to begin with Jesus, whether with his ministry, or with his birth, or with his crucifixion in which the clash with the evil powers took place. Thus the victory of goodness is an apparent defeat, and the theme of victory in the physical or even military sense, such as we find in other literature, including the Scrolls, is transposed into another key altogether. Jesus dies as the Son of God (Mark), as the incarnation of forgivingness (Luke), as he who could have summoned to his aid legions of angels (Matthew), or as a revelation of the Father and the mysterious source of cleansing and new power and new life (John); thus he conquers the powers, including that of death itself. Obvious though this is, it is necessary to draw attention to this manifest difference between the attitude of the Scrolls and of the Fourth Gospel (and indeed of all the Gospels) to the dualism which is suggested by the presence in the Gospel of the concept of the Spirit of Truth.

The introduction of the new element of Jesus as the Paraclete and Logos incarnate transforms every concept taken over by the New Testament writers from their heritage. The Paraclete who is to take the place of Jesus is identified with the Spirit of Truth but for those who are reading a Gospel about Jesus this identification must mean something different from its significance for the men of Qumran: the Paraclete-Spirit of Truth comes at the prayer of Jesus or in his name or even sent by him. If we explore the meaning of this we shall be in a position to understand in what sense the Paraclete can be called the Spirit of Truth as though the title were a synonym. We may take the passages in turn, after considering one important point belonging to the historical background.

The Fourth Gospel, for all its manifest strangeness, was written for a group of people (whether already in existence or to be called into existence by the work of the author) who shared with the rest of the Church a certain experience, usually described as the presence of Christ in his Church. It matters not at all whether the modern historian accepts this explanatory description of the phenomenon; he must admit its existence. If Mk 13:11[17] expresses an authentic prophecy of Jesus, its inclusion in that Gospel would still have been unlikely if it had not corresponded to something known to his readers; moreover, the composition of the Gospel would have been impossible. Thus if it is an authentic prophecy, it is also a fulfilled prophecy. If it is unauthentic, it points even more clearly to an experience known within the Church where, if not an authentic saying of Jesus, it must have originated. A further phenomenon to which all history (secular history sometimes rather ruefully) must give a place is the spread of the Christian Church over the Roman Empire and beyond, despite the persecution to which Mk 13:11 and much else in the New Testament bear witness, and the devotion of the martyrs and of many others in the process of this growth. It was a situation in which it was necessary to counter slander against not only Christians but Christ and to convince the adversary while defending oneself, and in which it was necessary as a naturally parallel activity to present a more and more articulated and reasoned structure of the faith that survived so many attacks; this was the situation which produced the doctrine of the Paraclete and the Spirit of Truth in the Fourth Gospel. Whether we read present or future of the verb "to be" at the end of Jn 14:17, Jesus' promise that the Paraclete-Spirit of Truth will stay and be in or among disciples exactly corresponds to their situation and experience.[18]

When therefore the author makes Jesus say, "I will ask the Father and he will give you another Paraclete..." (Jn 14:16), he is basing the dialogue on his own and his contemporaries' experience; this experience is interpreted partly in the light of his christological beliefs: he shows his confidence that what Jesus requests from the Father he will be granted, and indeed represents Jesus as claiming that the Father has granted him everything, even at the time of his earthly ministry. In the following verse (14:17) the Paraclete is explained as the Spirit of Truth. One reason for this title is easy to understand at once; in the Rule this figure (already discussed in connection with 14:26) is the constant helper of the sons of light (3:24f.; cf. 3:38f.) although God is also present to them in their need along with this spirit. However, in the Gospel the idea is developed to explain a recognizable situation. This Spirit of Truth the "world" cannot accept, having no vision or understanding of it; the imperviousness of the world to Christian witness reflects the intransigence of the contemporaries of Jesus as the author sees them, in spite of the signs which should have revealed the other-worldly character of Jesus to them (12:37–41). Christians understand this spirit because he dwells with them and will be (or is) in or among them. No better reason could be found for Christians' knowledge of the Spirit of Truth than this, that he is part of their experience; they do not meet him

---

17 Mk 13:11: "And when they bring you to trial and deliver you up, do not be anxious beforehand what you are to say; but say whatever is given you in that hour, for it is not you who speak, but the Holy Spirit" (RSV).
18 It is unnecessary therefore to say that members of the Church themselves fulfil the function of the Paraclete. Johnston, however, makes this assertion a main motif in his The Spirit-Paraclete in the Gospel of John,

as an exterior hitherto unknown phenomenon. Their knowledge arises out of, or may be said to be synonymous with, their analysis of their own self-understanding in their daily situation: it is an explanation of themselves in their Christian experience.

The next passage for examination is Jn 14:26, already mentioned in connection with what is said in it about the spirit. The phrase "Spirit of Truth" does not occur, but the Paraclete's function is clearly described: "he will teach you everything and remind you of all that I have said to you". He needs to be a Paraclete to help disciples in a situation where they are liable to persecution; he needs to be the Spirit of Truth (though not so called in this verse) in order to teach them everything and to help them preserve all his teaching; for his teaching, centred as it is on himself and his own function in the world, is the Truth. It is truth which must be learnt and must be "done" or practised. The idea was easily intelligible for a Jew: for him the Torah was a great body of teaching which he must accept as at once giving him his tasks and declaring to him the truth about God, God's actions and God's demands. The book of Tobit understood the phrase exactly in this way (4:6; and 13:6 according to the Sinaitic MS.): to "do the truth" means to obey and live by the Law. For those for whom the Fourth Gospel was written, the Torah had been superseded by the body of teaching from and about Jesus, and this was now the Truth. Jesus could be called the Truth (14:6) and 1 Jn 1:6 uses the phrase "do the truth" in the sense of to live honestly as a Christian without self-deception. This meaning has been anticipated in Jn 3:21, where a life of this quality, described in the same terms, seems to be contemplated as a possibility even before the death and resurrection of Jesus. The term Spirit of Truth is as naturally attached by the Fourth Gospel to the Paraclete as it was in Qumran to the spirit who maintains the faithfulness of the Qumran convenanters. In the former he is the revealer and preserver of all that Christians need in order to defend themselves against and ultimately to convince the world, in the latter he is the power which keeps them faithful to the already long-accepted Law.

Jn 15:26 may be interpreted in exactly the same way: the Spirit of Truth will witness about Jesus in a way parallel to the witness of the disciples, here clearly thought of as at least including those of the earthly Jesus, because they "have been with him from the beginning". Thus the Paraclete as Spirit of Truth helps those who preserve the tradition of the historical Jesus by witnessing to the reality of the Christ in his Church. In this verse it is said that the Spirit of Truth comes forth from the Father. Years of interpreting this in a metaphysical sense must not blind us to the simple explanation which offers itself when we see such terms against the now known historical background. The Paraclete is equated with the Spirit of Truth, here thought of—in the imagination of the author—as one of those spirit beings (or "angels") in whom heaven abounded. He "comes forth from" the Father as Gabriel does in Lk 1:19. This is not to affirm that the evangelist thought in literal spatial terms, but rather that if he is using a metaphor it is founded upon them.

Jn 16:7 has already been discussed to some extent, but the difficult passage, 16:8–11, remains. The interpretations given to these verses are numerous and it is unnecessary to summarize or list them here. Nor can we claim to offer anything original, but rather to present what seems to be the most reasonable interpretation in the light of our investigations into the background, especially that provided by the Scrolls, of the concepts used by the evangelist. It will be convenient to recapitulate certain conclusions: the Paraclete is a Spirit sent by God to take the place of Jesus, and his task is to assist and inform the disciples of Jesus, or the Christian Church, so that they can succeed in their task of self-defence. The task implies convincing and convicting the adversary, the "world"; for the "world", unable to understand the Truth which the Church holds,[19] persecutes those who hold it. It is natural therefore for him also to be called the Spirit of Truth. There can be no mistaking the scene or period in history of which the Jesus of the Fourth Gospel is speaking, for this is clear from the beginning of the chapter, 16:1–4a. Verses 4b–6 stress the fact that Jesus is about to "go away" and that this fills their hearts with sorrow; but part of the truth is that the departure of Jesus and the coming of the Paraclete are necessary (v. 7). The clue to the following verses, which are our problem, must therefore lie in the answer to the question, "Necessary for what?" The whole of our investigation and the description of the task of the Paraclete in verse 8 as being to convince or convict (*elenchein*) suggests that the answer to our question is that the absence of Jesus and the presence of the Paraclete are necessary to convince and convict the world. Verses 9 and 10 give the three subjects about which the Paraclete is to convince, and the second, always the hardest to explain, seems now to yield some meaning. The very absence of Jesus felt with such pain by disciples (not the pain of parting from the twelve only but the pain felt by persecuted disciples at the absence of their Lord) constitutes *dikaiosunē*. Remembering that the scene is understood according to a forensic model, that the word is here apparently contrasted with sin, and that the last of the three subjects is judgment, we must see this word in one of its radical meanings, which has been expressed in many translations of the New Testament by "justification" and must be explained as meaning "found and declared to be in the right", passing over into "before God inevitably a sinner but declared by him to be in the right". Thus it is the *dikaiosunē* of disciples that Jesus goes to the Father and they no longer see him; but this is scarcely intelligible and needs to be expressed in more positive terms. This can be achieved by attending to the passage a little further on, verses 16–24, where the question of the meaning of seeing Jesus no longer is resumed. It is often thought naturally enough that this passage refers to the grief which the disciples will feel at the crucifixion of Jesus and the joy which they will feel when he returns to them. At least two objections to this seem to be fatal: one is that such a meaning is obvious and straightforward whereas Jesus warns that he is speaking *en paroimiais* (v. 25); the other is that the entire passage (16:1–24) deals with a much more lasting absence, an absence

[19] For the Church as in some sense an infallible community, see Jn 5:24; 1 Jn 3:14; cf. Mt 16:18; 1 Tim 3:15.

for which the Paraclete is a *permanent* compensation. Moreover, the famous figure of the travailing mother is used to describe the experience not of Jesus but of disciples whose final joy (unlike the woman's baby) cannot be taken from them. Then they will ask nothing of Jesus but ask of the Father in his name. Thus their victory will be their own, won certainly with the aid of the Paraclete or Spirit of Truth, the supernatural helper sent by the Father, but *their* victory, the victory of the Church in its ceaseless battle with the world. There is another aspect of the "righteousness" or vindication of the disciples: the absence of Jesus is apparent only. Verses 12–15 show that the Spirit of Truth has more to tell the disciples which Jesus in his earthly ministry could not tell them because they could not bear the burden of it, yet verses 13b–14 show that what he tells them will really be from Jesus, or the Father (it is the same thing, as verse 15 makes plain). Verses 16ff. put the matter in another way: instead of the Paraclete's presence making the absence of Jesus merely apparent, Jesus is said to be absent only temporarily. The first way of putting it is spatial, the second temporal. Finally, the truth that Christians' victory is in some sense their own, is expressed in 1 Jn 5:4: "This is the victory which has overcome the world, our faith."

The translation (somewhat free) therefore here offered for 16:8b–11 is as follows: "... he will bring home to the world the truth about sin and about being in the right and about judgment. The truth about sin is that they do not believe in me; the truth about being in the right is that (you are shown to be so by the very fact that) I go to the Father and you no longer see me; the truth about judgment is that the ruler of this world has been judged." Jn 12:31 provides the best commentary on the last part of this passage; in 12:27–32 there is a curious multiplicity of scenes, not peculiar to this passage but striking here because it is threefold: there is the actual scene in which Jesus is addressing some listeners (the "Greeks" or the disciples, vv. 20–22), and there is the scene of the agony in the garden, unmistakably recalled by verses 27f., and there is the scene on the cosmic scale which the contest and victory of the garden signifies. This last scene is, like the constant battle of the Church with the world, the universe conceived of as the court in which God is the eternal judge. The victory of Jesus means the expulsion of the ruler of this world, the enemy Satan. This victory has to be extended into the world and into the future so long as time exists, and the battle is therefore continuous.

Some reference has already been made to Jn 16:13, the remaining verse where the Paraclete is called the Spirit of Truth. The passage is straightforward since it is obviously appropriate that the Spirit of Truth should lead disciples into all the truth. It is necessary only to be clear that the Truth is different from that so regarded by the covenanters of Qumran. As already claimed, this was for them the Torah, as interpreted by their leader or leaders, among whom is the author of the Hodayoth. In 1QH 2:13 and 18:11 the poet claims that God has made him an interpreter of mysteries, but these mysteries are those which are hidden in the scriptures, and he does not claim to go beyond their authority or such as belongs to human experience of and wonder at creation. In these passages the Hebrew word is *mēlîṣ*, found in Job 33:23 and Is 43:27, meaning something like "mediator" or spokesman. In the Job passage the *mēlîṣ* is a heavenly being and the Targum uses the Greek word *paraklētos* as a loan-word in Aramaic form. The claim of this Hebrew word to be one of those foreshadowing the concept of the Paraclete has already been discussed. It can hardly be the total explanation of the present passage, which must refer to the truth in a Christian context of the turbulent kind already described. The verb *hodēgēsei* may well have some special significance, especially in view of the variants of both this word and other phrases connected with it which are found in the apparatus criticus.[20] There seems to be no obscurity about the interpretation, for the key lies in the previous verse. Taken together the passage reveals the belief that the earthly Jesus could have revealed a whole body of doctrine concerning "heavenly things" if he had found listeners capable of accepting it. Neither Nicodemus, representing the ancient wisdom, nor disciples (whether contemporary with Jesus or with the author), representing the new revelation, could understand and therefore "bear" or "tolerate" some of the more advanced doctrine which the author evidently himself already entertained and at which he hints more than once in the course of the Gospel. See for example 3:12, 32; 5:41-44; 14:17, and note that 13:20 authorizes such development in the Church. The form of such doctrine can hardly be established, even if each interpreter of the Fourth Gospel may have his own suspicion of the direction in which the author believed the Spirit of Truth had since the time of Jesus "led" some at least of his followers. This is a subject lying outside our scope and a field in which many are already occupied.

---

20 The word is a *hapax legomenon* in the Johannine Gospel and Epistles.

4

The Calendar of Qumran and the Passion Narrative in John

A. JAUBERT

The title of this chapter requires a preliminary comment. It seems to us that the calendar attested by the Qumran documents was more ancient and widespread than the Qumran milieu. We believe that it is of biblical origin and rooted in the strata of the priestly code.[1] This calendar is advocated by the book of Jubilees and by the book of the Heavenly Luminaries of Enoch, which certainly had a wider area of influence than that of Qumran.

There has also been found at Masada a liturgical scroll concerned with the burnt offering of the Sabbath and maintaining the same calendar.[2] This discovery prompts reflection. Doubtless one can say that some Essenes who were participating in the Jewish revolt had carried the scroll to Masada.[3] It appears certain in fact that some Essenes had joined themselves to the Zealots in the war against the Romans,[4] although it has not been shown that there were any Essenes at Masada. In any case, if an Essene liturgical scroll was preserved at Masada, it is because it could be considered sympathetically in an environment as intransigent as that of the Zealots, impassioned for the traditions of their ancestors and regrouped around Eleazar, the descendant of Judas the Galilean.[5] The Masada discovery enlarges the range of the application of the Qumran calendar.

Additional reasons point in the same direction. Indeed the reappear-

---

[1] A. Jaubert, *La date de la cène* (Paris, 1957) 31–59. "Jésus et le calendrier de Qumrân", *NTS* 7 (1960) 2, n. 3. H. Cazelles, "Sur les origines du calendrier des Jubilés", *Bib* 43 (1962) 202–12. E. Vogt, "Note sur le calendrier du déluge", *Bib* 43 (1962) 212–16.

[2] Y. Yadin, *Masada* (Jerusalem, 1965) 81, 106–108.

[3] The opinion of Y. Yadin. To the contrary, C. Roth, "Qumran and Masadah", *RevQ* 5 (1964) 81–7. It is unlikely that the scroll had been left by Essenes during the time of Herod; cf. C. Daniel, "Les Hérodiens sont-ils des Esséniens", *RevQ* 6 (1967) 39.

[4] Josephus mentions John the Essene, a Jewish general who died during the assault made against Ashkelon, *War*, II, xx, 4, par. 567; III, ii, 1, par. 11, 19; see also II, viii, 10, par. 152 (the courage of the Essenes during the war against the Romans). Hippolytus derives the Zealots from the Essenes, *Elenchos*, IX, 26 (GCS 26, p. 260).

[5] *War*, II, xvii, 9, par. 447; VII, viii, 1, par. 253. The Galilean origin of the Zealot movement is notable. On the other hand the descent of the Sicarii on Engedi at the time of the Feast of Unleavened Bread suggests a difference in calendar between the assailants and the assailed; *War*, IV, vii, 2, par. 402.

ance of this calendar in Christian or Jewish settings obliges us to think that the Qumran Essenes were only one of the groups which followed this calendar, perhaps they were the ones who sought to observe it in its totality. In order to avoid the ambiguity of the name "Calendar of Qumran", and to simplify the title, the "old priestly calendar", we will call it the Zadokite calendar.

The problem to be dealt with is that of the connections between the Johannine passion narrative and the Zadokite calendar. Our purpose may appear to be a paradox, because John's Gospel is usually judged to be opposed to this calendar, and then this judgment is used as an argument against the long chronology of the Passion. According to the Gospel of John, in fact, Jesus dies at the moment when the Jews begin to sacrifice the Passover lambs in the Temple. The points of reference for the Fourth Gospel always appear as the official Jewish feasts, whether it concerns feasts which took place during the ministry of Jesus or the last Passover. As we have already had occasion to say, this point of view is normal in a catechesis addressed to a Hellenistic setting, which discerns especially the theological meaning that the Gospel attaches to the "feasts of the Jews": henceforth the only Temple—as the unique high-priest and the only victim—is Christ himself. The complexity of the calendar was experienced only in Palestine. We know from elsewhere that even among the Palestinian groups which were most attached to the Zadokite calendar, the Temple of Jerusalem had always exercised a real fascination.[6]

It is known, however—and this is one of the most important results of the literary criticism of the texts—that John's Gospel comes at the end of a long catechetical reflection which embodies some ancient elements while bringing them into new perspectives. Our problem then is to discover if beyond the Johannine presentation which attaches itself to the official feasts, the materials used by the Gospel of John are in contradiction to the Zadokite calendar or if, on the other hand, they are favourable to it.

Before discussing the narrative of the passion and especially that of the Last Supper, it is necessary to emphasize a curious correspondence between the Zadokite calendar and the Johannine resurrection narrative.

It is known that there are within John's Gospel some narratives built on a weekly schema. One of them is found at the beginning of the Gospel.[7] At the end of the Gospel, a week starts six days before the Passover (Jn 12:1) and ends on the Sunday of the Resurrection. This Sunday is common to the early Christian tradition, but the

---

[6] The site of the Temple was surely venerated by the Qumran sect, whose hope was turned towards the future temple. According to Josephus, the Essenes used to send offerings to the Temple, *Ant.*, XVIII, i, 5, par. 19.

[7] Three "next days" are noted (Jn 1:29, 35, 43); the wedding at Cana took place on the "third day" (2:1). However, the commentators diverge in their interpretation of these days. We would recall that the marriage of Jewish girls in ancient times was fixed to Wednesday. See Str-B 2, 398.

Gospel of John is the only one to tell of an appearance "eight days later" to the disciples, including Thomas (20:26).

That these eight days indicate the week following is the opinion of the commentators.[8] Now, there is no concern here for a weekly schema since this week would be completely empty (nothing happens between Resurrection Sunday and the following Sunday). The description of the eight days gives importance to the Sunday alone. If chapter 21, which is an appendix, is not taken into account, the eighth day of Jn 20:26 concludes the Gospel. It begins the whole period of the time of the Church, the period of "those who have not seen and yet believe". From a comparative study of the various resurrection narratives, the framework into which the evangelist places the appearance of Thomas must be of liturgical origin. The Sunday after the Passover would have therefore held a significance in the milieu of the author or in the tradition which he inherited. But from where could the importance of such a Sunday in certain sectors of primitive Christianity come?

If the question is addressed to the official Jewish calendar, there is nothing which favours making this Sunday prominent. In this calendar every feast is movable with respect to the days of the week and is dependent only on the day of the month. The 16th of Nisan, the day after the holiday of the Passover and the feast of the Sheaf, could fall on any day of the week. But, according to the evangelists, in the year of Jesus' death, 16 Nisan was a Sunday. Hence, the feast of the Sheaf fell on the same day in the official calendar, as in the reckoning of the Boethusians and the Samaritans, who interpreted Lev 23:15 literally, so that "the morrow after the Sabbath" was always a Sunday, the Sunday within the week of Unleavened Bread.[9]

In short, the Sunday of the Resurrection coincided with the offering of the Sheaf in several reckonings and the symbolism must have been perceived very early,[10] but the Sunday following did not correspond to anything in these reckonings; the feast of the Sheaf never had an octave. The feast of Unleavened Bread, which lasts seven days (or eight if 14 Nisan is counted—when 15 Nisan was on the Sabbath[11]), ended on Friday, not on Sunday.

In contrast, in the Zadokite calendar the day after the Sabbath following the Week of Unleavened Bread (the 26th of the first month) was an essential link, since the fifty days it opened regulated not only the date of the Zadokite Pentecost (the 15th of the third month) but that of the fifty days following, as the discovery of the Temple Scroll has confirmed.[12] In this calendar alone, as J. P. Audet first pointed out,[13] the Sunday of the appearance to Thomas can come

---

[8] R. Bultmann, *Das Evangelium des Johannes* (Göttingen, 1962) 538. C. K. Barrett, *The Gospel According to St John* (London, 1955) 476.

[9] *La date de la cène*, 21–22. J. Van Goudoever, *Fêtes et calendriers bibliques*, 3rd ed. (Paris, 1961) 31ff. M. Delcor, "Pentecôte", *VDBS* 7, 861f.

[10] As the allusion in 1 Cor 15:20 shows: "Christ, the first fruits of those who have fallen asleep".

[11] Str-B 1, 988.

[12] Y. Yadin, *Comptes rendus de l'Académie des Inscriptions* (Paris, 1968) 607–19.

[13] "Jésus et le 'calendrier sacerdotal ancien' ", *ScE* 10 (1958) 382. Cf. E. Vogt, *Bib* 40 (1959) 102–5.

from a liturgical source and support the symbolic significance that the author has given to it: the commencement for the time of the Church.

It is difficult to say if at the final stage of the Gospel of John the meaning of the second Sunday was still perceived with respect to the calendar of 364 days. It appears only under the form of the ogdoad ("eight days after") and it is thus that it has been preserved by the Christian liturgy.[14] A curious text of Eustratius calls this Sunday *deutero-prōtē*. One may interpret this expression as designating the *second* Sunday after the Wednesday of the Passover and the *first* Sunday of the seven weeks of Pentecost. Was this an archaic term which had significance with regard to the Zadokite calendar?[15]

Be that as it may, this Sunday lived on in the Gospel of John only in the state of a liturgical remnant, but this remnant was of necessity linked—at least originally—with the Zadokite Passover of Tuesday/Wednesday since it was calculated in accordance with it.[16] This discovery can only encourage the search to see if the Last Supper of Jesus according to John preserves any traces of the Zadokite Passover.

A later cross-checking raises the same question. In certain sectors of early Christianity the reading of the washing of the feet according to John was set for Tuesday/Wednesday of Holy Week. Such is the case for the Nestorian liturgy, the conservative character of which is recognized.[17] We should also note some early Syriac sermons on Holy Week attributed to Ephraim, in which the commentary on the washing of the feet is made on the night of Tuesday to Wednesday, and also point out the oldest known Roman lectionary which places on Tuesday evening the pericope of the washing of the feet.[18] These passages suggest that at an early time the reading of the washing of the feet conveyed with it the day of Tuesday/Wednesday, even in the settings where no memory of a Last Supper on Tuesday evening existed.

14 *Apostolic Constitutions*, V, 20, 1. *Pilgrimage of Etheria*, 40.

15 J. P. Audet, *ScE* 10 (1958) 361–83. The text of Eustratius places on this Sunday the death of the patriarch Eutychius, whom he considered a new Jacob, *Vita sancti Eutychii*, 96; PG 86, 2381.

16 Wednesday (15th of the first month) and Sunday (26th of the first month) could have been thought of as a liturgical unity, thus maintaining some stability when the calendar of 364 days was tending to break it up. The Wednesday of the Passover was calculated in accordance with the full moon and after the equinox. To keep this Wednesday, it was brought as near as possible to the beginning of the ideal year which had been effected on the fourth day of creation when God had created the luminaries. The moon had naturally been created full and it is often considered that there was in the Israelite calendar a transfer from the first to the fifteenth of the month. For Jews who faithfully observed the Passover according to this calendar the triple dimension (Wednesday, full moon, equinox) permitted the fourteenth day of the first month to be tested reliably, independently of the calendar of 364 days. The case of the Yezidis shows that this calculation is not purely theoretical, cf. A. Jaubert, "Le mercredi de nouvel an chez les Yezidis", *Bib* 49 (1968) 244–8.

17 A. Jaubert, "Une lecture du lavement des pieds au mardi/mercredi saint", *Mus* 79 (1966) 264–70. To the various sources indicated, add *Gannat Bussāmē*; see J. M. Voste, *RB* 37 (1928) 221–32; 386–419; and *RB* 42 (1933) 82.

18 *Mus* 79 (1966) 281–2.

The attempt at harmonization by the Diatessaron is significant.[19] The pericope of the washing of the feet is placed before the day of preparation for the Passover. Tatian was thereby led to break up the last meal of Jesus. Among the versions of the Diatessaron the precious codex of Fulda appears to give the most ancient order of the pericopes. The account of the washing of the feet "before the Passover" is placed just after the Synoptic passage in which Judas has the *intention* to betray Jesus (Mt 26:14). Now the liturgical tradition recorded by the Gospel of Matthew placed this episode on Tuesday.[20] This is an extra reason to think that the reading of the washing of the feet in the time of Tatian was made on Tuesday.

How is this anomaly of the reading of the washing of the feet before the preparation of the Passover to be explained? It may be noted that there exists in the Johannine account in 13:2 an allusion to the plan of the traitor to betray Jesus and that this plan could be linked liturgically with the plan of Judas in Mt 26:14. But could the simple recollection of the plan have changed the liturgical place of Jn 13:1–20, whose natural setting is the Last Supper? And how could this tenuous relationship have influenced important sectors of the Eastern Syriac tradition? In fact we think it is necessary to be attentive to the relationship which exists between Jn 13:2 and Mt 26:14–16, but by explaining it in another manner, at the very level of Johannine editing.[21]

What reason has urged Tatian to cut the washing of the feet from its context and to divide the last meal of Jesus? Tatian does not follow the tradition of the Last Supper on Tuesday evening, a tradition which he must nevertheless have known since it was alive for a long time within Syriac Christianity.[22] The only hypothesis which appears probable to us is that Tatian, who was bound by the Church's liturgy, had to follow the pressure of custom. Now it seems to us that only a custom inscribed in actions, that is to say a liturgical practice on Tuesday evening commemorating the washing of feet according to the injunction found in Jn 13:14f., could have forced this pericope to be placed before the day of preparation of the farewell meal.

According to our hypothesis, the Diatessaron (c. A.D. 175) would have preserved an early custom, which existed at least in the middle of the second century. We are drawing near to the date for the circulation of the Fourth Gospel. And this is why we think that the custom of a commemoration of the washing of feet on Tuesday evening came out of the Johannine circles themselves. In this case the farewell meal of Jesus and the last night that he spent with his disciples would have been commemorated—at least at some time—on the night of Tuesday to Wednesday corresponding to the Zadokite Passover. From this celebration only one clear testimony has

---

[19] *Mus* 79 (1966) 276–81.

[20] A. Jaubert, "Le mercredi où Jésus fut livré", *NTS* 14 (1967) 145–64.

[21] Cf. n. 52.

[22] A. Jaubert, "Une discussion patristique sur la chronologie de la passion", *RSR* 54 (1966) 407–10.

survived: the date for the washing of the feet, on account of its ritual character.

This liturgical information supplied by the early Church leads us to think that at least certain Johannine circles re-enacted on Tuesday evening the feet-washing ceremony. Moreover, we saw above that the Sunday of the appearance to Thomas obtains meaning only according to the Zadokite calendar. This Sunday is exterior to the week of Unleavened Bread; it is the second Sunday after the Tuesday/Wednesday of the Passover. A milieu which venerated this Sunday would have *also* celebrated the Passover on Tuesday evening. Hence, by two different observations we are driven to the same question: "Is there in the Johannine sources a trace of the commemoration of the eucharist on Tuesday evening?" Our primary task is now to attempt to discover if Jesus' last meal according to John contains any characteristics of the Passover.

Let us apply ourselves first to the farewell discourses—the plural is used because criticism has distinguished here three discourses: Jn 17, Jn 15-16, and Jn 13:31-14:31. Jn 14:31 is more closely connected to Jn 18:1 than it is to the other two discourses: "Rise, let us go hence" (14:31)—"Jesus went forth with his disciples . . ." (18:1). Jn 14:30 announced the coming of the prince of this world; in 18:2 Judas comes forward as the instrument of the devil (cf. 13:2). The discourse 13:31-14:31, even if it has been altered, probably belongs to the oldest stratum of the Gospel.

This first discourse presents a rather remarkable structure since it is punctuated by four interruptions on the part of the disciples of Jesus. Simon Peter says to him: "Lord, where are you going?" (13:36). Thomas says to him: "Lord, we do not know where you are going; how can we know the way?" (14:5). Philip says to him: "Lord, show us the Father, and we shall be satisfied" (14:8). Judas (not Iscariot) says to him: "Lord, how is it that you manifest yourself to us and not to the world?" (14:22). Of these four interruptions, three are interrogative in form (Simon Peter, Thomas, Judas); the fourth, that of Philip, induces the explanations of Jesus as well.

As is well known, it was customary at the Passover meal for the sons to ask for some explanations from the father of the family. In *Mekhilta Exodus* four questions from four types of sons are provided.[23] A passage in the *Talmud* foresees even that two rabbis may question one another.[24] In one type of Passover meal among men—and not a family affair—the participants could sometimes question one another or more normally question their master.[25] These successive questions could therefore reflect a Passover custom. This observation takes on added interest if it is recalled that the

23 Str-B 4, 68.
24 *Babylonian Talmud*, Pesahim 116a.
25 These questions are special to the first farewell discourse. In the second discourse it is said in contrast: "none of you asks me, 'Where are you going?' " (16:5); in v. 17 the disciples do not dare to ask and talk only among themselves; in v. 30 they recognize that Jesus does not need to be questioned.

customary form of farewell discourse is that of exhortations and injunctions;[26] it is not composed of interrogatives.

The themes treated are more important. The themes of the Passover vigil were the recall of the Exodus, the departure from Egypt, the waiting for the Messiah. During the Passover night in fact the Israelites, supporting themselves on the marvels of the past, were entirely turned towards the liberation to come, which the coming of the Messiah would usher in.[27] It is quite evident that these Jewish themes could only be changed in the Johannine presentation. But they are easy to locate. It is in fact a question only of the departure of Jesus and of his return—or of his coming.

The departure of Jesus, who passed from this world to the Father (13:1), indicates the great Exodus[28] in which the disciples would participate later. Hence, in the first discourse the questions concern the exodus of Jesus ("where are you going", 13:36; "how can we know the way?" 14:5). This departure is the pledge of the return of Jesus, who will come to take his disciples with him (14:2f.). One will note the insistence on the coming of Jesus, an especially paschal theme, which in the Johannine transposition is expressed also in the coming of Jesus with his Father and by the Spirit.

"And when I go and prepare a place for you, I *will come* again and will take you to myself..." (14:3). "I will not leave you desolate; I *will come* to you... you will see me" (14:18f.). "The Counsellor, the Holy Spirit, whom the Father *will send* in my name" (14:26). "You heard me say to you, 'I go away, and I *will come* to you'" (14:28).

Thus, in the first discourse the paschal theme of the coming of the Messiah is still very clear; however, the theme has evolved towards the idea of an interior coming of the Father, of the Son and of the Spirit.[29] The evolution is more marked in the second discourse in which the themes of departure and of coming in chapter 16 (vv. 5-7, 16, 19, 22, 28) move towards the idea of the coming of the Spirit (16:7, 12, 15), while in chapter 15 the allegory of the vine puts into relief the mutual indwelling. The evolution is even more advanced in the third discourse, chapter 17, which is a meditation in which the paschal theme is no longer discerned.

The paschal colour of the farewell discourses is softened in the last stage of composition. This is quite natural if one considers that its actual form moves the reader towards the Passover of the death of Jesus, that of Friday.

---

26 See the farewell discourses in the Bible and in the post-biblical literature (Jubilees, the Testaments of the Twelve Patriarchs). Consult J. Munck, "Discours d'adieu dans le Nouveau Testament et la littérature biblique", *Aux sources de la tradition chrétienne*, Mélanges Goguel (Neuchâtel, 1950) 155–70.

27 On the expectation of the Messiah at the Passover see E. Lohse, *Das Passafest der Quartadecimaner* (Gütersloh, 1953) 82f.; R. Le Déaut, *La nuit pascale* (Rome, 1963) 279–98; W. Huber, *Passa und Ostern* (Berlin, 1969) 213f.

28 Luke, who is often so close to John, calls the death of Jesus at Jerusalem an *exodus*.

29 It would be interesting to compare these themes to those of the *Epistula Apostolorum*, where the Johannine influence is very plain. The apostles must continue to share the (Passover) cup until the coming of Jesus which will also be the coming of the Father (*Ep. apost.*, 15–17).

As we now pass on to the first part of the Johannine evening (13:1–30), will we be able to discover any traits favourable to the paschal nature of the meal? The search is difficult because the evangelist must have retained only the elements which were still interesting to the Christian community. Neither in John nor in the Synoptics can we expect to find an exhaustive description of Jesus' last meal. The specialists, however, have attempted to disclose the details which argue for or against a paschal ritual.

We will not dwell on the reasons—strongly argued elsewhere[30]—which point in the direction of the paschal character: a meal where the guests are lying beside the table, a night meal, a night when one does not leave Jerusalem. These traits clearly distinguish Jesus' last meal from an ordinary meal.

But there is another point of which we would like to show the importance: that of the washing of the feet. We have presented the hypothesis that the rite was conserved as part of a celebration and that this celebration anciently had a paschal character. Is it possible to verify the merits of this hypothesis?

The atmosphere of the celebration is confirmed by the solemnity of the words which introduce Jesus' action: "Now before the feast of the Passover, when Jesus knew that his hour had come to depart out of this world to the Father, having loved his own who were in the world, he loved them to the end. And during supper, when the devil had already put it into the heart of Judas Iscariot, Simon's son, to betray him, Jesus, knowing that the Father had given all things into his hands, and that he had come from God and was going to God, rose from supper, laid aside his garments, and girded himself with a towel. Then he poured water into a basin, and began to wash the disciples' feet, and to wipe them with the towel with which he was girded" (Jn 13:1–5).

This sentence, which is curiously formed and extraordinary in length, is probably the result of modification. It has caused some ingenious explanations from literary critics, but these remain hypothetical due to the difficulties in reconstructing the prehistory of the text.[31] As this sentence stands at the present moment—and precisely by its length—it puts into striking relief the action which inaugurates and prefigures the passion according to John.

The scene of the washing of the feet is placed under the sign of the Hour. That Hour is frequently announced in the Gospel and concerns the passing to the Father under the sign of love carried to its peak.[32] Under the sign of betrayal, which is the rupture in this meal of love, the cross is already present through Judas, who hands over Jesus. As soon as the traitor has consummated the rupture, Jesus can say that the Son of Man has been glorified (13:31). Finally the

---

[30] J. Jeremias, *Die Abendmahlsworte Jesu* (Göttingen, 1960) 35–78; ET by N. Perrin, *The Eucharistic Words of Jesus* (New York, London, 1966) 41–84.

[31] Cf. W. K. Grossouw, "A note on John 13:1–3", *NT* 8 (1966) 124–31.

[32] *Agapē* is strongly emphasized in John. Now, the Passover meal in certain milieux at least (cf. Wis 18:6–9) must have been considered as a covenant meal. A. Jaubert, *La notion d'alliance dans le judaïsme aux abords de l'ère chrétienne* (Paris, 1963) 355–62; R. Le Déaut, *La nuit pascale* (Rome, 1963) 78–87, 173–8, 209f.; *Bib* 45 (1964) 444ff.

introduction terminates with this affirmation which sums up the mystery of the Word made flesh: "knowing . . . that he had come from God and was going to God".

After this solemn announcement one will note the precision of the details which describe the actions of Jesus: the rising, the laying aside of his garments, the pouring of water into a basin, the taking of a towel and girding himself with it, the washing, the drying with the towel. So meticulous a description is well explained by the hypothesis of an actual ritual in the Johannine community. In verse 12 Jesus takes up his garments and resumes his seat. Finally in verses 14f. comes the command to repeat the action: "You ought also to wash one another's feet. For I have given you an example that you also should do as I have done to you."

The ritual interpretation which has been suggested to us by the later patristic evidence appears to be well in accord with the commemorative setting furnished by the Gospel and equally with the mentality which craves for concrete and expressive gestures. Our opinion is not entirely new. G. Bertram thought that the washing of feet was based on a custom otherwise unknown.[33] The problem, therefore, is less to seek the significance of the feet-washing in the Johannine redaction[34] than to ask ourselves about a possible connection between this rite and the paschal celebration.

It will be noted that another allusion in the text, that of the bath, inserts itself easily into a paschal perspective. To the words of Peter, "Lord, not my feet only but also my hands and my head!" (Jn 13:9), Jesus responds, "He that has bathed does not need to wash, except for his feet; he is entirely clean" (Jn 13:10).[35] It would be inadequate, it seems to us, to see in the term *leloumenos* ("bathed") only an evocation of Christian baptism. In the Johannine presentation, the disciples have taken a bath before coming to the meal.

For an ordinary meal it was sufficient to wash the hands (cf. Mk 7:2ff.); in contrast, the paschal meal demanded a high degree of ritual purity.[36] It seems that at the time of Jesus bathing was rather widespread among the laity but obligatory according to the rabbinic sources only in certain cases.[37] The Gospel of John twice recalls the purifications necessary for the Passover (11:55; 18:28). If a bathing preceded the meal, it is an argument in favour of the meal's paschal character.

---

[33] G. Bertram, *Die Leidengeschichte Jesu und der Christuskult: Forschungen zur Religion und Literatur des Alten und Neuen Testaments* (Göttingen, 1922) 41.

[34] For the numerous interpretations of the washing of the feet, consult G. Richter, *Die Fusswaschung im Johannesevangelium* (Regensburg, 1967).

[35] The phrase "except his feet" is missing in some manuscripts. Perhaps this suppression came from a reaction against the washing of the feet, which would have been considered as dangerous to the significance of baptism, for the washing of the feet was often associated with it; cf. *Mus* 79 (1966) 273, 282-3. It is not unprofitable to point out that with the Mandaeans a washing of the feet follows baptism. See E. S. Drower, *The Coronation of the Great Sislam* (Leiden, 1962) 11.

[36] Esdras 6:20; 2 Chr 30:1-24; Num 9:6-13.

[37] The bath was necessary in case of ritual defilement. In the case of R. Hama (*Bab. Berakoth* 22b) the prepaschal bath prepared him to pronounce the blessing. According to J. B. Segal, *The Hebrew Passover from the Earliest Times to A.D. 70* (London, 1963) 262, the laws of ritual purity were interpreted leniently.

The washing of the feet poses more questions, not because it doubles the bathing (one can accept the common explanation of a complementary purification), but because it takes place in the course of the meal: Jesus rose from the table. It is true that one can suppose that within the meal some parts were important or of special "sanctity".

We should not, however, apply to Jesus' last meal the Mishnaic rules which governed the paschal meals of the family. The Last Supper was a meal among men, without women and children. According to the book of Jubilees, the Passover must be eaten in the sanctuary by men twenty years of age and over (Jub 49:16ff.). In the broad milieu which the book of Jubilees represents, the Passover was a very holy sacrifice which necessitated its being eaten in a holy place—in principle, in the Temple! It was impossible for the Zadokites to eat the Passover in the Temple, but one imagines that the Zadokite Passover, in conformity with the levitical traditions, had conserved the very strict rules of purification.[38]

Philo of Alexandria declares that at the Passover the whole nation acts as priest, "each for his part celebrating and performing his appropriate sacrifices".[39] "Each house at that moment assumes the likeness and the dignity of a temple.... Those who have assembled themselves for the banquet have been purified by the purificatory lustrations."[40] Philo, in the non-allegorical treatises, is an excellent witness to the Jewish rites before the ruin of the Temple; he may reflect a more traditional mentality than that which interpreted leniently the biblical rules of paschal purification. His testimony calls for a consideration of the influences by the levitical movements on the paschal practice. Certainly this was even more true of the Zadokite Passover.

If each house is like a temple, then one would have to observe there the rules of purification applicable to the Temple. These rules are known: bathings, purifications of hands and feet.[41] According to a ritual of which Jubilees and the Testament of Levi witness at the time, it is necessary to wash the hands and the feet before and after drawing near to the altar.[42] Other passages in the Testament of Levi speak of purifications during the sacrifice, and in the Greek edition of these texts the dialectal *louein* ("to bathe")/*niptein* ("to wash")[43] occurs in the narrative of the washing of the feet.

The analogy of the Testament of Levi is interesting since we can

---

[38] A. Guilding has pointed out that in Num 8:7,21 the great purification of the Levites precedes precisely the celebration of the second Passover; see *The Fourth Gospel and Jewish Worship* (London, 1960) 155.

[39] *De vita Mosis*, II, 224; cf. *Quaest. Exod.*, I, 2.

[40] *De spec. Leg.*, II, 148.

[41] Ex 30:18–21; 40:30–32; Yoma 3:2. According to E. Lohmeyer, the washing of the feet by Jesus put the disciples in the category of priests and made them qualified to become priests in the eschatological service; this is why the logion concerning the mission (Jn 13:16f.) follows the washing of the feet, "Die Fusswaschung", *ZNW* 38 (1939) 74–94.

[42] Jub 21:16; Test. Levi 18:2.

[43] Test. Levi 9:11. The second text is the Bodleian, in Aramaic, published by R. H. Charles (ed.), *The Greek Versions of the Testaments of the Twelve Patriarchs* (Oxford, 1908, reprinted 1962) 248, with the corresponding Greek fragment taken from MS. *e* from Mount Athos. For an English translation, see R. H. Charles, *APOT* 2, 364.

find nothing closer to a Zadokite milieu. Although it is an analogy, we do not believe that we overstep our sources by thinking that in a Zadokite milieu the celebration of the Passover by guests who were perceived as priests must normally have called for some supplementary purifications.

In the Johannine narrative of the washing of the feet the astonishment of the disciples did not arise from the strangeness of the rite but from the fact that the master put himself in the position of a slave. It is quite in the manner of the evangelist to show the alteration of the Jewish rites effected by Jesus. At Cana the water of the Jewish purifications was changed into wine. In Samaria, Jesus, a new Jacob, was offering the water of the Spirit which springs up from his own well; he was himself the new temple from which the source went out (Jn 7:38). Jesus was transforming the rite of the feet-washing by making it the sign of his love and a prelude to the humiliation of the cross. By this he also was reversing the hierarchy which appeared to have existed at the last meal;[44] and he was founding a new order of ministry.

The gesture of the washing of the feet, quite unexpected as it may be on the part of Jesus, did not appear as a bizarre gesture, deprived of immediate significance. It inserted itself with verisimilitude into a context of paschal purifications, current in some law-abiding milieux of the levitical traditions. It is a commonplace gesture that the evangelist has put into relief because of the new meaning which it assumes.

Should we say that the evangelist was dependent on a Zadokite source for Jesus' last meal? Do we not freely admit that the evangelist has preserved ties with the original Baptist, Essene and Levite milieux? Moreover, Zadokite influence appears proved in the case of the Sunday after Passover. Concerning the feet-washing, we think that if Jesus had not actually accomplished this act of humility, it would not have been ascribed to him. Why should the source not be the witness of the disciple whom Jesus loved?

The disciple whom Jesus loved must have been a disciple of John the Baptist, as the first chapter of the Gospel shows (Jn 1:35); and John the Baptist, according to Lk 1:5ff., was of a priestly family. His relations with the Temple appear to have been rather cold (Mt 1:7; 21:23–26; Jn 1:19ff.). This attitude connects him with the levitical circles which did not approve of the development of the cult in the Temple; foremost among those were the Essenes. Other chapters in the present book reveal some of the important relationships between the sources of the Fourth Gospel and the Zadokite milieux. Thus the cultural background of the Gospel is explained.

If we take up again the combined results of this analysis, we see that the Gospel of John can no longer be considered the great argument against Jesus' Last Supper being a Passover meal. The

---

44 The respective positions of Peter and John and the parallel passage in Luke (22:24f.) seem to indicate a dispute about precedence. Some have seen here possible Essene influence. But would this be a characteristic act of the Essenes or of the Therapeutae? Cf. Philo, *De Josepho*, 203: the custom of making guests sit according to their age or rank belongs to the tradition of the Hebrews.

sources used by the evangelist favour the paschal and Zadokite character of Jesus' Last Supper. This conclusion is revealed by the structure and the themes of the first farewell discourse, by the rites of purification presupposed by the washing of feet, and by the correspondence with the date of the appearance to Thomas.

In his actual presentation, however, the evangelist describes only one Passover celebration, that concomitant with the death of Jesus; he does not note any divergence in time between the Last Supper and the day of the crucifixion. This raises the question of the formation of the Johannine passion narrative.

According to our hypothesis, this narrative was formed by two commemorative celebrations inserted into the liturgical practice of the primitive Church: the evening of Tuesday/Wednesday and the day of Friday. Let us examine these in order.

The night of Tuesday/Wednesday began with the evening meal and ended when the cock crew. The importance of the crowing, which in the Gospels accompanies Peter's denial, may be explained in a liturgical framework: it marked the end of the evening celebration. The Synoptic tradition then mentions the tears of Peter; his sorrow must have been re-enacted by the early worshippers.[45] The sorrow of Jesus' followers is announced in the farewell discourse: "I say to you, you will weep and lament, but the world will rejoice" (Jn 16:20). Sorrow and fasting went together.

We are not informed about fasting in the Johannine community. In the liturgical tradition connected with the Gospels of Mark and Matthew, it is the treachery of Judas to which the fasting of Wednesday is attached; the sorrow must therefore originally have begun during the preceding night. In a Syriac canon attributed to Ignatius of Antioch a fast is imposed during the night of Tuesday/ Wednesday; the alleged motive, however, is not the treachery of Judas, but the sadness of the disciples (or of Jesus) before the announcement of the passion.[46]

[45] Mk 14:72; Mt 26:75; Lk 22:62. The sorrow of the disciples is described in the *Gospel of Peter* 26–27; see *Mus* 79 (1966) 152, n. 1.

[46] This text is pointed out by J. Van Goudoever in an additional note, *Fêtes et calendriers bibliques*, 3rd ed. (Paris, 1967) 260–1. There is an ecclesiastical canon which A. Mingana found in two different recensions and which he published in *Woodbrooke Studies* (Cambridge, 1927) vol. 1, 108–9. Here is the text which is common to them with the variant which interests us:
"We observe the night of Wednesday because in it our Lord announced his passion to his disciples and he was moved by affliction (Var: and they were troubled with sorrow). We observe the night of Friday because in it our Lord was seized by the Jews. We do not observe the night of Saturday because in it there was rest to all the Dead of Sheol, at the descent of our Lord to them."
In the introduction which he made to the texts published by Mingana, Rendel Harris suggested that this canon situated the Last Supper in the night of Tuesday to Wednesday, which appeared to him quite illogical in light of the rest of the text (*ibid.*, 15). We believe that this text maintains the tradition of a Supper on Tuesday evening: the distress of Jesus recorded in Jn 13:21 and the sadness of the disciples described in Mk 14:19 and Mt 26:32. But obviously this evidence is no longer understood. This ecclesiastical canon, which is surely later than Ignatius of Antioch, is a remarkable testimony to a more ancient tradition *concerning the observance on the night of Tuesday to Wednesday*. This observance can only be explained by bringing together this canon with all the other texts which, each in its own manner, celebrate this same night!

One cannot, however, reduce to a single liturgical type the life of the Church at the beginning of Christianity. A commemoration of Jesus' Last Supper on the night of Tuesday/Wednesday was scarcely able to survive except in circles which remained close to the priestly beginnings. The memory of it could only be sustained in conservative circles like those of the Didascalia or of the Nestorians. In these circles of the Johannine tradition in which the custom of the washing of feet continued, the night of Tuesday/Wednesday was preserved but its paschal character was lost. In contrast, the liturgical type represented by the *Epistola Apostolorum*, often considered as a Quartodeciman writing,[47] may have preserved the paschal character of the celebration, although it lost the day of the week. The vigil celebrated the Lord's action and "his love" until the cock's crow. We have seen that certain themes were connected with those of the Johannine vigil.[48]

The second liturigical support on which the passion narrative according to John is founded is the Friday of the Roman condemnation and of the crucifixion. This Friday was a commemorative day according to the Gospel of Mark in which the time of the crucifixion is divided up according to a liturgical schedule of three hours following three hours.[49] The strength of the primitive tradition of the coincidence of Jesus' death with the official Passover, with the correlative application to Jesus of the symbolism of the paschal lamb, while the Zadokite calendar was being forgotten, caused the transfer of the paschal emphasis to the day of the death of Jesus.

The author of the Fourth Gospel exploited the significance of the kingship of Jesus over against that of Caesar, by making the crowning with thorns a central scene on this day. All the episodes from the proceedings before Pilate could be commemorated on this day. In

---

[47] For E. Lohse this writing represents the Quartodeciman practice; see *Das Passafest*, 13–15. See the discussions by W. Rordorf, "Zum Ursprung des Osterfestes am Sonntag", *TZ* 18 (1962) 174; W. Huber, *Passa und Ostern*, 12. Is it not possible that the Quartodeciman usage derives from a rite of paschal vigil related entirely to the archaic Johannine vigil, but interpreted according to the official Passover, thus with the day of the week movable? The Quartodeciman practice is characterized by the commemoration at one and the same time of the death and resurrection of Jesus; now this is *a specific mark* of the Johannine evening: "I am going away and I am coming back to you."

[48] Cf. n. 29 above.

[49] We know that according to Mk 15:25 the crucifixion takes place at the third hour of the day, whereas John places the condemnation before Pilate at the sixth hour. The third hour should not be contested in Mark because it corresponds to the structure of the text. Mk 15:25 provides an older tradition because the form is Semitic: "It was the third hour *and* they crucified him" (*waw* of apodosis; cf. P. Joüon, *Grammaire de l'hébreu biblique*, 2nd ed. (Rome, 1947) par. 176f–g). Is the figure in John symbolic or due to a bad manuscript transmission as some ancients held? In favour of the sixth hour, see Benoit-Boismard, *Synopse des quatre évangiles* (Paris, 1965) on Mk 15:25. For the third hour see the documentation gathered in A. Jaubert, *La date de la cène*, 119–20 and in S. Bartina, "Ignotum episémon gabex", *VD* 36 (1958) 16–37. There must be added to these documents the Slavonic text of the Testament of Levi, where the darkness extends from the third to the ninth hour (R. H. Charles (ed.), *The Greek Version*, 259 and 269); certain texts which echo the *Apostolic Traditions* of Hippolytus—*Menologion* (PO 8, 617; 10, 40f.); and the Octateuch of Clement, translated by Nau in *Le canoniste contemporain* (Paris, 1909) 539. The later inversion is also found: condemnation at the third hour, crucifixion at the sixth, PO 8, 651.

this case the period in between, which according to our theory covers Wednesday and Thursday, remained a liturgical blank. This historical cavity is visible in Jn 18:28: nothing happens before Caiaphas. The memory of the Sanhedrin sessions was preserved only by the Synoptic tradition with varying arrangements.[50] John has no need of the Jewish trial; he has emphasized throughout his Gospel the full theological weight of the confrontation between the Jews and Jesus. He recalls only Jesus' coming before Annas, which was situated in the framework of the Passover night.

The Johannine passion narrative is thus formed from two ancient commemorations: the Passover night and the day of the crucifixion. Their juxtaposition has given the impression of a continuity between the night of the vigil of Tuesday and the day of Friday which appeared as the following day. Although the final redactor of the Johannine Gospel has conserved in a very exact fashion the chronological notations in relation to the official Passover (13:1; 18:28; 19:14), he has not sought to erase this impression. We have just seen that he has no theological interest in exploiting Jesus' appearance before Caiaphas. On the other hand, it is probable that at the last stage of the composition of the Gospel of John, there were already in circulation some differing traditions concerning the chronology of the passion. The Syriac groups preserved a conscious memory of Wednesday, but the Hellenistic circles forgot the Zadokite Passover and then lost the paschal character of the meal. The celebrated calendar of the official Jewish Passover—the only one known in these circles— helped to reduce the time of the passion in the Synoptic stream. The tradition recorded in Mark and Matthew, which came from a source which was very definite about the paschal meal, rejected the Wednesday as the prelude to the passion.[51] At the final literary stage of the Fourth Gospel, there must have been an interaction between the Johannine circles and the other streams of Christianity.[52]

The faithfulness of the redactor to his sources consisted in not going beyond them. He remains in the end nearer to the primitive outline than the Synoptic Evangelists, who had integrated information from different sources and who, in drawing the Passover meal nearer to the death of Jesus, had to transfer the Wednesday (the "two days" of Mt 26:2) before this meal. In order to rediscover the original outline it is necessary to refer to the various testimonies of the ancient Church, often through an unconscious liturgical "memory", and it is necessary to go back again to the Zadokite calendar which alone was able to give the key to a rather complex evolution.

---

[50] A. Jaubert, "Les séances du Sanhédrin et les récits de la passion", *RHR* 166 (1964) 143–69; and *RHR* 167 (1965) 1–33.

[51] Cf. n. 20 above, the article in *NTS*.

[52] The interpolated clause of Jn 13:2, "when the devil had already put it (the intention) into the heart of Judas Iscariot, Simon's son, to betray him", appears to us as a harmonization with the tradition of Matthew and Mark by the last Johannine redactor. In the Johannine setting the last meal of Jesus was commemorated on Wednesday, while in the tradition of Mark and Matthew the betrayal plan was recalled on Wednesday. The addition of verse 2, which lengthens unduly the sentence, was to harmonize the two traditions.

5

A Critical Comparison of the Dualism in 1QS 3:13–4:26 and the "Dualism" Contained in the Gospel of John[1]

JAMES H. CHARLESWORTH

Qumran dualism and its possible relation to Johannine "dualism" has been a subject of considerable interest and discussion. In the light of recent studies and with the subsidence of the Qumran fever, the time may be opportune for a fresh assessment of the evidence. In this chapter we shall confine ourselves to the crucial passage in 1QS 3:13–4:26. After examining the type of dualism reflected there, we shall proceed first to investigate the Johannine "dualism" separately,

---

[1] Originally published in *NTS* 15 (1968–69) 389–418. While the purpose of the present study is to define the type of dualism contained in 1QS 3:13–4:26 and in the Gospel of John, a brief note regarding the terminology employed in the following pages is appropriate. The term "dualism" refers to a pattern of thought, an antithesis, which is bifurcated into two mutually exclusive categories (e.g. two spirits or two worlds), each of which is qualified by a set of properties and ethical characteristics which are contrary to those under the other antithetic category (e.g. light and good *versus* darkness and evil). There are various types of dualism in the history of ideas: philosophical, anthropological, psychological, physical, metaphysical, cosmological, cosmic, ethical, eschatological, and soteriological. However, few phenomena in the history of religion would be representatively defined by only one of these terms. We have attempted to apply the following definitions: psychological dualism denotes two contrary inclinations which are found only within man; physical dualism means the absolute division between matter and spirit; metaphysical dualism signifies the opposition between God and Satan; cosmic dualism denotes the conception of two opposing celestial spirits or two distinct and present divisions of the universe; ethical dualism signifies the bifurcation of mankind into two mutually exclusive groups according to virtues or vices; eschatological dualism denotes the rigid division of time between the present aeon and the future one; soteriological dualism means the division of mankind caused by faith (acceptance) or disbelief (rejection) in a saviour. The type of dualism with which we are concerned is a modified dualism and not a polarity between two equal, eternal forces or concepts. It is precisely for this last observation that we cannot apply H. W. Huppenbauer's distinction between cosmic and cosmological dualism. See his *Der Mensch zwischen zwei Welten* (Abhandlungen zur Theologie des Alten und Neuen Testaments 34; Zürich, 1959) 9–10.

In this research I am indebted to the numerous conversations with Professor J. Strugnell of Harvard University, Professors D. M. Smith, Jr, and J. L. Price of Duke University, and especially with Professor H. Anderson of New College, the University of Edinburgh.

secondly to draw comparisons and contrasts, and finally to ask whether we are thereby led to any conclusions about the provenance of the Johannine tradition.[2]

The Dualism in 1QS 3 : 13–4 : 26[3]

1QS 3:13–4:26 begins with the clear purpose of instructing the Qumranic convenanters regarding man's nature. In the prologue (3:15b–18a) the scribe posits the belief that from the God of knowledge (*m'l hd'wt*) comes all that is. Everything, therefore, is not only derivative from the Creator, but is dependent upon him. In the first section of the body of this discourse (3:18b–4:1) the author records that "two Spirits" were allotted unto man that he

[2] It appears that the proper method to be employed is to separate at the outset the Johannine Epistles from the Gospel of John. This separation is necessary both because the old view that all were written by the same person is much criticized and because in 1 John, the Epistle closest in thought and expression to the Gospel, one finds different ideas and expressions. For example, in 1 John we find the term *antichristos* in 2:18, a strong strain of brotherhood (4:21) within a community that has, quite like Qumran, withdrawn from the evil world (v. 19), a developed ethic (*opheilei peripatein*, 2:6; see also 1:6) and an equation of sin not so much with unbelief as with lawlessness (*tēn anomian*, 3:4). Not unimportant is the observation that these differences move perpendicularly toward the Qumranic literature. Also a very striking parallel is found between 1 Jn 4:1–6 and 1QS 3:13–4:26.

[3] 1QS 3:13–4:26 teaches a dualism representative of the dualism found elsewhere in the Scrolls. While H. W. Huppenbauer has argued that we must speak not of one type of dualism but of many types of dualism in the Qumran Scrolls, he can still conclude that "Der Dualismus der Qumrangemeinde ist also ein *relativer*, *ethisch-kosmischer* Dualismus" (*Der Mensch zwischen zwei Welten*, 103, 113). It is precisely these three characteristics which our research has found to be emphasized in this treatise. Moreover, five independent examinations have found significant similarities between the dualism in this text and the dualism in other Qumran scrolls. Professor W. Foerster has exposed parallels between this passage and the Hodayoth; see "Der Heilige Geist im Spätjudentum", *NTS* 8 (1961–62) 129–31. More recently H. W. Kuhn has argued that the conception of two warring spirits and resultant predestination which is presented in 1QS 3:13ff. is also found in 1QH; see *Enderwartung und gegenwärtiges Heil* (SUNT 4; Göttingen, 1966) 121–5. Y. Yadin has shown that parallels exist between this passage and the War Scroll and suggested that the War Scroll was built upon the dualistic theory of 1QS 3:13–25; see *The Scroll of the War of the Sons of Light Against the Sons of Darkness*, trans. B. and C. Rabin (Oxford, 1962) 229–42. Although A. R. C. Leaney finds occasional contrasts between the dualistic doctrine of this passage and sections of other scrolls (e.g. 1QM 13:2–6), he suggests that 1QS 3:13–4:26 probably "exerted a great influence upon" the other passages and "may have once existed independently of its present context"; see *The Rule of Qumran and its Meaning* (London, 1966) 53–5. The contrast which Leaney finds between 1QS 3:16–18 and 1QM 13:2–6 is not in the texts since in 1QS 3:24 it is clearly stated that God and his "Angel of Truth" work together (see also the implications of 4:19); and moreover, in 1QM 13:2–6 we do not read of God warring against Belial but of God being the object of the sect's praises and Belial the recipient of the sect's curses. Finally, A. A. Anderson has argued that the difference between the dualism in 1QM, 1QH and 1QS is only apparent and probably results from the differences of authorship, date and nature of the writings. There is basically the same dualism, and "1QS may reflect the thought and practice of the whole community". See his "The use of 'Ruaḥ' in 1QS, 1QH and 1QM", *JSS* 7 (1962) 298.

If the author of the Fourth Gospel was influenced by 1QS 3:13–4:26, and we shall soon present evidence which convinces us that he was, then he probably knew it in its present context since "one doing the truth" in Jn 3:21 (and "we do not do the truth" in 1 Jn 1:6) is paralleled only in 1QS 1:5; 5:3; and 8:2.

should walk in them (*wyśm lw šty rwḥwt lhthlk bm*). The first is the "Spirit of Truth" (*h'mt*) which originates in "a habitation of light". The second is the "Spirit of Perversity" (*h'wl*) which originates in "a spring of darkness". The "Prince of Light" (*śr 'wrym*) has dominion over all the "sons of righteousness", and the "Angel of Darkness" (*ml'k ḥwšk*) has dominion over the "sons of perversity".

In the second section of the body of this discourse (4:2–8) one is informed about the ethical and religious attributes of the "sons of light" (*bny 'wr*) or the "sons of truth" (*bny 'mt*) and their reward "in perpetual life" (*bḥyy nṣḥ*). In the third section (4:9–14) the scribe presents the moral callousness and impiety of those who walk in the "Spirit of Perversity", and their reward of torment and bitterest misfortune until "they are destroyed" (*klwtm l'yn*). In the final section (4:15–26) one is taught that these two spirits continue a battle in which the "Spirit of Perversity" is eventually annihilated.

Before we get to the heart of the controversy over the dualism in 1QS 3:13ff., whether or not we are presented with a cosmic dualism, it is necessary to observe five of its important characteristics: the predominance of the light-*versus*-darkness *motif*, the ethical implications, the belief in an absolute determinism, the solution of the origin of evil, and the eschatological framework.

Perhaps the most conspicuous characteristic of the dualism in this document is the predominance of the light-*versus*-darkness *motif*. The contrast between the two warring spirits is immediately evident since the "Spirit of Truth" and the "Spirit of Perversity" are categorized on opposite sides of the mutually exclusive light-*versus*-darkness paradigm. Light or darkness denotes the origin and qualifies the actions of the respective spirit. Light is often used interchangeably for righteousness, and darkness is frequently applied alternatively for perversity.[4] Hence "Spirit of Truth" seems synonymous with "Prince of Light"[5] and "Spirit of Perversity" seems equivalent to "Angel of Darkness".[6] Indeed, the probability that these expressions are synonymous is strengthened by the observation that there are various names for God: *m'l hd'wt* ("from the God of Knowledge"), *w'l yśr'l* ("and the God of Israel"), and *'l nqmt* ("the God of Vengeance"). Surely no one would suggest that this observation uncovers a belief in four gods; rather it is clear that these expressions are also alternative names of the same reality.

The ethical implications of this paradigm are explicitly enumerated in 4:2–14. First, the ways of the "Spirit of Light" are described by

---

[4] So also W. Foerster, *NTS* 8 (1961–62) 128–9; and G. R. Driver, *The Judaean Scrolls* (Oxford, 1965) 545.

[5] So also A. R. C. Leaney, *The Rule of Qumran*, 148.

[6] So also W. D. Davies, *Christian Origins and Judaism* (London, 1962) 163–6; K. Schubert, *The Dead Sea Community* (London, 1959) 63; O. Betz, *Der Paraklet* (Leiden, 1963) 66–7; U. Simon, *Heaven in the Christian Tradition* (London, 1958) 173; O. Böcher, *Der johanneische Dualismus im Zusammenhang des nachbiblischen Judentums* (Gütersloh, 1965) 77, 101; K. G. Kuhn, "Johannesevangelium und Qumrantexte", *Neotestamentica et Patristica*, ed. W. C. van Unnik (Leiden, 1962) 119; A. A. Anderson *JSS* 7 (1962) 298–9; M. Burrows, *More Light on the Dead Sea Scrolls* (New York, London, 1958) 283–4; and F. Nötscher, "Geist und Geister in den Texten von Qumran", *Mélanges bibliques: rédigés en l'honneur de André Robert* (Trauvaux de l'Institut Catholique de Paris 4; Paris, 1956) 305–16.

means of a list of righteous attitudes and moral deeds. Next, the ways of the "Spirit of Darkness" (here called the "Spirit of Perversity") are presented by means of a list of immoral deeds and a perverse personality described in bodily terms (viz. "tongue", "eye", "ear", "neck", and "heart"). This observation reveals the treatise is essentially Jewish since these expressions presuppose an earthy and homogeneous anthropology distinct from the Greek transcendent and bifurcated concept.[7] We learn that there are two distinct and mutually exclusive groups of men, respectively characterized not only by light and darkness but also by virtues and vices.

The expression of ethical ideas in terms of the light-darkness paradigm is shared by this section in 1QS with other post-exilic Jewish documents. The germinal idea of this paradigm may be traced to the division of light and darkness in Genesis 1:3–5 (e.g. 1:4, *wyr' 'lhym 't h'wr ky twb*).[8] S. Aalen, however, has argued that the only important distinction between the meaning of this schema in the Old Testament and in the intertestamental literature is that in the latter it obtained an ethical dimension.[9] Finally, it should be observed that in no other Jewish document did this schema attain so high a level of sophistication.

Conjoined with this ethical dualism is the belief in an absolute determinism. 1QS 3:15 states that God is the sole creator of all that is and shall be, and that before things came into existence he determined (*hkyn*)[10] all their design (*mhšbtm*). In 1QS 3:16, moreover, it is stated that when things had come into being they fulfilled their work (functions, tasks) according to "their appointed roles" (*lt'wdwtm*), in accordance with his glorious design (*kmhšbt kbwdw*). Most scholars lean toward the view either that determinism is presented here although neither logically nor speculatively developed (so R. E. Brown),[11] or that this passage conveys a rigorous predestinarian formulation (so F. M. Cross, J. Licht, J. T. Milik, and H. Ringgren).[12] It is worth noting that to join the community was not a free act of choice[13] but an appointed task carried through by one

[7] Cf. K. Schubert's contention that this treatise is strongly influenced by Greek thought: "*Der gegenwärtige Stand der Erforschung der in Palästina neu gefundenen hebräischen Handschriften*", *TLZ* 78 (1953) 495–506.

[8] W. F. Albright has marshalled convincing archaeological evidence that this verse should be translated: "And God saw that the light was very good" ("The Refrain 'And God Saw KI TOB' in Genesis", *Mélanges bibliques: rédigés en l'honneur de André Robert*, 22–6).

[9] S. Aalen, *Die Begriffe "Licht" und "Finsternis" im Alten Testament, im Spätjudentum und im Rabbinismus* (Oslo, 1951) esp. 173–5.

[10] See Gen 41:32.

[11] "The Qumran Scrolls and the Johannine Gospel and Epistles", *The Scrolls and the New Testament*, ed. K. Stendahl (New York, 1957; London, 1958) 190.

[12] F. M. Cross, Jr, *The Ancient Library of Qumran and Modern Biblical Studies*, 2nd ed. (New York, 1961) 93; J. Licht, "An Analysis of the Treatise of Two Spirits in DSD", *SH* 4 (1958) 89; J. T. Milik, *Ten Years of Discovery in the Wilderness of Judaea*, trans. J. Strugnell (London, 1959) 119; H. Ringgren, *The Faith of Qumran*, trans. E. T. Sander (Philadelphia, 1961) 53–4.

[13] F. Nötscher argued that there is no determinism in this document but that freedom of the individual is upheld because the two spirits are struggling "um das Herz (wohl nicht: im Herzen) des Mannes (1QS 4:23)". While his translation is accurate, his exegesis fails to account for the deterministic statement found in 1QS 3:15–17, the importance of *gwrl* in this text (3 times), the strong predestinarian

predestined by nature to be a son of light (3:18).[14]

The preceding discussions prompt the following question: how does 1QS 3:13–4:26 account for the origin of evil? It appears that the author of this treatise felt that he had solved this pervasive riddle for post-exilic Judaism. Greed, falsehood, pride, deceit, hypocrisy, lust and all the other evils in the world are caused by one spirit, who is called the "Spirit of Perversity" or the "Angel of Darkness". It is conceivable, as some scholars have suggested,[15] that he is to be identified with the customary name for the "devil" in the Dead Sea Scolls,[16] Belial, which is mentioned four times in the two columns which precede this passage (1:18, 24; 2:5, 19).[17] In any case it is clear that our author wanted to attribute the cause of all evil to one spirit. His solution to this problem, however, is transparent precisely because he has not advocated an absolute dualism but has subjugated the evil spirit to one God who created all things (3:15b), established all things (3:25: "And He created the Spirits of Light and Darkness and upon them He established every act"), and ordained all things (3:15f.: "all that is and shall be ... fulfil their task ... according to His glorious design"). Hence, his monotheistic faith and concomitant belief in God's supreme sovereignty leads him unconsciously to attribute the cause of all things, even evil, to the "God of Israel" (3:24).

The attempt to solve the problem of evil found in this treatise is not as successful as other explanations found in post-exilic Jewish documents. An important distinction not made in this passage is found in the solution presented by both 1 Enoch 6:1–6; 7:1; 10:8–9 and the Book of Jubilees 5:1–2:[18] evil is not ultimately attributable to God but to the fallen angels' wilful corruption of their freedom. Two additional explanations for the cause of evil were prevalent in post-exilic Judaism: the contention found in the Apocalypse of Abraham 26 that sin originated with Adam's rejection of God's will and the rabbinic explanation found in the Mishnah at Berakoth 9:5[19] that evil is caused by the *yēṣer hā-rā'*, "evil inclination",

tone of *mbny 'yš* in 4:20 ("some men", see Psalm 4:3; also *mn* denotes "some", especially in late Hebrew, e.g. Ezra 2:68, 70; Neh 11:4, 25; Dan 11:35), and would tend to ascribe to the evil spirit the knowledge of who were his targets, i.e. the "sons of light", an ascription without support in the text. See F. Nötscher, *Zur theologischen Terminologie der Qumran-Texte* (Bonn, 1956) 79–80.

[14] So also Allegro's "astrological document" (e.g. 2:1–9); see "An Astrological Cryptic Document from Qumran", *JSS* 9 (1964) 291–4.

[15] E.g. A. R. C. Leaney, *The Rule of Qumran*, 149; Y. Yadin, *The Scroll of the War*, 236; O. Betz, *Der Paraklet*, 66–7; and M. Burrows, *More Light*, 287.

[16] See K. G. Kuhn, *Konkordanz zu den Qumrantexten* (Göttingen, 1960). It is significant that in 1QM 13:10–11 and in CD 5:18 the "Prince of Light" is opposed not by the "Angel of Darkness" but by Belial. However, it is surprising to find that in one of the most respected translations of the scrolls *bly'l* is habitually translated "Satan" (*śṭn*). See G. Vermes, *The Dead Sea Scrolls in English* (Harmondsworth, 1965).

[17] The "Spirit of Truth" may be identified with Michael (1QM 9:15–16; 17:6–7). So also Leaney, *The Rule*, 148; Yadin, *The Scroll of the War*, 236; Betz, *Der Paraklet*, 66–7; and Burrows, *More Light*, 284.

[18] Jubilees was known by the covenanters since fragments were found in cave 4. I am indebted in this discussion to D. S. Russell's comments in *The Method and Message of Jewish Apocalyptic* (Philadelphia, London, 1964) 249–54.

[19] See H. Danby, *The Mishnah* (Oxford, 1933) 10.

in man. Certainly 1QS's solution would also be weaker than either of these if it could be proved that Adam's sin and the "evil inclination" were conceived as something for which Adam or man himself were solely responsible, but there is evidence both for (Apoc. Abr 26; Gen 6:5; Test. Asher 1:6–9; 4 Ezra 8:56–60) and against (Gen 8:21, see Gen 9:7 in Midrash Rabbah) such an assumption. There is even evidence of the belief that the origin of evil is a mystery which man is incapable of understanding (4 Ezra 4:4–11). Of course there is a loophole even in these explanations for God must allow evil to exist since apparently in these texts he is also omnipotent. Nevertheless, it is important to observe that while in other intertestamental texts there is a possible attribution of evil to an angel's free will or to Adam's own responsibility or to man's own failure to control his "evil inclination" by means of his yēṣer haṭ-ṭôb, "good inclination", there is in 1QS 3:13–4:26 no similar recourse, for it is clearly stated that God created the "Spirit of Darkness", i.e. he was evil from the instant he was created; he did *not* fall from an original state of purity.[20]

In order to understand the dualism in this section of 1QS it is necessary to comprehend its eschatological nature. As one of the most striking features of the Qumran sect was its consciousness that it was living in the last days, so this passage in 1QS was written in an eschatological key.[21] While eschatology is present in the beginning of this discourse (3:18b: "until the time of His visitation"), it soon crescendos in a fugal pattern, as it were, appearing with intensity in the closing lines of each section of the teaching until it bursts forth to occupy the major portion of the final section (4:18b–26). To reiterate more specifically, in the closing lines of section one we read that God loves everlastingly the "Spirit of Light" but hates for ever[22] the counsel of the "Spirit of Darkness". The low eschatological tone in these verses reaches a much higher level in the closing lines of the second section, where we read about the rewards of the "sons of truth". Even more space is taken to describe the eschatological

[20] 1QS 3:25—whw'h br' rwḥwt 'wr wḥwšk. Significantly, we find the same peculiar belief emphasized in 1QM 13:10–11: "And you made Belial to corrupt, the Angel of Hatred, his dominion is in darkness and his counsel is to cause wickedness and guilt". In the preceding sentence lšḥt may be translated either ae "for the pit", taking šḥt as a noun in the dative case—so A. Dupont-Sommer, *The Essene Writings from Qumran* (New York, 1962) 189 and G. Vermes, *Dead Sea Scrolls*, 141—or as "to corrupt", taking the Pi. Inf. Cst. of the root šāḥat, so Y. Yadin (*The Scroll of the War*, 322). The latter translation is preferable because the passage is not referring to Belial's destiny but to his tasks, and the infinitive construct with lᵉ clearly expresses a *purpose*. Moreover, this interpretation seems demanded by the causative purposiveness of the two Hiph. Infin. Csts. which also have a prefixed lᵉ in the next line. As R. Meyer remarked, there is no teaching in the scrolls that the evil angel fell from the heavenly realm because of some fault; see *Die Qumranfunde und die Bibel* (Regensburg, 1959) 57.

[21] For two excellent discussions of the eschatological expectations of the covenanters, see K. Schubert, *The Dead Sea Community*, 61–3, 88–112; and J. Reuss, *Die Qumranfunde*, 110–12. The latest examination is by H.-W. Kuhn, *Enderwartung und gegenwärtiges Heil*.

[22] There is a minor inconsistency between this idea and the teaching that the "Spirit of Perversity" will be eventually destroyed found in 4:18–19. This inconsistency is minor precisely because there is no mention of the cessation of hatred and it is the counsel not the angel which God abhors.

fate of the "sons of perversity" at the close of section three. And in contrast to this section the final one allots almost three times as much space to eschatology.[23] Moreover, woven into the fugal pattern of this movement are two distinct eschatological levels. The eschatology in the closing lines of the first two sections is one which breaks into the present. When we reach the last lines of section three, however, we find both an emphasis on interim eschatology and also the introduction of a more distant time when the "Spirit of Perversity" will be annihilated. In the final section the progression of the fugal movement is complete as the emphasis is placed clearly upon the final judgment (4:19b–20a: 'd mw'd mšpṭ nḥrṣh).[24] In answer to the apparent question, how distant is the final judgment, the author of this treatise, as J. Licht remarked,[25] declares the unfathomable mystery of God's wisdom (4:18—w'l brzy śklw wbḥkmt kbwdw).

The consensus of scholarly opinion has been that 1QS 3:13–4:26 reveals a cosmic dualism between two warring spirits who are locked in a titanic warfare, although it is readily conceded that the cosmic dualism does break into the so-called "psychological" arena of each man.[26] Lately, however, P. Wernberg-Møller has argued for an entirely psychological interpretation.[27] He maintains that it is hard to com-

---

[23] W. D. Davies remarks that "it is only here that the spirit [of Truth] is ascribed a strictly eschatological significance at all in the scrolls" (*Christian Origins and Judaism*, 165).

[24] This phrase means literally "until the time of judgment which is decreed". Compare Is 10:23: wᵉneḥĕrāṣāh.

[25] *SH* 4 (1958) 96.

[26] K. G. Kuhn, "Die Sektenschrift und die iranische Religion", *ZTK* 49 (1952) 312. C. T. Fritsch, *The Qumran Community* (New York, 1956) 71. W. F. Albright, "The Bible After Twenty Years of Archeology", *RL* 21 (1952) 549. F. M. Cross, *The Ancient Library of Qumran and Modern Biblical Studies*, 210. A. Dupont-Sommer, *Essene Writings*, 78; and *The Jewish Sect of Qumran and the Essenes* (London, 1954) 118–19. J. M. Allegro, *The Dead Sea Scrolls* (Harmondsworth, Baltimore, 1956) 128. F. Nötscher, *Zur theologischen Terminologie der Qumran-Texte*, 80. H. J. Schonfield, *Secrets of The Dead Sea Scrolls* (London, 1956) 113. W. D. Davies, *Christian Origins and Judaism*, 164. A. R. C. Leaney, *The Rule of Qumran and its Meaning*, 43. K. Schubert, *TLZ* 78 (1953) 495–506; *The Dead Sea Community*, 62–6. G. R. Driver, *The Judaean Scrolls*, 559. J. Licht, *SH* 4 (1958) 92. R. Meyer and J. Reuss, *Die Qumranfunde*, 57. H. G. May, "Cosmological Reference in the Qumran Doctrine of the Two Spirits and in Old Testament Imagery", *JBL* 82 (1963) 1–14. M. Burrows, *More Light*, 280–1.

[27] P. Wernberg-Møller, "A Reconsideration of the Two Spirits in the Rule of the Community (1QSerek 3:13–4:26)", *RevQ* 11 (1961) 423. It appears that E. Schweizer would agree with Wernberg-Møller's interpretation since he emphasizes the ethical concern of this passage and denies the cosmic dimension. See his "Gegenwart des Geistes und eschatologische Hoffnung", *The Background of the New Testament and its Eschatology*, ed. W. D. Davies and D. Daube (Cambridge, 1956) 482–508, especially 490f. M. Treves clearly agrees with Wernberg-Møller's interpretation, for he wrote, "In my opinion these spirits are simply the tendencies or propensities which are implanted in every man's heart". It is quite surprising, however, to discover that Treves has examined this Qumranic treatise only by means of the interpretation of rwḥ found in the Old Testament, where it "never meant . . . an incorporeal being, such as an angel, a demon, or a fairy". But one dare not overlook the additional meaning obtained by this noun during the inter-testamental period. See his "The Two Spirits of the Rule of the Community", *RevQ* 3 (1961) 449–52. After examining the use of rwḥ in three of the most important scrolls, A. A. Anderson correctly remarked that "we meet with a further development and a change in emphasis. Thus in the scrolls Ruaḥ is used quite often

prehend how Dupont-Sommer's interpretation can insist both that the human personalities are made up of various mixtures of two metaphysical cosmic spirits, that all partake of both spirits, and that men can be divided into two exclusive groups. Consequently, he rejects Dupont-Sommer's view that "their works, with their classes" in 3:14 refers to the two catalogues of virtues in 4:2–6 and vices in 4:9–11.

At this point Wernberg-Møller uncovers a possible problem in the theology of the scroll,[28] but perhaps it can be resolved in the following manner. The Rule (1QS) suggests that men are divided into two mutually exclusive camps; they are either "sons of light" or "sons of darkness". This distinction is clearly made in 1QS 3:18ff. Two other observations, however, must be made. First, a particular individual exhibits varying degrees of virtues (4:2–6) and vices (4:9–11). Each person is a mixture of virtues and vices and is a "son of light" or a "son of darkness" according to the degree to which he displays respectively good or evil (4:16).[29] Secondly, a "son of light" may reveal eventually that he is actually a "son of darkness". The evil portion in a "son of light" may be removed by his own actions or will disappear with the final destruction of the evil spirit. The Rule was written to clarify by what criteria one was to be admitted into the community and by what standard a member of the congregation was to be promoted, demoted or ejected.

P. Wernberg-Møller contends, furthermore, that in 4:23 the scribe is not dealing with a kind of cosmic dualism represented by the two spirits.[30] He suggests that in this verse, "Until now the Spirits of truth and evil have been contesting in (for) the hearts of man" (*'d hnh yrybw rwḥy 'mt w'wl blbb gbr*), the scribe presents the idea that man was created by God with two spirits and that *rûaḥ* is used here as a psychological term. He derives this conclusion from the fact that the two spirits were created by God and dwell in man. However, the belief that the two spirits were created and are limited in time does not suggest that they must be inward or psychological forces. Likewise, there is no suggestion that the two spirits dwell in man exclusively. Rather in 3:18 we discover not that God created the spirits in man, but that he allotted them unto man (*wyśm lw*).[31]

to denote supernatural beings or angels and this is a considerable development in comparison with what we find in the Old Testament"; see *JSS* 7 (1962) 293.

[28] The problem originates with the attempt to uncover the original meaning of the Hebrew word *dor*. This noun can be translated "generation", "age", "race", or "class".

[29] So also Allegro's "astrological document" 2:7–8: "He has six (parts) spirit in the House of Light, and three in the Pit of Darkness." See also column 3:5–6: "He has [ei]ght (parts) spirit in the House of [Darkness] and one (part) from the House of Light." See J. M. Allegro, *JSS* 9 (1964) 291–4.

[30] "That *rwḥwt* is used here as a psychological term seems clear; and the implication is that the failure of man to 'rule the world' is due to man himself because he allows his 'spirit of perversion', that is to say his perverse and sinful propensities, to determine his behaviour. We have thus arrived at the rabbinic distinction between the evil and good *yeṣer*" (*RevQ* 3 (1961) 422).

[31] This Qumranic teaching is clearly distinguished from the rabbinic doctrine of the two inclinations in man (Berakoth 9:5) precisely because of the cosmic dimension of man's struggle, and because of the categorical difference between an imposed force and an inward inclination.

D

This verb, *śim*, when combined with the preposition *l^e*, means "to set for" (Gen 43:32; 2 Sam 12:20) or to "direct toward" (1 Sam 9:20; Dt 32:46). If this verb had been combined with the preposition *b^e*, which would probably have meant "to put in" (Gen 31:34), then a psychological rendering might have been possible. Furthermore, in 4:12 it is clearly stated that the "angels of destruction" (*ml'ky ḥbl*) plague all who walk in the "Spirit of Perversity" in a place which is neither in man nor on earth, but in the everlasting pit (*lšḥt 'wlmym*).[32]

P. Wernberg-Møller correctly asserts that the ethical demands of the community were so rigid that the members fell far short of the ideal; but what is more important to our investigation is that they knew they were far below these ethical demands. In 1QS 3:13–4:26 we find the differences between what the covenanters were eschatologically by divine election (*bny 'wr*), and what they were in reality during their sojourn here on earth. Consequently, he contends: "The darkness is not merely outside the community: it is present in the hearts of all the members. ..."[33] This statement seems to disclose that he has misread A. Dupont-Sommer, K. G. Kuhn, F. M. Cross, Jr, and others who advocate a cosmological dualism. These scholars do not argue that the cosmological dualism was "merely outside the community". One sentence from the scholar he seeks to correct clarifies this point: "The two 'spirits' live together within every man and are engaged in constant struggle."[34]

One of Wernberg-Møller's pivotal points is the contention that *twldwt* in 3:19 should be translated "characters" or "dispositions", or "minds", and that *twldwt/rwḥ* ("spirit") are synonymous.[35] If this translation, "in a dwelling of light is the disposition of truth", were accepted, then the passage might have a psychological connotation.

P. Wernberg-Møller and A. Dupont-Sommer suggest that *twldwt* in 3:13 denotes "the original source" of the "natures" of all men. To suggest, however, that in 3:19 it should be translated similarly distorts the proper meaning of this noun and overlooks the fact that context determines the precise meaning of a noun when it has considerable semantic range. W. Gesenius' lexicon as edited by F. Brown, S. R. Driver, and C. A. Briggs records that *twldwt*, a feminine noun which appears only in the plural, means "generations", or the account of a man and his descendants.[36] Nowhere has it been translated with any psychological connotation. It derives etymo-

32 As F. Nötscher argued, the "Angel of Darkness" is no abstract concept, "sondern *persönlicher Dämon*", the head of the evil spirits and the "kosmologisches Übel". See his article in *Mélanges bibliques: rédigés en l'honneur de André Robert*, 313–15.

33 P. Wernberg-Møller. *RevQ* 3 (1961) 435–6.

34 A. Dupont-Sommer, *Essene Writings*, 79. O. Böcher, *Der johanneische Dualismus*, 74: "Nicht nur das Mensehenherz, sondern die ganze Welt ist durchzogen vom Gegensatz zwischen Licht und Finsternis, Wahrheit und Verführung, Gut und Böse."

35 P. Wernberg-Møller, *RevQ* 3 (1961) 425.

36 F. Brown, S. R. Driver and C. A. Briggs (ed.), *A Hebrew and English Lexicon of The Old Testament* (Oxford, 1952) 410. So also L. Koehler and W. Baumgartner ed.), *Lexicon in Veteris Testamenti Libros* (Leiden, 1958) 1021.

logically from the verbal root *yld*, which in the Qal denotes "to bear", and in the Hiph'il means "to beget". Petrus Boccaccio, consequently, translates this passage with this denotation in mind: *historiam omnium filiorum hominis* (3:13), *origines veritatis—origines pravitatis* (3:19).[37] Moreover, contrary to Wernberg-Møller's suggestion[38] *'wr, 'mt* and *ḥwšk, 'wl* probably had dualistic overtones in post-exilic Judaism.[39] It seems certain to the present writer that at Qumran these terms did have dualistic overtones (1QS 3:25; 1QS 10:1; 1QM 1:1ff.; 1QM 13:15f.; etc.).

The preceding remarks, we believe, clearly show that 1QS 3:13–4:26 does not teach a psychological dualism. Accordingly, far from accepting Wernberg-Møller's position,[40] we contend that this passage clearly expresses a cosmic dualism, even though there may be some hints of a psychological perspective. For example, in 3:25 it is stated both that God created the two spirits and that he founded upon them every work. Since for post-exilic Jews angels (the terms angel and spirit are sometimes used synonymously throughout this section of 1QS)[41] were unquestionably cosmic beings and not merely psychological projections, anyone advocating a psychological rendering of this passage must necessarily explain why here particularly "Angel of Darkness" or "Angel of Truth" should be drained of their cosmic force.[42] He will also be forced to explain why the scribe

[37] P. Boccaccio, *srk hyḥd Regula Unionis Seu Manuale Disciplinae* (1QS) (Rome, 1958) 9.

[38] "'*mt*/'*wr* and '*wl*/*ḥwšk* are ethical terms without the dualistic overtones which are generally placed upon them" (P. Wernberg-Møller, *RevQ* 3 (1961) 425).

[39] See the following discussion regarding the antecedents of the dualism in 1QS and the observations concerning the similarities of the dualisms in these documents. While different Semitic nouns are employed in Test. Levi, which is clearly pre-Christian because of the fragments discovered at Qumran, the dualistic overtones have already been given to "light" and "gloomy" since the highest and lowest heaven are respectively characterized by light and gloom.

[40] As H. G. May remarked, Wernberg-Møller's contention that this treatise teaches a psychological dualism neither accounts for the apocalyptic framework of the teaching, nor does justice to the role of the "Angel of Darkness" and the "Prince of Light" in 1QS 3:20ff., nor recognizes the cosmic contexts of the use of *mmšlh* ("rule" or "dominion"). See *JBL* 82 (1963) 3–4.

[41] So also Y. Yadin, *The Scroll of the War*, 231; and E. Schweizer in *The Background of the New Testament and its Eschatology*, 491.

In contrast, however, M. Treves observed, "The mention of all the spirits allotted to the single Angel of Darkness (3:24) shows that here the terms 'spirit' and 'angel' are not synonyms". But the suggestion that there are many spirits under the command of the "Angel of Darkness" does not dismiss the possibility that the self-same angel is also called the "Spirit of Perversity". Moreover, it appears that Treves' suggestion that these two terms are not synonymous weakens the hypothesis of a psychological dualism which he had endeavoured to prove, since we would be left with an "angel" which was not a "spirit". See Treves' article in *RevQ* 3 (1961–62) 450.

[42] W. D. Davies correctly remarks that the fact that these spirits "are not merely inherent properties of man, as such, emerges clearly from the use of the term 'angel' to describe the two spirits: this preserves the 'otherness' of the two spirits even when they ap̲ ear to be merely immanent" (*Christian Origins and Judaism*, 164). Similarly, A. R. C. Leaney concludes: "The tendency to personify as angels the powers which control the stars and to identify God himself with the *Urlicht* may be paralleled by the identification of the two spirits with personal supernatural beings" (*The Rule of Qumran*, 43). Hence, as U. Simon so aptly put it, "The struggle in the heart of man is inseparable from the cosmic array of powers (1QS 4:18)" (*Heaven*, 173).

wrote *lw*, "for him", and not *bw*, "in him", in 3:18.[43]

Four other observations strengthen our argument that 1QS 3:13ff. presents a cosmic dualism. First, J. Strugnell has shown that the angelology of *Serek Šîrôt 'Ôlat Haššabbāt* is celestial. 4QS1 37–40 reveals that the Essenes imagined a heavenly sacrificial cult with celestial beings (or angels) who performed priestly functions. The cosmic dimension of this document increases the probability that the dualism in 1QS 3:13ff. is cosmic since both seem to date from the same early stage in the development of Qumran theology.[44]

Second, the astrological document from Qumran published by J. M. Allegro has striking similarities with 1QS 3:13–4:26. In this document we read of the influence of the stars upon men, and learn that, according to the time of his birth, a man has allotted unto him (*lw*) both portions of the Spirit *bbyt h'wr* and of the Spirit *bbwr hḥwšk* (2:7f.). The similarity between this passage and 1QS 3:18b–4:1 is impressive. For example, in 1QS 3:19 we read that the "Spirit of Truth" originates in "a habitation of light" (*bm'wn 'wr*), and in Allegro's document we read of a Spirit in "a house of light" (*bbyt h'wr*). In 1QS 3:19 we learn that the "Spirit of Perversity" originates in "a spring of darkness" (*wmmqwr ḥwšk*), and in Allegro's document we read of a Spirit in "a well of darkness" (*bbwr hḥwšk*).[45]

Third, Y. Yadin demonstrates that the War Scroll has cosmic dimensions: "Israel will overcome her enemies because God Himself and His angels fight in Israel's ranks."[46] It is significant that Professor Yadin suggests that the purpose of 1QM was to *apply* the dualistic doctrine defined in 1QS 3:13–15.[47]

Fourth, S. Holm-Nielsen and M. Delcor have shown that the Hodayoth have cosmic dimensions. For example, we read in 1QH 3:21–22: "And the perverted spirit Thou hast cleansed from the great transgression, to stand in the assembly with the host of the saints, and to come into communion with the congregation of the sons of heaven."[48] M. Delcor, therefore, correctly contends that one may speak of a sort of mystic communion between the sectarians and the celestial beings so that the community was thought of as a kind of "antichambre du ciel".[49] The conclusions from the researches of Professors Strugnell, Allegro, Yadin, Holm-Nielsen, and Delcor

---

[43] A. R. C. Leaney seems to find in 1QS 3:13–4:26 both an idea in harmony with the rabbinic thought of two inclinations in man and the belief that the two spirits are cosmic beings. This "inconsistency" seems less to be characteristic of the passage than it is attributable to Leaney's translation of *lw* in 1QS 3:18 as "in him" when it should be translated "for him".

[44] J. Strugnell, "The Angelic Liturgy at Qumran—4Q Serek Šîrôt 'Ôlat Haššabbāt", Supplements to Vetus Testamentum 7 (1959) 318–45.

[45] See J. M. Allegro, *JSS* 9 (1964) 291–4.

[46] *The Scroll of the War*, 237, 241f.

[47] *Ibid.*, 232–42.

[48] The translation is by S. Holm-Nielsen, *Hodayot: Psalms from Qumran* (Aarhus, 1960) 64; see also 68.

[49] M. Delcor, *Les Hymnes de Qumran* (*Hodayot*) (Paris, 1962) 40–52, esp. 41. K. Schubert seems to share Delcor's suggestion, for he remarks that the sect's services and prayers were for them an extension of the celestial liturgy (*The Dead Sea Community*, 64). Hence, O. Böcher correctly noted, "Die Grenzen zwischen Erde und Himmel sind für die Qumraniten fließend geworden" (*Der johanneische Dualismus*, 26).

strengthen our conclusion that 1QS 3:13–4:26 presents a cosmic dualism.

If in fact, therefore, we are dealing here with cosmic dualism, can we trace its antecedents? The scholarly answers given to this question can be arranged into two somewhat overlapping viewpoints: K. G. Kuhn,[50] C. T. Fritsch,[51] W. F. Albright,[52] F. M. Cross, Jr,[53] A. Dupont-Sommer,[54] D. Winston,[55] J. M. Allegro,[56] and H. Ringgren[57] argue that it has been influenced by the Iranian *Weltanschauung.* F. Nötscher,[58] J. van der Ploeg,[59] H. J. Schonfield,[60] and O. Böcher[61] argue that it reflects a further development of biblical thought.

The latter group point out that the dualism in 1QS 3:13–4:26 remains rooted in the monotheism of the Old Testament. However, striking similarities between the mythology of 1QS and a particular system developed in Iran may encourage us to look in that direction, namely to Zurvanism, which was current as early as the fourth century B.C.[62] and held belief in one supreme God.[63] This God of Time or Destiny, called Zurvan, transcended the spirit of light and the spirit of darkness as in 1QS 3:15ff.[64] Zurvan was the father of Ohrmazd, who "was on high in omniscience and goodness; for infinite Time he was ever in the Light. That Light is the Space and place of Ohrmazd: some call it the Endless Light."[65] Zurvan was also the father of Ahriman, who was "slow in knowledge, whose will is to

---

[50] "Die Sektenschrift und die iranische Religion", *ZTK* 49 (1952) 312.

[51] *The Qumran Community,* 73.

[52] "The Bible After Twenty Years of Archeology", *RL* 21 (1952) 549.

[53] *Ancient Library of Qumran,* 98; see also his comments in "The Dead Sea Scrolls", *Int. Bible,* vol. 22, 659.

[54] *The Jewish Sect of Qumran and the Essenes,* 118–19.

[55] "The Iranian Component in the Bible, Apocrypha, and Qumran: A Review of the Evidence", *HR* 5 (1966) 200ff.

[56] *The Dead Sea Scrolls,* 128.

[57] *The Faith of Qumran,* 78f.

[58] *Zur theologischen Terminologie der Qumran-Texte,* 86–92.

[59] *The Excavations at Qumran,* trans. K. Smyth (London, 1958) 100.

[60] *Secrets,* 113.

[61] *Der johanneische Dualismus,* 72.

[62] R. C. Zaehner contends that the earliest account of the Zurvanite myth is presented by Aristotle's pupil, Eudemus of Rhodes, and that there is no serious reason to doubt its authenticity; see *The Dawn and Twilight of Zoroastrianism* (London, 1961) 182. J. Duchesne-Guillemin believes both that Zurvanism predates Zoroaster (*c.* 628–*c.* 551 B.C.) and that the Zurvanite point of view was the religion of the common Iranian folk; see *Western Response to Zoroaster* (Oxford, 1958) 60ff., 18. Also see Zaehner's *Zurvan, A Zoroastrian Dilemma* (Oxford, 1955).

[63] Long after the above research had been completed, I was delighted to discover that at the colloquium on gnosticism, which met at Messina in April 1966, H. Ringgren remarked "I think the best parallels to the doctrine of the two spirits are found in Zurvanite texts. . . . My main objection is that it is impossible to explain the doctrine of the two spirits exclusively on the basis of the Old Testament doctrine." See *Le Origini dello Gnosticismo: Colloquio di Messina 13-18 Aprile 1966,* ed. U. Bianchi (Leiden, 1967) 385.

[64] It appears that the first scholar to perceive this connection was H. Michaud. "Un mythe zervanite dans un des manuscrits de Qumran", *VT* 5 (1955), 137–47.

[65] From the *Greater Bundahsin,* chapter 1, R. C. Zaehner's translation; see his *Zurvan, A Zoroastrian Dilemma,* 312. Although this work is late and reflects late Sassanian religion (seventh century A.D.), the passages quoted represent a much earlier tradition as evidenced by Eudemus' account.

smite; was deep down in the darkness: (he was) and is, yet will not be. The will to smite is his all, and darkness is his place: some call it the Endless Darkness."[66] The consonance of this dualism with Jewish monotheism,[67] the apparently clear solution to the problem of evil contrasted with the obscure, futile attempts within Judaism and the similarities between this aspect of Zurvanism and the ideas found in 1QS 3:15ff. prompt the view that our author may well have derived his dualism from the Zurvanites.[68] Moreover, the fact that Zurvanism was probably predominant in the time when Essene[69] thought developed, that both are qualified dualisms and contain a deterministic view, that both dualistic beliefs are cosmic and permeated by a similar light-*versus*-darkness *motif*, that both dualisms centre around two warring spirits, and that most scholars opt for Iranian dualism as the origin of post-exilic biblical dualistic thought[70] supports the idea that the Essenes were directly influenced by the Zurvanites. Conceivably indeed, when one reflects that the caravan routes between Iran and Egypt transected Palestine, the Essenes may have received this influence *viva voce* from the Zurvanites themselves.[71] It is also possible that the Jews, who were returning intermittently from Babylon, brought with them to Palestine these dualistic conceptions which they had received from their Zurvanite neighbours.

To sum up, we may say that the dualism in this treatise has seven[72] salient features.[73] First, we find a modified dualism both

[66] *Greater Bundahsin*, chapter 1, R. C. Zaehner's translation, *ibid.*

[67] Failure to consider Zurvanism led O. Böcher to contend that the religion of the Old Testament is distinct from the many other contemporary religions because the opposition between good and bad or God and Satan never became an absolute dualism since God remained the sole creator of all things. See O. Böcher, *Der johanneische Dualismus*, 119.

[68] M. Black contends that the sources and background of the dualistic thought of 1QS should be traced in the apocalyptic writings. The example he gives is from Test. Judah 20: "Know, therefore, my children, that two spirits wait upon man— the spirit of truth and the spirit of deceit"; see *The Scrolls and Christian Origins* (London, 1961) 134. Such passages from Jewish apocalyptic literature did influence the dualistic thought of Qumran; another influence was probably from Zurvanism.

[69] It is generally accepted by almost all scholars "that the Qumran sect was identical with the people known to the ancient historians as 'Essenes' "; see M. Black, *The Essene Problem* (London, 1961) 27. Also see A. Dupont-Sommer, *The Essene Writings from Qumran*, 39–67. Cf. G. R. Driver who contends that the Qumran covenanters may be identified in some sense with the Zealots (*The Judaean Scrolls*, 75, 118–19, 237–51). It might appear to some that Driver's hypothesis has been proved by the discovery of a Qumranic scroll at Masada, the fortress of the Zealots' last stand. (This fragment is "identical" to the Qumranic sectarian scroll 4Q Serek Šîrôt 'Ôlat Haššabbāt published by J. Strugnell.) However, I believe that Y. Yadin is correct to argue that the scroll probably belonged to one of the Essenes who joined the rebellion. See Y. Yadin, *Masada: Herod's Fortress and the Zealots' Last Stand* (London, 1966) 172–4. Also see the next chapter, especially note 3.

[70] One of the most recent scholarly examinations of this position is by D. Winston, *HR* 5 (1966) 183–216. Also see G. von Rad's *Old Testament Theology*, trans. D. M. G. Stalker (New York, London, 1962) vol. 1, 150.

[71] Cf. G. R. Driver, *The Judaean Scrolls*, 551.

[72] While J. Jeremias recognizes the cosmic dimension of this dualism, he prefers to isolate three main characteristics: the dualism is monotheistic, ethical and eschatological. See *Die theologische Bedeutung der Funde am Toten Meer* (Göttingen, 1962) 13–15. For ET see *CTM* 39 (1968) 557–71.

[73] In line with the logic of existentialism Huppenbauer argues that the point of

because the "Spirit of Truth" and the "Spirit of Perversity" are
subjugated to one God, and because the dualism is limited by the
finite existence of the "Spirit of Perversity"—he appeared after God
and will disappear at the final judgement (4:18). Second, the dualism
is explained in terms of the light-*versus*-darkness paradigm, which is
raised to a unique degree of sophistication. Third, there is an ethical
dualism in the sense that men are divided into two mutually exclusive
camps according to virtues or vices. Fourth, conjoined with this
ethical dualism is a belief in an absolute determinism. Fifth, although
the author attempted to solve the problem of evil by positing an evil
spirit, God becomes ultimately responsible because of the author's
monotheistic and predestinarian belief. Sixth, there is an eschatological
dualism both because the entire treatise is written in an eschatological
key, and because there are present rewards or punishments and future
rewards or punishments. Seventh, although the titanic struggle of
the two spirits seems to be centred in the heart of man (4:23), it is
not limited to man, but has cosmic dimensions which reflect the
influence of Zurvanism. In conclusion, the treatise presents a modified
cosmic dualism, under which is a subordinate ethical dualism, and
whose most conspicuous characteristic is the light–darkness paradigm,
and most pervasive feature is the eschatological dimension.

Johannine "dualism"

We now turn to an examination of the passages in the Gospel of
John which suggest a dualistic framework. In the Gospel we find the
belief in two worlds assumed;[74] assumed, in the sense that this belief
is neither introduced and defined before it is applied nor made the
intentional subject of any passage. The primary world is the "world
above" (*anōthen*) which is both the region[75] from which the angels

departure for the dualism of this treatise is, "in der lebendigen Situation der
Gemeinde zu suchen und zu finden" (*Der Mensch zwischen zwei Welten*, 42–4).
This contention appears unlikely for three main reasons. It would ascribe to the
origin of the Qumran community a sociological rather than an ideological or
theological cause. Secondly, references to contemporary historical events, found
couched in vague phrases in other scrolls, are conspicuously absent. Finally,
Huppenbauer's contention overlooks the fact that this treatise dates from the
earliest days of the community and most likely originally existed independently of
its present position. Is it not more likely that the cause of the origin of the Qumran
community was an acting out of a philosophy, which although certainly embryonic,
nevertheless adumbrated the sophisticated dualism now found in 1QS 3:13ff.?
This suggestion, however, would not weaken the probability, which appears quite
certain as Professor H. Anderson contended recently, that the Essenes believed
that "only within the group was there the light of total obedience to the will of God,
without there was nothing but the darkness of faithlessness and unrighteousness";
see "The Intertestamental Period", *The Bible and History* (London, 1968) 199.
Indeed, implicit in the Rule is the contention that only the Essenes were the "sons
of light".

[74] One wonders what relation there is between John and 2 Esdras: "The Most
High has made not one world but two" (2 Esdras 7:50). It appears that John
received his two worlds from such thoughts in late biblical Judaism. The idea, of
course, goes back to Gen 1:1ff.

[75] So O. Böcher, *Der johanneische Dualismus*, 26: "Dadurch wird es möglich,
das *anōthen* in Joh. 3:3 und 3:7 nicht nur temporal ('wiederum'), sondern auch
lokal, im Sinne des 'von oben', zu verstehen."

descend and to which they ascend (*anabainontas kai katabainontas*, see 1:51; 3:13; 3:31; 3:33; 6:41, 50, 51, 58, 62, *passim*), and the realm from which all emanates (in 1:3 and 1:10 it is stated that the Logos created all things, in 19:11 we read that Pilate receives his power "from above"). The "world above" is contrasted with the "world below" (*tōn katō*), which is comparatively limited in quality and quantity (6:51, 58, 63; 4:13f.), which is the object of action from above (1:11; 6: 38–40; 6:51; 17:6–10), and which hates (7:7) the "world above". It is important to note, moreover, that the "world below" does not signify the underworld or Hades. It signifies the inhabited earth which has rejected the revelation of Christ (n.b. the antithetic parallelism of 8:23 and the consequent similarity of *katō* and *kosmou*).

These two different worlds are represented by two sets of forces. The "force" from above is Christ (who is the Logos, 1:14, which is divine, 1:1, also the variant in 1:18 *monogenēs theos*, "only God"), who is opposed by "this world". The "force" from above is one (1:1, 14; 17:3, 21) but the "force" from below is manifold (8:23f. *et passim*, "the Jews"; 13:27; 12:31; 14:30; 13:2; 7:7).[76] The main actors within this framework are Jesus and the Jews. Jesus' twelve disciples display an ambiguous faith and are portrayed as intermittently moving between belief and doubt; consequently neither are they categorically *ek tou kosmou* (15:18–19) nor willing to commit themselves fully to Jesus since he must finally ask them *arti pisteuete?* ("Now do you believe?") (12:16; 16:32).[77]

The word *kosmos* plays a very important conceptual role in the theology of the Fourth Evangelist. It is used 8 times in Matthew, 3 times in Mark, 3 times in Luke, but 78 times in John. It appears as early as 1:9 where it is the place into which the light came (*to phōs* synonymous with *ho logos* and *ho Christos*). In the next verse it is stated that the cosmos did not always exist but came into being through the light, and that it did not know (*egnō*) him. Jesus is the one who has come down from above (6:51) in order to give light to the world (6:33; 8:1f.; 12:46) to save it (1:29; 3:16–17, 19; 4:42; *et passim*) and to sacrifice himself in the end vicariously for the sake of the world (6:51). John clearly points out that Jesus (*ho logos, to phōs, ho theos*) was sent *hina sōthē ho kosmos di' autou*, "so that the world might be saved through him" (3:17); but ironically it is the cosmos which hates him (7:7; 15:18f.).

W. F. Howard and M. Meinertz rightly point out that the Hellenistic concept of the cosmos as the realm of created things or the realm in which men live receives a theological meaning: "The mass of man-

---

[76] Nils A. Dahl sees the conflict between God and the world in forensic terms, with Jesus as the representative of God and the Jews as representatives of the world. See his article in *Current Issues in New Testament Interpretation*, ed. W. Klassen and G. F. Snyder (London, 1962) 124–42, esp. 139.

[77] The disciples are contrasted with Jesus. They display need for food "from below" (4:8, *trophas*) but he needs food "from above" (4:34, *brōma*). In 16:32 it is made clear that Jesus must face his suffering alone, yet in a higher sense he is not alone for his Father is with him.

kind mobilized in defiance of the divine power".[78] Likewise, C. K.
Barrett argues that the concept *ho kosmos houtos*, "this world"
(8:23; 9:39; 11:9; 12:25, 31; 13:1; 16:11; 18:36) is not simply
equivalent to the rabbinical *h'wlm hzh* (*ho aiōn houtos*, "this age"),
and hence contrasted with a future world, but is contrasted with a
world existing and above (*anō*).[79] It appears, therefore, that while the
cosmos was created by the Logos (1:10), it had not known the
Logos (1:10), but had rejected him (1:11, 14) who was the Word.
The cosmos, consequently, is an inferior and vulgar force in rebellion
against God.[80] How conceptually similar, as one can see from 8:23,
but not always synonymous, are the concepts *ho kosmos* and *tōn
katō* in the Fourth Gospel.

Two groups of antithetic categories contrast the two worlds. Light
(*phōs*) characterizes the "world above" (*anō*), and darkness (*skotia*)
distinguishes the "world below" (*katō*).[81] In John's thoughts light
comes first but is immediately opposed by darkness (1:4–5; 3:19).
Black is the paint by which he portrays man's resistance to belief.[82]
In 3:19 he states why men hate the light, "And men loved darkness
rather than light because their deeds were evil". Being in darkness is
equivalent to being in ignorance: "he who walks in darkness does
not know where he goes" (12:35).[83] The pericope of the man
born blind in chapter 9 sharply displays the two levels of being in
darkness: physical darkness and spiritual darkness. In verse 7 the
man who was born blind receives his eyesight but it is not until
verse 38 that he receives "the true light". Verse 41 clearly shows
that only spiritual blindness (unbelief) is condemned. In this
chapter we see the lucid application of the formula presented in
8:12: "Jesus spoke to them saying, 'I am the light of the world'"
(see also 12:35–36, 46). This exegesis reveals that for John "the light
of the world" describes what is "essentially a soteriological function
rather than a cosmological status".[84]

The question we must now face is, how is the Johannine "dualism"
operative on the human level? The overall belief of the Gospel is
that all men are in darkness (1:5) but have the potential to believe
and receive the light. If they believe then they are called children of
God (*tekna theou*, 1:12) but if they reject the light then they remain
in darkness and are not from God (*ek tou theou ouk este*).[85] Consequently, there are not two groups of men, i.e. those from above

[78] W. F. Howard, *Christianity According to John* (Philadelphia, 1946) 83; see
also M. Meinertz, *Theologie des Neuen Testaments*, zweiter Band (Bonn, 1950) 286.
[79] *The Gospel According to St John* (London, 1955) 135.
[80] J. Becker, *Das Heil Gottes* (Göttingen, 1964) 135.
[81] *Das Heil Gottes*, 218.
[82] R. Bultmann in his *Theology of the New Testament* (New York, 1955) vol. 2,
18f. correctly shows that the concept of darkness is provided by the possibility of
light and that it originates on man's side "by shutting one's self up against the
light", but his exegesis which follows reflects the imposition of existential logic
upon this passage and becomes distorted through his *Vorverständnis*.
[83] *ginōskein*, "to know", appears 56 times in John but only 59 times in the
Synoptics (Mt–21; Mk–18; Lk–20). It seems to be equated at times with power
and strength (4:32; 7:28, 29).
[84] C. K. Barrett, *The Gospel According to St John*, 279.
[85] The question of predestination is taken up in the following pages.

and those from below (as in 1QS 3:15ff.), but initially only Jesus is from above (*ek tou ouranou*, 3:13), though later *pas ho pisteuōn en autō* ("everyone who believes in him") obtains this quality. The division caused by ~~man's response to~~ Jesus is brought into sharp focus in chapter 8. In this chapter the Jews claim Abraham as their father (8:44). However, this statement does not reflect a comological or ontological connection but a practical and soteriological category as explained on the one hand by the charge "you are not from God", and on the other by the reasons given why they are so designated: they have rejected "the words of God" (v. 47). In vivid contrast Jesus' Father is God. He absolutely obeys God's will and so speaks the truth (5:30ff., and 8:45). Men are not divided into two mutually exclusive groups since the criterion is individualistic (*homo sui iuris*). The one who believes (*ho pisteuōn*: 3:16, 12:36) and the one who does not believe (*ho mē pisteuōn*: 3:18) categorize themselves by their response to the Word (3:16ff.; 5:29, 40; 6:40; 8:12; 11:26). In the sense, but only in the sense, that one's response to Jesus reflexively categorizes him as dwelling in darkness or in light, there are two exclusive groups in John.[86] In the Fourth Gospel, therefore, we find the idea that all men are in darkness and the suggestion that men are divided into different categories according to their response to Jesus.

We must now turn to a question which appeared in the preceding exegesis: "Is the devil portrayed as a cosmic spirit or as a figure of speech?"[87] As *ho kosmos* obtains the figurative meaning of all that rejects the light and defies God, so *ho diabolos* (6:70; 8:44; 13:2), *ho archōn tou kosmou toutou*, "the ruler of this world" (12:31; 14:30; 16:11), and *ho satanas* (13:27) have begun to lose their completely cosmic, hypostatic quality. Sometimes, it appears to me, these expressions symbolize the force of the collective temptations of this world.[88] The evangelist seemed to mean "not from God" by the expression "from your father the devil" (8:44–47). The opposite of *ho ōn ek tou theou* ("he who is of God") appears to be he who is described as *ek tou theou ouk ōn*, "not being of God", and so John is completely consistent with his monotheistic proclamation in 1:1–3.[89]

86 K. G. Kuhn, however, contends that in the Fourth Gospel "die Menschen teilt in die beiden antithetischen Gruppen der Leute". He also finds "einen praedestinatianischen Zug" in this Gospel. See his "Johannesevangelium und Qumrantexte", *Neotestamentica et Patristica*, 113.

87 Unfortunately there is as yet no detailed, critical publication regarding the demonology of the Fourth Gospel. Dodd and Barrett do not delve into this question and E. Langdon's otherwise excellent book, *Essentials of Demonology* (London, 1949), allots only two pages to the demonology of John while he assigns 71 to the New Testament generally and 14 to the book of Revelation.

88 There appears to be no distinction made between these expressions (e.g. compare the equation of *tou diabolou* in 13:2 with *ho satanas* in 13:27). While 13:2 and 13:27 may have originally signified a cosmic figure who opposed God, it appears that 6:70 can only have a symbolic meaning since Jesus remarked "Did I not choose you, the twelve, and one of you is a devil?"

89 V. Taylor remarked, "In the Fourth Gospel we approach nearest to the use of *theos* as a Christological title. . . . 'Only-begotten' is as far as John is prepared to go"; see "Does the New Testament Call Jesus God?", *ExpT* 73 (1962) 117–18. Space permits only a brief observation on this exegesis: it fails to do justice to

We believe that the devil in John is not fundamentally a hypostatic creature because of the following five observations:[90] (a) Jesus is not portrayed as struggling against an evil spirit, but against *ho kosmos*. (b) There are not two exclusive groups of men, but "of the devil" signifies the base condition of all men. (c) Man is no puppet, but *homo sui iuris*. (d) Satan is not characterized as a "spirit" or angel (cf. 2 Enoch (A) 31:4—"the devil is the evil spirit of the lower places...". (e) If one would argue with W. Bousset[91] that "the devil" is the *kosmokratōr tou aiōnos toutou*, "the ruler of this age", then, as W. F. Howard states,[92] the burden of proof lies with him to explain why *kosmokratōr* is not found in the Fourth Gospel. To be sure there are traces of the older view, that the devil is a personified creature (e.g. 8:44), but one should expect such ideas because of the *Weltanschauung* of John's day; however, the main thrust of this Gospel is that the devil has been demythologized. The reason for this Johannine characteristic is, of course, the belief that through his crucifixion Christ overcame the world (16:33) so that the devil is *now* defeated and destroyed (12:31; 16:11).

As we have just seen, the eschatological dimension of John's "dualism" is important. In John the eschatological view is not primarily futuristic, as in the apocalyptic literature; more than any biblical writer John emphasizes that the last things have already begun to break into the present. This interpretation seems verified by the formula: *alla erchetai hōra kai nun estin*, "but the hour is coming and now is" (4:23; 5:25) and the intimation of 12:23: *elēluthen hē hōra*, "the hour has come". The following passages elucidate the "realized" or "realizing" character of Johannine "dualism". Those who cling to the Law orient themselves around a past revelation (1:17), but those who come and believe in him whom God has sent (8:42) receive the light of a present revelation which has come but is also still to come (15:26; 4:16ff.). The contrast between the first wine which was inferior to "the good wine", which was held "until now" (2:10), and the contrast between the water from Jacob's well from which one would thirst again (4:12; see 6:58) and the water which Jesus gives (4:14) displays the present quality of John's eschatology. Even Solomon's Temple has become superseded by "the temple of his (Jesus') body" (2:21).

The futuristic eschatology so prevalent in the Synoptics has become modified in John so that despite 5:28–29; 6:39, 40, 44, 51c–58 and 12:48, which a few scholars believe are redactional,[93]

Jn 1:1 where the pre-existent Logos is called "God" and Jn 20:28 where Thomas exclaims: "My Lord and my God!" Moreover, in 1:18 we find the following authoritative variant for "only Son": *monogenēs theos* "only God".

[90] Hence how different John's demonology is from that of the Synoptics in which Jesus is portrayed in combat with Satan! See the excellent discussion on this topic by H. van der Loos. *The Miracles of Jesus* (Leiden, 1965) 204–11, 339ff.

[91] *Die Religion des Judentums im späthellenistischen Zeitalter* (Tübingen, 1926) 515.

[92] *Christianity According to John*, 82.

[93] See R. E. Brown, *The Gospel According to John* (I–XII) 219–21.

the *emphasis* is on "realized" eschatology.[94] If, however, these verses are not redactional, we cannot simply overlook them, any more than we can overlook the futuristic aspect of the repeated *erchetai hōra*, "the hour is coming", or the futuristic quality of *ho paraklētos* and *to pneuma tēs alētheias*, "the Spirit of truth", in chapter 16. One of the undeniable aspects of Johannine "dualism" is that, while the soteriological task of Jesus of Nazareth has been completed, God's revelation has not ended. The future holds the last judgment and final revelation.[95] Even so the eschatology of the Fourth Evangelist is *predominantly* "realized" or "realizing".

The thorny question of predestination in John, which has been approached only obliquely in the preceding pages, must now be examined directly because it points to the limits of his "dualism". In 1:12 the *tekna theou*, "children of God", are *all* who have accepted the Word and believed in his name. The commentators who argue for a predestinarian reading of John contend that this doctrine is espoused in verse 13. They hold that the "children of God" have believed precisely because they have come from God. However, there is no chronological division between being a "child of God" and believing.[96] The power (*exousia*) occurs with the decision to believe. Furthermore, this verse is accompanied by the belief that *all* things come from God (1:3) and the "true light" enlightens *all* men (1:9). There is no predestination here, for one is a "child of God" the moment he believes; he does not believe because he has been foreordained a "child of God".[97]

---

[94] C. K. Barrett (*The Gospel According to St John*, 57) and W. F. Howard (*Int. Bible*, vol. 8, 444) have presented a similar interpretation. Of course our discussion regarding the realizing eschatology of Johannine "dualism" in no way attempts to deal with the multifarious aspects of the contemporary debate concerning the eschatology of the Fourth Gospel. The most recent examination of the eschatology of the Fourth Gospel has been presented by P. Ricca, who approaches the problem from the Christological paradox that Christ is pre-existent, was incarnated, and continues to live in heaven as on earth through his *alter ego*, the Holy Spirit. Both Jesus' coming in the flesh and his return in the Spirit are final (*endgültig*). John both retains the distinction between the various *kairoi* of the *Heilsgeschichte* and exposes their essential interconnection since all time is grounded in Christ. Hence Ricca contends that the Johannine eschatology is a "*personalisierte*" eschatology precisely because the three acts of the eschatological drama—the end has come, is now and will come—are governed by Christ, "der gekommen ist, der da ist, der kommen wird". See *Die Eschatologie des Vierten Evangeliums* (Zürich, 1966).

For an excellent discussion of R. Bultmann's contention that 5:28–29; 6:39, 40, 44, 51c–58 and 12:48 are the additions of an ecclesiastical redactor, see D. M. Smith, Jr, *The Composition and Order of the Fourth Gospel* (New Haven, 1965), especially 134ff. and 217ff. An excellent general discussion of the composition of the Fourth Gospel is found in R. E. Brown, *The Gospel According to John (I–XII)* xxiv–xxxix.

[95] An interesting, and I think accurate, contribution has been made by C. F. D. Moule. He suggests that "The Fourth Evangelist's eschatology is much more 'normal' than is often assumed; and that, where it is of an emphatically realized type, there the individualistic tendency of this Gospel is also at its most prominent. . . ." See "The Individualism of The Fourth Gospel", *NT* 5 (1962) 182.

[96] Bultmann argues that "to be born of" does not attribute man's conduct to his nature but attributes all specific conduct to a man's being, in which his conduct is founded (*Theology of The New Testament*, vol. 2, 23).

[97] As R. E. Brown accurately remarks, "There is no hint, however, of anyone's being determined to evil without choice" (*The Scrolls and the New Testament*, ed. K. Stendahl, 191).

Is there an emphasis upon determinism in 6:37–45? In verse 37 it is stated, "All that the father gives to me shall come to me". One wonders to whom the *pan*, "all", refers? If it refers only to those who are given to Jesus then there is an element of determinism, since the "giving" precedes the "coming". But it is necessary to observe what this verse does not say: it does not say some are not given to Jesus. Hence, there are not two predetermined categories of men. There is no chronological precedence affirmed here but rather a theological precedence, i.e. God is prior to man; it is not that man's election is prior to his act of faith.

In verse 44 we read: "No man can come to me except the Father who sent me draws him." One must not remove this verse from its context. Jesus has addressed himself to the Jews who have just turned their backs on the present revelation; consequently they are not drawn by God because of their own actions.[98] Furthermore, this verse is followed by the statement: "Everyone who has heard and learned from the Father comes to me." The *pas* by itself indicates that everyone has the potential of being drawn by the Father.[99] Indeed, "to draw" (*helkein*) is the verb used by the evangelist when he has Jesus state: "When I am lifted up from the earth, I will draw all men to myself" (12:32). The fruits of the cross are available to *all* men.

In chapter 9 Jesus asks the man who had been blind from birth if he believes. Does this question not signify that man's will plays an important part in believing? An affirmative answer is required when one sees that in contrast to his confession, "I believe, Lord" (9:38), the Pharisees' spiritual blindness remains because they wilfully rejected the Light. Jesus' demand for faith goes forth to all. His words are not meant to instruct but to invite one to make a decision.

Throughout the Gospel men are asked if they want to remain in their present situation, i.e. in darkness: "I have come as light into the world, that whoever believes in me may not remain in darkness" (12:46). Many times the importance of man's decision is accentuated: "he who believes" (3:16, 36), "he who hears and believes" (5:24), "he who comes" (6:35), "he who follows" (8:12).[100] We conclude, therefore, that no doctrine of predestination is put forward in this Gospel,[101] nor is there any strong emphasis upon determinism. Man's destiny is balanced between God's sovereign initiative and man's response.

To sum up: we have argued that whereas there is no cosmic struggle between two warring spirits there is a cosmic dimension to the distinction between the world above and the world below (or this world). Light and darkness convey respectively the superiority of

---

[98] As G. H. C. MacGregor correctly stated, to say a certain number are not drawn to Christ is to say that unbelief in Christ is in many cases unintelligible for a believer like John. See *The Gospel of St John* (New York, 1928) 149.

[99] So R. Bultmann, *Theology*, 23.

[100] *Ibid.*, 21–2.

[101] Cf. J. H. Bernard, *The Gospel According to St John* (Edinburgh, 1928) who believes the Fourth Gospel is "Written from beginning to end *sub specie aeternitatis;* the predestined end is foreseen from the beginning" (vol. 1, 76). "The doctrine of predestination is apparent at every point in the Fourth Gospel, every incident being viewed *sub specie aeternitatis* as predestined in the mind of God" (vol. 2, 325).

tōn anō and the inferiority of *tōn katō*. There are not two distinct or predestined classes of men, but the struggle between light and darkness is portrayed as the struggle between Jesus and "the cosmos". Nevertheless, in the sense that belief or disbelief conditions whether one is of the light or of the darkness, there is some implication of two exclusive groups of men.

The devil in John is not *primarily* a cosmic spirit and the struggle between good and evil is not portrayed as Jesus *versus* an evil angel, hence there is no unqualified metaphysical dualism. John presents a realizing eschatology so that there is no distinct eschatological dualism. Neither do we find a physical dualism.[102] The Johannine "dualism" is essentially soteriological and ethical; soteriological and ethical, in the sense that the "dualism" is conceived as Christ opposed by the world, belief opposed by disbelief, light opposed by darkness, truth opposed by falsehood, righteousness opposed by sin, love opposed by hate, and life opposed by death.

A comparison of the "dualism" in the Gospel of John and that in 1QS 3:13–4:26

We are now in a position to take up the question whether John was dependent on 1QS. The task of discovering the antecedents of Johannine thought is rather more difficult than in the case of Qumran dualism. If we attempt to trace John's "dualism" to rabbinical thought we must first recognize that the rabbinical literature was not compiled until after the Gospel. Yet no doubt some of the rabbinical materials pre-date John. If we stress the similarities between John and the Testaments of the Twelve Patriarchs we must first allow for the possible redactions of post-Johannine Christians.[103] If we argue for the close parallels between Johannine "dualism" and the Ethiopic Book of Enoch we are faced with the possibility that chapters 37–71 may come from a Jewish-Christian hand of the second century A.D.[104]

John was probably not dependent in the literary sense upon the extant apocalyptic literature, although he probably was influenced by apocalyptic dualism.[105] In the first two sections of 1 Enoch,

---

[102] As the gnostic codices discovered at Nag Hammadi in Upper Egypt in 1945 clearly illustrate, e.g. Gospel of Thomas, Log. 29: "But I marvel at how this great wealth has made its home in this poverty." See also sayings 87 and 110. However, John's "dualism" is not physical as the gnostics'. It is important, nevertheless, to observe that in 3:6 and 6:63 there is not a dualism of two spirits, but a "dualism" of flesh and spirit. The soteriological "dualism" in John only adumbrated gnosticism and is typical of John. W. F. Howard correctly contends that 1:14 once and for all repudiates the gnostic antithesis of spirit and matter (*Christianity According to St John*, 83).

[103] De Jonge, Milik and Burrows argue that the Testaments of the Twelve Patriarchs was written by a Christian writer, using older Jewish material. Bickermann and Dupont-Sommer argue that the whole book originated in the Qumran community before the Christian era. This argument cannot be entered into in this paper; however, it appears that the weight of evidence is against a Christian author, and that a Christian redactor is more plausible.

[104] See J. T. Milik, *Ten Years of Discovery in the Wilderness of Judaea*, 33.

[105] So O. Böcher, *Der johanneische Dualismus*, 164. For one of the best examinations of the apocalyptic literature see D. S. Russell's *The Method and Message of Jewish Apocalyptic* (Philadelphia, London, 1964).

which are indisputably pre-Christian, we find the belief that the "spirits of the reprobate" and the "children of the watchers" (the unbelievers in John) are to be destroyed (1 Enoch 10:15) and that the "children of men" (the believers in John) shall receive "the store chambers of blessing which are in the heaven" (1 Enoch 11:1ff.). This belief in a great world judgment seems to be paralleled in John 5:28–29.[106] Likewise, the two worlds found in John's thought are parallel to the idea of a dusty earth on which man struggles and an obscure abode of Yahweh which permeates the canonical Old Testament.

Prior to the composition of John the conception of Satan in Jewish thought not peculiar to Qumran had evolved from God's obsequious opponent described in the prologue of Job to the full-blown dualistic conception of the Adversary in The Martyrdom of Isaiah.[107] In 2:4 of this work we are told that Beliar is "the angel of lawlessness, who is the ruler of this world...", an expression parallel to Jn 12:31: "the ruler of this world".

Clearly the search for the relation between the "dualism" in John and the dualism in 1QS 3:13–4:26 must be pursued on two levels. First there is the question of what the author of John and the author of 1QS both derived in common from the dualistic or incipient dualistic concepts in the Old Testament and the late non-canonical Jewish compositions. Second, there is the question of what ideas and expressions are unique to 1QS and of whether the author of John has been influenced by them. In answer to the first question our previous comments and studies of a number of scholars found elsewhere[108] have made it quite clear that both John and Qumran were influenced, if only in a limited degree, by the dualism in earlier Jewish writings. What is not so obvious is that John shares with 1QS a type of dualism which is unique. In the following pages we hope to clarify this contention.

It is significant to note that the characteristic dualism of late Judaism,[109] the thought of two ages or aeons sharply distinguished (hā'ôlām hazzeh, "this age"—and hā'ôlām habbā', "the age to come"), is modified by 1QS and John in precisely the same manner. Neither in

---

106 While the Old Testament, generally speaking, viewed death as being completely cut off from Yahweh (see Ps 87), a belief in a resurrection from the dead is promulgated in Is 26:19 and Dan 12:2 (see G. von Rad's *Old Testament Theology*, vol. 2, 350ff.). Of course one would not want to overlook the resurrection passages in the Old Testament Apocrypha and Pseudepigrapha (e.g. 2 Macc 7:9, 11, 14, 23, 29, 36; 12:43–45).

107 The evolution of this idea was not completed until after the composition of 1QS. R. H. Charles believed that the Martyrdom of Isaiah was probably composed in the first century A.D.; see *APOT* 2, 158–9. O. Eissfeldt suggests that it is much older and probably was composed in the first century B.C.; see *The Old Testament: An Introduction*, trans. P. R. Ackroyd (New York, 1965) 609. While it is difficult to date 1QS, it certainly is older than the first century A.D.

108 Above we mentioned that F. Nötscher, J. van der Ploeg, H. J. Schonfield, and O. Böcher argue that Qumranic dualism is a further development of biblical thought. We have argued above that Qumranic dualism has cosmic dimensions which reflect the influence of Zurvanism and hence obtained a dualistic belief which is unique in post-exilic Judaism.

109 See S. Mowinckel, *He That Cometh*, trans. G. W. Anderson (Oxford, 1956) 263ff.

1QS 3:13–4:26 (4:1, 3, 7, 8, 12, 16, 17, 22) nor in John (9:32; 4:14; 6:51; 8:51, 52; 10:28; 11:26; 8:35; 12:34; 13:8; 14:6) are these technical terms found. In 1QS 3:13–4:26 *'wlm* always indicates "everlasting"; in John, with the exception of 9:32, where it is a figure of speech signifying "the world", *aiōn* ("age") always indicates "everlasting". This observation raises the probability of interdependence, a probability which will be strengthened in the following pages. It seems convenient to begin a comparison of these two dualisms by discussing first the differences then the similarities between John and 1QS.

Despite similarities there are also notable differences. Whereas the Rule affirms that "God appointed for him (man) two Spirits", John does not teach that there are two hypostatic spirits.[110] In John, while there is a parallel to the "Spirit of Truth", as we shall see, there is no parallel to the "Spirit of Perversity" (but again one must note the pertinent qualifying remarks in the following discussion of similarities). In 1QS we read of the "Spirit of Truth" warring against the "Spirit of Perversity" (4:17–19). In John, however, there are not two warring spirits but only one man Jesus who is rejected, betrayed and persecuted by men.[111]

In 1QS the dualism is centred around two warring spirits. In John the ministry of Jesus is portrayed against a dualism of two worlds. In John the angels and "the son of man" ascend and descend from one world to the other: *kai tous angelous tou theou anabainontas kai katabainontas* (1:51; see also 3:13; 6:33, 38, 41, 50, 51, 58, 62; 20:17). It should be noted that the correlative Hebrew verb to *anabainein, 'lh,* is found in 1QS only at verse 12 and verse 24 and there it has no dualistic or cosmic overtones. The correlative Hebrew verb to *katabainein, yrd,* does not appear in 1QS.

While the dualism in 1QS involves determinism and predestinarianism, the "dualism" in John does not. The Rule is quite explicit about there being two distinct classes of men rigidly predetermined. John no more than implies two groups and is not predestinarian in anything like the full Qumran sense.

Another difference between the two types of dualism lies in their respective eschatologies. In the Rule there is a strong futuristic eschatological view, although the future is not far off, since the covenanters believed they were living in the last days. The day when truth shall arise (4:19) and the time of final judgment (4:20) are even so only in the future for Qumran. In John we find the view that with the incarnation of the divine Logos (1:14) truth came into the world (1:14, 17; 8:32; 14:6), though, paradoxically, it is

---

[110] R. E. Brown correctly argues both that John does not characterize Satan in the exact terminology of the Scrolls, and that Christ as "the light of the world" is a significant development beyond Qumran's "created" angel of light (*The Scrolls and the New Testament*, 188). F. M. Cross rightly argues that the "Spirit of Truth" in 1QS is an angelic creature who is a greater distance from God than the "Spirit of Truth", who in John is God's own Spirit (*The Ancient Library*, 213).

[111] Professor J. Reuss correctly remarked that in terms of their respective angelologies, "müssen wir nicht an eine direkte Abhängigkeit dieser Vorstellungen des Neuen Testaments von den Schriften von Qumran denken" (*Die Qumranfunde*, 110).

still to come (16:13). The advent of the Messiah brought judgment into the world (9:39; 12:31), and again, paradoxically, the judgment is in the future (e.g. 5:28–29; 6:39, 40, 44, 51c–58; 12:48). Consequently, in contrast to Qumran's futuristic eschatology, John emphasizes that the eschaton has already begun to break into the present. The crucial point is that for the Essenes the Messiah is yet to come, but for John he has already come and has completed his earthly ministry. While their respective eschatologies are different, one should note how similar to 1QS are the few passages in John which talk about the coming of the "Spirit of Truth" (14:17ff.; 15:26f.; 16:13ff.)[112] and the final judgment (5:28ff.; 6:38ff.; 12:48).

John's solution to the problem of evil is quite different from that of the Rule. While in 1QS sin is disobedience to God's laws (4:9–11), in John sin is primarily the rejection of Christ: *ho mē pisteuōn ēdē kekritai,* "he who does not believe is condemned already" (3:18, see also 8:24 and 6:9). The source of evil in 1QS is external and cosmic, the source of sin in John is within man himself.

In short, the two dualisms differ from each other in their angelology, their eschatology, their view of predestination, and their solution to the problem of evil. The differences between these two dualistic systems may be summarized as follows: the Qumranic dualism is based upon belief in two warring cosmic spirits; the Johannine "dualism" evolves out of an assumed belief in a spiritual world above and an evil world below. The stress of the eschatology in 1QS is upon the future, but the emphasis of the eschatology in John is upon the present. In 1QS the prominence of an absolute determinism results from a dualism which is primarily cosmic; in John the insistence upon personal decision causes his "dualism" to become essentially non-cosmic. In terms of *emphasis,* therefore, it is not misleading to suggest that Qumran's dualism is primarily cosmic and secondarily ethical, but John's "dualism" is essentially soteriological and only tacitly cosmic.

Now as to similarities: there is some similarity between John's two worlds and the scroll's two spirits. The world above, like the "Spirit of Truth", is characterized by light and truth, is the qualifying characteristic predicated of the righteous, and is opposed by the world below. This lower world, which is somewhat similar to the "Spirit of Perversity", is characterized by darkness and falsehood, and is the abode of the unrighteous. In the previous discussion we noted that there is no explicit reference to the "Spirit of Perversity" in John (cf. only two references in Paul to the spirit as an evil force: 1 Cor 2:12 and Eph 2:2). A qualifying observation, however, must be made. In Jn 12:31 we read, "Now is the judgment of this world, now shall the ruler of this world be cast out. . . ." Notice that "the world" performs the same function in John as the "Spirit of Perversity" in 1QS; observe that when John mentions the judgment the concept of "the ruler of this world" appears with the belief that "now he shall be cast out"; it is not improbable that John knew and deliberately toned down a rigid dualism which appears in Jewish thought only in the Scrolls.

112 See A. R. C. Leaney's chapter, pp. 38ff. above.

Both of these dualisms are modified. The Qumranic and Johannine opposites are not absolute. They are unequal—"the world above" and the "Spirit of Truth" are vastly superior to their respective opposites; they are limited in time—evil and perversity will eventually cease. Moreover, the opposites are subordinate to God—in 1QS 3:15 and Jn 1:3 we find the belief that God is supreme, the sole Creator. One of the most striking similarities is that both dualisms are so qualified.

In both the Rule and John light characterizes the righteous and darkness the unrighteous. Similarity on this point alone, however, proves very little with regard to the Rule's influence on John. The light-darkness *motif* was common in John's day, and was used to describe the contrast between good and evil in many writings (e.g. Fragment of the Book of Noah 108:11–15; Test. Zebulun 9:8; Test. Levi 2:8–3:1; 1 Enoch 58:5f.; 2 Baruch 17:4–18:2; 48:50; 59:2).

None of these texts emphasizes the light-darkness *motif* as do the author(s) of 1QS 3:13ff. and the author of John. Moreover, the light-darkness *paradigm* is not found in the Old Testament Apocrypha and Pseudepigrapha,[113] but it is found in the Rule and John. In the Rule and John light symbolically represents life, truth, knowledge, and eternal life; conversely darkness represents death, falsehood, ignorance, and annihilation. This similarity between the Rule and John is impressive.

In both 1QS and John there is the emphasis that the righteous shall be rewarded with an everlasting reward (1QS 4:7f.; Jn 3:16, *et passim*), and the wicked shall not receive eternal punishment, as in Dan 12:2, but shall be destroyed (1QS 4:14; Jn 3:16; 8:21, 24). There is strong agreement regarding the results of the final judgment.

On the whole the similarities between John and the Rule appear to be outweighed by such distinct differences as earlier noted. That the differences should stand out is not of course surprising. John's theology has been transposed into quite another key than Qumran's theology: he believes that Jesus is the long-awaited Messiah. To take but one instance of the radical differences demanded by John's belief that Jesus is the Christ, we need only hold up the affirmation of Jn 3:16 against that of 1QS 3:6–8. "For by the Spirit of true counsel concerning the ways of man shall all his iniquities be expiated in order that he may behold the light of life. By the Holy Spirit of the community, in his truth, he will be purified from all his iniquities."

After full account is taken of all the dissimilarities in theological perspective, we must ask whether in the realm of symbolism and mythology there exists between John and the Rule an underlying

---

113 See the following chapter, especially notes 15 and 16. In Zurvanism light signifies wisdom and goodness, darkness connotes falsehood and evil. See Zaehner, *Zurvan*, 209f. Much of the light-darkness paradigm, therefore, was already found in Zurvanism. It was the author of 1QS 3:13ff., however, who promulgated the light-darkness paradigm, adding life and eternal life to light, and death and annihilation to darkness. Indeed, the Zurvanites may have denied the existence of rewards and punishments. See Zaehner, *Zurvan*, 23f.

interrelationship of conceptual framework and literary expression.[114]
We may reasonably hold that the dualistic opposition between light
and darkness is not something each developed independently, but
rather something that betokens John's dependence on the Rule.[115]

The probability of dependence is increased by the following
observations.[116] There are four literary formulae which show that
John was probably directly influenced by the terminology and ideology
in 1QS 3:13–4:26. Both these documents use the expressions "Spirit
of Truth" and "Holy Spirit". Moreover, both called the righteous "sons
of light". This observation is quite important precisely because the
expression "sons of light" is characteristic only of Qumran and John.[117]
This expression is found neither in the Old Testament Pseudepigrapha
nor in the Old Testament Apocrypha (and of course it is not found
in the Old Testament itself). This observation heightens the importance of the fact that in both texts the reward of the "sons of light"
is eternal, or perpetual life.[118] The four shared linguistic formulae
which suggest a strong correlation between John and 1QS 3:13–4:26
are the following:

1	*to pneuma tēs alētheias* "the Spirit of Truth" (Jn 14:17; 15:26; 16:13; and variant in 4:24)	1 *rwh 'mt* "Spirit of Truth" (3:18–19; 4:21, 23)
2	*to pneuma to hagion* "the Holy Spirit" (Jn 14:26; 20:22)	2 *brwh qwdš* "by the Spirit of Holiness" (or Holy Spirit) (4:21)
3	*huioi phōtos* "sons of light" (Jn 12:36)	3 *bny 'wr* "sons of light" (3:13, 24, 25)

---

[114] Another possible means by which one could examine the relation of John
to 1QS is to search for reactions against Qumranic beliefs. This method, however,
is too subjective and has not produced any convincing conclusions.

[115] P. Benoit argues that the technical terms "sons of light" and "sons of
darkness" perhaps were coined by the Teacher of Righteousness, that Paul's
expressions are closely parallel to the light-*versus*-darkness paradigm found in 1QS,
and that John's connection is even closer; see "Qumrân et le Nouveau Testament",
NTS 7 (1960–61) 276–96, especially 289–90; ET in *Paul and Qumran*, ed. J. Murphy-
O'Connor, O.P. (London, Chicago, 1968) 1–30.

[116] In the following discussion I have been influenced by W. F. Albright's and
F. M. Braun's observations found respectively in *The Background of the New
Testament and its Eschatology*, 168–9, and in "L'Arrière-fond judaïque du quatrième
évangile et la communauté de l'alliance", *RB* 62 (1955) 12.

[117] The expression is found in only two other New Testament passages: "for all
of you are sons of light and sons of (the) day" (1 Th 5:5); "the sons of light"
(Lk 16:8). The first is not found in a context which is similar to the mythology of
1QS but can be explained as resulting from Paul's imagery of the dawning
eschatological *day*. The second is peculiarly non-Lucan and appears to belong to
his sources.

[118] The minor difference between these two similar expressions seems to be due
to the difference between the terrestrial eschatology of Judaism and the transcend-
ental expectation of primitive Christianity.

4 *zōēn aiōnion*
   "eternal life"
   (Jn 3:15, 16, 36; 4:14, 36;
   5:24, 39; 6:27, 40, 47, 54, 68;
   10:28; 12:25, 50; 17:2, 3)

4 *bḥyy nṣḥ*
   "in perpetual life"
   (4:7)

The terminological and ideological relationship between 1QS
3:13–4:26 and the Gospel of John, which has been exposed by
the fact that they share four such literary formulae, increases in
extension, strength and depth with the observation that there are
seven additional shared literary expressions:

5 *to phōs tēs zōēs*
   "the light of life"
   (Jn 8:12)

5 *b'wr hḥyym*
   "in the light of life"
   (3:7)

6 *kai ho peripatōn en tē skotia*
   "and he who walks in the
   darkness"
   (Jn 12:35)
   ou mē peripatēsē en tē skotia
   "he will not walk in the darkness"
   (Jn 8:12)

6 *wbdrky ḥwšk ythlkw*
   "and they shall walk in the
   ways of darkness"
   (3:21)
   llkt bkwl drky ḥwšk
   "to walk in all the ways of
   darkness"
   (4:11)

7 *hē orgē tou theou*
   "the wrath of God"
   (Jn 3:36)

7 *b'p 'brt 'l nqmt*
   "by the furious wrath of the
   God of vengeance"
   (4:12)

8 *typhlōn ophthalmous*
   "the eyes of the blind"
   (Jn 10:21; see also Jn 9:1, 2,
   13, 17–20, 24, 25, 32, 39, 40,
   41; 11:37)

8 *'wrwn 'ynym*
   "blindness of eyes"
   (4:11)

9 *plērēs charitos*
   "full of grace"
   (Jn 1:14)

9 *brwb ḥsdw*
   "in the fulness of his grace"
   (4:4)
   wrwb hsdym
   "and the fulness of grace"
   (4:5)

10 *ta erga tou theou*
   "the works of God"
   (Jn 6:28; 9:3)

10 *m'śy 'l*
   "the works of God"
   (4:4)

11 *hoi anthrōpoi . . . ēn gar
   autōn ponēra ta erga*
   "the men . . . because their
   works were evil"
   (Jn 3:19)

11 *m'śy tw'bh*
   "the works of abomination"
   (4:10)
   kwl m'śy gbr
   "all the works of a man"
   (4:20)

Examples three, five, six, and eight of the shared linguistic formulae show the strong correlation between the application, meaning and importance of the light–darkness paradigm in both texts. Concerning example nine, it is important to observe that in 1QS 4:2–5 we find a reference to God's "abundant grace" combined with the task of the "Spirit of Truth" to enlighten the "sons of truth". In Jn 1:17 we find the statement that "grace and truth came through Jesus Christ" (also see Jn 1:14). The probability that John's pattern of thought was influenced by the pattern of thought recorded in 1QS 3:13ff. becomes more certain since in both texts "abundant grace" is conjoined not with the usual biblical correlative concepts "glory" (e.g. Ps. 84:11; Eph 1:6) or "favour" (e.g. Est 2:17; Gen 6:8ff.; 19:19) but with "truth". Finally, it is significant that in both texts "the works of God" are antithetic to "the works of a man".

It is important to note that these eleven literary expressions are not shared by John with a voluminous work, but with only one and a half columns of 1QS. Certainly, it is difficult to overlook the probability that John was directly influenced by the Rule. These similarities, however, are not close enough nor numerous enough to *prove* that John directly *copied* from 1QS. But on the other hand, they are much too close to conclude that John and 1QS merely evolved out of the same milieu. John may not have copied from 1QS but he was strongly influenced by the expressions and terminology of 1QS.[119] Indeed, there is no closer parallel to John's dualistic mythology either in contemporary or in earlier Jewish or Hellenistic literature.[120]

Conclusion

The conclusion to our critical analysis and comparison of the dualism in 1QS 3:13–4:26 and the "dualism" in John is that John did not borrow from the Essene cosmic and communal theology.[121]

[119] D. Flusser argues that there must be some connection between early Christianity and Qumran because in Pauline and Johannine theology the question of predestination is presented within a dualistic framework; see "The Dead Sea Sect and Pre-Pauline Christianity", *SH* 4 (1958) 220.

[120] Although the symbolism of light for the divine is found frequently in the writings of Philo of Alexandria, the light-*versus*-darkness paradigm is conspicuously absent. As a loyal Jew he probably borrowed this symbolism from the Old Testament (e.g. Ps 27:1, "The Lord is my light . . ."). See F.-N. Klein, *Die Lichtterminologie bei Philon von Alexandrien und in den Hermetischen Schriften* (Leiden, 1962). J. Daniélou argued that although Philo thought the Essenes represented the Jewish ideal, the dualism found in 1QS 3:13ff. is foreign to him since his angelology is not dualistic. However, one should observe Daniélou's remarks on the ideas, which are odd for Philo, found in *Quaestiones in Exodum*. *Philon d'Alexandrie* (Paris, 1958) 53–7. While M. Simon finds striking analogies between this text and the Qumranic teaching of the two spirits found in 1QS 3:13ff., he also notes important differences (e.g. the two powers have created the world in Philo's text). See Simon's comments in *Le Origini dello Gnosticismo*, 371–2. E. Bréhier has argued that Philo borrowed his angelology from the Greeks; see *Les idées philosophiques et religieuses de Philon d'Alexandrie*, 2nd ed. (Paris, 1950) 126–75.

[121] So H. Braun: "Dazu kommt der für den johanneischen Dualismus typische christologische und eschatologische Rahmen, und dieser Rahmen entfällt in Qumran ganz. . . . Daher wird man den johanneischen Dualismus aus Qumran nicht ableiten dürfen" ("Qumran und das Neue Testament", *TR* 28 (1962) 194). He holds the same position in his recent publication, *Qumran und das Neue Testament* (Tübingen, 1966) vol. 1, 98.

But this conclusion does not exhaust the possible relation between John and 1QS. We have seen that John has apparently been directly influenced by Essene terminology. Moreover, Qumranic concepts would have been refracted by the prism of John's originality and deep conviction that Jesus is the Messiah[122] so that potentially parallel concepts would be deflected.[123] It is precisely this prism effect that explains why there is no "Spirit of Perversity" in John, and why the term "perpetual life" appears, because of the cosmic dimension of Jesus' resurrection, as "eternal life". These observations lead me to conclude that John probably borrowed some of his dualistic terminology and mythology from 1QS 3 : 13–4 : 26.[124]

If the Rule is behind Johannine "dualism", then another conclusion appears obvious: it becomes more probable that the *Sitz im Leben* of John's traditions is Palestinian. This probability arises because to our present knowledge there is no evidence that 1QS was read outside Palestine.[125] Hence, in contrast to the contention that all we

[122] K. Schubert remarked, "One frequently has the impression that a Christology for Essenes is being presented here. Thus one of the most important results of Qumran research has been to prove the Jewish origin of the Gospel of John conclusively" (*The Dead Sea Community*, 152). J. Reuss, who has critically compared the Johannine writings with the Qumran scrolls, clearly agrees with K. Schubert's judgment. See his discussion in *Die Qumranfunde*, 114–19. According to our research, although the above observations tend to lead toward this judgment, there is not sufficient evidence to verify such categorical conclusions.

[123] Failure to appreciate this important perspective led H. M. Teeple to ask, "Why should anyone think that John is very Jewish when its use of Jewish terms is, unlike Qumran, so far from Jewish usage?" Furthermore, his conclusion that "The Gospel of John is full of evidence that the author was a Gentile Christian" misrepresents the evidence. See his article in *NT* 4 (1960) 24.

[124] Cf. H. M. Teeple, *NT* 4 (1960) 6–25; and F. C. Grant, *Ancient Judaism and the New Testament* (Edinburgh, 1960) 20: "To return to the Qumran scrolls for a moment, it is perfectly obvious to scholars familiar with the whole broad world of first century religion that the contacts between the Dead Sea Scrolls and the New Testament are few in number and not really fundamental to either literature." Our research shows that the contacts between the Dead Sea Scrolls and the New Testament are not insignificant but fundamental.

[125] Apart from the scrolls found in the eleven caves near Khirbet Qumran, Qumranic scrolls have been found only at Masada, which is less than 35 miles south of Qumran, and in Cairo, if one would allow that CD is Qumranic, as it certainly appears to be. However, if anyone is tempted to argue that the Essenes migrated to Egypt because copies of CD were found over seventy years ago in the *genizah* of a Cairo synagogue, he must overcome three formidable objections: the synagogue only dates from the ninth century, the fragments probably are later than the tenth century A.D., and P. E. Kahle has presented a strong argument for the probability that these fragments are to be linked with the manuscripts brought from the Qumranic caves to Jerusalem about the year 800, and only subsequently found their way to Cairo. See his *The Cairo Geniza*, 2nd ed. (Oxford, 1959) 16–17.

In attempting to say something about the geographical limits of the Essenes, one must consider the meaning of "Damascus" in CD. R. North contends that the "Damascus" of CD does not refer to the city by that name, but probably is an appellation for the Nabataean kingdom from 87 B.C. to A.D. 103; see "The Damascus of Qumran Geography", *PEQ* 87 (1955) 34–48. F. M. Cross, Jr, holds that "the 'land of Damascus' is 'the prophetic name' applied to the desert of Qumran" (*Ancient Library*, 59). A. Jaubert argued that "Damascus" meant the place of refuge where the spiritually exiled will renew the covenant, and in this sense the thesis that the "land of Damascus" represents the region of Qumran is acceptable; see "Le Pays de Damas", *RB* 65 (1958) 214–48. N. Wieder contended that it refers to the region of Lebanon and Anti-Lebanon where the prelude to the messianic drama would be enacted and the messianic kingdom inaugurated; see

can state is that we no longer have to look outside Palestine for the antecedents of Johannine theology,[126] it is increasingly more probable that we should look to Palestine for the milieu which gave birth to John. Of course this conclusion does not *prove* that John was *written* in Palestine. It is possible, for example (as Braun, Cullmann and Brown have speculated),[127] that the author of John was formerly a disciple of John the Baptist, who was indoctrinated in Essene thought, or that the author of this Gospel saw the Rule in Palestine, perhaps only through the vivid memory of an Essene who had become a Christian, made notes on its contents, perhaps only mental ones, and then composed his Gospel in Ephesus. However, it is more probably at the present time that John was written, perhaps only in a first draft, in Palestine.[128]

The Judean Scrolls and Karaism (London, 1962) 7–10. These investigations show, it seems to me, that "Damascus" is an essentially religious term for the region in which the Essenes lived. It is important to note, therefore, that Père R. de Vaux, the leading archaeological authority on the Qumran community, remarked that it is conceivable that the Qumran community lived in huts and tents scattered along the cliffs adjacent to Khirbet Qumran. See his comments both in *Les "Petites Grottes" de Qumrân* (DJD 3; Oxford, 1962) 35; and in *Bible et Orient* (Paris, 1967) 323. S. E. Johnson suggested that it is easy to imagine that members of the Qumran sect lived in Jerusalem. See his article in *The Scrolls and the New Testament*, ed. K. Stendahl (New York, 1957) 142. It seems obvious from CD 7:6–8 and 12:19–13:1 that there were Essene camps outside the community. It seems, therefore, that 1QS was read elsewhere besides the monastery at Qumran, but so far there is no evidence that it was read outside Palestine. Cf. L. Cerfaux's speculation that the disciples of John (Acts 18:25–19:4) in Ephesus may have possessed Qumranic literature; see "Influence de Qumrân sur le Nouveau Testament", *La secte de Qumrân et les origines du christianisme* (RechBib 4; Louvain, 1959) 243.

126 To name but two scholars involved in the attempt to understand the relation of the Qumran scrolls to the New Testament, we have chosen one of the earliest and one of the most recent commentaries. M. Burrows, *The Dead Sea Scrolls* (New York, 1956) 340. H. Braun, *Qumran und das Neue Testament*, vol. 1, 98: "Das freilich wird man ... sagen müssen: in Palästina *kann* der johanneische Dualismus entstanden sein . . . ."

127 F. M. Braun argued that the author of the Fourth Gospel, who may have been a disciple of Jesus, possibly borrowed directly from Qumran (*emprunts directs*), but probably received most of his Qumranic influence through the medium of John the Baptist, of whom he may have been a disciple before following Jesus; see *RB* 62 (1955) 5–44 and *Jean le théologien et son évangile dans l'église ancienne* (Paris, 1959) 310–19. It is interesting to note that in the same year (1955) O. Cullmann and R. E. Brown independently entertained the same possibility. See their articles in *The Scrolls and the New Testament*, ed. K. Stendahl, 24–5, 207. See Raymond Brown's chapter above, pp. 1ff., and W. H. Brownlee's below, pp. 166ff.

128 Among the numerous discoveries which have prompted this conclusion are the following: The discovery of Rylands Greek Papyrus 457 and Egerton Papyrus 2 has shown that the composition of the Fourth Gospel can no longer be dated after A.D. 125. Other studies have increased the probability that the Johannine traditions betray Qumranic influences: of these studies the most noteworthy are A. Jaubert's contention that the Johannine tradition, which records that Jesus was crucified while official Judaism was sacrificing the paschal lambs, is vindicated by the observation that the Last Supper was held according to the Qumranic calendar; see her chapter above, pp. 62ff., and see also her book *The Date of the Last Supper* (Staten Island, N.Y., 1965), and J. de Waard's argument that the quotations found in Jn 12:40 and 13:18 are closer to the Old Testament text found at Qumran than they are to the Masoretic Text or to the Septuagint, in *A Comparative Study of the Old Testament Text in the Dead Sea Scrolls and in the New Testament* (STDJ 4; Leiden, 1965). Also compare E. D. Freed, *Old Testament Quotations in the Gospel of John* (NovTSup 11; Leiden, 1965) 122–3.

Professor Dodd has argued that "behind the Fourth Gospel lies an ancient tradition independent of the other gospels, and meriting serious consideration as a contribution to our knowledge of the historical facts concerning Jesus Christ"; see *Historical Tradition in the Fourth Gospel* (Cambridge, 1963) 423. A. J. B. Higgins has recently contended that "there is a certain amount of evidence that Jesus did not only speak as the synoptics report him to have done, but also used 'Johannine' phraseology and ideas"; see "The Words of Jesus According to St John", *BJRL* 49 (1967) 384.

Evidence has been disclosed that the Fourth Gospel is impressively familiar with the topography of Jerusalem and southern Palestine. See Albright's article in *The Background of the New Testament and its Eschatology*, 158–60; Dodd's comments in *Historical Tradition*, 244–5; and R. E. Brown's judgments in *The Gospel According to John (I–XII)*, xlii–xliii.

Of the attempts to show that an Aramaic source lies behind some of the Johannine traditions, certainly the most important is the perspicacious research of M. Black, *An Aramaic Approach to the Gospels and Acts*, 3rd ed. (Oxford, 1967) especially 272–4. Principal Black's judgments, which date from before the discovery of the Dead Sea Scrolls, have been supported by three separate discoveries: In Qumran cave 1 an important Aramaic document was found which dates from the time of Jesus; see E. Y. Kutscher's critical remarks in "The Language of the 'Genesis Apocryphon': A Preliminary Study", *SH* 4 (1958) 1–35. On Mt Olivet Aramaic ossuaries were unearthed which predate the Jewish War; see P. B. Bagatti and J. T. Milik, *Gli Scavi del "Dominus Flevit"* (Jerusalem, 1958) part 1, 70–109. Nine of the fifteen letters written in the time of the Bar Kochba revolt (A.D. 132–135), which Y. Yadin discovered in 1960, were written in Aramaic; see Y. Yadin, "More on the Letters of Bar Kochba", *BA* 24 (1961) 86–95. Also see H. Bardtke, *Die Handschriftenfunde in der Wüste Juda* (Berlin, 1962). Hence, it is no longer a pure conjecture but an established fact that Aramaic was both spoken and written by the Palestinian Jew during the first two Christian centuries.

Finally, John is strikingly close in terms of Christology, terminology and ideology to the Odes of Solomon, which is probably a late first-century Jewish-Christian hymn book; see the following chapter.

6

Qumran, John and the
Odes of Solomon

JAMES H. CHARLESWORTH

The chapters in this book show that John is influenced by Essene thought. There has been no question that John and the Odes are conceptually related; the question concerns the direction of influence. Recent research discloses that the Odes are indebted in many ways to the Essenes.[1] It is therefore appropriate to search for the relationship between Qumran, John and the Odes. Since dualistic thought[2] is found in each of these, and since the relationship between John and Qumran and also between the Odes and Qumran is most impressively evident when comparison is followed along the lines of dualism, it is wise to limit our present concern to an examination and comparison of the dualism found in these ancient manuscripts.

The development of the chapter is as follows. First, Qumran's dualism, John's "dualism" and Odes' "dualism" will be analysed separately. Second, the relationship between the Odes' and John's "dualism", the correlation between the Odes' "dualism" and Qumran's dualism, the comparison between John's "dualism" and Qumran's dualism, and the relationships among the "dualisms" in the Odes, in John, and in the Qumran Scrolls will be discussed consecutively. Third, the broader consequences obtained from this research will be organized as conclusions in retrospect and prospect.

The breadth of the subject and the brevity of this chapter demand that the remarks be merely programmatic. Our eyes will be focussed upon the texts, hence consideration of recent publications will be kept to a minimum.

---

[1] J. Carmignac, "Les affinités qumrâniennes de la onzième Ode de Salomon", *RevQ* 3 (1961) 71–102. J. Carmignac, "Un qumrânien converti au christianisme: l'auteur des Odes de Salomon", *Qumran-Probleme*, ed. H. Bardtke (Deutsche Akademie der Wissenschaften zu Berlin, Schriften der Sektion für Altertumswissenschaft 42; Berlin, 1963) 75–108. F. M. Braun, "L'énigme des Odes de Salomon", *RTh* 57 (1957) 597–625 [republished in *Jean le théologien et son évangile dans l'Église ancienne* (Paris, 1959) 224-59]. J. Charlesworth, "Les Odes de Salomon et les manuscrits de la Mer Morte", *RB* 77 (1970) 522–49.

[2] Definitions for the types of dualism mentioned herein may be found in the first footnote to the preceding chapter.

1. *Analyses*

The following analyses and comparisons are built upon conclusions obtained elsewhere. Most important of these are the following:

(1) The Dead Sea Scrolls antedate both John and the Odes and are Essene.[3]

(2) The extant Gospel attributed to John, herein abbreviated as John, was originally composed in Greek from numerous sources, some of which were Aramaic.[4]

[3] This conclusion is held by most scholars. See for example M. Black, *The Essene Problem* (London, 1961). The two major dissenting voices are G. R. Driver and S. Zeitlin. Rejecting the usual inferences from the archaeological (see especially p. 398) and palaeographical (see especially p. 416) data, G. R. Driver claims that the authors of the Scrolls should be identified with the Zealots. *The Judaean Scrolls* (Oxford, 1965) 75, 106–21, 237–51. Further, he dates the major scrolls between A.D. 46 and 132 (p. 373). Although Driver is exceedingly erudite, his hypotheses are highly improbable. See R. de Vaux, O.P., "Esséniens ou Zélotes? A propos d'un livre récent", *RB* 73 (1966) 212–35. For an English version of part of this article and one by M. Black on Driver's book see *NTS* 13 (1966–67) 81–104.

S. Zeitlin's position is even more extreme and untenable. He claims that the Scrolls are written by a fringe group of the Karaites in the Middle Ages. S. Zeitlin, *The Dead Sea Scrolls and Modern Scholarship* (Philadelphia, 1956). His articles are found in *The Jewish Quarterly Review*, of which the latest is "The Dead Sea Scrolls: Journalists and Dilettanti", *JQR* 60 (July, 1969) 75–9. Also see his "The Slavonic Josephus and the Dead Sea Scrolls: An Exposé of Recent Fairy Tales", *JQR* 58 (1968) 173–203. It is significant that an authority on Karaism, N. Wieder, argues that on purely theological grounds alone (dualistic world-view, predestination) it is extremely unlikely that the Qumran documents emanate from Karaite circles; *The Judean Scrolls and Karaism* (London, 1962) 253.

Under the influence of Driver's hypothesis Principal Black has qualified his position that the sect should be identified with the Essenes. He now holds that "the Essene group who held the fort at Qumran at the outbreak of the First Revolt" had "thrown in their lot with Zealot and Pharisaic groups"; *The Dead Sea Scrolls and Christian Doctrine* (London, 1966) 4. The men who had composed the Scrolls would still have been Essenes; hence, I prefer to agree with F. M. Cross, Jr, who has reaffirmed his earlier opinion that the men of Qumran were Essenes. See his "The Early History of the Qumran Community", *McCormick Quarterly* 21 (1968) 254.

[4] This position is held by most scholars. For the most recent publications, see especially the following: M. Black, *An Aramaic Approach to the Gospels and Acts*, third edition (Oxford, 1967) especially 75ff., 149–51. M. Black, "Aramaic Studies and the Language of Jesus", *In Memoriam Paul Kahle*, ed. M. Black and G. Fohrer (Berlin, 1968) 17–28. M. Black, "The 'Son of Man' Passion Sayings in the Gospel Tradition", *ZNW* 60 (1969) 1–8. S. Brown, S.J., "From Burney to Black: The Fourth Gospel and the Aramaic Question", *CBQ* 26 (1964) 323–39. H. Ott, "Um die Muttersprache Jesu: Forschungen seit Gustaf Dalman", *NT* 9 (1967) 1–25. M. Wilcox, "The Composition of John 13:21–30", *Neotestamentica et Semitica: Studies in Honour of Matthew Black*, ed. E. E. Ellis and M. Wilcox (Edinburgh, 1969) 143–56. R. E. Brown, S.S., *The Gospel According to John (i–xii)* (Anchor Bible 29; Garden City, New York, 1966; London, 1971) xxiv–xl, cxxix–cxxxvii.
There is presently keen interest in recovering the sources behind the Fourth Gospel. Two recent attempts are to be noted. R. Fortna, *The Gospel of Signs: A Reconstruction of the Narrative Source Underlying the Fourth Gospel* (SNTS Monograph Series 11; Cambridge, 1970). Also see his more recent article, "Source and Redaction in the Fourth Gospel's Portrayal of Jesus' Signs", *JBL* 89 (June, 1970) 151–66. The second recent attempt to diagnose the strata in the Fourth Gospel will be presented by E. Haenchen in his forthcoming commentary on John. Some of his ideas regarding the Evangelist's sources are conveniently collected in his *Gott und Mensch: Gesammelte Aufsätze* (Tübingen, 1965) and *Die Bibel und Wir* (Tübingen, 1968).

(3) The Odes of Solomon were originally composed in Syriac and are contemporaneous with John; both were composed around A.D. 100.[5]

QUMRAN'S DUALISM

It is well known that the Dead Sea Scrolls are characterized by dualism. In the preceding chapter discussion was limited to the treatise concerning the two Spirits (1QS 3:13–4:26). In the following examination we will attempt to see to what extent the features of this dualism are contained or modified in the major sectarian scrolls.

Putting aside for the moment the question of the development of dualism in Qumran theology,[6] it is necessary to emphasize that dualism appears in each of the major sectarian Scrolls. Observe the following representative excerpts:[7]

And to love all the sons of light,
 each according to his lot in the plan of God;
And to hate all the sons of darkness,
 each according to his guilt in the vengeance of God.

(1QS 1:9–11)

And He (The God of Knowledge) appointed
for him (man) two Spirits
in order that he should walk in them until
the time of His visitation;
they are the Spirits of Truth and Falsehood.

(1QS 3:18–19)

And then at the time of Judgment the sword of God will act quickly,
And all the sons of His tr[u]th shall be roused
to [destroy the sons of] wickedness;
And all the sons of iniquity shall be no more.

(1QH 6:29–30)

For in proportion to the Spirits
[Thou hast divi]ded them (men)
between good and evil.

(1QH 14:11–12)

---

[5] The date given to John is the one accepted by most scholars. That is the date of the extant Fourth Gospel. For the date attributed to the Odes see my *The Odes of Solomon* (Oxford, in preparation).

[6] Obviously this is not the place to discuss the date of composition for the instruction concerning two Spirits (1QS 3:13–4:26) or for portions thereof (especially 1QS 3:13–4:14). P. von der Osten-Sacken (*Gott und Belial: Traditionsgeschichtliche Untersuchungen zum Dualismus in den Texten aus Qumran*, SUNT 6; Göttingen, 1969) and J. Murphy-O'Connor, O.P. ("La genèse littéraire de la Règle de la Communauté", *RB* 76 (1969) 528–49) conclude their minute examinations by the contention that 1QS 3:13–4:26 is a later addition to the Rule. However, see also the position of A.-M. Denis, O.P., "évolution de structures dans la secte de Qumrân", *Aux Origines de l'Eglise* (RechBib 7; Louvain, 1965) 23–49.

[7] Unless otherwise noted, all translations are by the author.

For formerly Moses and Aaron arose
by the hand of the Prince of Lights;
but Belial raised Jannes and his brother,. . . .

(CD 5 : 17–19)

And no one who has entered the Covenant of God shall
take from or give to the sons of the Pit
except[8] through trade.

(CD 13 : 14–15)

. . . the war, The beginning is when the
sons of light stretch forth their hand in order
to begin against the lot of the sons of darkness. . . .

(1QM 1 : 1)

And Thou hast assigned us to the lot of light
for Thy truth. And from of old Thou
didst appoint the Prince of Light
to help us. . . .
And Thou didst make Belial, the
Angel of Hatred, to corrupt, his dominion is
in darkness.

(1QM 13 : 9–11)

The above excerpts from the Scrolls display Qumran's dualism. It was not an absolute dualism, however, because it was subsequent to, inferior to and dependent upon an overriding and fervent monotheism. As we look back at the above excerpts we note that according to 1QS 3 : 18–19 the "two Spirits" are under God's appointment and are to perform their functions only as long as he wills it ("until the time of his visitation; . . ."). Monotheism dominates the dualism found not only in the Rule but also in the other major sectarian Scrolls (see 1QH 1 : 1–20; CD 2 : 2–13; 1QM 1 : 8–14). The first characteristic feature of Qumran dualism is that it is limited in power, extent and time.

In these Scrolls we find the belief in two warring cosmic Spirits. In the Rule they are called by various names, the "Prince of Light" and the "Spirit of Truth" vis-à-vis the "Angel of Darkness" and the "Spirit of Perversity". In the Hodayoth several passages refer to the idea that there are two ruling Spirits, one evil, the other good (1QH 1 : 9, 17ff.; 4 : 31; 7 : 6–7; 11 : 12–13; 14 : 11–12; 16 : 9ff.; 17 : 23ff.). In the Damascus Document and the War Scroll the war rages between the "Prince of Lights" [or Light] (CD 5 : 18; 1QM 13 : 10)[9] and Belial (CD 4 : 13, 15 et passim; 1QM 1 : 1, 5, 13 et passim)

8 The Hebrew literally means "except hand for hand". The idiom clearly means that the member of the covenant of God must receive payment for what he gives and pay for what he receives.

9 H. Ringgren argues that in 1QM 13 : 2–4, "it is not a question of two spirits under God's supremacy but of God and Belial"; see *The Faith of Qumran: Theology of the Dead Sea Scrolls* (Philadelphia, 1963) 75 [an English translation of *Tro och liv enligt Döda-havsrullarna* (Stockholm, 1961)]. It would not be wise to build too much on the observation that the Levites (*et al.*) bless God but curse Belial. The "Prince of Light" is not mentioned in lines 2–4; however, it is appropriate to praise not the messenger from God but God himself.

and the "Angels of Destruction (Corruption)" (CD 2:6; 1QM 13:12). Behind the diversity of terminology lies the belief that the world is ripped into two realms by two warring, cosmic Spirits. This is the second characteristic of Qumran dualism.

Under the sheer brilliance of the dualism promulgated in 1QS 3:13–4:26 we often have the impression that Essene dualism is a system in which there are two warring Spirits, distinguished and separated by their identification either with light or with darkness. In fact J. Daniélou remarks that "the conflict between light and darkness ... is nothing else but the *leitmotif* of Qumran".[10] The remark is somewhat misleading because the Rule's dualism has been read into other documents. The Hodayoth do not contain the expression *bny 'wr*, "sons of light", or the term *bny ḥwšk*, "sons of darkness", nor do they have the phrase Prince, Angel or Spirit of Light. The Qumranic Damascus Document does not contain the word *ḥwšk*, "darkness". The light-darkness paradigm,[11] therefore, is not always the typical feature of Qumran dualism.

The omission of the terminology in the Hodayoth probably results from the focus of the speaker. The words are directed not to man's situation but to God. The speaker apparently assumes the light-darkness paradigm: "... and my light shines in Thy glory. For Thou hast caused the light to shine out of darkness ..." (1QH 9:26–27). The first two lines of the final column of the Hodayoth begin with the expression "Thy light". The author then confesses, "For with Thee is light ..." (1QH 18:3).

The observation that *ḥwšk* is not found in the Damascus Document should be combined with the recognition that in this same scroll we read that "the Prince of Lights" (CD 5:18) is opposed by "Belial" (CD 5:18). Since the noun Belial abounds in this Scroll (6 times) and since the composition is clearly later than the earliest portions of the Rule, it is possible that Belial was a frequent substitute by the *later* sectarians for the "Angel of Darkness". The possibility is strengthened by the observation that Belial is a favourite expression in the War Scroll (12 times), which is the latest of the major sectarian Scrolls. Further corroborative evidence is that the term Belial is found only in the preface (1QS 1:18, 24; 2:5, 19) and concluding hymn (1QS 10:21) of the Rule;[12] and these sections are dated by J. Murphy-O'Connor to approximately the same date: "The setting in life of the final hymn in 1QS is the same as that of 1QS 1:16–2:25a".[13] The time when these additions were made to the Rule corresponds approximately to the date of composition for the Dasmascus Document.

10 J. Daniélou, *The Dead Sea Scrolls and Primitive Christianity* (New York, Toronto, London, 1958) 107.

11 The light-darkness paradigm means more than that there is a dualism sometimes expressed in terms of light and darkness. It signifies that there are two opposites primarily described as light (which symbolically represents life, truth, knowledge and eternal life) or darkness (which tends to represent death, falsehood, ignorance and extinction).

12 "Belial" in 1QS 10:21 does not denote the cosmic evil Spirit. This observation alone, however, is not sufficient to place the hymn in the time of the Teacher of Righteousness.

13 J. Murphy-O'Connor, *RB* 76 (1969) 545.

What are we to say about the use of Belial in the Hodayoth, where it is also frequent (12 times)? Since the substitution of Belial for the "Angel of Darkness" would necessitate the cosmic conception of the former, we must ask another question: Is Belial conceived of as a hypostatic individual in the Hodayoth? Only in four passages does this term probably have a cosmic dimension (1QH 2:22; 3:28; 3:29; 3:32); in the other eight occurrences it has a non-cosmic or psychological meaning (1QH 2:16; 4:10; 4:13 [*bis*]; 5:26; 5:39; 6:21; 7:3). It is impressive to discover that each one of the latter group of passages is taken from sections that G. Jeremias has attributed to the Teacher of Righteousness.[14] The passages containing a cosmic meaning probably come from later stages in the life of the community. Moreover, in his *Konkordanz* Kuhn reports that the word Belial as *nomen proprium* does not appear in the Hodayoth (*q.v. ad loc.*). The evidence seems to converge towards the supposition that Belial as a synonym for the "Angel of Darkness" is peculiar to the later texts. By the time the Damascus Document was composed, "Belial" had become a surrogate for the "Angel of Darkness". The absence of the word "darkness" in this Scroll is not as stunning as formerly supposed.

We may now conclude our discussion of the light-darkness paradigm in the Scrolls. While the paradigm is not emphasized in each of the major sectarian documents, it is nevertheless characteristic of the Scrolls as a collection. This schema is so sophisticated in the Scrolls as to distinguish them from most literature with which they were contemporaneous.[15] The lone exception is the Testaments of the Twelve Patriarchs.[16] This document, however, may come from

---

[14] *Der Lehrer der Gerechtigkeit* (SUNT 2; Göttingen, 1963). G. Jeremias argues that in the Hodayoth "Belial" means "Bosheit, Ränke, nicht der Eigenname des göttlichen Gegenspielers..." (*Der Lehrer*, 194). M. Delcor also remarks, "Ce terme y sert à désigner des personnes ou des êtres mauvais ou qui veulent du mal, mais non le Démon lui-même" (*Les Hymnes de Qumran (Hodayot)* (Paris, 1962) 44; also see 37 and 185f.).

[15] This is certainly not the place to discuss the concepts of light and darkness in the intertestamental literature. Suffice it to state that in this literature "darkness" is not always portrayed as something intrinsically bad: for example in the Song of the Three Children (v. 48) light and darkness are exhorted to bless and praise the Lord. The authors of the Scrolls, Odes and John would never have conceived such an exhortation for darkness. The light-darkness paradigm is also not found in the rabbinic literature. It may, however, be behind some portions of the Ethiopic Book of Enoch (e.g. 58:3ff., 92:4ff.). The uniqueness of the light-darkness paradigm to Qumran (in contrast to other sects of pre-Christian Judaism) has recently been intimated by H. Kosmala: "Previous to the discovery of the Dead Sea Scrolls such expressions as 'the children of light', 'light' and 'darkness', 'enlightened', and many, many others were thought to be exclusively terms of the theological language of the New Testament and early Christian literature" ("The Parable of the Unjust Steward in the Light of Qumran", *Annual of the Swedish Theological Institute*, ed. H. Kosmala (Leiden, 1964) vol. 3, 114–21; the quotation is from p. 115). F. Nötscher discusses some of the peculiarities of Qumran's dualism in his *Zur theologischen Terminologie der Qumran-Texte* (BBB 10; Bonn, 1956) 103–48.

[16] E.g. Test. Levi 19:1–2, "choose... either the light or the darkness, either the law of the Lord or the works of Beliar" (cf. Test. Naphtali 2:7–10); Test. Joseph 20:2, "the Lord shall be with you in light, and Beliar shall be in darkness with the Egyptians." Even in the Testaments of the Twelve Patriarchs, as F. Nötscher and O. Böcher observed, the paradigm is not combined with the idea that there are two ways, which appears only once (Test. Asher 1:3–5); see *Zur theologischen Terminologie*, 114; *Der johanneische Dualismus*, 97, also see 96–101, 15.

Essene circles. Therefore the third characteristic of Qumran dualism is the light-darkness paradigm.

Pervading the Scrolls, as is well known, is the Essenes' belief that they were living in the last days, the future had irrupted into the present.[17] At times the Scrolls suggest that the post-biblical Jewish division of time between "this age" and "the age to come" had clearly dissolved. Often the Essene projects himself into the future and speaks as if the end has already come (1QH 3:23-36). At other times the Scrolls uphold a division within time. According to P. von der Osten-Sacken, the oldest form of Qumran dualism, found in the War Scroll and the first section of the Rule (1QS 3:13-4:14), emphasizes the imminent eschatological combat (*Endkampfdualismus*).[18] The decisive eschatological act still lay in the future. At the end of the impending conflict the "sons of light" will receive "every continuing blessing and eternal joy in eternal life, and a crown of glory with a garment of majesty in eternal light" (1QS 4:7-8; cf. 1QH 9:25). The "sons of darkness", however, will be annihilated "until they are exterminated without remnant or escape" (1QS 4:14; cf. 1QM 1:4-7). The fourth characteristic of Qumran dualism, therefore, is the eschatological dimension.

Each of the major sectarian Scrolls contains the idea that mankind is bifurcated into two mutually exclusive camps. Although the terminology changes, the dualism is clear and men are categorized either as "sons of light" (1QS and 1QM), "sons of truth" (1QS, 1QH and 1QM), "sons of Zadok" (1QS and CD) or as "sons of darkness" (1QS and 1QM), "sons of perversity" (1QS and 1QH), and "sons of the Pit" (CD). Since men are divided according to their virtues and vices, we have running through the Scrolls an ethical dualism. This is the fifth characteristic of Qumran dualism.

The ethical dualism is usually expressed in terms of preordination. Note the predestinarian strain in the following excerpts: "From the God of Knowledge comes all that is and will be, and before (things) were He established their complete design. And when they exist they fulfill their work according to their assignments[19] and His glorious plan" (1QS 3:15f.). "And in all of them He raised up for Himself those called by name that a remnant might be left for the land, ... But those whom He hated He caused to err" (CD 2:11-13). "And Thou hast cast upon man an eternal lot..." (1QH 3:22; 15:13-21). "And Thou hast caused us to fall into the lot of light for Thy truth. And from former times Thou didst appoint the Prince of Light to

A succinct comparison of the dualism contained in the Testaments of the Twelve Patriarchs with that in the Scrolls is found in P. von der Osten-Sacken, *Gott und Belial*, 197-205. Although Jubilees contains dualistic thought (e.g. "sons of perdition" [10:3]—"sons of the righteous" [10:6]), it does not contain the light-darkness paradigm.

[17] The point is developed with erudition in a recent monograph: H.-W. Kuhn, *Enderwartung und gegenwärtiges Heil* (SUNT 4; Göttingen, 1966). J. Carmignac has seriously questioned the appropriateness of the term "eschatology". See his "La notion d'eschatologie dans la Bible et à Qumrân", *RevQ* 7 (1969) 17-31.

[18] P. von der Osten-Sacken, *Gott und Belial*.

[19] H. Ringgren argues that *lt'wdwtm* means "according to His predestination"; see *The Faith of Qumran*, 53f.

help us,... And Thou didst make Belial to corrupt..."[20] (1QM
13:9–11). Other passages suggest the possibility of conversion from
sin ("to pardon them that return from sin": CD 2:5; cf. 1QS 10:20;
1QH 2:9; 6:6; 14:24), others attribute man's fate not to God's foreordination but to his foreknowledge ("For God did not choose them
from the beginning, and before they were established He knew their
works": CD 2:7–8),[21] but these ideas are exceptions. There is wide
agreement today that the authors of the Scrolls held a dualism that
contained predestinarian features.[22] This is the sixth characteristic of
Qumran dualism.

The most conspicuous feature of Qumran dualism is the ethical. The
cosmic struggle centres in the heart of man. Synonyms for the "sons of
light" and "sons of darkness" are respectively the "sons of righeous-
ness" and "sons of perversity". The pervasive eschatological tone of
the Scrolls clarifies the results of ethical dualism: eternal life for the
"sons of piety" (1QH 7:20), extinction for the "sons of transgression"
(1QH 5:7; 6:30; 7:11). Man's lot is predetermined. In summation,
mankind is divided not according to metaphysical but ethical categories.

JOHN'S "DUALISM"

In the following discussion we may conveniently summarize the results
of the analysis presented in the preceding chapter, and add only a few
new observations. In the following paragraphs it should become
evident that the most systematic dualism in the New Testament is
found in John.

A cosmic dualism is assumed by the author of John, not in the
sense of two opposing celestial spirits, but in the sense of two distinct
and present divisions in the universe. The universe is bifurcated into
the "world above", which is the source of all things, especially power
(1:3, 10; 19:11), and the "world below", which hates the "world
above" (7:7) and is similar in meaning to *kosmos,* which is an inferior
and vulgar force in rebellion against God. The cosmic dualism is
modified since the two worlds are not two equal and eternal concepts.
The "world below" is limited in quality and quantity: "And he (Jesus)
said to them (the Jews), 'You are from below, I am from above. You
are from this world, I am not from this world. Therefore, I declared
to you that you will die in your sins' " (8:23f., cf. 6:48–51, 58; 4:13–
14; 3:3ff., 31; 11:41; 19:11). The first characteristic of John's "dual-

[20] This idea frees Belial of responsibility for his sins. For a defence of the
translation see pp. 80ff. above.

[21] E. Cothenet entitles the section CD 2:2–13 "Prédestination des Justes et des
Impies" in *Les Textes de Qumran (II)* (Paris, 1963) 152. According to our interpretation the heading is misleading because *some* verses in the section intimate
foreknowledge not foreordination.

The omission of the word *ḥwšk* and the presence of passages that are not
"predestinarian" have led me to entertain the idea that CD was not directed to
those in the community. This idea is now developed by J. Murphy-O'Connor,
"An Essene Missionary Document? CD II, 14–VI, 1", *RB* 77 (1970) 201–29.

[22] Contrast A. Marx who argues that when talking about the Scrolls we ought
to avoid "le terme de 'prédestination' et de parler tout simplement de grâce!"
("Y a-t-il une prédestination à Qumrân?", *RevQ* 6 (1967) 163–81; the quotation
is from p. 181).

ism", therefore, is a modified cosmic dualism between the "world above" and the "world below".

Each world exhibits a force. From above the force is Christ, from below it is the *kosmos*. The main actors in the drama are Jesus and the Jews. Hence, while there is no metaphysical dualism (i.e., God is not opposed by an evil angel), there is a cosmic struggle between Jesus Christ and the *kosmos* (=the Jews). Since Jesus represents[23] God (5:36ff.; 12:50) and since the Jews symbolize the Devil (8:44) we are justified in calling this aspect of John's "dualism" an extremely modified metaphysical dualism.[24] This is the second characteristic of John's "dualism".

Pervading John's "dualism" is the light-darkness paradigm; his penchant for "light" and "darkness" distinguishes him from the other evangelists.[25] He uses the word "light" more than three times as much as either Matthew or Luke, and 23 times more than Mark (*phōs*, "light": Mt-7/Mk-1/Lk-7/Jn-23).[26] His application of the word "darkness" is slightly more frequent than the other evangelists, but his use of *skotia* to designate "darkness" is unique (Mt-2/Mk-0/Lk-1/Jn-8). The "world above" and the "world below" are respectively categorized by "light" and "darkness". All men are in darkness; however, the appearance of light brought judgment: "But this is the judgment: although light came into the world men loved *darkness* rather than *light*, because their deeds were evil" (3:19, italics mine). Ironically, judgment resulted from God's attempt to save man, since the appearance of Christ, "the light of the world" (8:12; 9:5) was for man's benefit: "I have come as *light* into the world, that whoever believes in me may not remain in *darkness*" (12:46, italics mine). Mankind, therefore, is bifurcated into two categories: on one side there is light, which is associated with belief (12:35f.), truth (3:21; 8:31f.), life (1:4; 8:12), and knowledge (1:9f.); on the other is darkness, which is linked primarily with evil (3:19f.) and ignorance (1:5; 12:35). He who does not believe "walks in the darkness" (12:35); he who follows Jesus "will not walk in *darkness*, but will have the *light* of life" (8:12, italics mine). John's cosmological and soteriological dualism, discussed below, are couched in terms of the light-darkness paradigm. This is the third characteristic of John's "dualism".

An important feature of John's "dualism" is the division of eschatology into the future that has broken into the present and the

---

23 Jesus is sent from God; it is not Jesus alone who speaks but God speaking through him, not Jesus himself who heals the sick but God's power manifest in and through him. The concept of Jesus as one sent and its relationship to the Old Testament and gnostic literature is now presented by J. Kuhl, *Die Sendung Jesu und der Kirche nach dem Johannes-Evangelium* (SIMSVD 11; Siegburg, Washington, 1967).

24 Some verses reflect the idea that Jesus has already fought and defeated the devil (e.g. 12:31; 16:33).

25 So also P. H. Bakotin, O.F.M., *De notione lucis et tenebrarum in Evangelio S. Joannis* (Croatia, Dubrovnik, 1943) and F. Nötscher, *Zur theologischen Terminologie*, 123.

26 For these statistics I am indebted to R. Morgenthaler, *Statistik des neutestamentlichen Wortschatzes* (Zürich, 1958) *loc. cit.* Also see R. E. Brown, S.S., *The Gospel According to John*, vol. 1, 515–16.

E

future that is about to break into the present. Like a cascading water-fall time has rushed on, leaving behind men who cling to a past revelation, the Law (1:17), and sweeping with it those who grasp the present revelation, Jesus (1:17; 8:12). John's realizing eschatology is the logical result of his Christology, the hour has come (12:23), the Devil is defeated (12:31; 16:11), Christ has overcome the world (16:33). In John, therefore, the distinct eschatological dualism between the present time and a future awaited day (the distinction between "this age" and "the age to come") has become modified.[27] Those who belong to the light have eternal life (3:16);[28] those who are of the darkness shall be destroyed (3:16, 18). This modified eschatological dualism is the fourth characteristic.

Although mankind is not initially divided into two mutually exclusive categories, an individual's response to Jesus' call for faith categorizes him either as "from God" (8:47; cf. "children of God" in 1:12) or "not from God" (8:47). After the invitation to believe, a man is categorized by his response; he is either "one who believes" (3:16; 12:36) or "one who does not believe" (3:18). The fifth characteristic of John's "dualism", therefore, is a soteriological dualism.

Consistent with his soteriology is John's insistence upon man's ability to choose.[29] While some passages tend to suggest preordination (1:12ff.; 6:37-45), the main thrust in John is that the invitation to believe is sent to *all* men: "For God so loved the world that he gave his only son, so that *everyone who believes in him* may not perish but have life eternal" (3:16, italics mine). Christ's death on the cross was not for an elect group alone, but for all men: "when I am lifted up from the earth, I will draw all men to myself" (12:32). Man's ability to choose is the sixth characteristic of John's "dualism".

The most important characteristic of Johannine "dualism" is the soteriological.[30] Pervading the Gospel is the emphasis upon the result of acceptance or rejection of Jesus Christ. John conceived of everything either being for or against Christ, in light or darkness, truth or

---

[27] There are exceptions posed by Jn 5:28-29; 6:39, 40, 44, 51c-58; and 12:48. For a discussion of these see pp. 93-4 above.

[28] S. Vitalini correctly notes that for John the reception of light signifies participation in "la vita divina" and the presence of eternal life; see *La nozione d'accoglienza nel Nuovo Testamento* (Studia Friburgensia, N.S. 35; Fribourg, 1963) 68-9.

[29] Contrast E. Käsemann's recent claim that for John faith is restricted to the elect: "To decide in favour of Jesus is a divine gift and possible only for the elect." This interpretation became possible because Jn 3:16 was judged to have come not from the Evangelist himself but from a "traditional primitive Christian formula", which was employed solely "to stress the glory of Jesus' mission, that is to say the miracle of the incarnation"; see *The Testament of Jesus: A Study of the Gospel of John in the Light of Chapter 17* (Philadelphia, London, 1968) 64, 60. It is quite likely, however, that Jn 3:16 is from the Evangelist; 3:1-21 is a well-organized discourse. So also R. E. Brown, S.S., *The Gospel According to John*, vol. 1, 136-7, 147.

[30] Perhaps this is what E. Käsemann meant when he declared that "The Johannine dualism marks the effect of the Word in that world in which the light has always shone into the darkness. . . . The decisions for or against the Word constantly take place on an earth which has already been separated into two hostile spheres through the event of the Word" (*The Testament of Jesus*, p. 63). Cf. A. Wikenhauser, *Das Evangelium nach Johannes*, 3rd ed. (Regensburger Neues Testament 4; Regensburg, 1961) 176.

error, righteousness or sin, life or death. Though cosmic dualism did
not originate from his soteriological dualism, it was reminted and
coloured by it. Everything is transposed into a higher key because of
the arrival of the promised *Sōtēr,* "Saviour"; hence the essential "dualism" is soteriological.

"DUALISM" IN THE ODES

Unlike the Scrolls and John, the Odes of Solomon have not been examined for their dualism. A cursory reading of the Odes would probably give the impression that there is relatively little, if any, dualism
in them. In the following pages we shall see that the Odes contain
a dualism, even if it is subdued.

Like the Scrolls and John the Odes are monotheistic. There is one
Creator upon whom all creatures and created things are dependent.
In Ode 4:15 we read, "And Thou, O Lord, hast made all". In
Ode 6:3-5 the Odist wrote the following:

For He (the Spirit of the Lord) destroys whatever is alien,
And everything is of the Lord.

For thus it was from the beginning,
And it will be until the end.

So that nothing shall be contrary,
And nothing shall rise up against him.

As we saw above when considering the Scrolls and John, the dualism
is decisively modified by the monotheistic belief.

In several verses the Creator is called the "Word" (12:10; cf.
7:7f.; 16:8-12, 19). In Ode 7:7, however, the Creator is specified
as the "Father of knowledge" (*'bwh dyd't'*). The striking parallels
between the former and John and the latter and the Scrolls will be
discussed below.

The Odist, like John, inherited the Old Testament idea that the
universe is separated into two worlds.[31] Occasionally the Odist
mentions the descent of the "Word" (12:5f.) and the Lord: "And His
(the Lord's) will descended from on high" (23:5). Elsewhere the
ascent of the believer is mentioned: "And I was lifted up in the
light,..." (21:6), "I rested on the Spirit of the Lord, /And she lifted
me up to heaven;..." (36:1). Like John, the cosmic dualism of two
worlds is modified because the "world above" is so vastly superior:

The likeness of that which is *below*
Is that which is *above.*

[31] O. Böcher correctly argues that according to the Old Testament the universe
is divided into the world above, heaven, and the world below, earth (Gen 1:1ff.;
14:19, 22). Sheol, the so-called "underworld" and abode of the dead (cf. especially
Is 14:9), is not a world separate and beneath the Earth, "but apparently on the
Earth itself"; see *Der johanneische Dualismus im Zusammenhang des nachbiblischen
Judentums* (Gütersloh, 1965) 23. Seen in this light Ode 22:1-2 does not reflect
belief in a trifurcated universe. It is also possible that these verses reflect the Odist's
belief that Christ descended from heaven, lived on the earth, died, descended into
hell, and then ascended into heaven again (Ode 42:11-20 is clearly about the
descensus ad inferos). According to Ode 29:4 Sheol is the abode of the dead on
the earth.

For everything is from *above,*
And from *below* there is nothing;
But it is believed to be by those in whom there is no understanding.
(Ode 34:4–5, italics mine)

The first characteristic of the Odist's "dualism", therefore, is a modified cosmic dualism of two worlds.

As one reads through the Odes he is confronted by a belief in two
Spirits, one good ("the Spirit of the Lord, which is not false,...":
3:10; "His (the Lord's) Spirit": 16:5, cf. 14:8; 7:3; 8:6; 21:2; 25:2),
the other bad ("the Evil One": 14:5). The dualism, however, does
not depict a cosmic struggle between two Spirits; here the good Spirit
(or the Lord) saves or has saved the believer from the evil Spirit
(14:4f.). Near the end of the collection we find a clearer expression
of this dualism; in Ode 33 the two "Spirits" do not fight each other
but vie for man's allegiance. Ode 33:3–7 reads as follows:

And he (the Corruptor) stood on the peak of a summit and cried
    aloud
From one end of the earth to the other.

The he drew to him all those who obeyed him,
For he did not appear as the Evil One.

However the perfect Virgin stood,
Who was preaching and summoning and saying:

O you sons of men, return,
And you their daughters, come.

And leave the ways of the Corruptor,
And approach me.

The dualism contained in this Ode, including the remaining verses,
may be expressed in diagram form as follows:

"the perfect Virgin" (33:5)	"the Corruptor" (33:1, 7) ="the Evil One" (33:4)
"the ways of truth" (33:8) "my (the Virgin's) ways" (33:13)	"the ways of that Corruptor" (33:7)
"obey me (the Virgin)" (33:10)	"all those who obeyed him" (33:4)
"be saved and blessed" (33:11)	"destruction" (33:8f.)
"possess incorruption in the new world" (33:12)	"perish" (33:9)

In Ode 38 we find a dualism between Truth and Error, both of
which are personified, and later a dualism between two sets of brides
and bridegrooms. Truth is not depicted as fighting against Error, but
as the protector of the Odist from Error, over whom he is definitely

superior ("For Error fled from Him, ...", 38:6). Likewise in the second section of this ode the "Bride who was corrupting" and the "Bridegroom who corrupts and is corrupted" do not confront but imitate "The Beloved and His Bride". The dualism contained in this ode may be outlined as follows:

The Lord (38:20)

Truth (38:1)	Error (38:6)
"light of Truth" (38:1)	
"the upright way" (38:7)	("The way of error" 15:6)
"I walked with Him (Truth)" (38:5)	("walking in error" 18:14)
"immortal life" (38:3)	death (38:8)
Truth (38:10)	the Corruptor (38:9)
"the Beloved and His Bride" (38:11)	"the Bridegroom who corrupts and is corrupted" (38:9) "the Bride who was corrupting" (38:9) ="the Deceiver and the Error" (38:10) "cause the world to err and corrupt it" (38:11)
(drink "from the Most High" 6:12, Ode 30 complete)	"the wine of their intoxication" (38:12)
wisdom and knowledge (38:13)	nonsense (38:13) no understanding (38:15)
the Truth (38:16)	the Deceivers (38:16)

In this ode, therefore, we find emphasis placed upon two ways, each of which is headed by a hypostatic figure.

In the Odes we have discovered a "dualism" of two opposing creatures. Since the two figures do not confront each other as they do in the War Scroll (viz. 1QM 7:6; 12:8; 16:11; 18:1), this aspect of the Odist's "dualism" can be called a modified metaphysical dualism. This is the second characteristic.

As with the Scrolls and John, the Odes express the dualistic ideas in terms of the light-darkness paradigm (cf. 5:4–6; 6:17; 7:14; 12:3; 25:7; 29:7; 31:1; 32:1; 38:1; 41:6, 14).[32] Note the following symbolic uses of "light" and "darkness":

"And to walk with watchfulness in His light" (8:2).
"the Lord ... possessed me by His light" (11:11).
Blessed are they who "have passed from darkness to light" (11:18f.).
"He is the light and dawning of thought" (12:7).

[32] Verses cited as examples in parentheses are usually meant to be representative not exhaustive.

the Lord "He is my Sun,/...
And His light has dismissed all darkness from my face" (15:2).

The Odist makes full use of this paradigm in 21:3 ("And I put off darkness,/And put on light") and 18:6:

Let not light be conquered by darkness,
Nor let truth flee from falsehood.

The synonymous parallelism shows that light is associated with truth (cf. 15:5) and darkness with falsehood. The third characteristic of the Odist's "dualism" is the emphasis put upon the light-darkness paradigm.

Like John, the Odes portray a realizing eschatology. The Odist believed that the Messiah had come (41:3f., 11–15), taking human form:

He became like me that I might receive Him.
In form He was considered like me
    that I might put Him on.

And I trembled not when I saw Him,
Because He was gracious to me.
Like my nature He became

    that I might understand Him.
And like my form
    that I might not turn away from Him.

(7:4–6)

The struggle between good and evil still continues (8:7; 9:6; 28:6; 29:9) but the decisive battle has been fought so that "the persecutors" are now "blotted out" (23:20; 42:5), because the Messiah has already captured the world ("I took courage and became strong and captured the world,/And it became mine for the glory of the Most High, and of God my Father": 10:4 [*ex ore Christi*]; cf. 29:10; 31:1f.), "possessed everything" (23:19), even conquering Sheol and death ("Sheol saw me and was shattered,/And death ejected me and many with me": 42:11 [*ex ore Christi*]; the remainder of this ode concerns the *descensus ad inferos*). As with John, so in the Odes "eternal life" is not merely a future reward but primarily a present actuality for the believer ("And He (the Lord) has caused to dwell in me His immortal life,...": 10:2, see 15:10). Some verses in the Odes, however, like Jn 5:28f., reflect a futuristic eschatology (e.g., "And they who have put me (the perfect Virgin) on shall not be falsely accused,/But they shall possess incorruption in the new world": 33:12). Nevertheless, throughout the Odes the concept of time is not that of the present versus the distant or even imminent future, but of the breaking in of the future into the present. The similarities with John are striking, hence we may refer to this fourth characteristic of the Odes' "dualism" as a modified eschatological dualism.

Pervasive in *sotto voce* throughout the Odes is a soteriological dualism. The Syriac word for "to save", *prq*, and its derivatives such as "Saviour", *prwq'*, are employed no less than 34 times. This frequency is remarkable, since it is roughly equal to the number of times "to praise" and its derivatives are used (35 times); and the Odes are primarily "thanksgiving hymns". Although the noun "Saviour" is found in only two verses (41:11; 42:18), the Odist continually praises the Lord for his salvation. His petition is for salvation from the Evil One ("... let me be saved from the Evil One": 14:5; cf. 18:7). Often he declares that he is saved ("And I walked with Him and was saved": 17:4; cf. 17:2, 15; 25:2, 4; 28:10; 35:2, 7; 38: 2f., 17). It is important to note that the Odist *is saved* from the Evil One (14:5), the "way of error" (15:6), and that it is because of salvation that the Lord ("the Son": 7:15) possesses everything (7:16).

Occasionally "the Lord" signifies "God" (29:6a), but usually it represents the Messiah (29:6b; 24:1), who is the One that rejects all who do not belong to the truth (24:10–12), the One that dispels darkness (15:1–2), and the Salvation-Bringer ("And because the Lord is my salvation,/I will not fear": 5:11; cf. 31:12f.) who is portrayed in dualistic terms:

The way of error I have forsaken,
And I went toward Him and received salvation from Him
    abundantly.   (15:6; cf. 21:2)

Like John, the Odes reflect the idea that the coming of the Saviour has split mankind into two groups, but unlike John, the Odes do not describe the division as "those who do not believe" and "those who believe". Only implicit in John but prominent in the Odes is the description of the two sections of mankind according to the paradigm error-ignorance vis-à-vis truth-knowledge. On the one hand are those who do not belong to the truth (24:10–12), the "vain people" (18:12), on the other are those who wear "the crown of truth" (1:2; 9:8ff.) and "the wise" (18:13). The division of men is frequently expressed in terms of two ways:

| "the way of error" (15:6) | "the way of truth" (11:3) |
| "walking in error" (18:14) | "walk in the knowledge of the Lord" (23:4) |

The bifurcation of mankind is also expressed in terms of an ethical dualism, although it is less prominent than the error versus truth schema. In two of the passages just cited knowledge is associated with "love" (11:2; 23:3; cf. Ode 3:1–7). Ode 17:2–5 implies that the Odist has been freed from the realm of "vanities" and condemnation to that of "salvation" and "truth". In Ode 7:20f. "knowledge" is not only contrasted with "ignorance" but "hatred" and "jealousy" as well. The ethical aspect is clearest in Ode 20:3–6 in which "the world" and "the flesh" are contrasted with "righteousness", "purity of heart and lips", "compassion", and other ethical norms. We may describe this fifth aspect of the "dualism" in the Odes as a soteriological dualism expressed frequently in terms of error versus truth and occasionally in terms of an ethical dualism.

Since the question of predestination in both the Scrolls and John has been examined, it is appropriate to say a few words about this subject in the Odes. As one would expect in a hymnbook, there is no discussion on this question; however, a few passages reflect that the Odist would have opted for the idea that man has a choice. The Odist apparently advocated universalism; he states that the stream (the spread of the good news; see 6:12ff.) "spread over the surface of *all* the earth,/And it filled *everything.*//Then *all* the thirsty upon the earth drank,/..." (6:10f., italics mine). In Ode 33, as we saw above, "the Corruptor" and "the perfect Virgin" are not playing chess with men as pawns; they are vying for man's allegiance. Note that "the perfect Virgin" is not described as teasing men, but as "preaching, summoning and saying: /... return, /... come" (33:5f.). The Odist's use of the term "the elect ones", therefore, does not mean men foreordained to election, but those who accept the invitation (see also 8:13–18; 23:2f.).[33] In 33:13 "My elect ones" is paralleled by "them who seek me". The sixth characteristic of the Odes' "dualism" is that men can choose.

Of these six aspects of the "dualism" in the Odes the fifth, soteriological dualism, is clearly the most important to the Odist. He composed these Odes to praise God for his recent action in history. Everything tended to be viewed from a soteriological perspective because he was joined to his Saviour:

> I have been united because the lover has found the Beloved,
> Because I love Him that is the Son,
> I shall become a son.   (3:7)

Not only in the entire third Ode but throughout the Odes we find evidence that the Odist is united with his Lord. Frequently it is difficult to discern whether the Odist or "Christ" is the speaker.

In conclusion it is necessary to state that unlike the author of 1QS 3:13ff. the Odist did not promulgate a theory concerning dualism. Unlike John the Odist did not write a Gospel or develop a theological position. He was a poet who wrote hymns. From this perspective and from the insight that the authors of the Hodayoth softened their own developed dualism, a new light is thrown upon the observation that the Odes contain a dualism. The above data are sufficient to show that the Odist held a rather sophisticated dualism. If he did not develop it, he probably inherited it from his predecessors or contemporaries. With this thought we enter the second section of the chapter in which the comparisons between the dualisms discussed above will be examined.

II. *Comparisons*

Critics who demand an exact quotation as the only proof that one document is dependent upon another need not proceed further. A

---

[33] Ode 8:13–18 refers not to foreordination but to foreknowledge; recognition (v. 13) precedes election (v. 18).

mind is needed with perceptions more keen and categories more subtle. An early Christian who borrowed from the Dead Sea Scrolls was dependent upon them regardless of whether he altered these traditions little or greatly. *A priori* we should assume that an early Christian would have reminted an inherited Jewish tradition in line with his shift in eschatology and messianism: the end of time has come, the long awaited Messiah is Jesus of Nazareth. Hence, as a prism refracts light so the belief in the new dispensation would have altered old traditions. During the present comparisons the problem of deciphering whether there is dependency on the Qumran Scrolls will be extreme precisely because both John and the Odes are characterized by the extent to which they rework their sources.[34]

THE "DUALISMS" OF THE ODES AND JOHN

Both the Odes and John inherit a modified cosmic dualism of two worlds. This similarity, at first glance, is unimpressive because most Christian texts written around A.D. 100 inherited from the Old Testament a dualistic cosmology. On closer examination, however, the similarity with which the Odes and John express this aspect of their "dualisms" and the conjoined thoughts raise the possibility that there is some dependence between them. It is significant that the Odes hold the Johannine belief that the universe was created by "the Word". This striking similarity is evident below (italics mine):

John	Odes
In the beginning was the *Word*, and *the Word* was with God, and *the Word* was God. He was in the beginning with God; *all things were made through him*, and without him was not anything made that was made.[35] In him was life, and the life was the	For *the Word* of the Lord searches out anything that is invisible, And reveals His thought. For the eye sees His works, And the ear hears His thought. *It is He who made the earth broad,* And placed the waters in the sea. He expanded the heaven, And fixed the stars. And He fixed the creation and set it up, Then He rested from His works. (Ode 16:8–12)

[34] This feature of John is well known and discussed in most of the commentaries. For the Odes, see my comments in *RB* 77 (1970) 522–49. Early Christians sometimes deliberately altered a passage borrowed (e.g. cf. 1 Enoch 1:9, *erchetai*, "he is coming", with Jude 14, *ēlthen*, "he came").

[35] Compare also 1QS 11:11, "And through his (God's) knowledge all is brought into being, and through his thought all life is established, and without him nothing is made." S. Schulz also sees a strong relationship between Jn 1:3 and 1QS 11:11. See his "Die Komposition des Johannesprologs und die Zusammensetzung des 4. Evangeliums", *Studia Evangelica*, ed K. Aland, F. L. Cross, *et al.* (TU 73; Berlin, 1959) 356. Also compare Jn 1:3 and 1QS 11:11 with Ode 16:18 ("And there is nothing outside of the Lord,/Because he was before anything came to be") and Ode 6:3 ("And everything is of the Lord").

light of men.	And they[36] were stimulated by *the*
The light shines	*Word*,
in the darkness,	And knew Him who had made
and the darkness	them,
has not overcome it.	Because they were in harmony.
(Jn 1:1–5 RSV)	(Ode 12:10)

It is clear that in both the Odes and John, the Creator is called the "Word" (see also Ode 7:7). The similarity between the Odes and John is increased by the observation that neither in the Old Testament[37] nor in the intertestamental literature[38] is there an *emphasis* upon the personification of the "Word". Unlike the other early Christian literature the Odes and John stand out by their thoroughgoing depiction of the Messiah (Odes 9:3; 41:14) as the "Word". Moreover, both of them conceive of the "Word" as pre-existent (Odes 32:2; 41:14; Jn 1:1f.), the Creator (Odes 7:7; 12:10; 16:8–14; Jn 1:3), incarnate (Odes 7:1–6; 39:9; 41:11f.; Jn 1:14), equated with light (Odes 10:1; 12:3; 16:14; 32:2; 41:14; Jn 1:4; 8:12), and the essence of love (Odes 12:12; Jn 13:34), truth (Odes 8:8; 12:3, 12; 32:2; Jn 14:6), and life (Ode 41:11; Jn 14:6), especially immortal life (Odes 10:1; 15:9; Jn 3:16 *et passim*). These similarities are too numerous, pervasive, and substantial to be mere coincidence. Numerous passages, many of which are cited below, are so close as to support the probability that there is some level of dependence between the Odes and John.

Numerous scholars, most recently R. Schnackenburg,[39] have argued that the Odes are dependent upon John. This conclusion is unlikely first because the evidence is equivocal: in one passage the Odes seem dependent on John, in another the reverse seems to be the case. It is improbable secondly and chiefly because of the following consideration. The Syriac texts of John use only *mell*ᵉ*thā'* to represent the divine "Word". This is true not only of the Peshitta and the Curetonian recensions (the first 24 verses of John are missing in the Sinaitic Palimpsest), but also of the Syriac commentaries on John.[40] In the Odes, however, *pethghāmā'* (10 times) as well as

---

[36] "They" are "the generations" mentioned in v. 7.

[37] Contrast the Odes and John with Genesis 1:1ff. and Ps 33:6 ("By the word of the Lord the heavens were made, . . . ").

[38] The Prayer of Manasseh 3 ("Who hast bound the sea by the word of thy command, . . .") is closer to Gen 1:1ff. than to Jn 1:1ff. Jubilees 12:4 (". . . the God of heaven, . . . has created everything by His word, . . . "), however, is closer to John and the Odes. The idea of creation by the word is also reflected in Ps 148:5, and 2 Pet 3:5, and 2 Bar 21:4 (if the text is emended from *bml'h* to *bmlt'*). Compare Acts of John 101. The translations from the Apocrypha and Pseudepigrapha are those found in R. H. Charles (ed.), *The Apocrypha and Pseudepigrapha of the Old Testament*, 2 vols (Oxford, 1913, reprinted 1963–68).

[39] *The Gospel According to St John*, trans. K. Smyth (London, New York, 1968) vol. 1, 145. See also F. M. Braun, *RTh* 57 (1957) 615–19.

[40] L. A. Herrick, who is presently working on Moses bar Kepha's commentary on John (MS Add. 1971 (Cambridge)), informs me that the *terminus technicus* for the divine Word in this MS. is *mell*ᵉ*thā'*; *pethghāmā'* is used exclusively in the sense of "text" or "phrase".

mell[e]thā' (11 times) signifies the divine "Word". This observation has not received the attention it deserves; it reduces the possibility that the Odes are dependent on John. If the Odes borrow from John's use of the "Word" then it is practically impossible to explain why in Ode 12, the only ode in which both *mell[e]thā'* and *pethghāmā'* are found, *mell[e]thā'* means "speech" but in four separate verses (3, 5, 10, 12) *pethghāmā'* denotes the divine Logos, to use the familiar Greek term.

The conclusion to this first comparison is that while both the Odes and John have borrowed some of their modified cosmic dualism from the Old Testament, other parts of it are so unique in the history of ideas and so similar to each other as to raise the question of some level of dependence. It is improbable that the Odist systematically borrowed from John. The most probable solution, at this stage in our research, is that both the author of John and the Odist contemporaneously shared not only the same milieu but perhaps also the same community.

In the discussion above we called the second aspect of John's and the Odes' "dualism" respectively "an extremely modified metaphysical dualism" and a "modified metaphysical dualism". To reiterate, the struggle in John is between Jesus, who represents God, and the Jews, who are frequently equated with the *kosmos* or Satan. In the Odes this aspect of the "dualism" is more pronounced and may be outlined as follows:

the Spirit of the Lord	the Evil One
the perfect Virgin	the Corruptor
Truth	Error
the Beloved and	the Bridegroom who corrupts and is corrupted
His Bride	the Bride who was corrupting the Deceiver

Since the Odist himself equates the Corruptor with the Evil One (33:4) and the evil Bride and Bridegroom with the Deceiver and the Error (38:10), it appears that he assumed the existence of one pair of evil creatures. Likewise, he thought that the good forces were also a pair: the Spirit of the Lord (the Beloved) and the perfect Virgin (his Bride).

Here the differences between the "dualisms" in the Odes and John are most extreme. First, in the Odes the imagery is more developed. As with the Scrolls, numerous names are given to the hypostatic creatures, and Truth and Error are clearly personified and juxtaposed. Second, in the Odes the evil creatures never confront the good figures, with the possible exception of Ode 33:1; they meet only obliquely as they vie for man's allegiance. In contrast, John portrays the Jews in confrontation with Jesus. Third, the names given to the opposing figures are strikingly different. The Odist's imagery of the Bride and Bridegroom is closer to letters attributed to Paul (2 Cor 11:2; Eph 5:25f.) than to John. Fourth, in the Odes the metaphysical dualism is less modified, hence closer to that of the Scrolls.

Some of the above differences could be the result of the poetic aspect of the Odes, which is in contrast to the "Gospel" character of John. Others can be due to the frequently anti-gentile characteristic in the Odes,[41] which is distinct from the occasional anti-Jewish bias in John (especially 8:12–9:41). However, we must not fail to observe that a considerable amount of independence must be accounted for when comparing the Odes and John.

In summary, the Odes are clearly closer than John to the Scrolls' concept of two warring cosmic Spirits. Observations made below raise the probability that some of the differences mentioned above between the Odes and John are caused by more direct Essene influence on the Odist.

One of the most impressive similarities between the "dualisms" in the Odes and John is that both have woven into the heart of their thought the light-darkness paradigm. Since neither of them develops the schema but presents it at a sophisticated level, it is clear that each has inherited the paradigm from an earlier tradition. Of all the dualisms by which the Odes and John could have been influenced, it is that developed in the Scrolls that comes closest as the source.[42] Only in the Scrolls, the Odes and John is light associated with truth, knowledge and everlasting (eternal) life, while antithetically darkness is linked with falsehood, ignorance and extinction. Both the Odes and John probably inherited this paradigm from the Essenes.

Some elaborations of this paradigm, however, come from the fact that both the Odes and John are Christian (hence the schema is seen soteriologically), but the conception that the Messiah (Christ) is "Light" suggests either some level of dependence between the Odes and John or that they both come from the same or contiguous communities. Compare Ode 41:14 ("And light dawned from the Word /That was before time in Him...") with the prologue to John, and Ode 10:1 ("The Lord directed my mouth by His Word, /And opened my heart by His light...") or Ode 15:2 ("Because He (the Lord) is my Sun, /...; /And His light has dismissed all darkness from my face")[43] with Jn 8:12 ("I am the light of the world;...").

In conclusion, therefore, the data suggest that both the Odes and John have been independently influenced by the light-darkness paradigm promulgated in the Scrolls, but that in developing it for the new dispensation they have been related dependently in some way, or independently influenced by a shared community.

It is not impressive that both the Odes and John present a modified eschatological dualism since both, as Christian documents, affirm that the Messiah has come and that the future has irrupted into the

---

[41] Ode 10:5, "And the Gentiles..., /I was not defiled by my love (for them)...." R. H. Charles correctly remarked that "Christ apologizes after a fashion for His reception of the Gentiles into the Church"; see *The Times Literary Supplement*, no. 430 (April 7, 1910) 124.

[42] See footnotes 15 and 16 above.

[43] Of all the variegated aspects of sectarian Judaism that we know today only the Essenes venerated the sun, and accentuated the symbolic importance of light.

present.[44] It is significant, however, that both depict the coming of the Messiah in such similar terms. Ode 12:12 ("For the dwelling place of the Word is man, /And His truth is love") is parallel to John 1:14 ("And the Word became flesh and dwelt among us ...").[45]

Two observations raise the possibility that on this point there is some relationship between the two documents. First, both clearly accentuate the reward of eternal life as the will of the Lord for all men (Ode 9:4; 10:2; 11:16f., *et passim*; Jn 3:15–16; 3:36; 4:14 *et passim*). Second, both describe "eternal life" as not a distant dream but a present reality for those who belong to the light (Ode 3:9; 11:12; 15:8–10; Jn 3:36; 4:14 *et passim*). The first point certainly does not suggest dependence upon the Scrolls, because of their exclusiveness (viz. 1QS 1:9f.). The second, however, might reflect the Essenes' contention that the "sons of light" would receive "perpetual life" (1QS 4:7) and the belief that their community was an antechamber of heaven.

We saw that the most important feature of the "dualism" in the Odes and John is the fifth aspect, soteriological dualism It would be difficult to show dependence between them here precisely because they share this characteristic with other Christian literature. A few observations, however, help clarify the possibility of dependence.

In contrast to Qumranic dualism, neither the Odes nor John portrays the bifurcation of mankind as a primordial fact but as the result of each man's response to the Saviour's call to repent. We mentioned above that both the Odes and John referred to the Creator as the "Word"; likewise both conceive of the Saviour as the "Word". It is clear that the author of John held this identification although he never says so explicitly, and the parallelism in Ode 41:11 shows that the Odist made the equation:

And His Word is with us in all our way,
The Saviour who gives life and does not reject us.

Two observations suggest that there is some level of dependence between the Odes and John in terms of the development of the soteriological dualism. First, both put an extraordinary amount of emphasis upon the salvific aspects of "to know" (*yd'* as a verb is employed 44 times in the Odes, *ginōskein* occurs 56 times in John). In both, "to know" is frequently synonymous with "to follow" or "to belong" to the Saviour, Jesus Christ. In Ode 42:3, "those who knew me [not]" is paralleled by "those who possessed me not", an idea which is similar to the dualistic dialogue in Jn 8:32–58 (cf. 14:20; 17:25). Correlatively, in both "Truth" is not only personified as the Saviour (viz. "The Truth led me": Ode 38:1; "I am ... the truth": Jn 14:6) but is also portrayed as the spiritual abode of the believer (viz. "And (Truth) became for me a haven of salvation ...": Ode 38:3;

---

[44] O. Betz correctly states that the Odes stress the present aspect of salvation even more so than John. *Der Paraklet: Fürsprecher im häretischen Spätjudentum, im Johannes-Evangelium und in neu gefundenen gnostischen Schriften* (AGSU 2; Leiden, 1963) 215.

[45] Also see Ode 39:9–13 and especially Ode 41:11–15.

"Every one who is of (*ek*) the truth hears my voice": Jn 18:37; cf. 8:44).[46]

Second, for both the distinguishing mark of one who belongs to the Saviour is "love". "For I should not have known how to love the Lord, /If He had not continuously loved me" (Ode 3:3) is strikingly similar to "We love him, because he first loved us" (1 Jn 4:19—I believe that 1 John and John are by the same author). Permeating the Odes is the emphasis put upon love (*'ḥb*, 25 times; *rḥm*, 24 times). The possibility of dependence, in some direction, is increased by the observation that only John records Jesus' commandment "to love" ("A new commandment I give to you, that you love one another; even as I have loved you...": Jn 13:34).

As we attempt to discover the level and direction of possible influence between the Odes and John we should make the following observation. In both, the Lord (=the Saviour) lifts up His voice (Ode 31:4; in Jn 17:1 Jesus "lifted up his eyes...and said") towards the Most High (Ode 31:4; in Jn 17:1 "to heaven") and offers to Him (Ode 31:4; Jn 17 *passim*, especially vv. 9f.) those whom "His Holy Father" (Ode 31:5; "Holy Father" in Jn 17:11) "had given to Him" (Ode 31:5; Jn 17:2, 6, 9 *et passim*), those who now possess "eternal life" (Ode 31:7; Jn 17:2f.). The similarities between Ode 31:4–5 and Jn 17 are sufficient to raise the question of some dependence. The initial reaction would be to assume that the Odist was influenced by Jn 17. This hypothesis, however, fails to convince on closer examination; there are too many expressions in these two verses of Ode 31 that are neither attributable to Jn 17 nor to the peculiar vocabulary of the Odist. Is it improbable that the connection could be traced to the same community from which the Odes and John might have come? Further research is needed before we can be certain.

The sixth characteristic of the "dualisms" in the Odes and John is that man has the ability to choose his own way. Perhaps it is here that both are farthest from Qumran and its exclusivism. Any relationship between the Odes and John at this point would be due not to dependence of one upon the other but to the universalism of burgeoning Christianity with its missionary zeal.

In concluding this comparison between the "dualism" in the Odes and John we may say that there are numerous and striking similarities. There is clearly some relationship between these two early Christian documents. The problems arise when one tries to analyse in which direction the dependence should be traced: are the Odes dependent on John, is John developing ideas found in the Odes, are the similarities the result of a shared community? The last possibility looms large not only in the light of the data amassed above, especially the observation that only the Odes employ *pethghāmā'* as a *terminus technicus* for the "Word", but also because it now seems highly probable that John is not the effort of a genius working alone

---

[46] Frequently the Odist's use of "truth" has a "Johannine" ring to it. In one verse (12:12) he conceptually combines "Word", "truth", and "love". In Ode 32:2 he writes, "And the Word of truth who is self-originate, ..."

but of a school of scholars.[47] There is certainly much yet to be done
before we can make sweeping generalizations about the relationship
between the Odes and John. Certainly we must become more aware
of our presuppositions and perceptions; because John is more
familiar to us, because we read it first, and because it is in the
canon are not sufficient reasons to proceed as if it must be the source
for the Odes.

"DUALISM" IN THE ODES AND DUALISM AT QUMRAN

Both the "dualism" in the Odes and the dualism in the Scrolls are
modified by an overriding monotheism. This idea and the belief that
the universe is bifurcated into heaven and earth display the Odist's
and Essenes' Old Testament heritage. A possible relationship between
them might be the shared conception of the community as an antechamber of heaven, the dwelling of "the holy ones". In Ode 22:12 we
read the following:

> And the foundation of everything is Thy rock.
> And upon it Thou hast built Thy kingdom,
> And it became the dwelling-place of the holy ones.

This imagery is similar to that of the Scrolls in which the "heavenly"
community—"the dwelling of perfect holiness" (1QS 8:8, cf. 1QM
12:2; 1QH 12:2; 1QSb 4:25)—is also conceived of as "founded upon
rock" (1QH 6:25).[48]

Here the possibility of dependence by the Odist upon ideas found
in the Scrolls is displayed by the observation that both specify the
Creator as *'bwh dyd't'*, "the Father of knowledge" (Ode 7:7) or *m'l
hd'wt,* "the God of Knowledge" (1QS 3:15; 1QH 1:26; 12:10;
fragment 4:15), peculiar concepts rarely found in the Old Testament
(the closest parallels are 1 Sam 2:3: *'l d'wt,* "God of knowledge", and
Is 11:2: *rwh d't,* "the spirit of knowledge"), the New Testament, the
Old Testament Apocrypha (contrast the closest parallel in Wis 9:2),
or the Old Testament Pseudepigrapha (contrast 1 Enoch 63:2). The
absence of parallels outside of the Odes and the Scrolls raises the probability that the Odist inherited the concept and expression from the
Scrolls, where it is found not only in the Rule but also in the
Hodayoth.

The two warring cosmic Spirits, which play such a prominent
role in Qumran's dualism, may be disguised in the Odes' "dualism",
even though the terminology is quite different. Also the cosmic figures
in the Odes are not described as warring with each other as they are,
for example, in the War Scroll and the Rule. The Odist may have
borrowed the broad lines of the Qumran dualistic imagery, but in
so doing he completely reminted the idea so that it is "the perfect
Virgin" who vies with "the Corruptor". Behind this Christian garb
may lie a disguised Qumran dualism of two warring Spirits, a possi-

---

[47] In my judgment the core of John ultimately goes back to the disciple John
the son of Zebedee, but the present form is the result of a Johannine school.
R. E. Brown, S.S., presents this solution as an *"ad hoc* theory" in *The Gospel
According to John,* vol. 1, xcviii–cii.

[48] See J. H. Charlesworth, *RB* 77 (1970) 529–32.

bility that should be taken seriously since both in the Odes (especially 33:3–7) and the Scrolls (viz. 1QS 3:18; 4:23) the struggle is for man's allegiance. Moreover, on two accounts the similarity is striking: the Odist's "the Spirit of the Lord, which is not false" (3:10) may be a reminted "Spirit of Truth" (1QS 3:19 *et passim*); "the Corruptor" (Odes 33 and 38) corresponds to the Essenes' "angels of destruction (corruption)" (1QS 4:12; 1QM 13:12; CD 2:6). It is logical to assume that here the Odist is influenced by Essene imagery.

The most striking similarity between the Odes' "dualism" and the Scrolls' dualism is the pervasiveness of the light-darkness paradigm in each. In both, "light", which represents "truth", is contrasted with "darkness", which signifies "falsehood". Compare for example Ode 18:6,

Let not light be conquered by darkness,
Nor let truth flee from falsehood.

with the Rule (1QS 3:19),

In a dwelling of light is the origin of Truth,
And in a fountain of darkness is the origin of Perversity.

We mentioned above that the development of the light-darkness paradigm is unique to Essene or Essene-influenced documents; it is found neither in the Old Testament nor in other intertestamental literature. We are left with two logical possibilities: either the Essenes and the Odist developed this paradigm independently, or the Odist has been influenced by Essene promulgations. The first possibility is unlikely because the Odist did not develop but inherited the paradigm. The second possibility looms probable and should be viewed in light of other striking similarities.[49] Moreover, it is significant that the Odes and the Scrolls are distinguished from documents with which they were contemporary by the inordinate degree to which they accentuate the importance of the sun (compare Ode 15:2 with 1QH 12:3–9; 11QPs[a] 26:4; 4Q *Morgen- und Abendgebete*).

The fourth characteristic of the dualistic thought found in the Odes and Scrolls is respectively the modified and unmodified eschatological dimension. It would be easy to report only how different the two eschatologies are: while the Odist repeatedly praises the marvellous advent of *the* Messiah, the Essenes yearn for the future coming of *a* Messiah(s); while the Odist proclaims that the decisive battle has been fought and that the Messiah has captured the world, the Essenes look to a future decisive battle. Behind these differences, however, there may be some impressive similarities, and we must not overlook the logic that an early Christian who borrows an idea or symbol from the Essenes is dependent upon them regardless of whether he remints or alters it in line with the eschatological ramifications of the new dispensation.

Under this fourth characteristic there is the striking similarity of

[49] See J. H. Charlesworth, *RB* 77 (1970) 522–49.

future rewards and punishments. Both stress that those who belong
to the light shall receive a "crown" (Ode 1:1–3; 9:8f.; 1QS 4:7–8;
1QH 9:25) and possess "eternal life" (viz. Ode 10:2; 15:10; 1QS
4:7–8); but that those who belong to the darkness shall receive not
eternal punishment (cf. Daniel 12:2; 1 Enoch 10:4–13; 67:4–13) but
extinction (e.g., Ode 33:8f.; 1QS 4:14). It is difficult to see these
similarities as mere coincidences; it is not impossible, however, that
the Odist received these ideas and images from the general Jewish
background.[50]

The fifth and most important characteristic of the "dualism"
in the Odes is that it is soteriological, while that in the Scrolls is
ethical. Earlier we noted that, unlike John, the Odes emphasized the
bifurcation of humanity according to the paradigm truth-knowledge
vis-à-vis error-ignorance. Note for example that the Odist and Essene
talk about the way or ways of truth (Ode 11:3; 33:8; 1QS 4:17)
and the way of error or unrighteousness (Ode 15:6; 1QH 14:26).[51]
Occasionally the Odist describes the soteriological dualism in terms
of an ethical dualism (compare Ode 20:3–6 with the long ethical
lists found in 1QS 4:2–11). Here the Odes are closer than John to
Qumranic dualism.

There are tremendous differences between the Odes and Qumran's
sixth characteristic feature. It is a difference that results from early
Christianity's universalism and missionary zeal, which was antithetical
to Qumran's exclusiveness (1QS 1:9ff.).

The similarities mentioned above are striking and pervasive. Certain
of these may be mere coincidences (e.g., the Odist's description of the
soteriological dualism); others might be the result of the general
Jewish background of the Odes to which Qumran thought belongs
(e.g., monotheism, angelology, the concept of future rewards or punishments). Others, however, are caused by ideas and images peculiar to
the Scrolls (e.g., the concept of the community as an antechamber of
heaven, terminology such as the description of the Creator as the
"Father of knowledge", the development of the idea that there are
two opposed cosmic figures, the centrality of the light-darkness
paradigm). The logical conclusion, therefore, is that the Odes are
probably influenced by the Scrolls; indeed in some passages they may
be directly dependent upon them.

JOHN AND QUMRAN

The preceding chapter and comments scattered above permit us to
make this section of the discussion brief. John and the Scrolls contain
a modified dualism; in John it is at first inconspicuous but in the
Scrolls almost blatant. John borrows his dualism, but the author(s)
of columns three and four in the Rule promulgates a dualism, employing ideas borrowed from elsewhere (viz. Zurvanism). John inherits the
concept of two worlds from the Old Testament, but animates the
worlds and sets them up as two opposing forces. The Essenes, on the

---

[50] See Brown's comments on pp. 1ff. above concerning our gain in understanding
of first-century Judaism.

[51] We should expect the Syriac *ṭ'ywt'* (Ode 15:6) to correspond to the Hebrew
tw'h, both of which mean "error"; but the Syriac noun is very close to the Hebrew
'wlh (1QH 14:26), which means "unrighteousness" or "wrong".

other hand, merely assume the existence of two worlds (viz. 1QH 16:3). John probably borrowed the light-darkness paradigm from the Essenes, who had developed it.[52] John's modified eschatological dualism, soteriological dualism, and concept of the freedom of the will are clearly distinct from the corresponding concepts in the Scrolls. These differences, however, are demanded by the affirmation that the long-awaited Messiah has come, and wills to save all men from destruction (viz. Jn 1:14; 3:16; 12:32). The similarities show that John probably has been influenced by Essene thought; this is especially evident by the terminology he employed to present his "dualism".

ODES, JOHN AND QUMRAN

In the following pages we shall attempt to organize the main observations regarding the relationships among the dualisms found in the Odes, John, and the Qumran Scrolls. The conclusions to the above analyses are conveniently arranged in the following chart (an asterisk marks the most conspicuous emphasis, italics signify the closest parallels):

Odes	John	Qumran
1. modified cosmic dualism of two worlds	1. modified cosmic dualism of two worlds	1. modified dualism
2. *modified metaphysical dualism*	2. an extremely modified metaphysical dualism	2. *2 warring cosmic Spirits*
3. *light-darkness paradigm*	3. *light-darkness paradigm*	3. *light-darkness paradigm*
4. modified eschatological dualism	4. modified eschatological dualism	4. eschatological dualism
*5. soteriological dualism (plus ethical dualism)	*5. soteriological dualism	*5. ethical dualism
6. choice	6. choice	6. predestination

First, the Odes, John and Qumran have inherited their basic cosmology from the Old Testament: there are two worlds, the one above, heaven, and the one below, earth. These two worlds are implicit in the Scrolls, explicit in the Odes, and emphasized with new dualistic connotations in John. We have seen that the similarities between the Odes and John on this first point are so impressive, especially in the shared terminology (viz. "Word"), as to warrant the probability that both come from an identical milieu, perhaps even the same community. While John, however, shows no dependence here on the Scrolls, the Odes are apparently influenced by their thoughts

[52] Contrast Bakotin, who argued that John inherited the paradigm from the Old Testament; however, he wrote before the Scrolls were discovered. He correctly saw that John's "dualism" should not be traced to Gnosticism (*De notione lucis et tenebrarum in Evangelio S. Joannis*, 84–87). See also G. Baumbach, *Qumran und das Johannes-Evangelium*, 51; and R. E. Murphy, O.Carm., *The Dead Sea Scrolls and the Bible* (Westminster, Maryland, 1956) 71–9.

and expressions. The conception of the community as an antechamber of heaven and the description of the Creator as the "Father of knowledge" suggest that the Odist has borrowed from the Scrolls.

From this first comparison we see that the Odist may have belonged to the same community as John, but apparently was more influenced by the Essenes than he. These possibilities could be accounted for by the assumption that Essenes lived in the community, by the hypothesis that the Odist had been an Essene before his conversion to Christianity, or both, since the two are not mutually exclusive.

Second, we have seen that the Odes, John and the Scrolls portray a cosmic struggle headed by two hypostatic figures, a concept only in the background of John's thought (e.g., Christ, the representative of God, against the Jews, the representatives of the Devil), but in the foreground of the Odist's and Essenes' metaphysics. We should not be mesmerized by differences; the Odes and Scrolls share images and expressions that are sufficiently similar as to warrant the hypothesis that the Odist has been influenced by the Essenes.

Third, and most significantly, the Odes, John and the Scrolls are distinguished by the inordinate degree to which they employ the light-darkness paradigm. No other documents dating from this time portray a dualism that is so permeated by light and truth versus darkness and falsehood. There can be little question that, as Christian writings essentially indebted to Judaism, the Odes and John probably inherited the paradigm from the dualistic ideas of pre-Christian Judaism. Therefore the probable source for this paradigm was the Essenes, who—as far as we can detect—promulgated and developed the light-darkness paradigm. It is highly improbable that the Odes have borrowed the schema from John or vice versa; it seems that both independently inherited the imagery from the Essenes.

Fourth, the chart above shows, on the one hand, that the eschatology in the Odes and John is similar, and on the other, that their eschatology is clearly distinct from that of the Essenes. Here particularly, however, we must allow for the prism effect of the Christian contention that the Messiah has come. Also, the similarities between the Odes and John should not be dismissed as merely one of the characteristics of early Christianity. The Odes and John are peculiar in two ways: the coming of the Messiah is described as the incarnation of the "Word", and victory is assured since the Messiah has overcome the world (compare Ode 10:4 with Jn 16:33).

Both the Odes[53] and John are distinguished by their emphasis upon the reward of eternal life for those of the light and the punishment of extinction for those of the darkness; moreover, both portray eternal life as a present possession. Certainly these striking similarities should be seen in conjunction with the observation that the Essenes taught the same rewards and punishments, and implied that they, the sons of light, already had eternal life since their community was

---

[53] E. Schweizer correctly remarks that in the Odes the Redeemer is frequently identified with the redeemed (p. 76). He also notes the terminological relationship between John and the Odes (p. 56). See his *Ego Eimi*, 2nd ed. (Göttingen, 1965). One of the difficulties confronted in translating the Odes is to decide when the Odist begins to compose *ex ore Christi*.

an antechamber of heaven in which angels were present.[54] Likewise, the Odes, John and the Scrolls accentuate that one who belongs to the light possesses "living water", a symbolism which frequently connotes the possession of eternal life. In pre-Christian literature the expression "living water" is not peculiar to the Scrolls, but it is clearly emphasized only in them.[55] Consequently, the presence of this concept in the Odes and John certainly strengthens the probability that they are influenced by the thought in the Scrolls.[56]

Fifth, the most conspicuous emphasis in the Odes and John is a soteriological dualism, that in the Scrolls an ethical dualism. In the Odes and John the bifurcation of mankind is caused by the appearance of the Saviour; in the Scrolls the division dates from the time the two Spirits were created. There seems to be some dependence between the Odes and John because both conceive of the Saviour as the "Word", accentuate the soteriological aspects of the verbs "to know" and "to love", and either explicitly (Odes) or implicitly (John) depict the division in terms of the schema error-ignorance vis-à-vis truth-knowledge. Here again we see that the Odes are a little closer to the Scrolls than John because they occasionally present the soteriological dualism in terms of an ethical dualism.

Another observation needs reporting at this time. All three denigrate the importance of sacrificing in the Jerusalem Temple (Odes 6; 12:4; 20:1–4; Jn 4:21–24; 1QS 9:3–5),[57] and accentuate the importance of bearing fruit, which in the Odes and Scrolls is frequently synonymous with "praise" (Odes 8:1f.; 11:1; 14:7f.; 16:2; Jn 15; 1QS 10:6–8).[58] These similarities are by no means mere coincidences; when they are taken with the numerous other parallels mentioned throughout this chapter, it seems likely that the Odes and John are influenced by the Scrolls.

Sixth, the tremendous difference between the Odes' and John's belief that man can choose and the Essenes' idea that man is predestined

---

[54] Contrast the surprising conclusion obtained by A. Feuillet in his "La participation actuelle à la vie divine d'après le quatrième évangile: les origines et le sens de cette conception", *SE* 1, 295–308, see especially 307: "More than all the other writings in the New Testament, it [John] seems turned toward the Greek world." Clearly such a statement is anachronic. Also, contrast our position with that of J. Carmignac, *Qumran-Probleme*, 89 and n. 42.

[55] See J. H. Charlesworth, *RB* 77 (1970) 534–7.

[56] O. D. Szojda has recently compared the symbolism of water in the Scrolls with the self-same imagery in John, and concludes that John probably knew the Essene symbolic and ritualistic use of water. He cautions, however, that John has completely reworked the symbolism of water so one must not claim that John is "directly dependent" on the Scrolls. "Symbolika Wody w Pismach Św. Jana Evangelisty i w Qumran", *RocTK* 13 (1966) 105–21.

[57] O. Cullmann contends that the type of Christianity represented by John is as old as that of the Synoptics primarily because there is such strong similarity between the nonconformist Jewish sects (Qumran), the Johannine group, and the Stephen-led branch of early Christianity. All three denigrate the present Temple cultus. See Cullmann's chapter in *Neutestamentliche Studien für Rudolf Bultmann* (Beihefte zur ZNW 21; Berlin, 1954) 35–41; and his article in *ExpT* 71 (1959–60) 8–12, 39–43 [=*NTS* 5 (1958–59) 157–73]. Also see J. Carmignac, *Rev Q* 3 (1961) 100f.

[58] These parallels are discussed by R. Borig, *Der Wahre Weinstock: Untersuchungen zu Jo 15, 1–10* (SANT 16; Munich, 1967). Borig correctly reports that there is no literary borrowing between the Odes and John; the relationship is probably through a shared milieu (p. 127).

should be viewed in the light of the missionary aspects of burgeoning Christianity, which has clearly left its mark on these two documents (Ode 6, 10;[59] Jn 20:31). No dependence can be traced here in any direction among the Odes, John and the Scrolls.

Conclusion

RETROSPECT

The numerous and pervasive parallels between the Odes and John cannot be explained by literary dependence of the Odist upon John or vice versa. The most likely explanation for the similarities analysed above is that the Odist and John shared the same milieu, and it is not improbable that they lived in the same community.

The Odes and John clearly share numerous parallels with the Scrolls; these similarities are seldom in terms of fundamental concepts, occasionally in images, and frequently in terminology.[60] Both the Odist and John could have been influenced independently by the Essenes or Essene literature, or could have received these influences at approximately the same time from Essenes living within or contiguous with their community. In the case of the Odist, we should take seriously the possibility that he is a converted Essene.[61] Subsequent research will reveal how possible or probable these tentative conclusions are.

PROSPECT

The discussion shows that we are no longer justified in speaking about the Odes and John as if they were late and gnostic.[62] Moreover, if both the Odes and John share the same milieu, as is extremely probable, and if the Odes were originally composed in Syriac, as recent research indicates,[63] then it would be well for us to look to

[59] A. A. T. Ehrhardt compares Ode 10 with 1QH 7:26–33 and claims that in particular what is new in the Ode is "a strong missionary spirit" (*SE* 1, 586f.).

[60] E. Best holds that "The Qumran material has led to a re-opening of the question of the background from which John was issued; for a dualism similar to John's appears in Qumran as well as in Hellenistic Judaism and in Gnosticism"; see "New Testament Scholarship Today", *Biblical Theology* 20 (1970) 22. I must disagree; the dualism in the Scrolls is dissimilar to that in Gnosticism, but it is similiar to that in John.

[61] See also J. Carmignac, *Qumran-Probleme*, 75–108.

[62] See my "The Odes of Solomon—Not Gnostic", *CBQ* 31 (1969) 357–69, and Professor H. Chadwick's lucid and brilliant "Some Reflections on the Character and Theology of the Odes of Solomon", *Kyriakon: Festschrift Johannes Quasten*, 2 vols, ed. P. Granfield and J. A. Jungmann (Münster, 1970) 266–70. See the excellent article recently presented by B. Reicke, "Da'at and Gnosis in Intertestamental Literature", *Neotestamentica et Semitica: Studies in Honour of Matthew Black*, ed. E. E. Ellis and M. Wilcox (Edinburgh, 1969) 245–55. Permit me to raise a question: is it insignificant that the Teacher of Righteousness is anonymous in the Scrolls, the Beloved Disciple is unnamed in John, and anonymity characterizes the Odes? See an interesting attempt at answering part of this question by J. Roloff, "Der johanneische 'Lieblingsjünger' und der Lehrer der Gerechtigkeit", *NTS* 15 (1968) 129–51. Roloff concludes, "dass das Johannes-Evangelium seine Wurzeln in dem gleichen sektererisch-täuferischen Milieu am Rande des palästinischen Judentums hatte, in dem auch die Qumran-Sekte beheimatet war" (p. 150).

[63] See J. A. Emerton, "Some Problems of Text and Language in the Odes of Solomon", *JTS* N.S. 18 (1967) 372–406; see also my *The Odes of Solomon* and my "Paronomasia and Assonance in the Syriac Text of the Odes of Solomon", *Semitics* 1 (1970) 12–26.

northern Palestine and Syria for the provenance of the Odes and of at least one recension of John.[64] Antioch, of course, should be considered as a prime candidate, and in this connection we must recall the numerous parallels between these two documents and the letters of Ignatius of Antioch, and the recent illustration of how these letters frequently resemble the imagery of the Scrolls.[65]

These observations raise questions that extend far beyond the scope of this chapter. Before we can adequately answer such questions and learn how and where John[66] and the Odes received their Essene influence, we need to know how geographically widespread the Essenes were, and when the Essenes ceased to be a strong influence upon Christianity.

The new perspectives obtained above show how far biblical research has advanced in the last few decades. In many ways we are dealing with issues undreamed of by our grandfathers. These exciting new insights into the origins of Christianity appear not primarily because of modern methods, but because of the recovery of such compositions as the long-lost Odes of Solomon, and manuscripts, like the Dead Sea Scrolls, actually copied or composed during the life of Jesus of Nazareth.

[64] Although T. E. Pollard's treatment of this issue is too brief, he tends toward the same conclusion (*Johannine Christology and the Early Church* (SNTS Monograph Series 13; Cambridge, 1970) 34). Contrast J. N. Sanders' contention that the numerous parallels between the Scrolls and John strengthen the indications that John Mark, "a member of the priestly aristocracy in Jerusalem", wrote the Fourth Gospel; but that he composed it at the end of his life in Ephesus; see *A Commentary on the Gospel According to St John*, ed. B. A. Mastin (New York, 1968), especially 50–1. Also contrast our position with Irenaeus' comment (*Adv. Haer.* III, xi, 1), recently developed by F. Neugebauer, that connects the origin of John with the imminent division in Christianity caused by Cerinthus' "heretical" cosmology and Christology (*Die Entstehung des Johannesevangeliums* (Arbeiten zur Theologie 1. Reihe, Heft 36; Stuttgart, 1968)). F. L. Cribbs is certainly correct in urging us "to make a reassessment of this gospel in the direction of an earlier dating and a possible origin for John against the general background of Palestinian Christianity" (p. 39) in "A Reassessment of the Date of Origin and the Destination of the Gospel of John", *JBL* 89 (1970) 38–55.

[65] V. Corwin argues that Ignatius knew some of the Odes and displays some of the frequent parallels between Ignatius, the Odes and John, in *St Ignatius and Christianity in Antioch* (Yale Publications in Religion 1; New Haven, 1960) especially 71–80.

[66] See Brownlee's chapter, pp. 166ff. below.

7

Qumran, John and Jewish Christianity

GILLES QUISPEL

Since the Second World War Jewish Christianity has been redis-
covered by specialists in Christian origins. The works of Hans
Joachim Schoeps drew the attention of many scholars to the Jewish
Christian elements in the Pseudo-Clementine Homilies and
Recognitions, until then generally considered to be novels without
any historical background. Jean Daniélou, in his *Theology of Jewish
Christianity,* gave a phenomenological description of the Jewish
Semitic categories, in which Christianity expressed itself before
coming into close contact with Greek philosophy in the time of the
Apologists.[1]

The definition of Jewish Christianity turned out to be difficult. Was
it a faction within the community at Jerusalem, obstinately faithful
to Jewish law and therefore opposed to Paul, which developed into
the sect of the True Prophet described in the Clementine writings?
Or was it rather the (orthodox) Christianity of the apostles, which
used Jewish notions like "angel" to describe the offices of Christ
and the Holy Spirit, but remained essentially faithful to the revelation
of its founder? We have reasons to suppose that there were different
currents among the descendants of the primitive community in
Jerusalem. Some of these Jewish Christians believed that Jesus was
born from a virgin, while others taught that Joseph was his father.
Some rejected Paul, and others appreciated his letters without relin-
quishing obedience to the Jewish law. All seem to have had in common
the conception that God has a form (is personal, not abstract), that
Christ is his angel, his messenger, an example for the life of his
followers, that the Holy Spirit is feminine, in fact a Mother, and that
the kingdom of God is to be expected on earth, in Jerusalem. All
of them stressed poverty and styled themselves as *'ebyônîm,* the voluntary poor for Christ's sake. Even if they did not accept the heretical
conceptions of a man like Elkesai, their religion differed substantially
from Greek Christianity. It soon appeared that these Palestinian Jewish
Christians must have been active missionaries. They probably founded
the Aramaic-speaking Syrian Church, which had its permanent centre
in Edessa (Urfa) in Mesopotamia. Tradition tells us that the founder
was Addai, the first to come from Jerusalem to preach the Gospel in
Edessa. Regardless of whether we consider this story a legend, there

[1] See my survey on the debate in "The Discussion of Judaic Christianity",
VigChr 22 (1968) 81–93.

remains little doubt that Syrian Christianity has Jewish Christian foundations: the Syrian Christians called themselves Nazaraeans, like those of Palestine, and considered the Holy Spirit a Mother; this is the case even in Philoxenus of Mabbug (sixth century). The Syrian Messalians, like the Jewish Christians, held that the faithful had to be so poor as to be unable to give alms. Many other indications suggest that Syrian Christianity came from Palestine and not from Antioch, the centre of Gentile Christianity.[2]

Similarly, Jewish Christian missionaries from Palestine were probably active in Alexandria at a very early date. Both Clement of Alexandria and Origen quote the Jewish Christian Gospel according to the Hebrews with some appreciation, thus showing that Jewish Christians had been active in Alexandria. A tradition, contained in the Pseudo-Clementine *Homilies* (1:9), records that Barnabas, described as a "Hebrew" and staunch supporter of Peter and James in their fight against Simon Magus, was the first missionary of the Gospel in Alexandria. Manfred Hornschuh has presented additional arguments which lead us to suppose that Jewish Christians brought Christianity to Egypt.[3] Moreover, Jewish Christians were active at an early date in Carthage, Rome, Asia Minor and elsewhere.[4] Generally speaking this new image of the history of the Church has met with widespread approval and reflects the present state of research.

The discovery of the Gospel of Thomas confirmed the consensus. This writing, a collection of 114 sayings attributed to Jesus, was probably composed in Edessa about A.D. 140. The author, not a Gnostic, but an Encratite (no wine, meat or wife) used a Jewish Christian source, an apocryphal Gospel or perhaps a collection of sayings, which contained a tradition of the logia of Jesus independent of our canonical Gospels. These logia show many similarities with the Gospel tradition of the Pseudo-Clementine writings, the *Diatessaron* of Tatian and the "Western Text" of our Gospel manuscripts (Codex Bezae, Old Latin and Old Syriac versions).[5] At the same time the Bodmer Papyrus of Luke and John (P75) revealed that the Egyptian text (Codex Vaticanus, Codex Sinaiticus, etc.) was very old and trustworthy, and had been copied by expert Alexandrine philologists.

Before these discoveries scholars supposed that an extra-canonical Jewish Christian Gospel tradition influenced, to a large extent, the "Western Text". As early as 1832, Credner had compared the quotations of Justin Martyr with those of the Pseudo-Clementines, with which they have very much in common. He concluded that the corruptions of the "Western Text" were largely due to the influence of a Jewish Christian Gospel, erroneously held to be the apocryphal and lost Gospel of Peter. Hugo de Groot saw clearly that when Tatian

[2] For more on this point consult my *Makarius, das Thomasevangelium und das Lied von der Perle* (Leiden, 1967).

[3] *Studien zur Epistula Apostolorum* (Berlin, 1965).

[4] See J. Daniélou's excellent survey in *The Crucible of Christianity*, ed. A. Toynbee (London, New York, 1969).

[5] See my articles in *VigChr* (1957–60).

composed the *Diatessaron* (about A.D. 170, probably in the East and probably in Syriac), he integrated some Jewish Christian Gospel material.

Subsequently the Bodmer Papyrus showed that most deviations of the "Western Text" resulted from either harmonization or extra-canonical influence and have no value for the reconstruction of the original text (for an editor of the New Testament must not ask what Jesus said, but what Matthew, Mark, Luke and John wrote). The Gospel of Thomas revealed that, at least in Mesopotamia, there existed an independent, Jewish Christian Gospel tradition, which influenced the "Western Text" and the *Diatessaron* and seems to have been known to such writers as Aphraates (fourth century). This new insight led Michael Mees to suppose that Clement of Alexandria had at his disposal a very good, Egyptian Text of the Gospels; the many variants he knew were probably taken from a free Jewish Christian tradition circulating at that time in Alexandria.[6] The many similarities of these passages with the Gospel of Thomas, the Clementines and Aphraates make this supposition highly probable. All these new discoveries mean that the Jewish Christian Gospel material has increased enormously.

The Jewish Christian Gospel material consists of the following:

(1) Fragments from the Gospel of the Hebrews, the Gospel of the Nazareans and the Gospel of the Ebionites;

(2) the sayings of the Synoptic type contained in the Gospel of Thomas;

(3) the extracanonical elements of the "Western Text";

(4) extracanonical material in the various versions of the *Diatessaron*;

(5) the Gospel quotations in the Pseudo-Clementine *Homilies* and *Recognitions*;

(6) extracanonical material in Clement of Alexandria;

(7) certain traditions in Aphraates, *Liber Graduum*, Macarius and other Syrian or Syriac authors (here it becomes difficult to distinguish between influences of the Gospel of Thomas, the *Diatessaron* and the Gospel of the Nazareans, all possibly known to the authors);

(8) other authors who agree with the Jewish Christian Gospel fragments, the Gospel of Thomas or the Pseudo-Clementines.

All this material must have evolved in part or totally from an independent, Palestinian tradition of the sayings of Jesus, transmitted by Jewish Christians. It is therefore important to ask to what extent the author of the Fourth Gospel used a special tradition of sayings of Jesus, not taken from Mark or other canonical Gospels, but ultimately derived from a Palestinian source. In the following we will discuss a few cases in order to show that the Jewish Christian Gospel tradition is relevant for this aspect of Johannine studies. Our basic assumption is that the Gospel of John is *not* quoted in the Gospel of Thomas.

C. H. Dodd[7] and Bent Noack[8] have demonstrated that the author

[6] M. Mees, *Die Zitate aus dem Neuen Testament bei Clemens von Alexandrien* Bari, 1970).

[7] C. H. Dodd, *Historical Tradition in the Fourth Gospel* (Cambridge, 1963).

[8] Bent Noack, *Zur johanneischen Tradition* (Copenhagen, 1954).

of the Fourth Gospel probably knew and used an independent tradition of the sayings of Jesus. The Johannine problem, however, is so
complicated and the solutions offered by serious scholars are so
diverse that we should make our position clear. As we see it, the
Gospel of John was written in Ephesus before A.D. 100 and has a
great deal in common with the Apocalypse of John. The author
used a source, perhaps the Gospel of his congregation, which
contained accounts of the baptism, miracles and death of Jesus. The
discourses in their present form, however, are the work of the author
himself. In the prologue a Christian, perhaps Aramaic, hymn was
used. The pericope of the woman taken in adultery formed no part
of the Fourth Gospel in its primitive form. The letters of John come
from the same circle as the Gospel. Probably 1 John and possibly
2 John and 3 John are by the same hand as the Gospel. To reiterate,
our aim is to show that all these parts have some affinity with the
Jewish Christian Gospel tradition and are firmly rooted in Palestinian
soil.

Baptism

The *Pericope adulterae* (Jn 7:53–8:11) is not found in the Vatican
and Sinaitic manuscripts, nor in P66 and P75, which reflect an earlier
stage of development of the same Egyptian text. This omission
confirmed the considered opinion of many scholars that the pericope
was not a part of the primitive Gospel and had been inserted later.
The oldest manuscript which contains this story is the Codex Bezae,
a representative of the "Western Text". This in itself could suggest
that the pericope had been taken from the Jewish Christian Gospel
tradition. Eusebius of Caesarea (*HE* III, 39, 17) tells us that it was
contained in the Jewish Christian Gospel according to the Hebrews.
Moreover, a manuscript of John from Mount Athos of the eleventh
century (MS. 1006) has a marginal note to the effect that "this chapter
comes from the Gospel according to Thomas". The pericope is not
found in the Coptic version of Thomas, found at Nag Hammadi in
1945–1946. Ulrich Becker, however, observes that in such a collection
of sayings a logion can easily be added or omitted in the course of
redaction.[9] He supposes that the pericope was contained in the
primitive edition of the Gospel of Thomas, which in this case used
the Gospel according to the Hebrews as a source. He holds that the
Jewish Christians transmitted the whole passage and that the pericope
may very well preserve an event in the life of Jesus. In this case the
influence of Jewish Christianity on the Fourth Gospel seems almost
certain; moreover the Gospel itself shows some affinity with the same
tradition. Its author does not mention explicitly the baptism of Jesus
by John in the river Jordan, but he evidently used a source which
contained a description of this event: "John testified further: 'I saw
the Spirit coming down from heaven like a dove and *resting upon
him (emeine)*'" (Jn 1:32). This underlying source cannot be Mk 1:10,
because the latter says that the Spirit came down and entered into him

---

[9] *Jesus und die Ehebrecherin* (Berlin, 1963) 149.

(*eis auton*). Moreover, we have in John a clear allusion to the prophecy of Is 11:2, according to which the Spirit of the Lord will *rest* (LXX, *anapausetai*) upon him (the Messiah). That John used an existing tradition, however, is shown by a preserved fragment of the Gospel of the Nazaraeans (Jerome, *In Is.* 11,2): "descendit fons omnis spiritus sancti et *requievit* super eum".

The Testament of Levi (18:7), one of the Testaments of the Twelve Patriarchs, which is a Jewish Christian writing according to J. Jervell,[10] reflects the same tradition: "Spirit will *rest* upon him in the water".

Close reading of the text reveals that the author of John in this case used a source which was not Mark but which contained a Palestinian tradition of the baptism of Jesus. This, of course, was not identical with the Gospel of the Nazaraeans, but it preserved the same tradition.

The author of John was well aware of the frictions between followers of John the Baptist and Jewish Christians in Palestine during the first century. He does not find it necessary to relate John's family relations and his call for repentance, but stresses the fact that John did not consider himself the Messiah: "I am not the Messiah" (1:20). Now in the Pseudo-Clementine *Recognitions* (I, 60) we find the echo of a debate between "a disciple of John" and the disciples of Christ. In its present form this discussion between the parties of the Jews and the twelve disciples is merely a literary device, but it is quite possible that such discussions occurred in Palestine. As long as scholars considered the Pseudo-Clementine writings to be a novel of late date, such data could inspire little confidence; however, now that we know these writings in some cases contain very valuable traditions, we may use them for the interpretation of the Fourth Gospel. "And lo, one of the disciples of John affirmed that John had been the Messiah and not Jesus." Our sources do not attest that John the Baptist himself made such a claim. Probably Jesus, and certainly his early disciples, proclaimed that he was the Anointed of Israel; if a disciple of the Baptist later said the same about John, this must have been a reaction to the Christian position. It is quite possible that in the debate between Christians and Baptists this was the case. It would seem, then, that the author of the Fourth Gospel, by attributing to the Baptist himself the denial that he was the Messiah, refuted by implication the views of the followers of John. He appealed to John himself against the latter's adherents. It is of course possible that there were in Ephesus disciples of John the Baptist who claimed that their master was the Messiah (cf. Acts 19:7). It seems also possible that such debates took place in Palestine. Therefore it is not excluded that the author found the saying of John, according to which he was not the Messiah, in a source.

It is very difficult to affirm anything with certainty in such cases, because the evidence is too limited. The author of the Fourth Gospel shows a certain familiarity with the Baptists of Palestine. He is the only one to tell us that Jesus at a certain period of his activity was

---

[10] C. Burchard, J. Jervell and J. Thomas, *Studien zu den Testamenten der zwölf Patriarchen* (BZNW 36; Berlin, 1969).

the leader of a group of Baptists in Judea (4:1-3). This seems very probable indeed. It is possible that he was personally aware of the schism in the group of Baptists, which caused some of them to follow Jesus, and others to reject him and form the nucleus of the Jewish Baptist sect, which continues as the Mandaean sect of Iran, still vehemently opposed to Jesus.[11] But in any case the Jewish Christian tradition about a clash between followers of the Baptist and followers of Jesus is relevant for the interpretation of the Fourth Gospel.

Wth this in mind we turn to the well-known passages about rebirth in the dialogue with Nicodemus:

"In truth, in very truth I tell you, unless a man has been born over again he cannot see the kingdom of God" (Jn 3:3).
"In truth I tell you, no one can enter the kingdom of God without being born from water and spirit" (Jn 3:5).

These are the only passages in the Fourth Gospel in which the kingdom of God is mentioned. This may be an indication that the Evangelist is here following a tradition. It might be a saying of Jesus preserved among others by the Pseudo Clementine *Homilies* (XI, 26, 2): "If you are not reborn ... you will not enter the kingdom of Heaven." This would seem to be a more primitive version than that of John, because it is more personal ("you") and because it speaks about the kingdom of Heaven, not the kingdom of God.

The point, however, is that the saying belongs to the Jewish Christian Gospel tradition, because it is found in the Pseudo-Clementines. If it is also found in Justin Martyr (*Apol.*, I, 61, 4), this only proves to be another argument showing that Justin was familiar with the tradition. It is also found in one of the newly discovered *Homilies* of Marcarius, though it is there tinged with influences from John: "If a man is not reborn from above, he will not enter the kingdom of Heaven" (III, 16, 3). Macarius was a Syrian mystic, belonging to the sect of the Messalians, who knew and used not only the Gospel of Thomas, but also the Jewish Christian Gospel tradition contained in the Pseudo-Clementine writings.[12] If he still quotes the saying in this form, he certainly must have borrowed it from Jewish Christian traditions, which persisted for a long time in Mesopotamia.

Rebirth, then, was not exclusively a Hellenistic, but also a Jewish Christian and so also a primitive Christian notion. This is understandable if, as Kretschmar[13] and Segelberg[14] have argued, Christian baptism had its prototype in the Jewish Baptist sects, of which the Mandaeans have still preserved the ritual pattern. The immersion of

---

[11] K. Rudolph, "Probleme einer Entwicklungsgeschichte der mandäischen Religion", *Le Origini dello Gnosticismo*, ed. U. Bianchi (Leiden, 1967) 583-97. R. Macuch, "Anfänge der Mandäer", *Die Araber in der Alten Welt*, ed. F. Altheim and R. Stiehl (Berlin, 1962) vol. 2, 76-190.

[12] G. Quispel, "The Syrian Thomas and the Syrian Macarius", *VigChr* 18 (1964) 226-35.

[13] G. Kretschmar, *Die Geschichte des Taufgottesdienstes in der alten Kirche* (*Leiturgia* 5, 31; Kassel, 1964).

[14] E. Segelberg, *Masbūtā, Studies in the Ritual of the Mandaean Baptism* (Uppsala, 1958).

adult people into the water of a streaming river spontaneously suggests to the ancient mind the idea of death and resurrection, a new birth.

The Mandaean and the Roman ritual of baptism have much in common: *immersio, vestitio, impositio manuum* etc.; the unction, symbol of the chrism with the Holy Spirit, seems to be specifically Christian. This gives a beautiful perspective to the words, "this is he who is to baptize in Holy Spirit" (Jn 1:33). As a matter of fact, the stress on the Spirit conveyed in and through the act of baptism is typically Christian when compared with Mandaean documents.

As is well known, the Baptist lived in the neighbourhood of Qumran. The Mandaeans share several ideas with the Essenes, and the language of the Scrolls is frequently similar to that in John: "and to purify him through holy spirit from all works of evil he will sprinkle upon him the spirit of truth as water of purification" (1QS 4:21–23).

As far as I know, however, nothing is said in the Dead Sea Scrolls about rebirth. The concept of rebirth, together with "the Spirit resting upon" Jesus during baptism, and the differences between Jesus and John the Baptist, form a consistent whole. To understand this, we should place the testimony of the Fourth Gospel in the perspective of Baptism rather than in that of Essenism.

The Brother[15]

In the Fourth Gospel the double commandment to love God and neighbour, so prominent in the Synoptic Gospels, is conspicuously absent. Nor do we find there an injunction to love God. In this respect, therefore, John probably did not follow the Synoptics; moreover, many scholars today think that John did not know the Synoptics at all. Nor does John record that the Christian should love his neighbour; the word *plēsion* is found in the *Corpus Johanneum* only at Jn 4:5 and there it means "near" not "neighbour".

The Fourth Gospel, however, and especially the Johannine Letters, do stress the essential importance of love. Jesus' new commandment emphasizes that his disciples should love one another (13:34–35). John teaches neither love of God nor love of neighbour, but brotherly love: only the man who loves his brother dwells in the light (1 Jn 2:10). It would seem that behind all these variations lies a saying of Jesus preserved in the Gospel of Thomas, logion 25: "Love thy brother as thy soul, guard him as the apple of thine eye." The expression "Love ... as thy soul" seems to be a Hebraism, found also in the Old Testament (1 Sam 18:1), and meaning "Love ... as yourself". As such it is found in the Testaments of the Twelve Patriarchs, which in its present form could be a Jewish Christian writing (Test. Sim. 4:6; Test. Benj. 4:3). In the same book we find the commandment to love your brother: "love every one his brother" (Test. Sim. 4:7; Test. Gad 6:1). The same saying seems to have been known to the author of the *Liber Graduum,* a Syriac writing of the fourth century:

[15] For the following see my article "Love thy brother", *Ancient Society* (Louvain, 1970) vol. 1.

"For he (Jesus) said to you: Love your brother more than your soul"
(16:4).

There is nothing gnostic in this saying: the Hebraism, the Semitic
parallelism, the fact that it is found in the Gospel of Thomas and
the Testaments of the Twelve Patriarchs, suggest that it was transmitted in Jewish Christian milieu. The differences from the Synoptic
wording are so enormous that the saying cannot have been borrowed
from Matthew, Mark or Luke. It has not, of course, been taken from
the Gospel of John, which contains no commandment of Jesus in this
form. It represents an independent tradition. This leads us to an
important conclusion: not only has the author of the Fourth Gospel
used a Palestinian saying, but his use of "brother" and of "brotherly
love" in this context is not due to his own redactional or theological
activity; the use has its roots in primitive Christianity and perhaps
in the teaching of Jesus himself.

What does "brother" mean in this context? In Lev 19:17–18, which
is the starting-point for this new commandment, it clearly means
"compatriot". But in the Damascus Document, an Essene writing
which has strong links with Qumran, it designates the member of
one's own sect: "Everyone shall love his brother as himself" (6:20).
It could very well be that "brother" has the same meaning in the
saying of Jesus. If we accept this perspective, it at once becomes
clear that there is a gap between Qumran and the saying of Jesus.
In the latter the letter of the Law is paraphrased with a freedom that
has no parallel in the Dead Sea Scrolls or in any contemporary
Jewish writing known to the present writer. John did the same. "Love
one another" is a far cry from Lev 19:17–18. It is possible, however,
that he has preserved the exact and exclusive meaning of the saying
of Jesus. The comparison of the Qumran material with John and the
saying of Jesus does not necessarily prove that John or Jesus was
indebted to Qumran in this case. The exclusivist and sectarian meaning of "brother" could also arise in a small community like that of
the Baptists. The parallel, however, may well show that the background of Jewish and Johannine Christianity is not to be found in
Pharisaism, but in that other sector of Judaism which in the course
of time was completely overshadowed by Pharisaism and rabbinic,
normative, orthodox Judaism. Our example was taken from the Farewell Discourses, which were redacted by the author. So the author
himself must have known the Palestinian tradition of logia.

Parallels with the Jewish Christian Gospel tradition

In the foregoing we have tried to show that the author of John was
familiar with sayings of Jesus found in Jewish Christianity. He may
have found part of it in his source, the so-called *Semeiaquelle*, which
possibly was the Gospel of the community to which he belonged. The
same parallels, however, are to be found in the Discourses, especially,
as we saw, in the Farewell Discourses. Behind John Bultmann sees a
Redenquelle, which is not Christian but pre-Christian and even gnostic
in its origin. The author of John supposedly demythologized this
source. Many impressive parallels from Mandaean and gnostic sources

have been adduced to prove the existence of such a *Redenquelle*.[16] This position has been challenged by Bent Noack. Writing before the discovery of the Gospel of Thomas, he convincingly argued that the author of John used a source of sayings, which he grouped together and amplified to form discourses. Of course it cannot be doubted that the Johannine discourses have a formal similarity with the Mandaean "discourse of revelation", as they also have with the literature of Hermes Trismegistos and other Hellenistic religious texts. Since Herodotus and Plato, however, it was the legitimate right of a Greek author to write discourses and dialogues in order to describe a historical situation as he saw it. Moreover, we see also in the Synoptic Gospels how sayings are combined to form a discourse. This, for instance, is the case with Matthew's Sermon on the Mount.

It would seem that the newly discovered Jewish Christian Gospel tradition offers ample material to corroborate the thesis of Bent Noack. It would require a whole book to show this in detail. We will therefore limit ourselves here to a few examples, leaving it to specialists to discuss this material more fully.

(1) The theme of the hidden Messiah, who is already present in this world, but not yet known, seems to have been inserted by the author of John into the traditional material of his source. After the well-known phrase, "I baptize in water", there follows, "among you stands the one whom you do not know" (1:26). This could have been an isolated saying of Jesus, since the theme of the hidden Messiah is frequent in the Gospel of Thomas:

"Know him, who is in thy sight, and what is hidden from thee will be revealed to thee" (1:5).
"I stood in the midst of the world and in flesh I appeared to them; I found them all drunk, I found none among them athirst" (1:28).
"You test the face of the sky and of the earth, and him who is before your face you have not known" (1:91).

(2) According to Jn 2:19 Christ said, "Destroy this temple and in three days I will raise it again". The Gospel of Thomas shows that this saying was to be found in the extracanonical tradition: "Jesus said: I shall destroy this house and no one will be able to build it again" (1:71). It is possible therefore that John did not take this saying from the Synoptics. It must be observed, however, that John is much nearer to the Synoptics than to the tradition of Thomas.

(3) Noack argues that John was not dependent upon the Synoptics, but borrowed from the free tradition, when he wrote: "a prophet has not honour in his own country" (4:44).[17] According to several critics, Thomas has preserved the original wording of the saying, "No prophet is acceptable in his village, no physician heals those who know him" (1:31). This seems to show that the logion was transmitted also out-

---

16 For details see R. Bultmann, *Das Evangelium des Johannes*, 13th ed. (Göttingen, 1953).
17 *Zur johanneischen Tradition*, 95.

side the Synoptics by the Jewish Christian Gospel tradition. It should
be observed, however, that John is nearer to Mark (6:4) than to
Thomas.

(4) In the second part of logion 38 Thomas says, "There will be days
when you will seek me and you will not find me". According to Noack
this saying was transmitted to John from an independent tradition.[18]
This hypothesis helps to explain why John alludes to this saying no
less than three times, always with small variations:

  7:34: "You will look for me, but you will not find me."
  8:21: "You will look for me, but you will die in your sins."
  13:33: "Then you will look for me, and, as I told the Jews, I tell
  you now, where I am going you cannot come."

(5) Jn 8:46: "Which of you convicts me of sin?"

  Thomas 1:104: "Which then is the sin that I have committed, or
  in what have I been vanquished?"

(6) Jn 10:7: "I am the door."

  Ps.-Clem. *Hom* III, 52, 2: "I am the gate."

(7) J. Schäfers published the following extracanonical saying of Jesus,
which probably goes back to a Syriac text:[19] "Every vine that was
planted in me and gives no fruit, is being rooted out." It would seem
that this remarkable version owes something to a Jewish Christian
saying preserved by the Gospel of Thomas (1:40): "A vine has been
planted without the Father and, as it is not established, it will be
pulled up by its roots and destroyed." This, then, would be the Jewish
Christian counterpart of Mt 15:13: "Any plant that is not of my
heavenly Father's planting will be rooted up." John, however, is nearer
to Thomas than to Matthew: "I am the real vine, and my Father is
the gardener. Every barren branch of mine he cuts away; and every
fruitful branch he cleans, to make it more fruitful still" (15:1f.). "He
who does not dwell in me is thrown away like a withered branch. The
withered branches are heaped together, thrown on the fire, and
burnt" (15:6).

If, when writing his discourses, John used a sayings source—and
this would seem rather probable—then in this case his own redactional
methods and his familiarity with Palestinian tradition seem rather
obvious.

The paraclete

John calls the Holy Spirit "the Paraclete". This word obviously has a
forensic meaning. In classical Greek *ho paraklētos* designates not only
the man who is called to one's aid in a court of justice, the legal assis-

18 *Zur johanneischen Tradition*, 139.
19 J. Schäfers, *Eine altsyrische antimarkionitische Erklärung von Parabeln des
Herrn* (Neutestamentliche Abhandlungen 6; Münster, 1917) 173.

tant or "advocate", but also the intercessor.[20] 1 Jn 2:1 preserves this meaning. Christ intercedes in heaven before God for the faithful: "but should anyone commit a sin, we have one to plead our cause with the Father, Jesus Christ." Christ can be called here "paraclete", because he is in heaven and prays for us.

The author of the Fourth Gospel also considers Christ to be a paraclete. According to him Jesus said in his farewell discourse: "I will ask the Father and he will give you another paraclete, who will be with you for ever, the Spirit of Truth" (14:16). If the Holy Ghost is a second paraclete, this implies that Christ also is a paraclete. We should expect then that in the view of the Fourth Gospel Christ and the Spirit pray and plead as advocates for sinful mankind before the throne of God. This assumption, however, is not the case.

As John sees it, the Paraclete is now on earth, in debate with the world, among the faithful and even within them. Nothing indicates that he has a forensic task here and now. This is astonishing, because elsewhere in the New Testament the Spirit is represented as praying and interceding for the Christians: "We do not know how to pray, but the Spirit himself is pleading for God's own people" (Rom 8: 26–28). John, therefore, uses the word "paraclete", but alters its original meaning of "intercessor" so that its actual function can only be designated as "helper" (of the faithful). Consequently the translation "comforter" is better than "advocate". This shift in meaning seems to show that John uses a specific tradition, in which the Spirit was called "paraclete" and had a forensic meaning, even though the latter connotation was omitted from the Gospel.

The second important observation is that John clearly regards the Holy Spirit as a person or at least as a hypostatic being with personal characteristics, distinct from Christ (not his force or spirit or function in the world). The author is so convinced of this personal being that he uses the Greek masculine pronoun *ekeinos* with the neuter substantive, *to pneuma tēs alētheias* (14:26, 17). This is not always the case in the New Testament, even in the Gospel of John: "He then breathed on them, saying: Receive the Holy Spirit" (20:22). This again suggests that John, when speaking about the paraclete, is using an existing idea transmitted to him by tradition. Where did it come from? Some have said that gnosticism must be the source of this idea. We would find here, then, the underlying idea of a succession of bearers of the revelation. The Mandaean *jawar*, thought to mean helper, is adduced as a proof of this hypothesis.[21] Against this it may be said that gnosticism abhors the idea of a paraclete.

In the *Epistula Jacobi Apocrypha*, the first book of the Jung codex, written in the second century A.D. in Egypt by a gnostic, possibly a Valentinian, the Johannine conception of the paraclete is seriously criticized. Jesus is quoted there as having said to his disciples James and Peter, "I intercede for you with the Father and he will forgive you much". But when the disciples, narrow-minded as they are, become joyful because this is said to them, they must hear that the true gnostic

---

20 See H. G. Liddell, R. Scott, *A Greek-English Lexicon*, rev. H. S. Jones and R. McKenzie (Oxford, 1968) *ad loc.*
21 R. Bultmann, *Das Evangelium des Johannes*, 437.

F

does not need an intercessor, because he possesses grace as a permanent possession and can speak to God freely without a mediator:
"But when he saw us rejoicing, he said, 'Woe to you, O you that need
an intercessor (*paraklētos*), woe to you that need grace. Blessed shall
they be who have spoken openly, and have acquired grace for themselves' " (11:10–17). Moreover, it has been observed that *jawar* does
not mean "helper", but "brilliant one". The idea of a succession of
revealers, so prominent in Manicheism, was taken by Manes possibly
from Jewish Christianity, which he had known in Babylonia. The
idea is found, for example, in the Pseudo-Clementine writings.[22]
Nevertheless, this gnostic material is useful for the interpretation of
John, because it suggests the possibility that the Holy Spirit in this
Gospel is the successor, the only legitimate successor of Jesus on earth.

The Dead Sea Scrolls are less helpful here. It is true that the expression "The Spirit of Truth" is found there (1QS 3:18–19; 4:21–23),
but the same is the case with the Pastor of Hermas, *Mandates*, III, 4.
Hermas, writing in Rome in the first half of the second century
A.D., did not know the Gospel of John, yet he has much in common
with Qumran and was familiar with Jewish Christian ideas (cf. his
adoptionism). Both he and John may have taken the expression from
a primitive, Jewish Christian tradition which was indebted to Qumran.
John, at least in this case, has not used the writings of the Essenes,
but knows an Essene expression through the intermediary of Palestinian Christianity.

When we stress the personal character of the Holy Spirit in John,
it may perhaps be illuminating to state that in the Qumran Scrolls
the Prince of Light and Angel of Light, possibly Michael, is identified
with the Spirit of Truth (1QS 3:21). This, however, is merely a
parallel, not a source. John speaks of two paracletes and presupposes a
certain trinitarian schema. There are not two angels of light in the
Scrolls. Until now no passage in the Dead Sea Scrolls has been discovered which says explicitly that an angel intercedes with God on man's
behalf while the devil accuses him. As for the origin of the paraclete
in John, Qumran is a blind alley.[23] Rabbinic parallels are rather late,
but they once refer to the Spirit as *snygwr*, the equivalent of Greek
synēgoros, practically identical with *paraklētos* (Lev R. 6:109a). Moreover, in one case, the Spirit intercedes in favour of the people to
placate the wrath of God (Dt R. 3:12).[24] Nowhere in rabbinic literature, however, do we find two paracletes. ,

This material opens our eyes to the essential fact that the conception
of the paraclete in John is of Jewish origin and must be examined in
a Jewish perspective. According to the Old Testament an angel intercedes in heaven in favour of man (Job 16:19; 33:23; Zech 3:3). Only
in Jewish Christian sources, however, do we find the exact parallel
for the underlying idea in John. According to the Ascension of Isaiah

---

22 For Jewish Christian influences upon Manicheism see my article "Manicheism",
Man, Myth and Magic (London, 1971).
23 For a different opinion see O. Betz's *Der Paraklet* (Leiden, 1963), and Leaney's
chapter above, pp. 38ff.
24 S. Mowinckel, "Die Vorstellungen des Spätjudentums vom Heiligen Geist als
Fürsprecher", *ZNW* 32 (1933) 97–130.

(9) the Lord and a second angel, the Angel of the Holy Spirit, are standing before the throne of God, adored as divine beings and adoring God themselves.

The Jewish Christian Elkesai (A.D. 100), when staying in Parthia, received a vision of the Messiah and opposite him the Holy Ghost in the form of a female being.[25] In the Testaments of the Patriarchs the following passages are found:

> "I am the angel who intercedeth for the nation of Israel, that they may not be smitten utterly, for every evil spirit attacketh it" (Test. Levi 5:6).
> "Draw near unto God and to the angel that intercedeth for you, for he is a mediator between God and man, and for the peace of Israel he shall stand up against the kingdom of the enemy" (Test. Dan 6:2).

If, as J. Jervell supposes, the Testaments of the Twelve Patriarchs in their present form are Jewish Christian, then the Angel of the Lord in these passages must be the Messiah. In the Septuagint at Is 9:5 (v. 6 in English versions) the Messiah was regarded as "the Angel of the Great Council". This is the starting-point for the curious interpretation of the Old Testament to be found later in Justin Martyr and so many other Christian authors, who identified Christ with the Angel of the Lord in the Old Testament. It is also the root of the angel-Christology of the Jewish Christians, which is not necessarily heterodox, because even in the Old Testament the Angel of the Lord can be another term for the Lord.

When, however, in the Testaments of the Twelve Patriarchs and in the Pseudo-Clementine *Recognitions* (II, 42) this angelic Messiah is entrusted exclusively with the care of the people of Israel, it seems rather probable that he has assumed the functions of Michael, who is the intercessor for the Jewish people.[26]

Does this not reveal the Palestinian Jewish background of John's idea? Since the word "paraclete" is not found outside John, it may have been a technical term current in the congregation to which John belonged, Ephesus. The trinitarian schema, however, has Palestinian roots. In this perspective we discern how John freely used his traditional material. Against the Jewish Christians he held that since the advent of Christ the Spirit was on earth, a personal God among his people, leading them towards the truth and refuting the pretensions of the world.

The name

In the farewell discourses, especially in chapter 17, Jesus speaks about the Name: "I have made thy Name known to the men whom thou didst give me out of the world. They were thine, thou gavest them to me, and they have preserved thy word (*logos*)" (17:6); "Protect them

---

25 Hippolytus, *Refutatio* IX, 13.

26 For the Jewish Christian origins of the doctrine of the Trinity see G. Kretschmar, *Studien zur frühchristlichen Trinitätstheologie* (Tübingen, 1956).

by the power of thy Name which thou hast given me" (17:11); "I made thy Name known to them, and I will make it known" (17:26). Christ has received the Name of God from God and reveals it to his disciples, and he is in a sense the Name. This is the revelation which his followers have received and preserved; not a word, or a command-ment, but the "Word" which contains the Name. *Logos*, "Word", and *Onoma*, "Name", are interchangeable and, in a way, identical in 17:6. This interchangeability implies that the Name was hidden and un-known before Jesus revealed it. The Name of a god or goddess has important implications in practically all religions. This applies also in magic, for magical acts are often performed by the power of the name of a divine being, which the magician knows and can manipu-late. The interchangeability also presupposes a Jewish background; nowhere is the Name so important as in Judaism. Nobody was allowed to pronounce the tetragrammaton, except the high priest on the Day of Atonement. Instead of the tetragrammaton the word *Adonai*, "Lord", was read; in private reading it was replaced by the technical term *haššēm*, "the Name". The Name is the hidden, unutterable Name, the *šem hammᵉpōrāš*.

There is here a distinct difference between Judaism and Hellenistic philosophy. The latter holds that the divinity is completely unknown and unknowable; it has no name. Judaism, on the contrary, firmly believes that God has a Name, but that it is completely incompre-hensible. Moreover, modern scholars have been unable to give a satis-factory etymology of the tetragrammaton.

These observations show that Judaism and Christianity, in this respect, have more in common with the religions of the world than with philosophy; the Name is a typically religious category. Judaism and Christianity are not only faiths, but also religions. We cannot enter into the long and complicated story of the Name in the Old Testament and in intertestamental Judaism; for our purposes it is enough to state that the Name can be described as the essential revelation of God's being. When John describes Christ as the Name of God, he means that Christ is the essential revelation of God. The Gospel of Truth, a gnostic, Valentinian meditation written about A.D. 150, contains very long and elaborate speculations about Christ as the Name, even the Proper Name of God.[27] The following pass-age may be quoted:

> "But the Name of the Father is the Son. It is He, who, in the begin-ning, gave a name to him who came forth from Him and who was Himself and whom He begat as a Son. He gave him His Name which belonged to Him" (Gospel of Truth 38:5ff.).

God has given his Name to his Son, whom he has begotten before all ages and who is consubstantial, identical with himself. The Name, of course, can be none other than the tetragrammaton, the Name of the Jewish God, the Lord.

[27] K. Grobel, *The Gospel of Truth* (New York, 1960) 180-90.

"Since the Father is unbegotten, it is He alone who begat him for Himself as a Name, before he had begotten the Aeons, in order that the Name of the Father should be over their head as Lord, he who is the authentic Name, firm in its authority and its perfect power".

How could the Name be Lord, unless the Name was "Lord"?

"He (Christ) is the Proper Name. It is not as a loan that he received the Name, ... but he is the Proper Name. There is no other to whom He has given It."

It became immediately clear to the editors of the Gospel of Truth how enormous the Jewish influence had been upon this writing.[28] For them there was no doubt that this Name was the tetragrammaton and that these elaborate speculations could not be due to the influence of the Gospel of John or the New Testament writings in general, though these were no doubt practically all known to the author of the Gospel of Truth, who was perhaps Valentinus himself.

New Testament scholarship in general remained sceptical and hesitated to adopt these new insights for the interpretation of the Fourth Gospel.[29] Some scholars tend to ignore what is new. If commentators read the Gospel of Truth, their commentaries on John certainly did not betray this secret. Moreover, at this time it was extravagant and even shocking to relate gnosticism to Judaism, which were held to have nothing at all in common (Martin Buber). Gnosticism was either considered to be a religious philosophy, brought forth by Hellenism, or it was thought to have its origin in an imaginary Iranian myth of the Saved Saviour (Bultmann, Widengren). It is not easy for a professor to revise his considered opinion. One, an eminent scholar, who was well versed in Coptic but knew little Greek, thought the translation "Proper Name" was faulty. He preferred to translate "Lord of the Name". This is impossible; *dzjaeis ñren* certainly renders the Greek *kyrion onoma*, and the Gospel of Truth had been translated from the Greek into Coptic. If any lingering doubts remained as to the extent and significance of the Jewish contribution to gnosticism, subsequent discoveries and researches should be sufficient to remove them completely.

In the first place then Proper Name in relation to God is typically Jewish: *šem hammeyuḥad*.[30] It is found only once in a Greek papyrus: "the Proper Name, which is Ogdoas Theos, who orders and governs everything".[31] But, as Gershom Scholem has pointed out, this text was strongly influenced by esoteric Jewish lore.[32] As far as I know, no other Greek document exists in which it is said that a god has a "Proper Name". The expression of course is Stoic. We may perhaps

---

[28] G. Quispel, "Christliche Gnosis und jüdische Heterodoxie", *EvT* 14 (1954) 1–11.
[29] See my "Het Johannesevangelie en de Gnosis", *NTT* 11 (1957) 173–203.
[30] W. Bacher, *Die exegetische Terminologie* (Darmstadt, 1965) vol. 1, 159 and 186.
[31] A. Dieterich, *Abraxas* (Leipzig, 1891) 194.
[32] G. Scholem, "Some Problems of Jewish Gnosticism", *Atti del VIII congresso internazionale di storia delle religioni* (Rome, 1955; Florence, 1956) 283–5.

wonder why the Jews picked up such a technical, grammatical term, in order to express their deepest mystery, but the fact is that they did. The Gospel of Truth is no exception to the rule. Many Valentinian writings speak about Christ as the Name: an example is *Excerpta ex Theodoto*, extracts made by Clement of Alexandria from Valentinian sources (22, 4–6; 26, 1; 31, 3). Most illuminating was the Gospel of Philip, a Valentinian collection of short remarks and observations, probably written at Antioch about A.D. 200. In section 12 of this writing we read: "One single Name they do not utter in the world, the Name which the Father gave to the Son, which is the Name of the Father. For the Son would not become Father, except he *clothes himself* with the Name of the Father." The expression, "to clothe oneself with the Name", *enduesthai to onoma*, is very peculiar. I know of no other Greek or Latin text which contains it, but it was current in Valentinian circles. A liturgical formula of the Valentinians speaks about "the Name ... which Jesus invested" (Irenaeus, *Adv. Haer.*, I, 21, 3). The same term is found in esoteric Judaism of a later date: the magician descends into the water and *puts on* the *Name*, i.e. performs a symbolic act by clothing himself in a garment into whose texture the Name has been woven and so impregnates himself with the great Name of God.[33]

Exactly the same expression is found in Samaritan sources, especially in the *Memar Marqa*.[34] According to this text, Moses, the great prophet of the Samaritans, was vested with the Name on the top of Mount Horeb. It is very important for the Fourth Gospel to see how the Samaritans, heterodox Jews, could exalt a man like Moses: "Moses was vested with the Name";[35] "I have given him (Moses) my Name";[36] "this Name fills the whole world and contains it";[37] "I have vested you with my Name";[38] "exalted is the great prophet Moses, whom the Lord vested with his Name";[39] "by that Name Moses slew the unbelievers";[40] "it is with his Name that he is vested";[41] "... vested me with thy Name, by which Thou didst create the world"[42] (here we find the idea, so well known from esoteric Judaism, that the world was created through the intermediary of the Name); "the Name with which he was vested on the top of Mount Horeb".[43]

The same writing says that the "Taheb" (Messiah) will reveal the truth: "When the Taheb comes, he will reveal the truth."[44] This presents a fine parallel to the remark of the Samaritan woman in the Gospel of John: "I know that Messiah (that is Christ) is coming.

---

[33] G. Scholem, *Major Trends in Jewish Mysticism* (New York, 1941) 77. The name of the writing in which this ceremony is described is called *Sefer Ha-Malbush*.
[34] See J. Macdonald (ed.), *Memar Marqah* (Berlin, 1963).
[35] *Ibid.*, 4.
[36] *Ibid.*, 14.
[37] *Ibid.*, 17.
[38] *Ibid.*, 32.
[39] *Ibid.*, 80.
[40] *Ibid.*, 81.
[41] *Ibid.*, 139.
[42] *Ibid.*, 158.
[43] *Ibid.*, 194.
[44] *Ibid.*, 70.

When he comes he will tell us everything" (Jn 4:25). I find no evidence, however, that according to the Samaritans the Taheb will be vested with the Name.

These parallels serve our purposes. In the first place they show us that the technical expression of the Valentinians has a Jewish ring and must have been taken from a Jewish milieu. Secondly, it now becomes clear that a theology of the Name could very well arise in a Jewish milieu, to such an extent that a man, Moses, could be identified with the Name of God. This is the more important if, as J. Bowman has shown, the *Memar Marqa* contains a curious mixture of orthodox Samaritanism and the gnosis of Dositheus (first century A.D.), which has relations with Qumran.[45] In the Dead Sea Scrolls, however, the expression "to put on the Name" is not found. The question then arises whether the passage on the Name in the Gospel of Truth has a Jewish or Jewish Christian origin.

Jewish precedents do exist. In Ethiopic Enoch (69:14) we find that heaven and earth have been created by the Name. Esoteric Judaism borrowed this theme from apocalyptic. In *Hekkaloth Rabbati* (ch. 9) it is said: "Great is the Name by which heaven and earth were created." The same is found in 3 Enoch (13:1; 41:1) and later in the mystical book of creation, *Yezira*.

In the Apocalypse of Abraham (ch. 10) the Angel of the Lord, God's vicegerent, second only to God himself, called Jao-el, has received the Name (Iao) from God himself: "I am called Jaoel by Him who moveth that which existeth with me on the seventh expanse upon the firmament, a power in virtue of the ineffable Name that is dwelling in me." The Name dwells in the Angel of the Lord (cf. Ex 23:21). This certainly is an interesting parallel, both for John and Valentinus, but neither of them seems to have known these Jewish, esoteric speculations directly. It seems more likely that the Christology of the Name reached them through Jewish Christian channels.

Traditions about the Name had been current in Ephesus. The Apocalypse of John (19:14) contains the following: "written upon him (Christ) was (the) Name known to nobody but himself... and his Name is called the Word of God." We see here that the Word is not just a word, or many words, but the one word which reveals God's essential being. And this could be very well the case with the Logos in the prologue of the Gospel of John. Moreover the expression "to put on the Name" is found in the Odes of Solomon 39:8: "Put on, therefore, the Name of the Most High and know Him: and you shall cross without danger, while the rivers shall be subject to you." The argument would be decisive if we could be sure that the Odes of Solomon were Jewish Christian, as is often said.[46] But this is not certain. We do not know whether they were written at Edessa, in Palestine or elsewhere, in Greek or in Syriac. Certainly they are not gnostic, and they reflect a religiosity very much akin to that of the author of the Fourth Gospel. But they could be encratitic, whereas the Jewish Christians, as far as we know, were not.

45 J. Bowman, *Samaritanische Probleme* (Stuttgart, 1967).
46 J. H. Charlesworth, "The Odes of Solomon—Not Gnostic". *CBQ* 31 (1969) 357–69.

Speculations about the Name are not limited to Jewish Christian writings. Clement of Rome speaks about "your (God's) Name which is the origin of the whole creation" (*archēgonon*, 57, 3). It is not certain that Christ is meant here, and Clement could have taken this view from Jewish Christians in Rome. The Didache (10, 2) speaks about the "Name, which thou madest dwell (*kateskēnōsas*) in our hearts". Here again we may hesitate about the real significance of the phrase.

The expression has parallels in Jewish literature. In the Psalms of Solomon it is said: "we will find mercy, when your Name dwells (*kataskēnoun*) among us" (7:6). This of course is the best imaginable parallel for John 1:14: "the Word became flesh; he came to dwell among us"; it shows how Jewish is the wording of John and how close are the meanings of *Logos* and *Onoma*. It could be that the Didache, when speaking about the Name dwelling in the heart of the faithful who have partaken in the eucharist, means to say that Christ is that Name; if so, this might reflect Jewish Christian teaching.

In an article entitled "La première communauté chrétienne à Jérusalem" Lucien Cerfaux has argued that there existed in the primitive community of Jerusalem an archaic Christology of the Name.[47] Miracles are performed there "through the Name of thy holy servant Jesus" (Acts 4:30). Men are granted no other Name by which they receive salvation than the Name of Jesus (Acts 4:12). In fact already in the congregation of Jerusalem, Old Testament passages in which "the Lord" is mentioned are applied to Jesus, and it seems plausible that the oldest confession "Jesus Lord" has its origin in this community.

If Paul, when writing Phil 2:6–11, is using an old Palestinian hymn, this view would seem to be confirmed: "Therefore God raised him to the heights and bestowed on him the Name above all names (the tetragrammaton), that at the Name of Jesus every knee should bow—in heaven, on earth and in the depths—and every tongue confess 'Jesus Christ is Lord' to the glory of God the Father".

According to this hymn the Name has been given to Jesus after his resurrection. Valentinus or the Valentinians hold that the Name descended upon Jesus during his baptism at the river Jordan (*Excerpta ex Theodoto*, 22, 4–6). This would seem to presuppose the well-known adoptionist Christology of the Jewish Christians, according to which Jesus became the Messiah at baptism. We may conclude then that the Valentinian speculations about Christ as the Proper Name of God and as "vested with the Name" were taken from Jewish Christians. This borrowing could have occurred in Egypt. Not only was Valentinus born in Egypt, but the *Epistula Jacobi Apocrypha*, possibly Valentinian, certainly gnostic and written in Egypt in the second century A.D., has revealed to what extent the gnostics of Egypt have been influenced by Jewish Christianity.

This apocryphon, allegedly written by James, the brother of the Lord and chief of the whole Church, goes so far as to call Jesus "the

[47] "La première communauté chrétienne à Jérusalem", *Recueil Lucien Cerfaux* (Gembloux, 1954) vol. 2, 125–56.

Son of the Holy Spirit",[48] an expression which has its parallel in the Gospel according to the Hebrews.[49]

Although these speculations on Christ as the Name were current in Jewish Christian circles of second-century Egypt, they ultimately go back to the primitive community in Jerusalem. It is from there that they reached the author of John in Ephesus, thus showing to what extent he is indebted to Palestinian tradition.

[48] Puech-Quispel, *Epistula Jacobi Apocrypha* (Zürich, 1968) 6, 20–1.
[49] *Ibid.*, 55.

8

The First Epistle of John and the
Writings of Qumran

MARIE-EMILE BOISMARD, O.P.

Of all the writings in the New Testament, the First Epistle of John,[1] along with the Epistle to the Ephesians, presents perhaps the greatest number of theological contacts with the writings from Qumran. This study will take as a basis for comparison the teaching concerning the two spirits which is set out in columns three and four of the Rule (1QS), although other passages drawn from the Qumran Scrolls will be used to complete it.

Dualism

It has been noted for a long time that the collection of writings from Qumran is permeated by a dualistic conception of the world, inherited probably from Zoroastrianism. This dualism expresses itself by means of two pairs of opposites, light and darkness, truth and iniquity. That the two pairs are closely linked is proved by this passage: "From one fountain of light (is) the origin of truth and from one source of darkness (is) the origin of iniquity" (1QS 3:19). Men are divided into two classes: one consists of the "sons of light" (3:13, 24, 25), who are also called "sons of truth" (4:5, 6, 17); the other consists of the "sons of darkness" (1:10), called also "sons of iniquity" (3:21). Two spirits contend for the heart of man: "the spirit of light" (3:25) or "the spirit of truth" (3:18, 19), and "the spirit of darkness" (3:25) or "the spirit of iniquity" (3:18, 19). Finally, these two worlds have at their head two "angels" or "princes" who struggle to keep power over men. The "prince of light" (3:20), who is called elsewhere the "angel of truth" (3:24), is opposed by the "angel of darkness" (3:21). Later we shall return to the meaning of these different categories of beings.

However, it must be specified immediately that this dualism is essentially moral. Light and darkness are respectively used as the symbols of truth and iniquity, a symbolism which is already known from Zoroastrianism. From another point of view, truth and iniquity designate all human action which is performed in accord with, or in

---

[1] For the bibliography and a discussion of the various works published on this subject, see: H. Braun, *Qumran und das Neue Testament* (2 vols; Tübingen, 1966) vol. 1, 290–306. Also see the bibliography at the end of the present book.

opposition to, the will of God and the divine Law. The sons of righteousness "walk" in the ways of light, while the sons of iniquity "walk"
in the ways of darkness (1QS 3:20f.). This verb "to walk" indicates
in the Rule the moral behaviour of man, as it often does in the Old
Testament. 1QS 4:2ff. contains first a long list of good actions, which
are accomplished by those under the influence of the spirit of truth,
then a second list of wicked actions, which are performed under the
influence of the spirit of iniquity. At the time of the final judgment,
according to these actions, good or evil, the sons of light will be
rewarded and the sons of darkness punished. Hence, light and truth
on one side, darkness and iniquity on the other, define in a very general
way Good and Evil (1QS 4:26) in relationship to the divine will.

We noted above that Qumran dualism originated partly in
Zoroastrianism. It is distinguishable always at a fundamental point:
it is a "modified" dualism, in the sense that light and darkness, and
the spirits of light and darkness, have been created by God and
remain dependent on him (3:25), as does everything which exists
(3:15). This allows the contemplation of a future time when iniquity
will disappear from the world, while the truth of God will purify every
man and triumph for ever (4:18-23). Or, to use the expressions of a
hymn from Qumran: "When those who bring forth iniquity are shut
up, evil will pass away before righteousness as darkness before light,
and as smoke disappears and is no more, so will evil disappear for
ever."[2]

After an introduction of four verses, the First Epistle of John
begins in this way: "This is the message we have heard from him
and proclaim to you, that God is light and in him is no darkness at
all..." (1:5). So from the outset of the Epistle we find ourselves in
the presence of the opposition between light and darkness, which is
characteristic of the Qumran Scrolls. God is preeminently light, without any darkness; but men are divided into two categories, according
to whether they walk in the light or in the darkness (1 Jn 1:6, 7). This
theme is taken up again in the process of grouping in 1 Jn 2:8-11, the
last passage where the opposition between light and darkness is set
forth. As in the Scrolls, the perspective is essentially moral; we find
the expression "to walk in the light" or "to walk in the darkness",
which occurs frequently in the Scrolls and which, as we have already
noted, indicates the moral conduct of man. Moreover, it is easy to
understand that the categories "light" and "darkness" speak with
reference to the love one has for his brethren or the hate he bears
towards them (1 Jn 2:9-11). Finally, as the Scrolls, the Epistle affirms
the final victory of light over darkness: "The darkness is passing
away and the true light is already shining" (2:8), a text which approximates the fragment of hymn quoted above: "... evil will pass away
before righteousness as darkness passes away before light."

We have seen that in the Qumran Scrolls the opposition between
light and darkness is complemented by an opposition between truth
and iniquity, which merges with it. It is the same in the First Epistle
of John. The one who "walks in the light" is said to possess "the truth
in him" (1 Jn 1:8; cf. 2:4). This term "truth" must be understood

2 Cf. R. de Vaux, "La Grotte des Manuscrits Hébreux", *RB* 56 (1949) 605.

in its biblical sense and so embody everything which concerns the actions of a man with reference to the will of God; not only correctness of faith (cf. 1 Jn 2:21f.), but also the fulfilment of the command to love one's neighbour (1 Jn 3:17–19). Again we meet the Scrolls' phraseology in which "light" and "truth" designate the whole sphere of goodness, which is understood as the conformity of human behaviour to the demands of the divine will. It must be recognized, however, that in 1 John 1:5–2:11, although the opposition between "light" and "darkness" is clearly marked, the opposition between "truth" and "iniquity" is much less apparent. Yet, later in 4:6, the author juxtaposes "the spirit of truth" with "the spirit of error", which corresponds to a large extent with the contrasting pair in the Rule; "the spirit of truth" and "the spirit of iniquity" (1QS 3:18f., et passim). The difference in vocabulary is not very important since, according to 1QS 3:21, it is "the spirit of iniquity" which causes men to stray and misleads them. The Johannine expression is found elsewhere in the Testaments of the Twelve Patriarchs (Test. Jud. 20:1), of which the affinities to the Qumran Scrolls have long been established. Lastly, let us note that in 1 John the dualism expresses itself again in 2:29–3:10, but with a distinct preference for the opposition between righteousness and sin. Once again men appear divided into two categories, according to whether they are "of God" and practise righteousness, or "of the Devil" and commit sin.

So it can be concluded that, as in the Qumran Scrolls, especially the Rule (1QS), the First Epistle of John is structured according to a dualism which has no equivalent in the Old Testament, and which is found in such an accentuated form only in some exceptional passages in the New Testament. Influence from Qumran theology is difficult to deny. It will appear even more obvious when we have considered the analogies of the various "characters" who perform in front of this backdrop: men, the two spirits, and the two angels.

The two categories of men

In the writings from Qumran, men who follow faithfully the demands of the divine Law are called "sons of light" or even "sons of truth" (1QS 1:9; 2:16; 3:13; 24f.; 4:5f., et passim). Although the expression "sons of light" is found in the Gospel of John at 12:36 and in some other texts in the New Testament,[3] it is absent from 1 John. The expression "sons of truth" never occurs in the New Testament. However, if we take into consideration that "sons of..." signifies adherence to a certain category of persons or to a certain kind of life, we can make an equivalence between the Qumran expression "sons of truth" and the Johannine expression "those (who are) of the truth" (1 Jn 2:21; 3:19). There exists in the same way a relationship between the Qumranic contrast between "the men of the lot of God and the men of the lot of Belial" (1QS 2:2, 5), and the Johannine contrast between "those (who are) of God and those (who are) of the Devil" (1 Jn 3:8, 10, 12; 4:4, 6; 5:19). It must be recognized, however, that the author of 1 John does not seem to have attached special importance to the

3 See above, p. 101, n. 117.

manner by which the Qumran writings refer to those who belong to the two opposing worlds, that of light and that of darkness.

According to the historian Josephus, the Essenes "practise mutual love more than others" (*War*, II, viii, 2, par. 119). An identical testimony has been given to us by Philo of Alexandria: "Their sect does not exist on the basis of race ... but is motivated by zeal for virtue and by a passion for the love of men" (cited by Eusebius of Caesarea, *Praep. Evang.* VIII, xi, 2). The Community Rule confirms the indication given by these two historians. In 7:1ff., among the punishments specified against those who transgress the customs of the community, a great number penalize lapses in brotherly love: unjust accusation addressed to another, arrogant words spoken against a neighbour, behaving with arrogance towards a neighbour, becoming angry unjustly against a neighbour, spreading slander against a neighbour, complaining unjustly against him, etc. In numerous passages in the Rule, love of one's neighbour appears as one of the principal objectives to which members of the sect should offer themselves: "All will be in true unity, in good humility, with merciful love, and with righteous purposes, each one towards his neighbour" (1QS 2:24f.); "... to practise the truth in common, and righteous humility, justice and merciful love" (5:3f.); "they must correct each other with truth, humility and merciful love towards each one" (5:24f.); "... to practise truth, righteousness, justice and merciful love, and to walk humbly, each one with his neighbour" (8:2f.). Let us quote as well a passage from the Damascus Document: "... for each one to love his brother as himself and to care for the wretched, the poor and the stranger and for each one to seek the well-being of his brother" (CD 6:20f.). Of course this commandment of brotherly love was already recorded in Leviticus 19:18: "You shall love your neighbour as yourself"; but what is remarkable is the importance given to this commandment. It was of such importance that it appears as one of the characteristics of the Essenes mentioned by Josephus and Philo. Finally we will note that this love is only exercised towards the members of the Essene community, towards the "sons of light" or the "sons of truth". In contrast, numerous texts call for hate towards those who are "sons of darkness" and of the lot of Belial, in other words, towards those who are not part of the Essene community.

In the New Testament, the Johannine writings are not alone in insisting on the commandment to love one's neighbour, but the Fourth Gospel and the First Epistle of John give quite a special place to this commandment. According to Jn 13:35 Jesus says to his disciples: "By this all men will know that you are my disciples, if you have love for one another." This is to say explicitly that brotherly love is the distinctive sign of the disciple of Jesus, as it was the principal characteristic of the Essene, according to Josephus and Philo. This commandment of brotherly love returns as a constant refrain throughout the First Epistle of John. The setting forth of the contrast between light and darkness (1:5–2:11) is concluded with an appeal for brotherly love (2:9–11); and it is clear that brotherly love distinguishes those who walk in the light from those who walk in the darkness. In 1 Jn 3:10 we learn that brotherly love is the criterion which allows the children of God to be distinguished from the children of the Devil; then comes a recollection of Jesus' teaching: "We should love one another" (3:11). The author of the Epistle subsequently gives some concrete examples of what this love must be in reality (3:12–18), concluding his argument by affirming that it is love which permits the recognition that "we are of the truth" (3:19). In 3:23, the teaching of Jesus seems to lead to the double commandment: to believe and to love. From 4:7 to 5:3 the sole subject is love for one's neighbour, which is rooted in God's love for us. Brotherly love is indeed the distinctive mark of the disciple of Jesus. From this perspective it is interesting to compare 1 Jn 4:20f. with 1QS 8:2f. The Johannine text establishes such a close relationship between love for God and love for neighbour that one is conditional upon the other: "If any one says, 'I love God', and hates his brother, he is a liar; for he who does not love his brother whom he has seen, how can he love God whom he has not seen? And this is the commandment we have from him, that he who loves God should love his brother also." The text of the Rule quotes Micah 6:8: "... to practise truth ... justice and merciful love, and to walk humbly, each with his neighbour." The end, however, is changed! Micah says: "to walk humbly with your God"; the Qumran text replaces "God" with "neighbour". Does not the alteration result from the contention that love for God can be expressed only by love for one's neighbour?

Together with brotherly love, another characteristic of the Scrolls is the idea of "community" (yaḥad). This term ought to be taken in its strongest sense: a "community" founded on *the unity* between ideal and life. For example, we read in 1QS 5:1f.: "And such is the rule for the men of the community who agree ... to separate themselves from the community of the men of perversion in order to form a community with respect to the Law and possessions." The term yaḥad, "community", is rarely employed as a noun in the Old Testament (Dt 33:5; 1 Chr 12:18). Frequently in the Scrolls, however, it designates the "sons of light". They form "the community" (1QS 1:1, 16; 3:12; 5:1; 8:1, 5; *et passim*), the "community of God" (1QS 1:12; 2:22), and the "community of the truth of God" (2:26; 3:6). It is to emphasize this community ideal in the service of God that the Essenes of Qumran habitually held all their goods in common, and took their meals together (in common) (1QS 1:12; 5:2; 6:2f.). If men wished to be united in a holy community, it was so that they could return *together* to the divine covenant (1QS 1:8; 5:14, 20; 9:6; cf. 5:22).

From the Acts of the Apostles (2:44; 4:32) we learn that, at least in Jerusalem, the first Christian community held all their possessions in common and endeavoured to achieve a heart-felt unity in the service of God. Many commentators see here an influence of the Essene ideal upon primitive Christianity in Jerusalem. Elsewhere, the Gospel of John insists in a characteristic manner on the *unity* which joins together all Christians (10:16; 11:52; and especially 17:11, 20–22). This being so, it is probably not by chance that the First Epistle of John employs four times in three verses (1:3, 3, 6, 7) the word "community" or "fellowship" (*koinōnia*), which corresponds exactly to the Hebrew word *yaḥad,* which was used to designate the "community" formed by the people of Qumran. This word, *koinōnia,* signifies not only the "fellowship" of Christians among themselves (1:3a, 7), but also the "fellowship" of Christians with the Father and with his Son Jesus Christ (1:3b, 6). From the opening of his Epistle, John wishes to recall discreetly the ideal of "fellowship" among all who are in God's service. This emphasis brings to mind the ideal of the Essenes.

The "confession of sins" was a theme already known in the Old Testament (Lev 5:5; Num 5:7) and consisted principally of recognizing transgressions of the covenant made by all the people of Israel (Lev 26:40). This confession of sins, however, is accentuated in the Qumran community. It occupies an essential part in the ceremony for the admission of neophytes: "All who enter the covenant make their confession after them (the Levites), saying, 'We have sinned, we have been guilty, we and our fathers before us in walking contrary to the precepts of truth'" (1QS 1:24f.; cf. CD 20:28B). Now, this theme of the confession of sins, which is very rare in the New Testament, is found in 1 John immediately after the section concerning the "fellow-ship" among brothers: "If we say we have no sin, we deceive ourselves, and the truth is not in us. If we confess our sins, he is faithful and just, and will forgive our sins and cleanse us from all unrighteousness. If we say we have not sinned, we make him a liar, and his word is not in us" (1 John 1:8-10).

Let us point out yet one more link between 1 John and the Qumran writings with regard to the members of the community. In the course of the initiation ceremony for the neophytes, the priests give this warning: "Cursed be the one who, in order to walk with *the idols* of his heart while he enters into this covenant, yet stumbles in his sins and keeps his intention to backslide.... On account of *these idols* which have caused him to stumble into sin, his lot will be assigned with those who are cursed for ever" (1QS 2:11-17). In the catalogue of the fruits of the spirit of truth, it is mentioned: "... the purity of the soul detests all the idols of impurity" (4:5). Finally, in the Damascus Document it is said of the apostate who returns to his sins after having become part of the covenant: "These are people who have put idols on their hearts and who walk in the obstinacy of their hearts" (CD 20:9f.). In all these texts the word *idol* is used in a meta-phorical sense; in combination with the word heart (to put idols on his heart, to keep the idols of his heart), it designates the action of turning one's heart to what is evil, towards what one loves but God detests. If this sense is given to the word "idol", would it not explain the conclusion of the First Epistle of John: "Little children, keep your-selves from idols" (5:21)? This admonition is strange; nowhere earlier has the Epistle spoken of idolatry in the proper sense. Would the author of the Epistle not speak of the "idols of the heart" in a metaphorical sense, as in the Qumran texts? This suggestion is all the more plausible, because in the preceding verse it is said that God has given us *dianoia,* a word which translates quite regularly in the Septuagint the Hebrew word *lēb,* which properly signifies heart.

The two spirits

"God has put before him (man) two spirits so that he may walk in them until the time of his visitation; these are the spirits of truth and iniquity" (1QS 3:18f.). According to the present arrangement of verses in the Rule, these two spirits seem to merge with the two Angels (or Princes), who are spoken of in 1QS 3:20-24. In fact, this little passage about the two angels is an insertion. The theme of the two spirits is taken up again at the end of line twenty-five and throughout column four. It seems, therefore, that these two "spirits", one good and the other evil, correspond to the rabbinic concept of the two "inclinations", which lead a man to good or evil. So these two spirits are not persons, but inclinations within man. It is as a result of these two spirits that a man accomplishes the good or the evil actions, which are listed in 4:2-11. Every man shares in both spirits: "Until now the spirits of truth and iniquity strive in the heart of man" (4:23b); but with some, the spirit of truth dominates; with others, the spirit of iniquity. This doctrine leads to a conclusion which has great importance in the Rule: before admitting a beginner, or in order to establish the rank of each one in the community, it is essential for the leaders of the community to be able to "discern" the spirits of each. The instruction concerning the two spirits begins with these words: "To the instructor, teach and instruct all the sons of light the nature of all men, according to the kinds of their spirits, the distinguishing signs according to their works..." (1QS 3:13f.). Later we read: "If any one enters the covenant to live according to these precepts... they shall examine his spirit in community among themselves, concerning his understanding and his works in the Law" (5:20f.). Each will then receive the rank which suits him according to his spirit. The text adds: "They shall examine their spirit and their works each year in order to promote each according to his understanding and the perfection of his conduct, or to demote him according to his offences" (5:24; cf. also 9:14). From these texts it is clear that the works of each man, in conformity or not with the divine Law, show the quality of each man's spirit, the spirit of truth or the spirit of iniquity.

We have already noted that the opposition in 1 Jn 4:6 between "the spirit of truth" and "the spirit of error" corresponds to the opposition in the Scrolls between "the spirit of truth" and "the spirit of iniquity". Yet the Johannine text calls for a number of remarks. To begin with, in contrast to Jn 14:17; 15:26; 16:13, the expression "spirit of truth" does not signify the third person of the Trinity, but a disposition of the human soul which comes to us "from God" (4:2). Similarly, "the spirit of error" is an evil disposition of the human soul which comes from the Antichrist (4:3). So once again we meet the sense which the expressions "spirit of truth" and "spirit of iniquity" bore at an early phase in the Qumran writings. Then again, each "spirit" can be recognized by a sign: if he believes that Jesus is the Christ, he comes from God; if he refuses to believe, he comes from the Antichrist (4:2f.). Hence, these verses clarify the conclusion: "By this we know the spirit of truth and the spirit of error" (4:6). It should be noted, however, that in 1QS 3:25ff. it is "works" which manifest the spirit of truth and the spirit of iniquity; in 1 Jn 4:1ff. it is "faith" in Jesus Christ. In spite of this difference, we discover in 1 John, as in 1QS, the principle of the discernment of spirits, which is asserted in 1 Jn 4:1: "Beloved, do not believe every spirit, but test the spirits (to see) whether they are of God." It is difficult not to recognize here an influence of Essene theology on the First Epistle of John.

The two angels

The theme of the two angels or the two princes finds its most complete expression in 1QS 3:20–25. These two persons are sometimes called the "angel of truth" and the "angel of darkness" (3:21, 24), sometimes Prince of light (3:20) and sometimes, for the angel of darkness, Belial (1:24; 2:19, et passim). Their role is well defined in 3:20f.: "In the hand of the prince of light is the rule over all the sons of righteousness; it is in the ways of righteousness that they walk; in the hand of the angel of darkness is the rule over all the sons of iniquity; it is in the ways of darkness that they walk." Thus, from the perspective of the Scrolls, the moral conduct of men, their faithfulness or unfaithfulness to the Law of God, is to a certain extent conditioned by the "power" that the angel of light and the angel of darkness exercise over them. Such a conception seems to imply an unquestionable determinism. Each angel has received rule, whether over the sons of light to cause them to act in conformity to the Law of God, or over the sons of darkness to make them live in opposition to the Law of God. The same idea is found in the Damascus Document: "At the beginning Moses and Aaron arose through the hand of the prince of light, but Belial, in his wickedness, raised up Jannes and his brother ..." (CD 5:17f.). Unhappily for the sons of light, the activities of the angel of darkness are not exercised exclusively on the sons of darkness: "And through the angel of darkness all the sons of righteousness stray and all their sins, their faults, their defilements and their acts of disobedience are caused by his rule" (1QS 3:22). This theme had already found expression in the "confession of sins" made by the Levites during the initiation ceremony of the neophytes: "And the Levites shall recite the iniquities of the sons of Israel and all their guilty rebellions and their sins, accomplished under the power of Belial" (1:22–24). In order to cause the sons of light to fall, the angel of darkness, Belial, raises against them persecutions by the sons of darkness: "(they pledge themselves)... not to turn aside from God before any fear, terror, ordeal or persecution (made) by the strength of Belial" (1:17f.; cf. 3:23). Happily, God has provided a means to come to the aid of the sons of light: "... and all the spirits of his lot (of the angel of darkness) exist to cause the sons of light to stumble, but the God of Israel and his angel of truth come to the aid of the sons of light" (3:24f.). If the case of the sons of darkness seems definitely determined, that of the sons of light is not; the two angels fight one another for their subject. The angel of darkness and his assistants, on the one side, do their best to cause the sons of light to fall and to deny God and his Law, and thus become sons of darkness. The Angel of light, on the other, has received a divine mission to help the sons of light against the enterprises of the angel of darkness, so that they may remain faithful to God.

In the First Epistle of John, we find these themes, but they have been transposed into another key. The angel of light is Christ himself, who is called in the Gospel "the light of the world" (Jn 8:12; cf. 9:5; 12:46). The angel of darkness or Belial is the devil. Let us first reread 1 Jn 3:8–10: "He who commits sin is of the devil; for the devil has sinned from the beginning. The reason the Son of God appeared was to destroy the works of the devil. No one born of God commits sin, for his nature (seed) abides in him, and he cannot sin because he is born of God. By this it may be seen who are the children of God, and who are the children of the devil." The author of the Epistle avoids the determinism of the texts of Qumran and refuses to say that the sons of light or the sons of darkness are "in the power" of the two angels. Yet, when he writes that "he who commits sin is of the devil", he wishes to insinuate that the sins of men are instigated by the devil. From another point of view, those who are born of God cannot sin, because they have within themselves the "seed" of God, that is the Word of God (2:14) or the Son of God (see below). We meet the Scrolls theme again: the sons of light act well because they are in the power of the angel of light. Lastly, the struggle between the two angels, one seeking to cause the sons of light to fall and the other protecting them, is expressed in the following sentence: "The reason the Son of God appeared was to destroy the works of the devil" (1 Jn 3:8). This idea had already been expressed in 1 Jn 2:14: "I write to you, young men, because you are strong, and the Word of God abides in you, and you have overcome the evil one." It will be taken up again at the end of the Epistle: "We know that any one born of God does not sin, but he who was born of God (=the Son of God) keeps him, and the evil one does not touch him" (5:18). As in the Scrolls, the evil one or the devil seeks to cause the children of God to fall; but God and his Son keep them and protect them from the attacks of the devil. Even if the author of 1 John does not use exactly the vocabulary of the Scrolls, he uses the essential theme of the struggle between the two angels.

Conclusion

The aim of this chapter has been to show how the First Epistle of John put forward a certain number of themes which are present in the Scrolls, and which directly depend on a dualistic view of the world: darkness opposes light, truth opposes iniquity. Even if he does not always take up the vocabulary of the Scrolls, the author of 1 John appears to be closely dependent on their theology.

If the reader accepts not only the relationships at the beginning of the Epistle between the terms "fellowship" (koinōnia) and "community" (yaḥad), but also the relationship at the end of the Epistle between the admonition "to keep yourselves from idols" (1 John) and "idols of his heart" (1QS), he will be tempted to think that the Epistle is addressed to a Christian community whose members to a large extent had been Essenes. These converted Essenes could understand without difficulty the allusions contained in these expressions. If we maintain the traditional idea, according to which the Johannine writings received their final form at Ephesus, we would be able to conclude that there existed at Ephesus an Essene community, perhaps more or less connected to the disciples of John the Baptist, whose existence at Ephesus is attested by Acts 19:2ff.

9

Whence the Gospel According to John?

WILLIAM H. BROWNLEE

This Gospel's place and time of origin, its inception and its development comprise an enormous subject to which the present volume should contribute something. Though it may not yield a final solution, at least it should provide data to be studied in further consideration of such fundamental matters. Without the advantage of having read the contributions of the rest, it is my task to make suggestions as to how Qumran ideas may have been mediated to this Gospel. This implies that there are affinities to be explained, and this my own study has led me to believe.[1]

The question of transmission is inseparable from that of authorship and place of origin for the Gospel; for if the whole was written by John the Apostle in the Holy Land before A.D. 70, then the solution to our question will be different from that of the whole being composed by John the Elder at Ephesus in A.D. 100. It is not that these are the only positions as to authorship and date worth considering, but that these are the opposite poles, between which lie all the mediating positions. So enormous is the scholarly literature on this subject in the last one hundred years, that I must claim more ignorance than knowledge of the subject. If I am to contribute anything to the solution, it must be more from insight than from erudition. All proposals must be tentative and suggestive; for I cannot claim to have discovered the answers, but only to have erected my Ebenezer as of the present date, with the hope and the prayer that there may be something in my presentation which may help others

---

[1] I called attention to important affinities in the final page of my article, "A Comparison of the Covenanters of the Dead Sea Scrolls with Pre-Christian Jewish Sects", *BA* 13 (1950) 50–72. My translation of *The Dead Sea Manual of Discipline* (BASOR Supplementary Studies 10–12; New Haven, 1951) contained many notes calling attention to possible New Testament correlations, including references to John. W. Grossouw, "The Dead Sea Scrolls and the New Testament", *StCa* 26 (1951) 289–99; *StCa* 27 (1952) 1–8, depends largely on my notes. See also my article, "John the Baptist in the New Light of Ancient Scrolls", *The Scrolls and the New Testament*, ed. K. Stendahl (New York, 1957) 33–53, 253–6. Most recently, in my article, "Jesus and Qumran", *Jesus and the Historian*, ed. F. T. Trotter (Philadelphia, 1968) 52–81, I have written concerning John, as well as the other Gospels.

who are more knowledgeable than I to achieve the final victory in comprehending the whence and how of this Evangel.

The historical rootage of the Gospel

Any adequate theory of the history of the traditions in the Fourth Gospel must take cognizance of John's familiarity with Palestinian geography, not only of the country as a whole, but of the city Jerusalem itself.[2] Thus the existence of the pool of Bethesda (Jn 5) has been confirmed and its character has been clarified through the combined study of archaeology and ancient literary references, including one in the Copper Scroll (3Q15).[3] There may be symbolic as well as literal significance assigned by the Evangelist to the event and place, yet the spot is none the less historical.

One question as to John's knowledge of the country has arisen in connection with "Bethany beyond the Jordan" (1:28) as distinguished from "Bethany, the village of Mary and her sister Martha" (11:1), the latter being near Jerusalem. These may for convenience be dubbed Bethany I and Bethany II respectively. In the third century A.D., Origen in his quest of biblical sites failed to locate any trace of a village that he could identify with Bethany I. He therefore proposed that the text be corrected to read Bethabara.[4] However, the village of this name is now believed to lie west of the Jordan, so it has been suggested that one should take Bethabara in its etymological sense as meaning only "place of crossing". In this case Bethabara simply designates the ford where John preached and baptized.[5] Nevertheless the most ancient manuscripts favour the reading "Bethany" for 1:28, so that most scholars posit the existence of a village Bethany opposite Jericho, across the Jordan. The spot is even located on biblical maps.

Fortunately, John has given us two passages dealing with Bethany I in which the walking time between it and other places is fixed. On the third day after leaving Bethany I, Jesus and his disciples attended a wedding at Cana of Galilee (1:28, 43; 2:1-11). One day, or at most two, was spent in making this journey. The distance is too great from either the ford east of Jericho or from Bethabara (some 80 and 65 miles, respectively) to make it seem likely that Jesus and his disciples had walked to Cana in such a short time. In Jn 10:40-11:17, they travel from Bethany I to Bethany II in four days. This would be

---

[2] See J. H. Bernard, *A Critical and Exegetical Commentary on the Gospel according to St John* (ICC; Edinburgh, 1928) vol. 1, lxxxf.; R. D. Potter, "Topography and Archaeology in the Fourth Gospel", *Studia Evangelica*, ed. K. Aland, F. L. Cross, et al. (TU 73; Berlin, 1959) 329-37.

[3] J. Jeremias, *The Rediscovery of Bethesda, John* 5:2 (New Testament Archaeology Monograph 1; Louisville, Kentucky, 1966).

[4] See R. Brown, *The Gospel according to John (i-xii)* (The Anchor Bible 29; New York, 1966; London, 1971) 44ff. Cf. M. E. Boismard, *Du Baptême à Cana* (*Jean* 1, 19-2, 11) (Paris, 1956) 37-9.

[5] If the Baptist in any sense used the Jordan for crossing over into the promised land, it is suggestive that something of this kind may have been practised by the people of Qumran in their annual "passing over into the covenant" (1QS 1:16); for despite the precedent of Dt 29:11, their use of '*br* as a synonym of *bw*' might be misunderstood as meaning "transgress the covenant". Cf. CD 1:20 (1:15) and the note *ad loc.* in *APOT* 2, 802.

too much time to allow, if they were travelling to Bethany II from the lower region of the Jordan. One might allow that from some such location they might have walked only as far as Jericho the first day (under the assumption that they got a late start); but then they would surely have pressed forward in a single day from Jericho through the desolate wilderness up to Bethany II. Thus two days would be the maximum time to allow for this trip. This latter estimate of the time required can be made to agree with the text of Jn 11 only if one assumes that Lazarus died on the same day that Jesus learned of his illness; for Jesus waited two days before starting for Bethany II; and when he arrived, Lazarus had been dead for four days. However, one should probably infer that Lazarus was not dead at the beginning of the story, for Jesus declared, "This illness is not unto death", whereas two days later he stated, "Lazarus is dead". We should probably understand that Jesus knew when Lazarus died and that the four days began at that point.[6] We are therefore constrained to seek to locate Bethany I within only one or two days from Cana, but as much as four days distant from Bethany II.

The nineteenth-century suggestion that "Bethany beyond the Jordan" means Batanaea, the highlands of upper Transjordania, demands reconsideration.[7] This was a populous area, through which flowed the Yarmuk River and its tributaries; so it would be easy to find an appropriate baptismal site within forty miles of Cana and eighty miles of Bethany II, to which Jesus could travel within two and four days respectively. It may be significant that Bethany II alone is called a village (*kōmē*), whereas Bethany I is referred to once simply as a "place", "area" or "region" (*topos*, 10:40). Admittedly, the Evangelist could have made the identification of Bethany I clearer by the use of the article with this name, as he does for other regions, such as Judea, Samaria and Galilee. However, in Hebrew and Aramaic the area was referred to both with and without the article; and there

---

[6] Actually, of course, Jesus' words are to be understood also to mean that death will not have the last word. Such *double-entendre* is characteristic of John. Jesus' knowledge of the occurrence of Lazarus' death is like that of Ezekiel's knowledge of the date of the destruction of the Temple. See Ezek 24:25–27 and 33:31f. in *The Interpreter's One-Volume Commentary on the Bible* (Nashville, 1971). The only uncertainty is whether the words of Martha (11:21) constitute a rebuke or only a lament. As a rebuke her words should imply that during the two days that Jesus tarried at Bethany I, he could have made the journey to Bethany II and saved the life of Lazarus. Thus, though four days of ordinary travel were required to make the trip between the two Bethanys, it might have been possible through extreme exertion and unusual haste, or by unusual transportation (as by mule), to make the trip in two days. One is so aware of Jesus' delay that it seems most natural to interpret Martha's words as a rebuke. W. H. Cadman, "The Raising of Lazarus", *SE* 1, 423–34, especially 426, says that Jesus is "allowing Lazarus to die".

[7] See Claude Reigner Conder in the quarterly statements of the *Palestine Exploration Fund*, "The Site of Bethabara", 1875, pp. 72–4; "Bethany Beyond Jordan", 1877, pp. 184–7. Conder argued that even the reading of "Bethabara" in Jn 1:28 could be assigned to a northern locale, since the principal ford north of Beisan bore the Arabic name *Makhadhet 'Abara* ("Ford of the Crossing Over")— a site twenty-five miles from Cana. Thanks are due to M. E. Boismard for drawing my attention to the *PEF*. Other works (which I have not seen) are A. Henderson, *Palestine* (Edinburgh, 1884) 154 and C. R. Conder, *A Handbook to the Bible*, 2nd ed. (London, 1880).

may have been theological reasons for his making the two names appear as similar as possible.

The Greek designation Batanaea is a Hellenized form of the Aramaic equivalent of the Hebrew name Bashan ([hab]-bāšān). Various Aramaic spellings and punctuations are listed by Jastrow: bôtᵉnayyê, bôtᵉnāyyim, bôtᵉnᵉyîn, bûtᵉnan, and bātᵉnayyāy'.⁸ The area is known in Arabic as el-Bottein, or el-Betheneyeh.⁹ This last comes the nearest to the Evangelist's Bēthania, which may be compared with bytnyyn in the Jerusalem Talmud (presumably vocalized bêtnᵉyîn or bêtnayyîn, which in determined form would be bêtᵉnayyāʾ).¹⁰ We are not at all certain as to the Aramaic spelling of Bethany II; but the names are probably non-identical, being simply assimilated one to the other in the Fourth Gospel. Probably the Bethany near the Holy City was spelt in Aramaic byt hyny (bêt hînê) or in determined form byt hynyyʾ (bêt hînayyā).¹¹ However, a Hebrew spelling of bêt ʿᵃnîyyâh has also been proposed.¹² Further, it appears probable that Judith 1:9 refers to Bethany II as Baitanē or Batanē, which comes very close to the spelling Batanaia employed by Josephus and Irenaeus for the region Batanaea.¹³

The original names of Bethany I and Bethany II were probably etymologically different, but still they were close enough to each other in orthography for the Evangelist to assimilate them one to the other in his spelling. His theological motivation is probably to be discerned in the fact that there are three different six-day periods calculated from a stay in Bethany: (1) from the time that Jesus comes to the Baptist at Bethany I until the wedding at Cana,¹⁴ (2) from the time when at Bethany I Jesus hears of Lazarus' illness until he makes his way to Bethany II, (3) from the time that he arrives at Bethany II until he is crucified at Jerusalem. Each six-day period was climaxed in a manifestation of his glory (2:11; 11:4, 40; 12:23; 13:31; 17: 1-5). Each trip from Bethany I foreshadowed the glorification of the Son of Man at Calvary and his ultimate glory as the risen Lord.

---

⁸ A Dictionary of the Targumim, The Talmud Babli and Yerushalmi, and the Midrashic Literature (New York, 1950) vol. 1, 115b.

⁹ So given in John McClintock and James Strong, Cyclopaedia of Biblical, Theological and Ecclesiastical Literature (New York, 1867; reprinted 1969) vol. 1, 681a, in the article on "Bashan".

¹⁰ This form, cited by Jastrow, Dictionary, loc. cit., is not vocalized. He lists only the undetermined form. We have no way of knowing for sure whether this variant form represents a dialectical variation, or a scribal error of yōd for wāw; but, in view of other variants as to the first vowel (as in the two different forms of the Arabic), we should not eliminate this as a real variant.

¹¹ Cf. M. Jastrow, Dictionary, vol. 1, 348b. The determined form is not listed; but such a termination seems to be implied by the last two letters of Bēthania.

¹² This alternative is given by McClintock and Strong, Cyclopaedia, vol. 1, 771b. Cf. Ananiah of Neh 3:23.

¹³ Josephus, Ant., IX, viii, 1 (par. 159); Eusebius, Onomastica, s. v.

¹⁴ I follow Boismard, Du Baptême à Cana, 82ff., in reading prōi at 1:41 instead of prōton or prōtos. In that case the six days are as follows: (1) 1:29–34; (2) 1:35–40; (3) 1:41f.; (4) 1:43–51; (5) en route, 2:1; (6) at Cana 2:1ff. However, if one rejects this reading, one may calculate the first day as 1:19–28, beginning before Jesus makes his debut—in which case the third day would consist of 1:35–42. See Thomas Barrosse, "The Seven Days of New Creation in St John's Gospel", CBQ 21 (1959) 507–16.

Included within Bashan was the Levitical city of Golan; and just as the former gave rise to the name Batanaea, so the latter gave rise to the designation Gaulanitis, which Josephus knew as the name of both a town and a district. A person with a biblical perspective would claim Gaulanitis as simply a subdistrict of Batanaea (or Bashan), for every time Golan is mentioned in the Old Testament it appears in the expression "Golan in Bashan".[15] Any standard Bible atlas will show Gaulanitis extending around the north shore of the Sea of Galilee to the Jordan River, and including the lakeside city of Bethsaida. Thus, from a biblical perspective, Bethsaida would be located in Bashan-Batanaea or to use John's terminology,"in Bethany". This leads to the important conclusion that the stories of Jn 1 probably took place north of the Sea of Galilee, on the east bank of the Jordan River in the area ruled by Herod Philip. Although we have become accustomed to thinking of the Baptist's ministry as lying further south, Lk 3:3 does state that "he went into *all the region about the Jordan*", and there is no reason to exclude from this the area north of Galilee.

A reexamination of Jn 1 in the light of this hypothesis makes this location of "Bethany beyond the Jordan" highly reasonable, for three of Jesus' newly found disciples are from Bethsaida (1:44), Nathaniel is from Cana (21:2), and Jesus himself is from Nazareth. They are all Galileans or "Botaneans", unless it be the unnamed disciple, who, if one of the sons of Zebedee, would also be a Galilean! There is nothing startling about Jesus' first calling of his disciples by the Sea of Galilee; but we had not been accustomed to interpreting Jn 1 this way. Yet some scholars who have analysed the traditions of this chapter conclude that we have here simply a variant of the Synoptic account of the Galilean vocation of the apostles.[16] Our varied approaches to the problem tend to complement and confirm one another, and they are considerably reinforced by Jesus' specified itinerary. When at Jn 1:43 Jesus decides to go to Galilee, all he has to do is to leave the vicinity of Bethsaida and very shortly cross the Jordan River which separates Gaulanitis from Galilee. From Bethsaida to Cana it is only some twenty miles, so that the disciples could have spent most or all the first day in the vicinity of Bethsaida (where Jesus called two more disciples). Then they would have made it in an easy journey the second day to Cana, where they spent the night, before participating in the wedding festivities of the third day. When, later on, the journey from Bethany I to Bethany II was made in four days, they might have needed to travel a distance of some ninety miles, but this would still be within the realm of possibility. The three six-day periods (mentioned above) are perhaps symbolic, the two six-day journeys being made to agree with the six days of Jesus' last week at Jerusalem. Even if this is so, we need not deny the author at least the possibility of achieving verisimilitude. In fact, it is this very achievement which (along with much else) strongly suggests a Palestinian source for these stories.

15 Dt 4:43; Jos 20:8; 21:27; 1 Chr 6:71.
16 E.g. C. H. Dodd, *Historical Tradition in the Fourth Gospel* (Cambridge, 1963) 305.

The Evangelist's geography, while rooted in history, is no doubt symbolic. Just as he explains the meaning of the pool of Siloam as "sent" (9:7), a term loaded with theological meaning for him,[17] so we suspect that a special significance was attached to Bethany I = Bashan. In this case, however, the significance may not lie in the meaning of the name, but rather in the biblical connotations of the place. It was an area noted for its flocks and herds, which would elicit the thought of the "lamb of God" (1:29, 36).[18] There may also be shepherd terminology as the disciples "follow" Jesus (1:36, 43). In the Aramaic original of 1:15 also, the Baptist may have said:[19]

He who is coming after me
before me will become,
that he may take the lead.

To "come after" someone is to follow him.[20] Jesus is now following John, as a sheep its shepherd; but Jesus is destined to go ahead of John and himself become the shepherd of the flock.[21] Mic 7:14f. should be considered as of some influence:

Shepherd thy people with thy staff,
　the flock of thy inheritance,
who dwell alone in a forest
　in the midst of a garden land;
Let them feed in Bashan and Gilead
　as in the days of old.
As in the days when you come out
　of the land of Egypt
I will show them marvellous things.　　　(RSV)

[17] The term is used mainly of Christ himself (Jn 1:6; 3:17, 28, 34; 4:38; 5:36, 38; 6:29, 57; 7:29; 8:42; 10:36; 11:42; 17:3, 8, 18, 21, 23, 25; 20:21), but also of the disciples (17:18; 20:21). In chapter 9 there may also be an allusion to Is 42:19: "Who is blind but my servant, or deaf as my messenger whom I send?"

[18] Cf. Dt 32:14; Ps 22:13 (=22:12); Ezek 39:18; Am 4:1.

[19] Cf. the text as reconstructed by C. F. Burney, The Aramaic Origin of the Fourth Gospel (Oxford, 1922) 104. However, he renders the last clause as "because He was the first (of all)". I would tentatively propose altering the last clause to dyqdm, which I suppose was then misread or reinterpreted as dy qdm[y] in order to bring it into line with the prologue. Matthew Black, An Aramaic Approach to the Gospels and Acts, 2nd ed. (Oxford, 1954) 107f. [3rd ed. (Oxford, 1967) 145f.] also suggests that the original meaning was not one of pre-existence. In Int 9 (1955) 85-9, I explored the possibility of the Baptizer's having spoken of a pre-existent messiah, perhaps Elijah redivivus.

[20] See both in the Hebrew and in the Aramaic Targums: Gen 37:17; 2 Kg 13:2; 23:3; Is 65:2. "Come after" means "follow" also in Mk 1:17; 8:34; Mt 16:24; Lk 9:23; 14:27. Yet the temporal sense is present in Mt 3:11; Mk 1:7.

[21] One may also add, "as a peripatetic teacher leads his disciples". Just as the people of Qumran expected the future messianic leadership to arise from their own community, so likewise John expected the Messiah to arise from among his own followers, one "who will come after" him, not only temporally, but as a disciple who is destined to go ahead of his own teacher. Cf. 3:30 and also Mt 11:11. as interpreted by O. Cullmann in "The Significance of the Qumran Texts for Research into the Beginnings of Christianity", JBL 74 (1955) 218f. and by M. J. Suggs, Wisdom, Christology, and Law in Matthew's Gospel (Cambridge, Mass., 1970) 45-8.

Jesus becomes the shepherd of the flock who promises Nathaniel a vision of "the angels of God ascending and descending upon the Son of man" (1:51). Jer 50:19f. may also have contributed to the thought of John:

> I will restore Israel to his pasture, and he shall feed on Carmel and in Bashan, and his desire shall be satisfied on the hills of Ephraim and in Gilead; In those days and in that time, says the LORD, iniquity shall be sought in Israel, and there shall be none; and sin in Judah, and none shall be found; for I will pardon those whom I leave as a remnant.   (RSV)

When the flock is restored to its pasture, the Lord will remove all sin, and this is the work of "the lamb of God" (1:29).[22] Also suggestive is Ps 68:15f.:

> The hill of Bashan is a hill of God indeed,
> a hill of many peaks is Bashan's hill.
> But, O hill of many peaks, why gaze in envy
> at the hill where the LORD delights to dwell
> where the LORD himself will live [tabernacle] for ever?   (NEB)

By meditating upon this and other passages, the meaning of God's tabernacling with men (Jn 1:14) may have been shaped in the mind of the Evangelist. In the passages cited from Micah and Jeremiah, it is noteworthy that Bashan does not appear alone and that both mention also Gilead. It may well be that "Bethany beyond the Jordan" stands for more than the immediate vicinity of Bethsaida, that it is intended to make us think of Transjordania as a whole. In this case, there are four regions, encompassing the entire land of Israel, which enter into the geographic symbolism of the Gospel: Transjordania, Galilee, Judea and Samaria.[23] For this reason the locale of Bethsaida is referred to so obscurely, as the Evangelist draws upon the semantic development of Bashan>Batanaea>Bethany. The place where Jesus called his first disciples was given a preeminent place because the scriptures encouraged the Evangelist to believe that Messianic hopes were centred there; and by assimilating the name of Batanaea to that of the village Bethany, he linked the north shore of the Sea of Galilee with the redemptive events at Jerusalem.

If indeed John the Baptizer did preach and baptize near Bethsaida (either in the river or the lake, or both),[24] what is its historical significance? The least one can say is that it serves to illustrate Luke's assertion that the Baptist "went into all the region about the Jordan, preaching a baptism of repentance". If one follows tradition in locat-

---

[22] On this, see note 44 below.

[23] On the geographical symbolism, see W. A. Meeks, "Galilee and Judea in the Fourth Gospel", *JBL* 85 (1966) 159–69; *The Prophet King, Moses Traditions and the Johannine Christology* (Leiden, 1967) 35–41, 313–18.

[24] Cf. 1QS 3:5, "nor sanctify himself with seas [=lakes] or rivers", together with my annotation in *The Dead Sea Manual of Discipline*, 13, note 11.

ing the "Aenon near Salem" of 3:23 near the Jordan, south of
Scythopolis, he finds another illustration of this. In fact,'the strategy
of John's three baptismal sites might be thought of as appealing to
the people of the whole land: the place in the south attracting people
in Judea and Peraea; the place near Aenon attracting people from
Decapolis, Samaria and lower Galilee; the place near Bethsaida
attracting people from Batanaea, Gaulanitis and upper Galilee. In
this case the Jordan River may have been thought of as a central
line running through the land. Even if "Aenon near Salem" be located
in Samaria,[25] we are still indebted to the Fourth Gospel for our
knowledge of two of the three places of John's baptism.

If one interprets Jn 1:29-34 as describing events happening on the
very day of Jesus' baptism, then one will need to claim the Fourth
Gospel as evidence that Jesus' baptism in the Jordan River occurred far
to the north, and not at the Jordan opposite Jericho. In that case
the Synoptic Gospels have telescoped John's activity in the south with
an account of Jesus' baptism which had actually occurred in the north.
There is nothing intrinsically improbable about this; yet I do not think
that Jn 1:29-34 depicts the day of Jesus' baptism. It is rather a
theological reflection upon the earlier event. It is not at the baptismal
event as such, but it is when John sees Jesus coming to him on a later
occasion, that he makes his proclamation, "Behold the lamb of God".
Neither is there any room here for the forty days of temptation in
the wilderness, as each eventful day follows another. Probably, then,
we have a theological transposition in John similar to the Galilean
setting of the discussion of the eucharist at 6:25-65. By this I do not
intend to deny that John the Baptizer and Jesus may not have been
associated together near Bethsaida; for this is highly reasonable. Why
should not Jesus wish to return to John, after the wonderful experience which was his at the moment of his baptism?[26] One infers
simply that if the Evangelist wished to begin the story where he himself became an observer, he could not tell of Jesus' baptism as it
originally transpired, but he could only relate John's witness to Jesus
at a later date.

So natural is this Galilean setting for the coming together of the
Baptist, Jesus and his disciples, that it seems well nigh self-authenticat-
ing.

This thesis has an important bearing, also, upon the question
of whether Jesus or any of his disciples were ever residents at Qumran.
I find nothing that would indicate any such direct connection. Jean
Steinmann has suggested that the disciples who left John to follow
Jesus had at one time lived together at Qumran.[27] Although I never
did see any need for such a hypothesis, Steinmann could at least claim
a certain justification for his view, in that not only the Baptist, but

---

[25] It is located there by W. F. Albright, "Recent Discoveries in Palestine and
the Gospel of John", *BNTE* 153-71; see especially pp. 159ff. Cf. R. E. Brown, *The
Gospel according to John*, vol. 1, 151.

[26] Note that in Jn 3:22 Jesus carries on a baptismal ministry parallel to that
of John.

[27] *Saint John the Baptist and the Desert Tradition*, trans. M. Boyes (New York,
1958) 60.

also his Galilean disciples, were all attracted to a place so near Qumran. If, however, the calling of the disciples took place near Bethsaida, the hypothesis of any connection between the apostles and Qumran appears all the more unlikely. The two men who left John to follow Jesus were Galileans who appear together in a Galilean setting. Most likely, then, they were neophytes who heard John for the first time during his "Batanaean" ministry.[28] It is only John the Baptist who at any time may have resided at Qumran (or at some other centre of Essenism); and what the story of Bethany I discloses is that John brought personally whatever Essenism that had influenced his own thinking into the vicinity of Galilee itself. It was through his preaching by the shores of Galilee as well as elsewhere, that John the Baptist was Jesus' forerunner. We shall never know for sure whether the unnamed disciple of Jn 1:35-40 was John the son of Zebedee, but it is a reasonable suggestion. We shall never know for sure how much of the Qumran colouring which may be found in the Fourth Gospel is due to the Baptist's influence upon Jesus or how much is rather due to the Baptizer's influence upon John the son of Zebedee, but it appears reasonable to suppose that it may be due to a combination of both, for the Evangelist seems to refract all the light from both John and Jesus and to bring it all to a focus upon the Son of Man. To the Evangelist, John was "a burning and shining lamp" (5:35); but only Jesus, in his view, is "the light of the world" (1:6-8; 8:12).

Behold the man

Jesus was hailed twice by John the Baptist with the words, "Behold the lamb of God" (1:29, 36) and twice by Pilate: "Behold, the man" (19:5) and "Behold, your king" (19:15). These four public presentations, two at each end of Jesus' ministry, are surely intended by the Evangelist as literary parallelism.[29] Whatever may have been Pilate's supposed intention, the Evangelist wanted us to understand far more in "Behold the man" than "Here is the culprit whom you wish me to crucify".[30] In fact, this statement like the rest was meant by the Evangelist as a part of the Christian declaration. Many things in John are directed to the Samaritans, some to the Pharisees, some to the followers of John the Baptist, some to the Greeks, and some perhaps even to the Essenes. If nothing is explicitly directed to the Essenes, at least much is directed to concepts and ideas that were made current by them. As I have shown elsewhere, the Messianic "Man" is a peculiar feature of John's christology, which in some way must be dependent upon the *geber* of Qumran messianism.[31] I wish to discuss this figure further here, by way of bringing to bear new evidence which

---

[28] This explains why they had not yet given up their fishing trade to become full-time disciples, as would have been necessary if they had been long-established disciples of the Baptist in the lower Jordan.

[29] On this type of literary parallelism, see W. H. Brownlee, *The Meaning of the Qumrân Scrolls for the Bible with Special Attention to the Book of Isaiah* (New York, 1964) 247-59. This book will be cited hereafter as *Meaning*.

[30] See my discussion in *Jesus and the Historian*, ed. F. T. Trotter, 64.

[31] "Messianic Motifs of Qumran and the New Testament", *NTS* 3 (1965) 12-30, 195-210, especially 23-30; see also *Jesus and the Historian*, ed. F. T. Trotter, 59-64.

reinforces much that has been said in this book concerning the significance of Qumran for the Fourth Gospel.

The Messianic Man must pass through the womb (or "refining furnace") of mother Israel in order to emerge as the Wonderful Counsellor, according to one important Qumran hymn (1QH 3:7–12).[32] In a key passage of the Rule (1QS 4:19ff.), man's present predicament of the inner struggle between the spirits of truth and error will be resolved when God refines one *geber* more than other sons of men and cleanses him with the Spirit of Truth. Then the truth will be made to triumph through him, coming forth undefiled and giving all upright insight into the knowledge of the Most High. Thus all perversity will be overcome. In my previous studies of this passage,[33] I did not take into account 4QTestimonia, with its peculiar readings of Num 24:15–17:[34]

15 And he intoned his allegory and said:
"The oracle of Balaam the son of Beor:
An oracle about the *Man* [*geber*] *whose iniquity is purged*,
16 an oracle about the Man who hears the words of God,
who knows the *knowledge of the Most High*,
who the vision of the Almighty sees,
entranced, but open-eyed.
17 I see him, but not now;
I behold him, but not nigh:
A Star strides forth from Jacob,
and a Sceptre [*or* Comet] arises from Israel.
It will crush the forehead of Moab
and break down all *the sons of the Pit*."

In the above translation, some key points are italicized. The first of these calls attention to a variant reading which results in a phrase similar to one concerning the "Man" in the Rule. Instead of reading *štm h'yn* (*š^etum hā'āyin* or *šetām hā'āyin*), "opened of eye"[35] or

---

[32] On this passage, see *Meaning*, Appendix C, 274–81; but on the key point of syntax, not dealt with there, which proves the messianic interpretation, see Brownlee, "The Significance of 'David's Compositions' ", *RevQ* 5 (1966) 569–74, especially 572ff.

[33] For the passage as a whole, see Brownlee, "The Servant of the Lord in the Qumran Scrolls. II", *BASOR* 135 (1954) 33–8, especially 36ff., notes 30 and 33. For fresh arguments from syntax and parallelism, see *Meaning*, Appendix A, 261–70.

[34] Cf. J. M. Allegro, "Further Messianic References in Qumran Literature", *JBL* 75 (1955) 174–87, especially 182–7; DJD 5, 4Q*175* on pp. 57–60 and plate XXI. However, Allegro's readings are inaccurate at the following points: in line 10, read *h'wn*, not *h'yn*; and in line 16 read *lyd'tykhy* (the last letter is a *yod*, not a *waw!*). The last word stands for *l' yd'tykh* and *l' yd'tyky*—in a deliberate conflation of both the feminine and the masculine pronominal suffixes, since Levi is supposed to have addressed each parent separately. Allegro complained in his article in *JBL* (p. 182) that "the present work is characterized by carelessness and a rather strange orthography", but this judgment was largely premature, through failure to understand the scribe's intention. Only the omission of the *aleph* of the negative particle appears to be a scribal error.

[35] One might also read *š^etum* ("*closed* of eye") in order to obtain the sort of sense with which Libellus I of the *Corpus Hermeticum* begins.

"whose eye is perfect",[36] the manuscript reads rather *šḥtm h'wn* (*šeḥutam he'āwôn* or *šeḥātēm he'āwôn*), "whose iniquity is purged" or "who has purged [destroyed] iniquity". The resultant text of Numbers assimilates the passage to 1QS 4:20f.:

20 Then God will purify through his truth
     all the needs of a man [*geber*]
     and refine him more than the sons of men
     in order to purge [*le̔hātēm*] every Spirit of Perversity
21   from the inner parts of his flesh,
     and to purify him through the Holy Spirit
     from all wicked practices.
     And he will sprinkle upon him the Spirit of Truth
     as water for removal of impurity,
     (to cleanse him) from all deceitful abominations
22   and from wallowing in the Spirit of Impurity
     so that he may give the upright insight
     into the knowledge of the Most High (*da'at 'elyôn*)
     and the wisdom of the heavenly beings,
     that he may make wise the perfect of way;
     for God has chosen them for an eternal covenant,
23   and theirs will be the whole glory of Adam.
     And (thus) there will be no more perversity,
     to the shame of all works of fraud.

When God gets through "purging away [*le̔hātēm*] every Spirit of Perversity", the Man of God's refining will emerge as one "whose iniquity is purged" (*šeḥutam*). Such a Man is also one "who has purged away (*šeḥātēm*) iniquity"[37] and who imparts "insight into the knowledge of the Most High". Note that the phrase "knowledge of the Most High" occurs in both 1QS 4:22 and Num 24:16. It is clear then that the text of Numbers has been assimilated to that of 1QS, and what makes this particularly impressive is that the same scribe wrote both texts![38]

One may note also another variant in the text of Numbers, the reading of *šyt* (*šît*, "pit") for *št* (*šēt*, "Seth" or "Shuthite").[39] Although this difference in orthography might be explained as purely orthographic (a *yōd* appearing for the *ṣērē*), the text may very well provide us with the rabbinic word "pit" in order to heighten the eschatological role of the future deliverer who will "break down all the sons of the pit".

[36] Cf. the LXX rendering *ho alēthinos horōn* ("who truly sees"). Is there any connection between this and Jn 1:47–49?

[37] Cf. Dan 9:24: "Seventy weeks of years are decreed ... to finish the transgression and to purge away [*lhtm*] sins and to expiate iniquity ['*wn*]". For the former word I follow the *qe̔rē*.

[38] So Allegro has observed in both of his publications: *JBL* 75 (1955) 182, and DJD 5, 58 in a note to line 1.

[39] The Hebrew text probably gives an archaic name for Moab, referred to as Shutu in an Egyptian execration text from the period of the Middle Kingdom. See J. A. Wilson, "The Execration of Asiatic Princes", *Ancient Near Eastern Texts Relating to the Old Testament*, ed. J. B. Pritchard, 2nd ed. (Princeton, 1955) 328f. The New American Bible renders, "all the Shuthites".

Now in the above Text of 4QTestimonia we seem to have trans-
ferred to the man of the future what originally referred to Balaam
himself. What was originally "an oracle *of* the man whose eye was
perfected" (namely, Balaam) has become "an oracle *about* the Man
whose iniquity is purged"[40] and "who also has purged away iniquity".
It is evident that the author of the Testimonia did not cite verses
15-16 in order to honour Balaam, but rather he has found here a
reference to a future *geber*. If the whole citation from Numbers be
applied to the Davidic Messiah, as some scholars propose, then he
is to be endowed with an oracular and teaching function as well as a
military role. However, the Damascus Document interprets the "star"
as the "expounder of the Law who is coming to the land of Damascus"
and the "sceptre" as "the prince of all the congregation" who "will
break down all the 'sons of Sheth' [*or* 'sons of battle din'?]".[41] This
latter figure is the royal messiah expected at Qumran. It is entirely
possible, therefore, that all three hoped-for messianic figures of
Qumran are to be discerned in this passage : the prophet, as the
geber of verses 15-16; the Messiah of Aaron, as the "star" of verse
17; and the Messiah of Israel, as the "sceptre" of verse 17. It may
be that more than one interpretation of the passage existed among
those associated with Qumran, so that as one encounters the *geber*
in various passages, one is not always sure which eschatological figure
is meant.[42] In any case, "Behold the man" in John's intention means
the same as Pilate's other words, "Behold your king"—a king whose
purpose is "to bear witness to the truth".[43]

In connection with the Man one should examine the pronouncement
of the Baptizer in Jn 1 : 29—"Behold, the lamb of God who takes
away the sin of the world". Several scholars have argued with good
reason that behind this "lamb" lies the Aramaic word *ṭᵉlēh* (or, in
determined form, *ṭalyā'*), a word which could mean either "lamb"

---

[40] In general, the word used for "oracle" here (MT *nᵉ'um*) should receive only a
subjective genitive. However, *Gesenius' Hebrew and Chaldee Lexicon to the Old
Testament Scriptures*, trans. S. P. Tregelles (Grand Rapids, 1949) *loc. cit.*, interprets
n'm pš' of Ps 36:2 as "an utterance (song) concerning wickedness". Although
more recent interpreters are probably correct in preferring the subjective genitive
even here ("the inspiration of transgression"), analogical reasoning from the
synonym *maśśā'*, which frequently receives the objective genitive (e.g., Is 13:1;
15:1; 17:1) may have led to the other interpretation at Qumran. If, nevertheless,
one insists on the rendering "an oracle *of*", then Balaam must be interpreted as a
type of the future *geber*. Ancient Samaritans also derived their messianic hope
from this Balaam oracle. Cf. J. Macdonald, *The Theology of the Samaritans* (London,
1964) 363, 414, n. 1.

[41] CD 7:14-21 (9:5-10).

[42] Since in 1QH 3:10 the *geber* is called "the wonderful counsellor" (Is 9:6),
he should be Davidic. Note the use of *haggeber* for David in 2 Sam 23:1. Yet
specifically royal traits are lacking in 1QS 4 and in Num 24:15f., unless one
translates "the man who *destroys* iniquity".

[43] Such a theory of the witness-king reminds one of the philosopher-king of
Plato. Yet the description of the Lord's servant as a witness may have contributed
to this (Is 42:1-4; 43:10-12). Cf. 1QS 8:6, "witnesses of truth with regard to
judgment [or religion]". In Jub 1:12, the prophets are referred to as witnesses:
"And I will send witnesses unto them, that I may witness against them, but they
will not hear, and will slay the witnesses also." Cf. 2 Chron 24:19; 36:15f.; Jer
25:4; Mt 23:34; Lk 11:49. Thus the witness-role of the Christ in John (a prominent
motif) is that of the prophet-king and servant of the Lord.

or "servant". However, the more likely meaning on the lips of the
Baptizer, they argue, was: "Behold the servant of God who removes
the sin of the world."[44] This will seem highly probable, if one
considers the immediate reference to the coming of the Spirit upon
Jesus (vv. 32f.); and it becomes almost certain, if one follows the
well-attested reading "I have seen and have borne witness that this
is God's *chosen*" (rather than "God's son"), for this leads one to see
in the text a threefold allusion to Isaiah 42:1:

Behold, my servant, whom I uphold,
    my chosen in whom my soul is pleased.
I have put my Spirit upon him;
    he will bring justice to the nations.

Yet the author of the Gospel and/or of the Aramaic source undoubtedly also understood "lamb" as well as "servant" for the meaning of $t^e l\bar{e}h$. In this way he assimilated the Baptist's statement to
Is 53:7, where the suffering servant was compared to a lamb. However, on the lips of the Baptist, taking away the sins of the world may
not have had a sacrificial connotation, but have rather meant the same
as *šeḥātēm heʿāwôn* ("who destroys [or purges away] iniquity"). The
eschatological Man of the Rule was to be one upon whom God "will
sprinkle the spirit of truth" and whom God "will purify through the
Holy Spirit"—again corresponding closely to the Baptist's testimony.[45] In fact, as has been shown elsewhere, the passage cited from
the Manual probably alluded also to Is 52:15 as read in 1QIs[a]—
"Because of himself, he will sprinkle many nations"—i.e., because of
his own anointing with God's spirit, he will in turn sprinkle others.[46]
This last element which is merely implicit in the texts of Qumran
becomes explicit only in Jn 1:33—"He on whom you see the Spirit
descend and remain, this is he who baptizes with the Holy Spirit."
It is Jesus as the sinless man ("whose iniquity is purged"), in whom is
no demon (since God was "to purge every Spirit of Perversity from
the inner parts of his flesh"), and also God's servant and lamb, whom
Pilate unwittingly proclaims when he cries out, "Behold the man!"
Also, just as "the man" of the Qumran hymn is born through the

---

[44] Burney, *Aramaic Origin*, 104–8, was the first to suggest that underlying this
expression "the Lamb of God" is the Aramaic which by deliberate ambiguity
means "the child", "servant", or "lamb of God". Primary, however, is the meaning
"servant of God". This argument may now be reinforced by the strong attestation
of the reading "chosen of God" at 1:34. See Boismard, *Du Baptême à Cana*,
56–60; R. E. Brown, *The Gospel According to John*, vol. 1, 57.

[45] On the relation of John the Baptist to Qumran, see Brownlee, "John the
Baptist in the New Light of Ancient Scrolls", *The Scrolls and the New Testament*,
ed. K. Stendahl, 33–53, 252–6. Most of the points made in this article have been
reinforced by C. H. Scobie, "John the Baptist", *The Scrolls and Christianity*, ed.
M. Black (London, 1969) 58–69. In *BASOR* 135 (1954) 37, note 31, I stressed the
relationship of the "man of God's refining" with the suffering servant of the Lord.
In the present context, cf. the *anēr* of Jn 1:30, equivalent to Aramaic $g^e bar$.

[46] Cf. W. H. Brownlee, "The Servant of the Lord in the Qumran Scrolls. I",
BASOR 132 (1953) 8–15, especially 10. In this interpretation I am supported by
F. F. Bruce, *Biblical Exegesis in the Qumran Texts* (Grand Rapids, Michigan, 1959)
51, 56, and by R. K. Harrison, *The Dead Sea Scrolls* (New York, 1961).

birth-pangs of mother Israel, so through rejection and crucifixion, amid the sympathetic suffering of his disciples, the *anthrōpos* (Christ) is born into the world.[47] Here then is an important element of the christology of John which has unmistakable links with the eschatological language of Qumran. How did the Gospel writer or his source come by this? Had he himself ever belonged to an Essene community? Perhaps, but we really have no reason to suppose this. We should rather take seriously the testimony of the Gospel itself, that the Baptizer had in his teaching at Bethany I given expression to ideas like this, and that both Jesus and his disciples were present to hear him preach. Thus the manuscripts of Qumran strengthen the conviction that the Fourth Gospel is deeply rooted in the religious history of Palestine, and that an authentic apostolic tradition lies behind it.

Could this Gospel have been written in Palestine?

Other facets of religious thought in the Fourth Gospel must not be submerged and lost sight of in any pan-Qumranian approach, for that would be to refract only one ray of light from the Evangel and to be blind to all other rays. Those who compare John's theology with that of the Samaritans do so with good reason, and surely not all the similarities should be dismissed as Christian influence on the Samaritans. Rather, one should recognize the probability that John's high christology and his doctrine of Jesus as prophet-king may be at least partially rooted in the Samaritan high estimate of Moses and in their expectation of a messianic restorer (*tāhēb*) who is to come as a new Moses.[48]

Yet, as C. H. Dodd has exemplified again and again, the doctrine of Christ in the Fourth Gospel may be compared with rabbinic claims concerning the Torah; for both are identified with the creative principle of the universe, are the light of men, the water of life, etc.[49] In this connection one should not overlook the significance of targums for understanding some of the concepts in the Fourth Gospel.[50] No matter what state, through oral development, the actual texts of the Aramaic targums had attained in the first century A.D.,[51] one pervasive element was surely the frequent avoidance of anthropomorphisms by attributing visual experience of God to a vision of his shekinah (glorious presence) and auditory experience to the hearing of his word (*mêmrā'*). Much of divine action in this world also was through his Word. Here is conceptual substance which relates to the prologue

---

[47] Cf. the remarkable parallel in Rev 12:1-6.

[48] On the Taheb, see J. Macdonald, *The Theology of the Samaritans*, 81ff., 280, 351, 362-71, 394.

[49] *The Interpretation of the Fourth Gospel* (Cambridge, 1954) 74-96, and frequently throughout. See also R. E. Brown, *The Gospel according to John*, vol. 1, lxif.

[50] Not only for its concepts, but also for its method of interpreting and expanding the words of Jesus, this Gospel may be profoundly influenced by targums. Cf. W. F. Howard, *The Fourth Gospel in Recent Criticism and Interpretation* (London, 1931) 227-9.

[51] Cf. Brownlee, "The Habakkuk Midrash and the Targum of Jonathan", *JJS* 7 (1956) 169-86. From 11Q has come a targum of Job, to be published by A. S. van der Woude and J. van der Ploeg of the Netherlands.

G

of John, which is not dependent upon the reading of any particular verse in the targums. One is concerned simply with a stream of tradition according to which "No one has ever seen God", but all direct knowledge of God is but the seeing of his glory or the hearing of his word. It is this knowledge, according to Jn 1:18, that has been disclosed by the Christ.

In the light of the preceding, one should not be amazed at the theory first developed by C. F. Burney that the prologue was originally a hymn in Aramaic honouring the Christ. Burney reconstructed the underlying Aramaic poem, along with the prose commentary to it, as both deriving from the same author.[52] His results, however, were readily available for a keenly critical mind like Rudolf Bultmann as a starting-point for the source criticism of the Fourth Gospel.[53] Prose and poetry pointed to two different sources, which the final author (the Evangelist) put together. One of these sources consisted of revelatory speeches (*Offenbarungsreden*) which were taken over from the Baptist movement. These were Aramaic poems honouring John the Baptist. The first poem honoured the Baptizer as the Word, referring to him in the third person; but the rest consisted of first-person discourses ascribed to the Baptist. These formed a gnostic-like document which contained no narrative, but consisted solely of self-disclosure, revelatory speeches. The Evangelist had himself been a disciple of the Baptist; but after being converted to Christianity, he appropriated these gnostic hymns and combined them with a narrative concerning Christ, which Bultmann called the signs source. The Evangelist then found ready-made a theology of the pre-incarnate Logos manifest to men on earth; and he proceeded to historicize this myth by uniting it to a history of the Christ. For his narrative material, the Evangelist appropriated two other documents, an account of seven signs performed by Christ (the signs source) and a passion story. He may also have included some other independent traditions.[54]

This much is correct about Bultmann's theory; the Gospel does consist of prose narrative and poetic discourses, and an important contribution has been made by the New American Bible in translating and printing the poetic sections as poetry. It appears to me, however, that most of the narrative and most of the revelatory speeches of the Fourth Gospel stem from the same author, that what we are concerned with in this Evangel is material which originally did not consist of literature, but of apostolic witness, of preaching.

How these different styles (*Gattungen*) of preaching relate to each other will be discussed below.

---

[52] C. F. Burney, *Aramaic Origin*, 28–48.

[53] "Der religionsgeschichtliche Hintergrund des Prologs zum Johannes-Evangelium", *Eucharistērion* (Göttingen, 1923) 2nd part, 3–26—which I have not seen— but see D. M. Smith, *The Composition and Order of the Fourth Gospel* (New Haven, London, 1965) 1f., 3–7. Bultmann's fullest treatment is in his *Das Evangelium des Johannes* (Göttingen, 1952) 1–57.

[54] Bultmann's views in his *Das Evangelium des Johannes* are summarized, with the different sources reconstructed in Greek, by D. M. Smith in *The Composition and Order of the Fourth Gospel* as follows: The Revelatory Speeches, 15–34; the Signs Source, 34–44; the Passion Source, 44–56.

Robert T. Fortna has advanced an intriguing theory of a rudimentary Signs Gospel which began with the story of John the Baptist
and Jesus and concluded with the crucifixion and resurrection.[55] Such
a Gospel would be brief enough, it seems to me, to have been delivered
frequently by its author as a single sermon designed to elicit faith in
Jesus as the Messiah. The scope of such a Gospel fits precisely that of
the apostolic witness according to Acts 1:22: "beginning from the
baptism of John until the day when he was taken up from us—one
of these men must become with us a witness to his resurrection".
Such a Gospel would also meet the need of the Jews, who according
to Paul "demand signs" (1 Cor 1:22). However, the same author
might well have also included, at least on occasion in his witnessing,
words of Jesus which brought out their rich symbolism.[56] In this
way, single incidents (such as the feeding of the five thousand) could
be enlarged into a brief, self-contained sermon for the edification of
the believer, or for appeal to interested persons who wished to hear
more concerning Jesus. The use of the rudimentary Signs Gospel
would be to awaken faith (or at least inquiry) and the use of the
narrative plus speech would be to bring out the deeper import of the
signs. Thus the speeches assigned to Jesus as well as the Signs Gospel
were preached material of the Evangelist, but speeches were added
to narrative selections largely as *didachē,* whereas the Signs Gospel

[55] "Source and Redaction in the Fourth Gospel's Portrayal of Jesus' Signs",
JBL 89 (1970) 151–66; *The Gospel of Signs: A Reconstruction of the Narrative
Source Underlying the Fourth Gospel* (SNTS Monograph Series 11; London, 1970).
Fortna is in a large measure dependent upon the prior work of W. Wilkens, *Die
Entstehungsgeschichte des vierten Evangeliums* (Zollikon-Zürich, 1958), reviewed by
J. M. Robinson in "Recent Research in the Fourth Gospel", *JBL* 78 (1959) 242–6.
Since many of Fortna's deletions from the narrative are necessarily tenuous and
subjective, his claim to have recovered in large measure a "pre-Johannine" source
is unconvincing, and the resultant narrative is sometimes so dull that it sounds
more like an abstract than an original composition. A more valid goal, it seems
to me, is the recovery of a proto-Johannine narrative, which (since it is by the same
author as much else) it will never be possible to separate completely from the other
Johannine contributions. The justification for seeking this source is what Fortna
calls *aporia.*

[56] To ascribe difference of authorship on the basis of contrasts in meaning of
signs in the miracle stories and in the sermons fails to take into account sufficiently
the different purposes for which the simple stories and those enriched with discourses were intended. Only in *didachē* ("teaching"), for example, are these warnings
as to the dangers of misapprehending the miracles proclaimed in *kērygma*
("proclamation"). Wilkens, in contrast with Fortna, recognizes that the Signs
Source instead of being pre-Johannine is actually the earliest Johannine stage. See
his latest work, *Zeichen und Werke: Ein Beitrag zur Theologie des 4. Evangeliums
in Erzählungs und Redestoff* (AThANT 55; Zürich, 1969), reviewed by R. T. Fortna
in *JBL* 89 (1970) 457–62.

The difference between initial announcement (belonging to *kērygma*) and cautious
exposition (belonging to *didachē*) may be illustrated by comparing my earlier with
later statements concerning the significance of Hab 2:4 as interpreted at Qumran.
Thus G. Jeremias, *Der Lehrer der Gerechtigkeit* (SUNT 2; Göttingen, 1963) 142f.
could take issue with my early, brief, one-sentence comment. In so doing he argued
a position similar to my own in *Meaning,* 126f., the ideas set forth there having
been taught by me for many years. It is not that meanwhile I changed my mind
(though of course one's views mature) which explains the difference in presentation,
but it is rather my different purpose, for at first it seemed more important to call
attention to the simple correlation between 1QpHab and Paul, and to leave detailed
exegesis for treatment elsewhere.

was used largely as *kērygma*.[57] The Evangelist died, without ever producing a manuscript incorporating all the material sequentially arranged, with the result that the ecclesiastical editor responsible for the present arrangement made certain mistakes or was faced with unavoidable breaks in sequence which he did not seek to smooth out by rewriting or by freely supplying transitional material.

The latest stage of this Gospel, according to J. L. Martyn, addresses itself to the problem created by the synagogue in the expulsion of Christians from their midst (9:22; 12:42; 16:2).[58] He thinks that this reflects the introduction of the curse upon Nazarenes (i.e., Christians) and Minim (heretics) into the twelfth of the Eighteen Benedictions which were recited in the synagogue. This curse was no doubt intended to make Christians and other heretics uncomfortable so that they would leave on their own volition rather than participate in such a curse. Also, secret believers in Jesus could be put on the spot by being asked to lead the congregation in the Eighteen Benedictions; and if one did so, but faltered or left out the malediction against Minim, he would then be called down from his praying. After this, according to Martyn, "He is then, presumably, 'drummed out' of the synagogue fellowship".[59] In a note, Martyn elucidates further:[60]

> I suppose, as my expression "drummed out" suggests, that just as a delegate of the congregation who stumbled on Benediction number 12 would be called down from his post, so perhaps after careful questioning of the sort portrayed in John 9, he would [be] excluded from the synagogue.

In other words, the malediction was a method of detection and it does not relate to any legal act of exclusion, which still remains only a supposition. It may be that the supposition is correct, even though we cannot yet prove it. But then Jn 12:42 must describe the earlier situation which called forth this "benediction":

> Nevertheless, many even of the authorities believed in him, but for fear of the Pharisees they did not confess it, lest they should be put out of the synagogue.

Again the Gospel's rootage in early Christian-Jewish history is apparent, even though we do not know what powers of excommunication were exercised by the synagogue at that early date.[61] The evidence

---

[57] Since both, however, concerned the historical Jesus, the Evangelist probably included both as *martyria*, testimony as to what one has both seen and heard.

[58] J. L. Martyn, *History and Theology in the Fourth Gospel* (New York, 1968); "Source Criticism and *Religionsgeschichte* in the Fourth Gospel", *Jesus and Man's Hope* (Perspective Book 11; Pittsburgh, 1970) 247–73.

[59] *History and Theology*, 24–40, with this quotation on p. 39.

[60] *Ibid.*

[61] Our problem is that too often we assume a "normative Judaism" for the period of the "Second Temple", whereas much variety may have existed, including synagogues which could excommunicate as peremptorily as Qumran. It could be, on the other hand, that Martyn's expression "drummed out" is correct, if given a less formal definition—harassment leading to "voluntary" withdrawal from the synagogue.

of the rabbinic malediction introduced about A.D. 85 points rather to an earlier and not to a later date for the Fourth Gospel.

It is here assumed that an apostolic witness to the Christ in Palestine is more likely to have existed before than after the first Jewish revolt against Rome (A.D. 66–70). If, then, the sources of the Fourth Gospel consist largely of such apostolic preaching, the first question to ask is whether this witness originated largely in Palestine or whether the Gospel sources point to some other provenance. The second question to ask is where the editor who put these sources together performed his labour of love.

In answer to the first question it seems clear that the sources betray an intimate knowledge of Palestinian geography, history and religious thought, and that their author addresses himself in his symbolic geography to all parts and factions of the country. Galilee, Bethany (i.e. Batanaea, representing the whole trans-Jordan area), Samaria and Judea are all prominent in the narrative. The ambiguity of "Jew" or "Judean" often arises, since the same word may be translated either way; but sometimes in John the term means "Judean" in antithesis to "Batanaean" or Galilean. As a religious term, also, it stands in antithesis to Baptist, Samaritan and disciple of Jesus.[62] Standing above all factional divisions, the author of this witness does not call believers Jews (even though many Jews believe); the believer is a "disciple" or "an Israelite", and Jesus is "the King of Israel". Already at Qumran, "Israel" was used restrictively to refer to the true Community of God,[63] but John intends this inclusively as he seeks to bring both Jews and Samaritans to see God in Jesus Christ. Jn 3:38 clearly points to a knowledge of the Christian evangelism of Samaria, and according to Acts 8:14f., the apostle John was one who participated in it.

[62] As opposed to Batanean, see 1:19; 11:8; as opposed to Galilean, see 7:11; as opposed to Baptist, see 3:25; as opposed to Samaritan, see 4:9, 22; 11:54(?); as opposed to disciples, see 13:13. In a passage like 3:25, it might conceivably mean "*another* Jew". However, John's disciples might be included implicitly among the *Israelites*, as the earliest members of the true Israel. In connection with Jewish observances and festivals in which Jesus himself participates, the term is neutral (2:6, 13; 5:1; 6:4; 7:2; 11:55; 18:20; 19:40, 42), even though ultimately Jesus is to supersede these festivals, as the antitype replaces the type. Sometimes the term "Jew" is neutral, as in 3:1; 8:31 (editorial?); 19:20. The Evangelist accepts the title "king of the Jews" as a true witness to Christ (18:33, 39; 19:19, 21); but Pilate's intention was one of scorn. John himself would have preferred "king of Israel" (1:49; 12:13). The term refers to Jesus' fellow nationals generally in 6:41, 52 ("Bataneans" and Galileans); 5:11, 15; 10:19–21 (context Jerusalem); 11:19, 31, 33, 36, 45 (context Bethany II). However, in many passages they are Jesus' opponents, and implicitly the Jewish leaders in Jerusalem: 2:18, 20; 5:10, 15f., 18; 8:22, 48, 52, 57; 9:18, 22; 10:24, 31, 33; 18:12, 14, 31, 36, 38; 19:7, 12, 14f., 31, 38; 20:19. In these cases, the "Jews" may have also the connotation "Judeans", and even the sense non-Israelites (not belonging to the true Israel). Seldom does it ever mean Jew as opposed to Gentile (18:35f.), though as read by a Gentile it might easily be so understood. On the other hand, as preached among the Samaritans, much of this Gospel would be understood by them as differentiating these opponents of Jesus from themselves. See G. W. Buchanan, "The Samaritan Origin of the Gospel of John", in *Religions in Antiquity*, ed. J. Neusner (Numen Supplementary Studies 14; Leiden, 1967) 148–75. In view of all these considerations, it is a misinterpretation of this Gospel to charge it with anti-Semitism.

[63] See my discussion in *Jesus and the Historian*, 70ff. On "Israel" in John, see Boismard, *Du Baptême à Cana*, 95–131.

In view of alleged Hellenisms in Johannine thought and vocabulary, it is important to ask whether a Palestinian witness to Christ could have been influenced by Greek literature, such as the Wisdom of Solomon, Philo or the Septuagint.[64] We must not exclude some acquaintance with Greek thought and language; for, ever since the conquest of Alexander the Great, Greek had become a cultural factor to be reckoned with in the Holy Land. In fact, there was a synagogue of the Hellenists at Jerusalem itself. There were also Greek-speaking communitities, for many Palestinians were non-Jews. Of these, some were Greek-speaking, such as colonists settled by Alexander at Samaria, many of whose descendents were still living in the land.[65] Jerusalem was the centre for religious pilgrims from all over the world, and an early effort was made to convert them to "the way". Here was a witness who needed Greek as well as Aramaic. The Evangelist who preached so eloquently in Palestine may therefore have been concerned with Greek-speaking Jews who went to Jerusalem at festival time (12:20). Wherever else this Evangelist preached, the substance of his message seems to have been worked out in the living context of the varied population of the land of Israel, and there he proclaimed Jesus as the prophet-king and Saviour of Israel.

The Gospel according to John is in my view substantially the testimony of the apostle John. It is very different from the Gospel according to Mark, to be sure, which is generally believed to be dependent upon the witness of Peter. The teaching of Jesus is also very different from the moral teaching of Q, the supposed source of much of the common teaching of Matthew and Luke. If one accepts Fortna's theory of a rudimentary Signs Gospel, however, a comparison with Mark becomes more fruitful, and the differences are attributable to the perspective of a different author. As for Synoptic material in general, it seems likely that the Fourth Gospel and its sources reflect some acquaintance with the traditions which lie behind those Gospels, without knowing the Synoptics themselves. In fact, one should conceive of this Johannine witness as born within a milieu where many people were intimately acquainted with the deeds and words of Jesus not mentioned in this Gospel. Therefore, the Evangelist is apologetic about not including many familiar stories.[66] The

---

[64] Most notably, cf. the soteriological interpretation of the serpent in the wilderness (3:14f.; Wisdom 16:6f.), the doctrine of the Logos in Philo, and the translation of Is 52:13 in the LXX, from which the Fourth Gospel gets its terms "lifted up" and "glorified" for the crucifixion and exaltation of the Christ. On Hellenistic influence in Palestine, see W. D. Davies, *Paul and Rabbinic Judaism*, rev. ed. (London, New York, 1955) 1–16.

[65] See G. E. Wright, *Shechem, the Biography of a Biblical City* (New York, Toronto, 1965) 175–81. Herod the Great carried out extensive building operations in the city of Samaria, renaming it Sebaste (=Augusta). See Josephus, *War*, I, xx, 2 (par. 403). There were also the Greek cities of the Decapolis, all of them in Transjordan, except for Scythopolis (=Old Testament Bethshan). Josephus refers also to Gaza, Gadara and Hippus as "Greek cities" in *Ant.*, XVII, xi, 4 (par. 320). Cf. also the Grecians (or Hellenists) living in Jerusalem, according to Acts 6:1; 9:29.

[66] Cf. 20:30–31, the conclusion to the primitive Gospel of Signs as written; but I suggest that this material was first of all preached. Note the prominent place given to narration in the sermons of Stephen (Acts 7:2–53), Peter (10:34–43) and Paul (13:16–41). In Acts 10:37 Cornelius and his friends are reported as knowing a great deal about Jesus from the oral Gospel.

Fourth Gospel is not to be thought of as intentionally supplemental to the Synoptics, though it is supplemental to their underlying traditions.[67] Thus the Evangelist may refer to abiding in Christ's word and to keeping his commandments, without indicating wherein their substance lies.[68] If, indeed, there was a source Q available for Jesus' teachings, embodying perhaps apostolic memory of Jesus' kingdom ethics, the Evangelist would surely have commended it to his congregations for further spiritual nurture. The vagueness with which he refers to the moral imperatives of the Christian life demands this; but still the essence of the ethical requirement was no doubt Jesus' "new commandment, that you love one another as I have loved you".

It has always seemed anomalous to me that the apostolic origin of Matthew and John should be rejected for opposite reasons: Matthew because it is too much like Mark and Luke, and John because it is too unlike Matthew, Mark and Luke. If Matthew is to be rejected as apostolic on the grounds that an apostle would not copy from a non-apostolic source (such as Mark or Q), then what of John which did not copy from any of these? If what one is looking for as apostolic is a fresh and independent witness, John has it—and not as fabrications of the imagination stemming from some late period of the Gospel tradition, but as the voice of a living witness from the cultural context of the early decades of Christianity in Palestine![69]

Were there Aramaic sources for the Evangel?

The Palestinian matrix of the Gospel is reinforced by the presence of Aramaisms in its text, and probably also by a few mistranslations.[70] One may suspect an Aramaic background, where the idioms and expressions are congruent with Aramaic idiom, even without being able to demonstrate it conclusively.[71] Thus Bultmann acknowledged

---

[67] This is indicated by allusions to events that were known but not related, e.g., (1) John's baptism of Jesus, (2) the institution of the Lord's Supper, (3) the ascension.

[68] One must abide in Christ's word (8:31, 37) or have it abiding in one (5:38; 15:7). This includes more than doctrine (i.e., christology), for one is also to keep Christ's words (14:32) and his commandments (14:15, 21; 15:11). The ethical character of the Christian life is indicated also by 3:19–21; 5:28f. 1 John, perhaps written by the apostle to churches where he had formerly preached, certainly has a strong ethical emphasis.

[69] Cf. W. F. Albright's article in *BNTE* and also his earlier article, "Some Observations Favoring the Palestinian Origin of the Fourth Gospel", *HTR* 17 (1924) 189–95; J. A. T. Robinson, "The New Look on the Fourth Gospel", *SE* 1, 338–50 [reprinted in his *Twelve New Testament Studies* (London, 1962) 94–106]. It used to be argued that the historical tradition in John was derived from Palestine, but that the ideas are non-Palestinian. The articles of the present volume, however, abundantly refute the qualification, demonstrating the "new look" of which I wrote in *Int* 9 (1955) 90.

[70] On the Aramaic origin of this Gospel, see C. F. Burney, *Aramaic Origin;* C. C. Torrey, *Our Translated Gospels* (London, 1937); M. Burrows, "The Original Language of the Gospel of John", *JBL* 49 (1930) 95–139; J. De Zwaan, "John Wrote in Aramaic", *JBL* 57 (1938) 155–71. See also note 4 to chapter 6 above, p. 108.

[71] Thus Dr E. C. Colwell, *The Greek of the Fourth Gospel* (Chicago, 1931) sought to dispose of translation theories by finding in Greek works illustrations of the idioms alleged to be Aramaisms. See also O. T. Allis, "The Alleged Aramaic Origin of the Fourth Gospel", *PTR* 26 (1928) 531–72.

the possibility of an original Aramaic text underlying the revelatory speeches, but he regarded the Signs Source and the Johannine passion narrative as having been composed in an Aramaizing Greek.[72] If the Apostle wrote the whole, one might even consider the possibility that he wrote some of the material in Aramaic and some in an Aramaizing Greek. But if, as both Bultmann and Fortna propose, the signs narrative began with the ministry of John the Baptist and Jesus' calling of his disciples, then also in that document (as indicated above) there may be inadequate translations from Aramaic.

In one of John's free, composite biblical quotations, the first step of the solution as to meaning is to be found in discovering the biblical sources of the composite quotation. It is the much controverted 7:38, "From his belly will flow rivers of living water". C. F. Burney was correct in seeking a relationship to Joel 4:18 (=3:18); Ezek 47:1–12; and Zech 14:8.[73] In Joel, "A fountain will come forth from the house of Yahweh and will water the Wady [nahal] Shittim", flowing toward the Mediterranean. In Ezekiel, water issues from beneath the altar of the Temple and becomes a mighty river (nahal) as it flows to the Dead Sea. As M. Delcor has observed, Zech 14:8 combines the imagery of these two passages by having water flow from Jerusalem in both directions.[74] Here is the best source for John's "rivers". However, in this plural there may also be the influence of the word "river" (nahălayim) in the dual form at Ezek 47:9.

The second step towards understanding Jn 7:38 is to examine the verse in the light of the underlying Aramaic. Burney was perhaps right in positing behind the translation ("belly") the Aramaic word ma'yān, which may mean either "belly" or "fountain".[75] On the other hand, C. C. Torrey proposed that the underlying word was gaw, meaning either "midst" or "belly".[76] In his view the translator

---

[72] Bultmann, *Das Evangelium des Johannes*, 5, 68 (note 7), 131 (note 5), 155 (note 5), 177 (note 4), 250 (note 1), 301 (note 2), 491f. That Semitisms should appear most prominent in the speeches of Jesus, one may argue, is due to the special reverence given to the words of Jesus by the translator who employs even the fulfilment formula in an editorial comment at 18:32.

[73] *Aramaic Origin*, 109–11.

[74] "Les sources du Deutéro-Zacharie et ses procédés d'emprunt", *RB* 59 (1952) 385.

[75] *Aramaic Origin*, 110.

[76] *Our Translated Gospels*, 108–11. Torrey's objection to Burney's restoration is partially justified; for where Burney has *ma'yān*, one would expect either *ma'yānā'* ("*the* fountain") or *ma'yāneh* ("its/his fountain"). This, however, would not be confused with *me'ôhî* ("his belly", as spelled in Dan 2:32). However, in rabbinic Aramaic *ma'yān* as well as *me'în* can mean "belly"; we do not know the precise linguistic background of the translator, or whether this ambiguity was unknown in Jerusalem. After all, Babylonian Jews made pilgrimages to the Holy City. Torrey's insistence that the primary reference is to Ps 46:5–8 (4–7, English) seems to be unjustified; for whereas this could account for the word "river", it cannot account for the plural "rivers". M. E. Boismard suggested that contrariwise the reference was to the water which flowed from the rock struck by Moses, and that John drew upon a Palestinian targum to Ps 78:16. His article, " 'De son ventre couleront des fleuves d'eau' (Jo. VII, 38)", *RB* 65 (1958) 523–46, was followed by a series of articles reinforcing or modifying its position: P. Grelot, *RB* 66 (1959) 369–74; M. E. Boismard, *RB* 66 (1959) 374–8; J. P. Audet, *RB* 66 (1959) 379–86; P. Grelot, "A propos de Jean VII, 38", *RB* 67 (1960) 224f.; "Jean, VII, 38: Eau du rocher ou source du temple?", *RB* 70 (1963) 43–51. In this last article Grelot answers his own question by saying it is both the messianic rock (typified by Moses striking

misinterpreted the pronominal suffix in *gawwah* ("her midst") as *gawwēh* ("his bowels"). Thus the original reference to water flowing out from the Holy City was missed. However, both Joel and Ezekiel depict the water as flowing from the Temple—for which the various words are masculine! Jesus was standing in the Temple on the occasion of the water-drawing ceremony of Tabernacles when he spoke. If, then, the quotation read, "From its [the Temple's] fountain rivers of living water will flow", one must think of Christ's body as the Temple (Jn 2:21) and the Spirit which fills him as the source of the living water (4:10). In either reconstruction of the underlying Aramaic, the indefiniteness of the pronominal reference was probably to allow for the dual reference to both the temple and Christ himself: "From the fountain [*or* the midst] of the Temple [namely, Christ] will flow rivers of living water." Even in Greek, the possessive pronoun *autou* would be appropriate to either Christ or the Temple, regardless of whether one chooses a masculine noun (*naos*) or a neuter noun (*hieron*) for "temple". If only the translator had used some other word than *koilia,* to translate the Aramaic, the ambiguity of the pronominal antecedent would have been perfectly represented in the Greek. However, one would need to punctuate the text so as to read: [77]

If anyone thirsts, let him come to me;
  let him drink who believes in me—
just as the scripture has said:
  "From its/his fountain will flow
  rivers of living water."

The assumption of the underlying Aramaic is too helpful in the elucidation of the Fourth Gospel to be easily set aside, and this at least reinforces the Palestinian origin of its sources.

Where then was the Gospel of John written?

Supposing the apostolic sources to have been written mainly in Aramaic, when and where were they translated? A full answer will not be attempted at this point, but one should not rule out the possibility that the work of translating John's Gospel may have begun

---

the rock) and the spring flowing from the Temple. He thereby acceded to the soundness of the arguments of A. Feuillet, "Les fleuves d'eau vive de Jo., VII, 38", *Parole de Dieu et Sacerdoce,* ed. E. Fischer and L. Bouyer (Paris, Rome, New York, 1962) 107–20, who reinforced the Temple reference by interpreting this verse in relation to Rev 21:22; 22:1f., 17. None of these follows Burney in restoring the actual word "fountain". Yet the reference to the "fountain *from* the house of Yahweh" in Joel 4:18 strongly favours Burney's basic solution. The preposition "from" has been deliberately shifted to the preceding noun, and "the house of Yahweh" has become "his/its" by way of creating a deliberate ambiguity—"its" (in English) meaning the Temple and "his" meaning Jesus, the new spiritual Temple.

[77] On the punctuation, see Burney, *Aramaic Origin, loc. cit.;* Torrey, *Our Translated Gospels, loc. cit.;* M. E. Boismard, *RB* 65 (1958) 523–40. This punctuation is followed by JB, NEB and NAB.

in Palestine. The final chapter of Greek Esther attests the expertness
of some Jerusalemites in Greek:

> In the fourth year of the reign of Ptolemy and Cleopatra,
> Dositheus, who said that he was a priest and a Levite, and Ptolemy
> his son brought to Egypt the preceding letter of Purim, which they
> said was genuine and had been translated by Lysimachus the son
> of Ptolemy, one of the residents of Jerusalem.

In other words, the passage declares that a Jerusalemite had translated a Hebrew (or Aramaic) work into Greek, before it was taken
to Egypt.[78] The date has been variously interpreted as falling under
Ptolemy VIII, and therefore as 114 B.C., or under Ptolemy XIV, and
therefore 48 B.C. Similarly, the prologue to the Wisdom of Jesus Son
of Sirach states that the Greek translation was prepared by a grandson
of the author who was from Palestine, but in this case it was after
he had resided for some time in Egypt, where presumably he may
have become more proficient in Greek. Both possibilities must be
considered for the Gospel according to John: compilation and translation in the Holy Land, or the accomplishment of this task elsewhere. One should not be dogmatic concerning this, but the latter
alternative merits serious consideration.

Either the apostle himself wrote his sermons or a disciple took
them down from his mouth, but the Gospel as we have it seems to
have been dependent upon written sources, which the final writer or
editor translated and put together. Where then was this work done?
One might answer this question by declaring: "The Gospel could
have been written anywhere by the apostle himself or a disciple of his
may have gone, bringing with him copies of John's sermons."

One might then fall back upon tradition and answer this question
by stating that John the apostle went to Ephesus and there lived to
write his own Gospel from records of his earlier preaching; or, fail-
ing to finish his task, he left this work unfinished to be completed by
his disciple John the Elder.[79] This tradition, however, is insecure,

---

[78] On the knowledge of Greek in Palestine, see W. D. Davies, *Paul and Rabbinic
Judaism*, 5ff. See also J. N. Sevenster, *Do you know Greek? How much Greek could
the first Jewish Christians have known?* (NovTSup 19; Leiden, 1968); J. A. Fitzmyer,
"The Languages of Palestine in the First Century A.D.", *CBQ* 32 (1970) 501–31,
especially 507ff.

[79] On John as an unfinished Gospel, see W. F. Howard, *The Fourth Gospel in
Recent Criticism* (London, 1931) 141; W. Wilkens, *Entstehungsgeschichte*, 171–4;
D. M. Smith, *The Composition and Order of the Fourth Gospel*, 99, proposes this
as an alternative to the fragmentary state of an already completed Gospel with
which, according to Bultmann, the ecclesiastical editor worked. I suggest that there
may have been individual sermons of the apostle recorded on separate leaves,
which confronted the translator-author with the problem of where to insert certain
of these sermons or paradigmatic discourses. Some of these may have been event
plus discourse, and where the event coincided with one in the Gospel of Signs,
there would be no problem. Other sermons attributed to Jesus may have appeared
on leaves without a historical context. Sometimes there may have been more than
one draft of sermon material to be combined, producing conflations. My graduate
assistant, Mr Gerald Frens, has brought to my attention Matthew's expansions
upon the miracle stories of Mark as an illustration of John's use of individual events
as a basis of conversation and discourse. See H. J. Held, "Matthew as Interpreter

for it depends upon an alleged claim of Papias to have known the apostle himself during his residence at Ephesus.[80] Eusebius questioned this tradition on the basis of another statement of Papias to the effect that he did not know any of the apostles, but that whenever any visitors arrived from abroad who had known any of the apostles (including John), those eager to learn would always ask for their reminiscences.[81]

If one is hesitant or unconvinced regarding the Ephesian tradition, the only approach to the place of composition is to find a variant tradition[82] or to ferret it out by inference on the basis of internal evidence. Although I would not rule out Palestine as a possibility, I find Jn 7:35 as very suggestive:

> The Jews said to one another, "Where does this man intend to go that we shall not find him? Does he intend to go to the dispersion among the Greeks and teach the Greeks?"

Whoever wrote this verse was familiar with the Christian mission in the diaspora, and certainly such language could even have been written in a Greek milieu.[83]

If then one seeks a non-Palestinian place of composition for the Fourth Gospel, it seems probable to me that Alexandria meets all the requirements for a milieu in which the preaching of John would be especially appropriate.[84] At Alexandria there was a large Jewish population, and also a large Samaritan population.[85] The Jews of Alexandria sometimes found themselves in conflict with the Greeks

---

of the Miracle Stories", *Tradition and Interpretation in Matthew*, ed. G. Bornkamm, G. Barth, H. J. Held (Philadelphia, London, 1963) 165–299.

[80] Eusebius, *Ecclesiastical History*, V, xx, 4–8.

[81] *Ibid.*, III, xxxix, 1–7.

[82] See for example, the tradition of the early martyrdom of the apostle John in Palestine, examined critically by J. H. Bernard, *A Critical and Exegetical Commentary on the Gospel According to St John* (ICC; Edinburgh, 1928) xxxvii–xlv. Perhaps one should consider the Muratorian Canon as attesting the tradition that John at least began to write his Gospel before the dispersion of the apostles from Jerusalem. See Markus Dods, *The Expositor's Greek Testament* (Grand Rapids, n. d.) vol. 1, 661.

[83] Bernard, *John*, vol. 1, 280, states: "It is an instance of the 'irony' of the evangelist that he does not stay to make the obvious comment that what Jewish critics of Jesus thought so absurd was afterwards accomplished by the first preachers of His Gospel, which embraced both Greek and Jew." However, according to J. A. T. Robinson, "The Destination and Purpose of St John's Gospel", *NTS* 6 (1960) 117–31, the term "Greek" in John means a Jew of the diaspora as distinct from a Palestinian Jew. John was primarily an apostle to the circumcised (Gal 2:9)!

[84] Among those who have advocated an Alexandrian location for John are Kirsopp and Silva Lake, *An Introduction to the New Testament* (London, 1938) 53, but they greatly exaggerated in arguing "the Gospel is extremely Philonic". J. L. Martyn, *History and Theology in the Fourth Gospel*, 58, note 94, argues for a Greek city with a large Jewish quarter ruled by its own magistrates, probably Alexandria.

[85] On the settlement of Samaritans at Thebes, see *Ant.*, XI, viii, 6 (par. 345). According to Ralph Marcus, *Josephus* (Loeb Classical Library, Josephus 6; Cambridge, Mass., London, 1937) 481, there was a village in the Fayum, 65 miles south of the Delta, called Samareia. See V. A. Tcherikover, *Corpus Papyrorum Judaicarum* (Cambridge, Mass., 1957) vol. 1, 5, note 12. Samaritans in Alexandria are mentioned in *Ant.*, XIII, iii, 4 and in Egypt generally in *Ant.*, XIII, i, 1.

there, in disputation as to who were the real citizens of that city.[86] This argument may be reflected in the claims of Jesus' opponents (8:33): "We are descendants of Abraham, and have never been in bondage to anyone." Jesus' own teaching, "You shall know the truth and the truth will make you free", might have seemed especially convincing in a city where Philo produced his tractate *Quod omnis probus liber sit.*

Alexandria was also a fanatical city, where sometimes blood flowed, as Jew brought about the death of Samaritan,[87] and where Greek and Roman persecuted the Jew.[88] The same fanaticism may also have brought about the death of some early witnesses to the Gospel of Christ. Therefore, even though Jn 16:2 may be applicable to a Palestinian situation (such as the persecution of Saul of Tarsus), it may also have been pertinent at Alexandria. Not all Alexandrian Jews thought and spoke profoundly theological language like Philo, but many were much more akin in their thinking to the author of 3 Maccabees, a rather simple and non-philosophical Jew who wholeheartedly approved of the massacre of apostate and idolatrous Jews.[89] The preaching of the divinity of Christ may have been regarded by men with his frame of mind as sufficient cause for expulsion from the synagogue, or even for stoning (8:58f.; 10:29-39). If either John the apostle, or one of his disciples bearing John's Gospel message, came to Alexandria, he would find inside boisterous Alexandria most of the parties to whom the Fourth Gospel is addressed. He would even find there disciples of John the Baptist, who might need to be told (1:8), "John was not the light, but came to bear witness to the light".[90] In short, he would find a little Palestine all within one city, and the preaching of the Evangelist would fit exactly the need of such a city.[91] Indeed, Jesus' prayer for the unity of believers (Jn 17) would appear as one grand hope for bridging the alienations which separated men at Alexandria, for "the children of God who are scattered abroad" must now be gathered into one (11:51f.).

The apostle John may himself have preached in Alexandria, and

---

[86] According to the Epistle of Aristeas (12–27, 33–37) Ptolemy Lagos had taken many Jewish captives to Egypt where they were enslaved, but Ptolemy Philadelphus freed them. On the whole question of Jews in Egypt, see Tcherikover's three-volume work: *Corpus Papyrorum Judaicarum*, especially vol. 1, 1–85; vol. 2, 36–55, 78ff.

[87] Josephus, *Ant.*, XIII, iii, 4.

[88] See here 3 Macc; Philo, *On the Embassy to Gaius;* Josephus, *Against Apion.*

[89] On 3 Macc, see V. A. Tcherikover, "The Third Book of Maccabees as a Historical Source", *SH* 7 (Jerusalem, 1961) 1–26; see also Brownlee in *IDB* vol. K–Q, 210b–212a.

[90] Cf. Acts 18:24f.; 19:1–5, and the discussion by S. G. F. Brandon in *The Fall of Jerusalem and the Christian Church*, 2nd ed. (London, 1957) 24f.

[91] Contrast the situation at Ephesus as described by H. E. Dana, *The Ephesian Tradition: An Oral Source of the Fourth Gospel* (Kansas City, 1940) 94–149. Dana ascribes the origin of the historical traditions to Palestine, and constantly stresses the fact that the Palestinian aspects of the narrative would be largely irrelevant to Ephesus where the Gospel was written. On the other hand, Dana builds a connection between Caesarea and Ephesus (pp. 40ff.) to account for the transmission of the tradition. W. C. van Unnik, "The Purpose of St John's Gospel", *SE* 1, 382–411, believes that the book is addressed to Jews of the diaspora and was written at Ephesus.

even if he made use of an interpreter, there may have been an undetermined influence of Alexandria upon his Evangel. His preaching would need to be translated to meet the needs of the preponderantly Greek-speaking population, for this is the city where as early as the third century B.C. it was deemed desirable to translate the Torah into Greek. The philosophical thought which characterized some leading circles at Alexandria must have prepared them to find in the simple, though profound "philosophical thinking" of John something warmly appealing; for once the hymn which begins his Gospel was translated into Greek and the *Mêmrā́* became the *Logos,* Jesus would be seen not only as the fulfilment of Jewish messianic hopes, but also as the answer to Greek speculation regarding the Logos.

Before the Fourth Gospel consisted of much more than written sources, the apostle himself had died; the Gospel was put together from the manuscripts left behind by the original Evangelist. The author of the Gospel as we have it translated whatever materials required translation from Aramaic and put the whole story together. However, his work was largely like that of the editor, for the "Rudimentary Signs Gospel" provided the framework into which he needed to fit other samples of Johannine preaching. Supposing this author-translator to have been John the Elder, one may suggest that he, like Apollos, may have eventually made his way from Alexandria to Ephesus[92] and there completed the translation and editing of the Fourth Gospel. The aged John, of whom we hear in ecclesiastical tradition and who down to the reign of Domitian continued to exhort his congregation saying, "Little children, love one another", may therefore have been this John the Elder.[93]

Who was the beloved disciple?

Here is a question which affects the authorship of this Gospel; for if one approaches the question from tradition alone, the probable inference is that he is John the apostle, who is (according to 21:20, 24) both the beloved disciple and the author of the Gospel. If, however, one approaches this question from internal evidence alone, the

---

[92] Acts 18:24–28. The bearer of the Johannine tradition had not yet reached Alexandria before the departure of Apollos, for Jn 1:33 distinguishes the baptism of Jesus from that of the Baptist. However, 3:25ff. assigns a period to Jesus' career in which the baptism of the Christ himself would appear to be that of the Baptist! This was before the gift of the Spirit.

[93] To posit at least the publication of the Fourth Gospel at Ephesus is to ascribe a minimal historical value to the tradition of Papias; and, if the publisher was one John the Elder, a former disciple of the apostle, one can readily understand the confusion. J. N. Sanders, *IDB*, vol. E–J, 941*b*–942*a*, suggests that Paul's letter to the Colossians and John's Gospel are addressed to a like situation of the Asian churches. One can see how this Gospel would be relevant in that geographic and spiritual context; but there is insufficient evidence that its contents were shaped in that milieu. See, however, H. C. Snape, "The Fourth Gospel, Ephesus, and Alexandria", *HTR* 47 (1954) 1–14. Snape supplies a deficiency of Brandon's work, a discussion of the Fourth Gospel. If, however, this Evangel represents Palestinian preaching, introduced early in Alexandria, this calls for radical revisions in Brandon's theses.

conclusion is that the beloved disciple is Lazarus of Bethany II.[94]
The two lines of evidence would therefore seem to collide in Jn 21,
where one will need to choose between Lazarus and John the apostle
as the author of the Gospel or of its embodied sources.

When word reached Jesus at Bethany I that Lazarus at Bethany II
was critically ill, the message read: "Lord, he whom you love is ill."
Then when Jesus eventually came to Bethany II, "Jesus wept. So the
Judeans said, 'See how he loved him!' " When Jesus came again to
Bethany II, "Lazarus was one of those at table with him".[95] Against
this background, when we come to the Last Supper and read, "One
of his disciples, whom Jesus loved, was lying close to the breast of
Jesus" (13:22), all the clues that we have for identifying this disciple
point only to Lazarus. The "other disciple known to the high priest"
(18:16), who figures in Jesus' trial before Caiaphas, could also reasonably be Lazarus, for as a resident at Bethany he was a frequent
visitor to Jerusalem and may well have been known to its chief priests.
The disciple who stood by the cross of Christ, to whom Jesus
commended the care of his own mother, is clearly identified as "the
disciple whom he loved" (19:26f.). If "from that hour the disciple
took her to his own home", this is also reasonable, for Bethany was
near at hand. John the apostle had probably long before given up
whatever home he ever had, but if he had any, it would have been
at Capernaum.[96] If again it was Lazarus who outran Peter in reach-
ing the tomb of Christ on the morning of his resurrection, it is he
who above all others would know how impossible it is to free oneself
from the swaddling cloths of the dead, and instantly recognize there
in the still-rolled cocoon-like garments the clear proof of a supernatural resurrection.

The symbolism of John's history also favours this interpretation,
for if it was at Bethany I that Jesus had called his first disciples, then
it was fitting that he should have at least one disciple from Bethany II.
What then constitutes the call of Lazarus to become Jesus' disciple?
Is it not when Jesus cried, "Lazarus come out!"? For here in summoning Lazarus from death to life, from the darkness of the tomb
to the light of life, we see what it really means to become a disciple
of Jesus; for as Jesus said on another occasion (5:25), "The hour is
coming, *and now is,* when the dead shall hear the voice of the Son
of God, and those who hear will live." The parallelism teaches us
that this had already happened to those whom Jesus called at Bethany
I; but then it took the physical resurrection of Lazarus to represent this
in the symbolic history of the Fourth Gospel.

[94] See F. V. Filson, "Who was the Beloved Disciple?", *JBL* 63 (1949) 83-8;
"Beloved Disciple", *IDB*, vol. A–D, 378f.

[95] Jn 11:3, 35f.; 12:1.

[96] How much was included in "everything" the "disciples left" (Lk 5:11)?
Contrast the less absolute statements of Mk 1:20 and Mt 4:22. Alternatively, the
family of Zebedee lived at Bethsaida; for the arrival of Jesus and his disciples at
Capernaum, according to Mk 1:21, was subsequent to the call of the disciples,
and the two towns were close enough to each other for this sequence of events.
Mk 1:29 places the house of Peter and Andrew at Capernaum, but they may have
been natives of Bethsaida (Jn 1:44). Actually, they probably fished back and forth
across the lake between the two villages.

In the beloved disciple, therefore, we should see not just Lazarus, but every disciple. Naturally, it was not possible for every one of the disciples to "lie close to the breast of Jesus", but Lazarus could do this and thereby illustrate how Jesus who had "loved his own who were in the world, loved them to the end" (13:1). If one argues, therefore, that Lazarus as the ideal disciple is non-historical, this may be a reasonable point of view, but I think it is overhasty, for in John real history and symbolic expression have a way of coinciding. If from the Synoptic Gospels we learn only of the presence of the Twelve at the Last Supper, this may be due to a preoccupation with the importance of the twelve, a theme which is only incidental in John's Gospel.[97] In other words, the surprise of finding Lazarus at the Lord's Supper in the upper room of Jerusalem is the sort of shocking thing that late tradition would not allow, but it is the very thing that an eye-witness would tell.

The description of the beloved disciple as reclining in the bosom of Jesus means far more than a relationship of affection and intimacy, as is shown by Jubilees 22:26 where "Jacob slept in the bosom of Abraham". This occurred when the older patriarch was about to die, but he first conferred his final blessing (along with much moral exhortation) on his grandson. Lying in the testator's bosom seems to designate one as the true son and heir. In Lk 16:19-23 it is Lazarus the poor beggar who lies in the patriarch's bosom. It was just like Jesus to show in this way that the social outcast rather than the rich man is the true son of Abraham.[98] Jubilees 22:26 is in the context

[97] The twelve are mentioned only in the context of Judas' defection (6:66-71) and of Thomas' absence (20:24), i.e., when the wholeness of the apostolic company is threatened or impaired. E. L. Titus, "The Identity of the Beloved Disciple", *JBL* 69 (1950) 323-8, has correctly observed that in 13:21-30 the beloved disciple seems to be juxtaposed to Judas the betrayer. From this he infers that the former succeeds the latter. Since in Acts 1 it is Matthias who is Judas' successor, he proposes identifying the beloved disciple with him. The internal evidence, however, militates against this logical conclusion. Rather, we are in the presence of a rival tradition as to who filled Judas' vacancy—unless, of course, Lazarus and Matthias are different names for the same person. Some, indeed, may have regarded Paul as the true successor to Judas.

[98] This partial parallel, together with the rich man's request that Lazarus be raised from the dead, might seem to favour the view of Titus, 323, note 1, that Lazarus is actually only a fictive character historicized by John through combining Lk 10:38-42 and 16:19-31. Could the Evangelist, however, have considered it plausible that Mary and Martha, who entertained others, allowed their own brother to lie hungry with unattended sores at the rich man's gate? Lk 16:27-31, however, may well be secondary, a *post eventum* allusion of Jesus' resurrection. Although Lazarus was such a common name, that one might argue that the identity of names is pure coincidence, the uniqueness of giving a name to a parabolic figure suggests that the tradition of Lazarus' resurrection led to the naming of the "poor man". The original parable like that of Nathan (2 Sam 12:1-4) left the characters anonymous.

That already at Jn 11:3 Lazarus is described as one whom Jesus loved implies an earlier acquaintanceship not recorded elsewhere. It is very reasonable to suppose that on numerous visits to Jerusalem, some of them prior to his public ministry, Jesus lodged in Bethany. Thus Lazarus may have been a friend of much longer standing than any of the apostles. It may be that Lazarus does not figure in Lk 10:38-42 simply because this was Martha's house, whereas Lazarus was married and had a home of his own at Bethany. On the other hand, Lazarus may have been a little brother not involved in the controversy of Lk 10.

of Abraham's final blessing and testamentary exhortation. It is on a
like occasion that the beloved disciple lies on Jesus' breast. This
means that he and all true disciples (whom he symbolizes) inherit the
task, the Spirit, and the peace which Jesus has bequeathed.[99] Similarly, the divine Logos as God's only begotten is one "in the bosom of
the Father" (1:18), for he is the heir of all things to whom all that
the Father has belongs (16:15).[100]

What then are we to make of Jn 21, in which it appears that the
beloved disciple is also the author of the Gospel? This chapter must
surely be the conclusion of the compiler of this Evangel. The original
conclusion of John's Signs Gospel was at 20:30f., but the compiler
of the whole Johannine tradition added chapter 21, and it is he
who is responsible for identifying the beloved disciple with the
Evangelist. We cannot be sure, but perhaps the beloved disciple who
figures in this story is actually John, for the sons of Zebedee are
said to have been present at the lake shore; and if in this resurrection
appearance of Jesus it really is John who becomes the beloved disciple,
then we can understand why 21:24 insists upon identifying the beloved
disciple with the Evangelist.[101] Those who see in John the apostle the
theologian *par excellence* may here perceive a certain justification;
for, whatever happened at the Last Supper, the words of John are
those of one who had "leaned on Jesus' breast".

---

[99] Belonging to this same testamentary context is Jesus' "New Commandment"
(13:34; 15:12). In the Testaments of the Twelve Patriarchs the Hebrew equivalent
of the Greek *diathēkē* ("testament"), *ṣawwāh* ("command"), had long been used
of the final arrangements of one about to die (2 Sam 17:23; 2 Kg 20:1). See
APOT 2, 283. The corresponding Aramaic verb employed in the targum is *pᵉqad*
and its cognate noun is *pᵉqadtā*, "order", 'last will'. This is probably the word used
by Jesus. Now according to Jubilees and the Testaments of the Twelve Patriarchs,
moral exhortation had become an important part of testamentary activity. This
appears also in Mattathias' farewell to his sons (1 Macc 2:49–69). The testamentary
context, therefore, shows that Christ's new *entolē* is not only commandment, but
also last will and testament.

[100] M. E. Boismard, " 'Dans le sein du Père', (Jo., I, 18)", *RB* 59 (1952) 23–39,
restores: "No one has ever seen God, except the only Begotten; into the Father's
bosom, that One brings [his sons]."

[101] Though it has been reasonably proposed that the rumour that the beloved
disciple should not die had been based on his previous resurrection, this is not the
point of 21:23. The translator and compiler of the Gospel as we have it has
probably drawn on a Johannine tradition for chapter 21; but meanwhile the
language of that story may well have been shaped by the misunderstanding of the
beloved disciple as none other than John the son of Zebedee. In any case, since
there is no tradition of Lazarus as the author of this Evangel, we must assume that
21:24 has in mind John the apostle as both the beloved disciple and the Evangelist.
Titus, *JBL* 69 (1950) 328, has well stated: "There is little doubt that it [the appendix]
is the work of a redactor and that it was his intention to identify the beloved
disciple with John the son of Zebedee." The death of the apostle would create a
problem for those who interpreted literally Mk 9:1, if we assume with tradition
that John outlived the others; but would this call for a date beyond A.D. 70 or 80?
In so far as 21:22 relates to believers generally, it could be very early. Cf. 1 Th
4:13–18.

Select Bibliography
on John and Qumran

Albright, W. F., *New Horizons in Biblical Research*, London, New York, Toronto, 1966. See especially pp. 43–6.

——, "Recent Discoveries in Palestine and the Gospel of St John", *The Background of the New Testament and Its Eschatology*, ed. W. D. Davies and D. Daube, Cambridge, 1956, 153–71.

Allegro, J., *The Dead Sea Scrolls: A Reappraisal*, 2nd ed., Harmondsworth, Baltimore, 1964. See especially pp. 142–5.

Baumbach, G., *Der Daulismus in der Sektenrolle [1QS] im Vergleich mit dem Dualismus in den spätjüdischen Apokalypsen und dem Johannesevangelium*, Diss. ev. theol. Humboldt-Universität, Berlin, 1956.

——, *Qumrān und das Johannes-Evangelium. Eine vergleichende Untersuchung der dualistischen Aussagen der Ordensregel [1QS] von Qumrān und des Johannes-Evangeliums mit Berücksichtigung der spätjüdischen Apokalypsen* (AVTR 6) Berlin, 1958.

Becker, J., *Das Heil Gottes. Heils-und Sündenbegriffe in den Qumrantexten und im Neuen Testament* (SUNT 3) Göttingen, 1964. See especially pp. 217–37.

Benoit, P., "Qumrân et le Nouveau Testament", *NTS* 7 (1960–61) 276–96. (ET: "Qumran and the New Testament", *Paul and Qumran*, ed. J. Murphy–O'Connor, London, Chicago, 1968, 1–30.)

Bergmeier, R., "Glaube als Werk? Die 'Werke Gottes' in Damaskusschrift II, 14–15 und Johannes, 6, 28–29", *RevQ* 6 (1967) 253–60.

Betz, O., *Offenbarung und Schriftforschung in der Qumransekte* (WUZNT 6) Tübingen, 1960. See especially pp. 60f.

——, *Der Paraklet: Fürsprecher im häretischen Spätjudentum, im Johannes-Evangelium und in neu gefundenen gnostischen Schriften* (AGSU 2) Leiden, 1963. See especially pp. 36–72, 113–16, 117–212.

——, "Zungenreden und süsser Wein: Zur eschatologischen Exegese von Jesaja 28 in Qumran und im Neuen Testament", *Bibel und Qumran*, ed. S. Wagner, Berlin, 1968, 20–36.

Bishop, E. F. F., *Skotos* and *Skotia* in the New Testament", *ALUOS* 2 (1959–61) 48–53.

Black, M., *The Scrolls and Christian Origins: Studies in the Jewish Background of the New Testament*, London, Paris, New York, 1961. See especially p. 134.

——, "Theological Conceptions in the Dead Sea Scrolls", *SEA* 18–19 (1953–54) 72–97. See especially pp. 79–80.

Böcher, O., *Der johanneische Dualismus im Zusammenhang des nachbiblischen Judentums*, Gütersloh, 1965.

Boismard, M.-É., "L'Évolution du thème eschatologique dans les traditions johanniques", *RB* 68 (1961) 507–24.

——, "L'importance de la critique textuelle pour établir l'origine araméenne du Quatrième Évangile", *L'Évangile de Jean* (RechBib 3) Louvain, 1958, 41–57.

——, "La literatura de Qumrán y los escritos de San Juan", *CB* 12 (1955) 250–64.

Bonnard, P., "Les manuscrits du désert de Juda et l'Évangile", *FV* 57 (1958) 79–93.

Borig, R., *Der Wahre Weinstock: Untersuchungen zu Jo 15, 1–10* (SANT 16) Munich, 1967. See especially pp. 127–8, 191–2.

Braun, F.-M., "L'arrière-fond du 4e Évangile", *L'Évangile de Jean: Études et Problèmes* (RechBib 3) Louvain, 1958, 179–96.

——, "L'arrière-fond judaïque du quatrième évangile et la Communauté d'Alliance", *RB* 62 (1955) 5–44.

——, "L'Évangile de Saint Jean et les grandes traditions d'Israel", *RTh* 59 (1959) 421–50; 60 (1960) 165–84, 325–63. See especially 60 (1960) 180–4, 333–4.

——, "Hermétisme et Johannisme", *RTh* 55 (1955) 22–42, 259–99. See especially pp. 290–5.

——, *Jean le Théologien*, 3 vols, (ÉtBib) Paris, 1959–66. See especially vol. 1, pp. 37–8, 226–31, 310–19; vol. 2, pp. 134, 253–76; vol. 3, pp. 43–7.

——, *Où en est l'étude du Quatrième Évangile?*, *ETL* 32 (1956) 535–46.

Braun, H., *Qumran und das Neue Testament*, 2 vols, Tübingen, 1966. See especially vol. 1, pp. 96–138; vol. 2, pp. 118–44.

——, *Spätjüdisch-häretischer und frühchristlicher Radikalismus. Jesus von Nazareth und die essenische Qumransekte* (BHT 24) Tübingen, 1957.

Brown, R. E., "The Fourth Gospel in Modern Research", *TBT* 20 (1965) 1302–10. See especially pp. 1303–4, 1308.

——, *The Gospel According to John*, 2 vols, (The Anchor Bible 29, 29a) Garden City, New York, 1966, 1970; London, 1971. See especially vol. 1, pp. lxii–lxiv.

——, "The Paraclete in the Fourth Gospel", *NTS* 13 (1967) 113–32.

——, "The 'Paraclete' in the Light of Modern Research", *SE* 4, part 1, 158–65.

——, "The Problem of Historicity in John", *CBQ* 24 (1962) 1–14. (Republished in R. E. Brown, *New Testament Essays*, Milwaukee, 1965; London, 1966, 143–67.)

——, "The Qumran Scrolls and the Johannine Gospel and Epistles", *CBQ* 17 (1955) 403–19, 559–74. (Republished in *The Scrolls and the New Testament*, ed. K. Stendahl, New York, 1957, 183–207, and in R. E. Brown, *New Testament Essays*, Milwaukee, 1965; London, 1966, 102–31.)

——, "Second Thoughts: X. The Dead Sea Scrolls and the New Testament", *ExpT* 78 (1966) 19–23. See especially pp. 21–2.

Brown, S., "From Burney to Black: The Fourth Gospel and the Aramaic Question", *CBQ* 26 (1964) 323–39.

Brownlee, W. H., "John the Baptist in the New Light of the Ancient Scrolls", *Int* 9 (1955) 71–90. (Revised and republished in *The Scrolls and the New Testament*, ed. K. Stendahl, New York, 1957, 33–53.)

——, *The Meaning of the Qumrân Scrolls for the Bible*, New York, 1964. See especially pp. 122–3.

——, "Messianic Motifs of Qumran and the New Testament", *NTS* 3 (1965) 12–30. See especially pp. 28–30.

Bruce, F. F., "The Dead Sea Scrolls and Early Christianity", *BJRL* 49 (1966) 69–90.

——, "Holy Spirit in the Qumran Texts", *ALUOS* 6 (1969) 49–55.

——, "Jesus and the Gospels in the Light of the Scrolls", *The Scrolls and Christianity*, ed. M. Black, London, 1969, 70–82. See especially pp. 78–9.

——, "Qumran and the New Testament", *FT* 90 (1958) 92–102. See especially pp. 97–9.

Buchanan, G. W., "The Samaritan Origin of the Gospel of John", *Religions in Antiquity: Essays in Memory of Erwin Ramsdell Goodenough*, ed. J. Neusner (SHR 14) Leiden, 1968, 149–75.

Bultmann, R., *Theology of the New Testament*, 2 vols, trans. K. Grobel, New York, 1951–5. See especially vol. 2, p. 13, note.

Burrows, M., *The Dead Sea Scrolls*, New York, London, 1955. See especially pp. 338–40.

——, *More Light on the Dead Sea Scrolls*, New York, London, 1958. See especially pp. 61, 123–32.

Carmignac, J., "Les affinités Qumrâniennes de la onzième Ode de Salomon", *RevQ* 3 (1961) 71–102. See especially pp. 97–101.

——, *Le Docteur de Justice et Jésus Christ*, Paris, 1957. (ET by K. G. Pedley: *Christ and the Teacher of Righteousness*, Baltimore, 1962.)

——, "Un Qumrânien converti au Christianisme: l'auteur des Odes de Salomon", *Qumran-Probleme*, ed. H. Bardtke (DAWB 42) Berlin, 1963, 75–108.

——, *Recherches sur le "Notre Père"*, Leiden, 1969.

Castellini, G. M., "Due note Giovannee", *RiB* 3 (1955) 229–34.

Cerfaux, L., "Influence de Qumrân sur le Nouveau Testament", *La secte de Qumrân et les origines du Christianisme* (RechBib 4) Paris, 1959, 233–44.

Charlesworth, J. H., "A Critical Comparison of the Dualism in 1QS III, 13–IV, 26 and the 'Dualism' Contained in the Fourth Gospel", *NTS* 15 (1969) 389–418 [reprinted above, pp. 76–106].

Clark, F., "Tension and Tide in St John's Gospel", *ITQ* 24 (1957) 154–65.

Colwell, E. C., "The Interpretation of a Gospel", *En* 25 (1964) 3–40.

Coppens, J., "Le don de l'Esprit d'après les textes de Qumrân et le Quatrième Évangile", *L'Évangile de Jean: Études et Problèmes* (RechBib 3) Louvain, 1958, 209–23.

Cribbs, F. L., "A Reassessment of the Date of Origin and the Destination of the Gospel of John", *JBL* 89 (1970) 38–55.

Cross, F. L. (ed.), *Studies in the Fourth Gospel*, London, 1957. See especially pp. 99–100.

Cross, Jr, F. M., *The Ancient Library of Qumran and Modern Biblical Studies*, rev. ed., Garden City, New York, 1961. See especially pp. 206–16.

——, "The Dead Sea Scrolls", *The Interpreter's Bible*, ed. G. A. Buttrick *et al.*, New York, Nashville, 1957, vol. 12, 645–67. See especially pp. 660–2.

——, "The Scrolls and the New Testament", *ChCen* 72 (1955) 968–71.

Cullmann, O., "L'Opposition contre le Temple de Jérusalem, motif commun de la théologie johannique et du monde ambiant", *NTS* 5 (1959) 157–73. (ET: "A New Approach to the Interpretation of the Fourth Gospel", *ExpT* 71 (1959) 8–12, 39–43.)

——, "Das Rätsel des Johannesevangeliums im Lichte der Neuen Handschriftenfunde", *Vorträge und Aufsätze 1925–1962*, ed. F. Fröhlich, Tübingen, 1966, 260–91.

——, "Secte de Qumran, hellénistes des Actes et Quatrième Évangile", *Les manuscrits de la Mer Morte: Colloque de Strasbourg 25–27 Mai 1955*, Paris, 1957, 61–74, 135–6.

——, "The Significance of the Qumran Texts for Research into the Beginnings of Christianity", *JBL* 74 (1955) 213–26.

Dąbrowski, E., "Nowy Testament w Świetle Współczesnych Odkryć Biblijnych", *Znak* 12 (1960) 155–79. (Title means: "The New Testament in the Light of Modern Biblical Discoveries".)

——, *Odkrycia w Qumran nad Morzem Martwym a Nowy Testament*, Warsaw, 1960. (Title means: *The Discoveries at Qumran near the Dead Sea and the New Testament*.)

Daniélou, J., "Église primitive et communauté de Qumran", *Ét* 90 (1957) 216–35. See especially pp. 226–8.

——, *Les manuscrits de la Mer Morte et les origines du Christianisme*, Paris, 1957. See especially pp. 99–106. (ET by Salvator Attanasio: *The Dead Sea Scrolls and Primitive Christianity*, Baltimore, 1958. See especially pp. 103–11.)

Davies, A. P., *The Meaning of the Dead Sea Scrolls*, New York, 1956; London, 1957.

Davies, W. D., "The Dead Sea Scrolls and Christian Origins", *RL* 26 (1957) 246–64. (Republished in *Christian Origins and Judaism*, Philadelphia, 1962, 97–119.)

Dodd, C. H., *Historical Tradition in the Fourth Gospel*, Cambridge, 1963. See especially pp. 263ff., 300.

Driver, G. R., *The Judaean Scrolls: The Problem and a Solution*, Oxford, 1965. See especially pp. 544–61.

Emerton, J. A., "Melchizedek and the Gods: Fresh Evidence for the Jewish Background of John X. 34–6", *JTS* 17 (1966) 399–401.

Feine, P., and Behm, J., *Introduction to the New Testament*, re-ed. W. G. Kümmel, Nashville, New York, London, 1966. See especially pp. 154–61.

Feuillet, A., "The Johannine Writings", *Introduction to the New Testament*, ed. A. Robert and A. Feuillet, New York, Rome, Paris, 1965. See especially pp. 646–7.

——, "La littérature de Qumrân et les écrits johanniques", *RCE* 3 (1959) 440–56.

Fitzmyer, J. A., *The Genesis Apocryphon of Qumran Cave I* (BO 18) Rome, 1966. See especially p. 134. [2nd ed., 1971.]

——, "The Use of Explicit Old Testament Quotations in Qumran Literature and in the New Testament", *NTS* 7 (1960–61) 297–333. (Republished in his *Essays on the Semitic Background of the New Testament*, London, 1971, 3–58.)

——, "The Aramaic 'Elect of God' Text from Qumran Cave 4", *CBQ* 27 (1965) 348–72. (Republished in his *Essays on the Semitic Background of the New Testament*, London, 1971, 127–60.)

Flusser, D., "The Dead Sea Sect and Pre-Pauline Christianity", *Aspects of the Dead Sea Scrolls*, ed. C. Rabin and Y. Yadin (*SH* 4) Jerusalem, 1958, reprinted 1965, 215–66.

——, "The Dualism of 'Flesh and Spirit' in the Dead Sea Scrolls and the New Testament" [in Hebrew], *Tarb* 27 (1958) 158–65.

——, "Die Sekte aus der Wuste Juda und das Christentum", *Ijunim bimegilloth Midbar Jehudah*, Jerusalem, 1957, 85–103.

Freed, E. D., *Old Testament Quotations in the Gospel of John* (NovTSup 11) Leiden, 1965. See especially pp. 122–3.

Fritsch, C. T., *The Qumrân Community*, New York, 1956. See especially pp. 116–18.

Grant, R. M., *Gnosticism and Early Christianity*, New York, 1966. See especially pp. 163–9.

Grossouw, W., "The Dead Sea Scrolls and the New Testament. A Preliminary Survey", *StCa* 26 (1951) 289–99; 27 (1952) 1–8.

Gryglewicz, F., "Der Evangelist Johannes und die Sekte von Qumran", *MTZ* 10 (1959) 226–8.

——, Św. Jan Ewangelista a Qumrańczycy", *ZNKUL* 2 (1959) 121–5.

Henderson, M. W., *The Priestly Ministry of Jesus in the Gospel of John and the Epistle of the Hebrews*, diss. The Southern Baptist Theological Seminary, Louisville, Ky, 1966.

Higgins, A. J. B., *The Historicity of the Fourth Gospel*, London, 1960. See especially pp. 16–17, 61–2.

Howlett, D., *The Essenes and Christianity. An interpretation of the Dead Sea Scrolls*, New York, 1957. See especially pp. 166–8, 177–8.

Hunter, A. M., *According to John*, London, Philadelphia, 1968. See especially pp. 23–34.

——, "Recent Trends in Johannine Studies", *ExpT* 71 (1959–60) 164–7, 219–22.

Huppenbauer, H. W., *Der Mensch zwischen zwei Welten: Der Dualismus der Texte von Qumran (Höhle I) und der Damaskusfragmente [CD]. Ein Beitrag zur Vorgeschichte des Evangeliums*, Zürich, 1959. See especially pp. 53, 95–6.

Irwin, A. L., *Conflict Spirit-Dualism in the Qumran Writings and in the New Testament*, diss. Hartford Theological Seminary, Hartford, Conn., 1960.

Jaubert, A., *La date de la cène: calendrier biblique et liturgie chrétienne* (ÉtBib), Paris, 1957. (ET by I. Rafferty: *The Date of the Last Supper*, Staten Island, 1965.)

Jeremias, J., "Qumrân et la theologie", *NRT* 85 (1963) 674–90. See especially pp. 685–6.

——, "The Qumran Texts and the New Testament", *ExpT* 70 (1958) 68–9.

——, *The Rediscovery of Bethesda, John 5:2* (New Testament Archaeology Monograph 1) Louisville, Ky, 1966. See especially pp. 34–8.

——, *Die theologische Bedeutung der Funde am Toten Meer*, Göttingen, 1962. (ET by D. Zersen: "The Theological Significance of the Dead Sea Scrolls", *CTM* 39 (1968) 557–71.)

Johnston, G., *The Spirit-Paraclete in the Gospel of John* (SNTS Monograph Series 12) Cambridge, 1970. See especially pp. 7–12, 54–5, 96–118.

Käsemann, E., *Jesu letzter Wille nach Johannes 17*, Tübingen, 1966. (ET by G. Krodel: *The Testament of Jesus: A Study of the Gospel of John in the Light of Chapter 17*, London, Philadeplhia, 1968. See especially pp. 59, 66.)

Kahle, P., "The Greek Bible and the Gospels. Fragments from the Judaen Desert", *SE* 1, 613–21.

Koch, G. A., *An Investigation of the Possible Relationship between the Gospel of John and the Sectarian Documents of the Dead Sea Scrolls as Suggested by Certain Recent Authors*, diss. Eastern Baptist Theological Seminary, Philadelphia, 1959.

Kocsis, E., "János Iratainok Néhány Helye a Holttengeri Leletek Megvilágitásában", *Református Egyház* 14 (1962) 248–50. (Title means: "Some Passages from St John's Writings in the Light of the Dead Sea Discoveries.")

Kuhl, J., *Die Sendung Jesu und der Kirche nach dem Johannes-Evangelium* (SIMSVD 11) St Augustin/Siegburg, 1967. See especially pp. 22–6.

Kuhn, K. G., "Die in Palästina gefundenen hebräischen Texte und das Neue Testament", *ZTK* 47 (1950) 192–211. See especially pp. 209–10.

——, "Johannesevangelium und Qumrāntexte", *Neotestamentica et Patristica* (NovTSup 6) ed. W. C. van Unnik. Leiden, 1962, 111–22.

Lákatos, E., "El Cuarto Evangelio y los Documentos de Qumran", *RevTh* 21 (1956) 67–77.

LaSor, W. S., *Amazing Dead Sea Scrolls and the Christian Faith*, Chicago, 1956. See especially pp. 211–14.

Laurin, R. B., "The Problem of Two Messiahs in the Qumran Scrolls", *RevQ* 4 (1963) 39–52. See especially pp. 42–3.

Lazure, N., "La convoitise de la chair en I Jean II, 16", *RB* 76 (1969) 161–205.

Leaney, A. R. C., *The Rule of Qumran and Its Meaning*, London, Philadelphia, 1966.

——, "The Scrolls and the New Testament", *A Guide to the Scrolls,* ed. A. R. C. Leaney, London, 1958, 79–122. See especially pp. 95–103.

Lee, E. K., "The Historicity of the Fourth Gospel", *ChQr* 167 (1966) 292–302. See especially pp. 298–301.

Licht, J., "An Analysis of the Treatise of the Two Spirits in DSD", *Aspects of the Dead Sea Scrolls,* ed. C. Rabin and Y. Yadin (*SH* 4) Jerusalem, 1958, 215–66.

Livshiťs, G. M., *Proiskhozhdenie Khristianstva v svete rukopiseĭ Mertvogo moriâ,* Minsk, 1967. See especially pp. 192–3. (Title means: *The Origin of Christianity in the Light of the Dead Sea Scrolls.*)

Marsh, J., *The Gospel of St John* (PelGosCom) Harmondsworth, Baltimore, 1968. See especially pp. 37–40.

Mayer, R., and J. Reuss, *Die Qumranfunde und die Bibel,* Regensburg, 1959. See especially pp. 114–19.

Meeks, W. A., *The Prophet-King: Moses Traditions and the Johannine Christology* (NovTSup 14) Leiden, 1967. See especially pp. 171–5.

Molin, G., *Die Söhne des Lichtes: Zeit und Stellung der Handschriften vom Toten Meer,* Vienna, Munich, 1954. See especially pp. 181–6, Anhänge 4 and 5.

Morris, L., *The Dead Sea Scrolls and St John's Gospel* (The Twelfth Campbell Morgan Lecture) London, 1960. (Republished in L. Morris, *Studies in the Fourth Gospel,* Grand Rapids, Michigan, 1969, 321–58.)

Mowry, L., "The Dead Sea Scrolls and the Background for the Gospel of John", *BA* 17 (1954) 78–97.

——, *The Dead Sea Scrolls and the Early Church,* Chicago, 1962. See especially pp. 236–7, 242–4.

Murphy, R. E., "The Dead Sea Scrolls and New Testament Comparisons", *CBQ* 18 (1956) 263–72.

——, *The Dead Sea Scrolls and the Bible,* Westminster, Maryland, 1956. See especially pp. 64–79.

——, "Insights into the New Testament from the Dead Sea Scrolls", *AER* 135 (1956) 9–22.

Nakano, K., "Shikai-shahon to Yohane-den", *Tôk* 22 (1958). (Title means: "The Dead Sea Manuscripts and the Gospel of John".)

Nauck, W., *Die Tradition und der Charakter des Ersten Johannesbriefes* (WUZNT 3) Tübingen, 1957. See especially pp. 165–82.

Neill, S., *The Interpretation of the New Testament 1861–1961,* New York, Toronto, London, 1964. See especially pp. 308–24.

Nötscher, F., "Geist und Geister in den Texten von Qumran", *Mélanges Bibliques: Rédigés en l'honneur de André Robert* (TrInstCaP 4) Paris, 1956, 305–16.

——, *Gotteswege und Menschenwege in der Bibel und in Qumran* (BBB 15) Bonn, 1958. See especially pp. 97–122.

——, *Vom Alten zum Neuen Testament* (BBB 17) Bonn, 1962.

——, *Zur theologischen Terminologie der Qumran-Texte* (BBB 10) Bonn, 1956.

O'Neill, J. C., *The Puzzle of 1 John,* London, 1966.

Parente, F., "Il problema storico dei rapporti tra Essenismo e Cristianesimo prima della scoperta dei Rotoli del Mar Morto", *PP* 86 (1962) 333–70.

Pollard, T. E., "Cosmology and the Prologue of the Fourth Gospel", *Vig Chr* 12 (1958) 147–53.

——, "The Fourth Gospel: Its Background and Early Interpretation", *AusBR* 7 (1959) 41–53.

——, *Johannine Christology and the Early Church* (SNTS Monograph Series 13) Cambridge, 1970. See especially pp. 10–15, 234–5.

Potterie, I. de la, "L'arrière-fond du thème johannique de vérite", *SE* 1, 277–94.

Price, J. L., "The Search for the Theology of the Fourth Evangelist", *JAAR* 35 (1967) 3–15.

Quispel, G., "Het Johannesevangelie en de Gnosis", *NTT* 11 (1956–57) 173–203.

Ramlot, L., "L'Évangile selon saint Jean et la critique historique", *BiViChr* (1961) 80–7.

Ringgren, H., *The Faith of Qumran*, trans. E. T. Sander, Philadelphia, 1963. See especially pp. 151, 245–7.

——, "Qumrân and Gnosticism", *Le origini dello gnosticismo*, ed. U. Bianchi, Leiden, 1967, 379–88.

Robinson, J. A. T., "The New Look on the Fourth Gospel", *SE* 1, 338–50.

——, *Twelve New Testament Studies* (SBT 34) London, 1962. See especially pp. 11–27, 99–101, 132.

Roloff, J., "Der johanneische 'Lieblingsjünger' und der Lehrer der Gerechtigkeit", *NTS* 15 (1968) 129–51.

Rowley, H. H., *The Dead Sea Scrolls and the New Testament*, London, 1957. See especially pp. 24–8.

Sanders, J. N., "John, Gospel of", *IDB* 2, 932–46. See especially pp. 940–3.

——, *A Commentary on the Gospel According to St John*, ed. B. A. Mastin, New York, 1968. See especially pp. 50, 352–5, 359.

Schaedel, K., *Das Johannesevangelium und die "Kinder des Lichtes". Untersuchungen zu den Selbstbezeichnungen Jesu im 4 Evangelium und zur Heilsterminologie des " 'En-Fešḥa-Sekte"*, Diss. ev. theol., Vienna, 1953.

Schelkle, K. H., *Die Gemeinde von Qumran und die Kirche des Neuen Testaments*, Düsseldorf, 1960. See especially pp. 103–8.

Schmitt, J., "Les écrits du Nouveau Testament et les textes de Qumran", *RScRel* 29 (1955) 381–401; 30 (1956) 55–74, 261–82.

Schnackenburg, R., "Anbetung in Geist und Wahrheit ... 2. Vergleich mit Qumran-Texten", *Christliche Existenz nach dem Neuen Testament*, Munich, 1967, vol. 2, 83–9.

——, "Die Anbetung in Geist und Wahrheit (Jo 4, 23) im Lichte von Qumrân-Texten", *BZ*, N.S. 3 (1959) 88–94.

——, *Das Johannesevangelium*, 2 vols, Freiburg, 1965. (ET by K. Smyth: *The Gospel According to St John*, New York, 1968. See especially vol. 1, pp. 105–11, 128–35.)

——, "Logos-Hymnus und Johanneischer Prolog", *BZ* 1 (1957) 69–109.

Schubert, K., *Die Gemeinde vom Toten Meer: Ihre Entstehung und ihre Lehren*, Munich, 1958. See especially pp. 131–3. (ET by J. W. Doberstein: *The Dead Sea Community: Its Origin and Teachings*, London, 1959. See especially pp. 151–4.)

Schulz, S., "Die Komposition des Johannesprologs und die Zusammensetzung des 4. Evangelium", *SE* 1, 351–62.

——, *Komposition und Herkunft der Johanneischen Reden* (BWANT 5 Folge 1) Stuttgart, 1960. See especially pp. 94–102, 152–70, 184–7.

Sibinga, J. S., "1 Johannes Tegen de Achtergrond van de Teksten van Qumran", *VoxTh* 24 (1953–54) 11–14.

Sidebottom, E. M., *The Christ of the Fourth Gospel in the Light of First-Century Thought*, London, 1961. See especially pp. 3–9.

Simon, U., *Heaven in the Christian Tradition*, London, 1958. See especially pp. 174–5.

Škrinjar, A., "Prima Epistola Johannis in theologia aetatis suae", *VD* 46 (1968) 148–68.

Smith, D. M., "The Sources of the Gospel of John: An Assessment of the Present State of the Problem", *NTS* 10 (1964) 336–51. See especially pp. 350–1.

Stanley, D. M., "The Johannine Literature", *TS* 17 (1956) 516–31.

Stauffer, E., *Jesus und die Wüstengemeinde am Toten Meer* (ColHef 9) Stuttgart, 1957 (ET by H. Spalteholz: *Jesus and the Wilderness Community at Qumran*, Philadelphia, 1964.)

——, "Probleme der Priestertradition", *TLZ* 81 (1956) 135–50, 255ff.

——, "Qumran und die Evangelienforschung", *Universitas* 14 (1959) 487–95.

Szodja, D., "Symbolika Wody w Pismach Św. Jana Ewangelisty i w Qumran", *RocTK* 13 (1966) 105–21. (Résumé: "Le symbolisme de l'eau dans les écrits de S. Jean Évangéliste et de ceux de Qumran", 120–1.)

Teeple, H. M., "Qumran and the Origin of the Fourth Gospel", *NT* 4 (1960) 6-25.

Vanderlip, D. G., *A Comparative Study of Certain Alleged Similarities between the Literature of Qumran and the Fourth Gospel*, diss. University of Southern California, Berkeley, Calif., 1959.

Vawter, B., "The Gospel According to John", *The Jerome Biblical Commentary*, 2 vols, ed. R. E. Brown, s.s., J. A. Fitzmyer, s.j., R. E. Murphy, O.Carm., Englewood Cliffs, N.J., 1968; London, 1969, vol. 2, 414–66. See especially vol. 2, p. 417.

Vermes, G., "'He is the Bread': Targum Neofiti Exodus 16:15", *Neotestamentica et Semitica: Studies in Honour of Matthew Black*, ed. E. E. Ellis and M. Wilcox, Edinburgh, 1969, 256–63.

Via, D. O., "Darkness, Christ, and the Church in the Fourth Gospel", *SJT* 14 (1961) 172–93.

Waard, J. de, *A Comparative Study of the Old Testament Text in the Dead Sea Scrolls and in the New Testament* (STDJ 4) Leiden, 1965. See especially pp. 65–6.

Wilcox, M., "Dualism, Gnosticism, and other Elements in the Pre-Pauline Tradition", *The Scrolls and Christianity*, ed. M. Black, London, 1969, 83–96.

Wildberger, H., "Der Dualismus in den Qumrânschriften", *AsSt* (1954) 163–77.

Wilson, E., *The Dead Sea Scrolls 1947–1969*, New York, 1969. See especially pp. 95ff.

Young, F. W., "A Study of the Relation of Isaiah to the Fourth Gospel", *ZNW* 46 (1955) 215–33.

Note on Contributors

Raymond E. Brown, S.S., Professor of Biblical Studies at Union Theological Seminary and Woodstock College, studied at the Catholic University of America in Washington, D.C., the Gregorian University in Rome, St Mary's Seminary and Pontifical University in Baltimore, from which he received a doctorate in theology (S.T.D.), Johns Hopkins University in Baltimore, from which he received the Ph.D., and the Pontifical Biblical Commission in Rome. Before accepting the present position at Union, Father Brown was Professor of Sacred Scripture at St Mary's Seminary in Baltimore. In 1958–59 he was Fellow of the A.S.O.R. in Jerusalem. He is a member of numerous professional societies, including the American Schools of Oriental Research, the Catholic Biblical Association, the Society of Biblical Literature, and the *Studiorum Novi Testamenti Societas*.

Father Brown is a most prolific New Testament scholar. His articles and reviews have appeared in many technical and popular journals, and his books include:

The Gospel of St John and The Johannine Epistles (NTRG 13) Collegeville, Minn., 1965.

New Testament Essays, Milwaukee, 1965; London, 1966.

The Gospel According to John, 2 vols, Garden City, New York, 1966–70; London, 1971 [Anchor Bible].

Jesus, God and Man, Milwaukee, 1967, London, 1968.

The Semitic Background of the Term "Mystery" in the New Testament, Philadelphia, 1968.

(with others) *The Jerome Biblical Commentary*, 2 vols, Englewood Cliffs, N.J., 1968; London, 1969.

Priest and Bishop: Biblical Reflections, New York, London, 1971.

Father Brown is recognized by Protestants, Catholics, and Jews as one of the most informed scholars concerning the relationships between John and Qumran.

James Ligon Price, Jr, Professor of Religion, Vice Provost and Dean of Undergraduate Education at Duke University, studied at Washington and Lee University, Union Theological Seminary in Virginia, Princeton Theological Seminary, The University of Cambridge, from which he received the Ph.D., and the University of Zürich. Professor Price is a member of numerous professional societies. He was president of the American Academy of Religion in 1965, and president of the

Southern Section of the Society of Biblical Literature in 1961-62. Professor Price has published articles in numerous scholarly journals. His *Interpreting the New Testament* (2nd rev. ed. to be published in 1971) is a standard reference work in many major universities in the United States. Professor Price is widely respected for his theological sensitivity and interpretation of Paul and John.

A. R. C. Leaney, Head of the Department of Theology and Professor of Christian Theology at Nottingham University, earned the B.D. and D.D. from Oxford University. A member of many professional societies, he is presently serving on the British and Foreign Bible Society's Old Testament Translator's Panel, and has been Secretary of *Studiorum Novi Testamenti Societas*.

Professor Leaney has contributed to several scholarly periodicals, and his books include:

(with others) *A Guide to the Scrolls: Nottingham Studies on the Qumran Discoveries*, London, 1958.

A Commentary on the Gospel According to St Luke, London, New York, 1958.

The Epistles to Timothy, Titus, and Philemon: Introduction and Commentary, London, 1960.

The Rule of Qumran and Its Meaning, London, Philadelphia, 1966.

The Letters of Peter and Jude: A Commentary on the First Letter of Peter, A Letter of Jude and the Second Letter of Peter, Cambridge, 1967.

(with R. Davidson) *Biblical Criticism*, Harmondsworth, Baltimore, 1970.

Professor Leaney is especially known and respected for his important contributions to the understanding of Qumran's *Rule*.

Annie Jaubert, maître de recherche in Christian Origins at Centre National de la Recherche Scientifique, is a member of several professional organizations, including the *Studiorum Novi Testamenti Societas*.

Professor Jaubert has published numerous articles, and her books include:

La Date de la Cène: Calendrier biblique et liturgie chrétienne, Paris, 1957.

Origène, *Homélies sur Josué*, Paris, 1960.

La notion d'alliance dans le judaisme aux abords de l'ère chrétienne, Paris, 1963.

Les premiers chrétiens, Paris, 1967.

Clement de Rome, *Epître aux Corinthiens*, at the publisher.

Professor Jaubert is recognized internationally for her pioneering work on the calendar at Qumran and its possible influence on burgeoning Christianity.

James H. Charlesworth, Assistant Professor of Religion at Duke University, studied at Ohio Wesleyan University, Duke Divinity School, Duke Graduate School, from which he earned the Ph.D., the University of Edinburgh, and the École Biblique de Jérusalem, from which he earned the É.T. He has been a Dempster Fellow, a Fullbright Fellow, and Joseph Henry Thayer Fellow of the American School of Oriental Research in Jerusalem. He is a member of several professional societies, including *Phi Beta Kappa* and the *Studiorum Novi Testamenti Societas*, and is at present Secretary of the Pseudepigrapha Project of the Society of Biblical Literature. Dr Charlesworth has published articles in philosophical and biblical periodicals. For five years he has been working on a critical edition of the Odes of Solomon.

Marie-Émile Boismard, O.P., Professor at the École Biblique de Jérusalem, is a member of numerous professional organizations, including the *Studiorum Novi Testamenti Societas*. He has contributed numerous articles to the *Revue Biblique* and *Lumière et Vie*. His books are the following:

L'Apocalypse, Paris, 1950.
Le Prologue de Saint Jean (Lectio Divina 11) Paris, 1953.
Du Baptême à Cana (Lectio Divina 18) Paris, 1956.
(with others) *L'Évangile de Jean: Études et Problèmes*, Brussels, 1958.
Quatre Hymnes baptismales dans la première épître de Pierre (Lectio Divina 30) Paris, 1961.
(with others) *Synopse des Quatre Evangiles*, 2 vols, Paris, 1965.
Père Boismard is an internationally respected authority on the Johannine literature.

Gilles Quispel, Professor of History of the Early Church, State University, Utrecht, studied at Leiden, Groningen, and Utrecht. His books include:

De bronnen van Tertullianus' Adversus Marcionem, Leiden, 1943.
M. Minucii Felicis Octavius, Leiden, 1949.
Gnosis als Weltreligion, Zürich, 1951.
Het getuigenis der ziel bij Tertullianus, Leiden, 1952.
Ptolemée, Lettre à Flora (Sources Chrétiennes 24) 2nd ed., Paris, 1966.
Makarius, das Thomasevangelium und das Lied von der Perle, Leiden, 1967.
(with others):
Evangelium-Veritatis, Zürich, 1956.
The Gospel According to Thomas, Leiden, London, 1959.
Evangelium Veritatis. Supplementum, Zürich-Stuttgart, 1961.
Epistula Jacobi Apocrypha, Zürich-Stuttgart, 1968.
Professor Quispel is one of the world's authorities on Gnosticism and Jewish Christianity.

William Hugh Brownlee, Professor of Religion at Claremont Graduate School, studied at Sterling College, Pittsburgh-Xenia Theological Seminary, and Duke University, from which he earned the Ph.D. From 1947–48 he was Fellow of the American School of Oriental Research in Jerusalem. He was one of the first scholars to see the Dead Sea Scrolls, to recognize correctly their antiquity, and to photograph them.

He has participated in excavations at Bethel and on Mt Gerizim. He has been a Fellow of The American Association of Theological Schools, American Council of Learned Societies, and The American Philosophical Society.

Among his numerous writings on the Dead Sea Scrolls and on biblical subjects, the following may be singled out:

The first translations of the Dead Sea Habakkuk Commentary (1948) and the Manual of Discipline (1951).

The Hebrew facsimiles and transcriptions of the first three Qumran Scrolls (1950–51, assisting Millar Burrows and John C. Trever).

The Text of Habakkuk in the Ancient Commentary from Qumran (SBL Monograph Series 11) Philadelphia, 1959.

The Meaning of the Qumran Scrolls for the Bible: With Special Attention to the Book of Isaiah, New York, 1964.

Index of Names and Subjects[1]

[1]All Indexes in this book have been prepared by Brenda Hall, M.A., Registered Indexer of the Society of Indexers.

Zadokite calendar:
  connections between Johannine passion narrative and, 63, 73–5, 105n
  connections between Johannine resurrection narrative and, 63–5
  origins, widespread use of, 62–3 and n
Zadokite priesthood, Teacher of Righteousness descended from, 1
Zaehner, R. C., 87n, 100n
Zealots:
  association with Essenes, 62 and n

association with Qumran community, 88n, 108n
origins in Galilee, 62 and n
Zeitlin, S., 108n
Zoroastrianism, and origins of Qumran dualism, 87n, 156, 157
Zurvanism, and origins of Qumran dualism, 87–9, 103n, 131
Zwaan, J. de, 185n

Index of Scriptural References

Index of Pseudepigraphal References

Index of Dead Sea Scrolls References

Some other books on biblical studies

Essays on the Semitic Background of the New Testament

Joseph A. Fitzmyer SJ

Fr Fitzmyer is one of the world's leading Aramaic scholars. Sixteen of his most important articles have been revised, updated and put together to form this book.

The essays are arranged according to subject-matter into five sections: the use of the Old Testament; the Semitic background of various Gospel passages; Pauline passages; the epistle to the Hebrews; early Christianity.

'In my judgment, Joseph Fitzmyer is the most skilled Catholic New Testament scholar in the English-speaking world. This is a truly representative collection of his work and should enable a wider audience to appreciate the value of his contribution to biblical studies.' *Raymond E. Brown SS*

'Joseph A. Fitzmyer's contributions to Aramaic studies and to our understanding of the Semitic background of the New Testament have long since established him as a leading scholar in these fields. The present work, which draws together into one handy volume some sixteen of his essays, hitherto scattered over several journals and other publications, is a valuable addition to our literature in the subject. Qumran, New Testament Semitisms, historical questions in Judaism and early Christianity—all are represented and treated with imagination, thoroughness, and restraint. The result is a volume which will be a "must" for all serious students of the New Testament and of the Judaism of its time.' *Max Wilcox*

'I am familiar with all the articles and rate them highly indeed—from every point of view. In my opinion, Fr Fitzmyer's work on the relation of the Qumran manuscripts to the New Testament is extremely good. It is based on a thorough knowledge of Aramaic.... He is also at home in the New Testament field and its Old Testament background as well as in all the necessary languages and he is uniquely qualified to write the studies contained in this volume. I have no doubt whatever that it will speedily become one of the standard books in its area.' *William F. Albright*

225.48884.1   544pp   cased   £5

The Anchor Bible

The Gospel According to John

VOLUMES I AND II

Translated with an introduction and notes by
Raymond E. Brown SS

This commentary on John has already been widely acclaimed. A long and important introduction deals with such questions as the present state of Johannine studies, the tradition behind the Fourth Gospel, unity and composition, Johannine theology, and language, text and format.

Raymond Brown provides a translation which is both accurate and contemporary. The translation is divided into sections, and each section is followed by detailed notes and more general comment.

A special feature is the appendices: they cover Johannine vocabulary, the 'Word', 'Signs and works', *Ego eimi*, and the paraclete. For ease of reference, volume II contains the translation of chapters 1–12 as an appendix. There is also an index of authors and an index of subjects to cover both volumes.

Raymond Brown's work—particularly his exposition of Johannine philology and theology—is an original contribution to scholarship and marks an important step in studies on the Fourth Gospel. At the same time these books have been written in such a way that they will also appeal to the non-specialist: all Semitic and Greek words are transliterated, and 'Comment' sections deal with the broad scope of the Gospel's thought and composition.

'This is an excellent book, and every student of Johannine literature will make grateful use of the large amount of information it contains.... The author has every right to expect admiration for one of the most helpful contributions to Johannine studies in this century.' *C. K. Barrett in Journal of Biblical Literature*

'It will rank with the outstanding commentaries on this Gospel.'
E. C. Blackman in Canadian Journal of Theology

'As a comprehensive, clear, and up-to-date conspectus of the vast and complicated range of modern study of the Fourth Gospel, this work has no equal in English.'
Owen E. Evans in The Expository Times

Vol. I: John I–XII (second edition)
225.66061.X   684pp   cased   £3·50

Vol. II: John XIII–XXI
225.66071.7   688pp   cased   £3·50

Paul and Qumran

Edited by Jerome Murphy-O'Connor

This is a collection of essays in which New Testament scholars examine the possible influence of Qumran on St Paul's formation and on his theology. The first of these essays lays down solid principles on which any honest attempt to draw parallels and infer sources should be based.

The scholarliness of the work does not put it out of the reach of the general reader, who will find it an education in the complexity and delicacy of this field of study.

Contributors: P. Benoit, J. A. Fitzmyer, J. Murphy-O'Connor, J. Gnilka, J. Coppens, W. Grundmann, M. Delcor, K. G. Kuhn, F. Mussner.

'Such volumes as *Paul and Qumran* are of immense value to a wide circle of readers.... The authors are a distinguished team, including scholars of great eminence, and all are concerned to give a sober and honest assessment of the facts.... All these are learned and instructive essays.' *Times Literary Supplement*

225.27548.1   256pp   cased   £1·50